# Welfare and the Great Recession

# Welfare and the Great Recession

## A Comparative Study

*Edited by*
Stefán Ólafsson, Mary Daly,
Olli Kangas, and Joakim Palme

OXFORD
UNIVERSITY PRESS

**OXFORD**
**UNIVERSITY PRESS**

Great Clarendon Street, Oxford, OX2 6DP,
United Kingdom

Oxford University Press is a department of the University of Oxford.
It furthers the University's objective of excellence in research, scholarship,
and education by publishing worldwide. Oxford is a registered trade mark of
Oxford University Press in the UK and in certain other countries



First Edition published in 2019



Published in the United States of America by Oxford University Press
198 Madison Avenue, New York, NY 10016, United States of America

British Library Cataloguing in Publication Data
Data available

Library of Congress Control Number: 2018950706

ISBN 978–0–19–883096–2

# Preface

This book stems from a Nordic project aimed at learning lessons from Great Recession experiences and the ways in which governments managed their crisis responses. With a joint workshop in Reykjavík in September 2016 the project was extended to become a wider European project by including representatives from more countries and by aiming to undertake comparative analyses across 30 European countries, as well as by focusing on selected country case studies.

The origin of the project can be traced to Iceland's premiership of the Nordic Council of Ministers between 2014 and 2017. The Ministry of Welfare in Iceland wanted to highlight lessons from different approaches to crisis reactions with a primary focus on how populations were protected or not against crisis consequences. Stefán Ólafsson directed the project and worked with Agnar Freyr Helgason and Kolbeinn Stefánsson on the comparative research work and data processing.

We thank all the authors of the country case studies for their cooperation and hard work as well as anonymous referees for useful comments. The editors are all members of the European Social Policy Network (ESPN), which is a network of independent experts from all over Europe, working for the European Commission, in the areas of employment, social affairs, and inclusion. We thank Eric Marlier, the director of the network, and all its members for enlightening discussions and reporting during the last decade.

The Icelandic team thanks Ingi Valur Jóhannsson, Sigríður Jónsdóttir, and Siv Friðleifsdóttir at the Ministry of Welfare for their invaluable help and the Nordic Council of Ministers for financial support. They also thank Anton Örn Karlsson at Statistics Iceland for his invaluable advice on both methodology and substance.

Edda Centre of Excellence at the University of Iceland hosted the project and we thank Irma Erlingsdóttir and Valur Ingimundarson for support throughout.

# Table of Contents

# List of Figures and Tables

## Figures

## Tables

# Notes on Contributors

**Jørgen Goul Andersen** is Professor of Political Science at Aalborg University (Denmark). He was founder and director of Centre for Comparative Welfare Studies, from 1995 to 2009 and 2016 to 2017. In 1998–2003 he was a member of the group in charge of the Danish Power and Democracy Study. From 1998 to 2007 Jørgen chaired the Danish Election Project. He has written a large number of books on welfare problems, welfare policy, political power, and democracy, political behaviour, and on Danish society in general.

**Sergio González Begega** is a Senior Lecturer in the Department of Sociology, University of Oviedo (Spain). He is member of the research networks Promoting Work and Welfare in Europe (University of Oviedo, Spain), Worker Participation in Europe, and GoodCorp (European Trade Union Institute: ETUI). He has enjoyed research fellowships at Manchester Business School-Manchester University (Manchester), ETUI (Brussels), Cultures et Sociétés Urbaines-Centre National de la Recherche Scientifique (Paris), and Institute of Public Goods and Policies of the Spanish National Research Council (Madrid). His research lines include European industrial relations, social dialogue and industrial conflict, and comparative social policy. He has participated in edited books with several publishers including Oxford University Press. He has also published articles in journals such as *Employee Relations, Transfer, Critical Perspectives on International Business, European Journal of Social Security, Rural Extension and Innovation Systems*, and *Review of International Studies*, among others.

**Fran Bennett** is a Senior Research and Teaching Fellow in the Department of Social Policy and Intervention at the University of Oxford. She has a particular interest in social security policy, gender issues, poverty, income distribution, and participation. Fran has written extensively on social policy issues for the UK government, non-governmental organizations, and others. With Professor Jonathan Bradshaw, she is one of the UK team of independent experts in the European Social Policy Network for the European Commission. Fran chairs the editorial board of the *Journal of Poverty and Social Justice*, having been a co-editor. She is a Fellow of the Academy of Social Sciences and an associate of its international advisory group. Fran is an active member of the Women's Budget Group and chairs the policy advisory group for Oxfam's work on poverty in the UK.

**Mary Daly** is Professor of Sociology and Social Policy at the University of Oxford. Among the fields on which she has published are welfare state, gender, family and the labour market, and poverty. Much of her work is comparative, set in a European and international context. She is a member of a number of networks and boards on topics related to the welfare state, employment, family, and gender, and is an editor of the journal *Social Politics*. She is the Irish coordinator of the European Network on Social Policy. Her latest book is *Families and Poverty: Everyday Life on a Low Income* (co-authored with Grace Kelly, 2015).

**Jon Erik Dølvik** is Senior Researcher and Coordinator of Comparative Labour Research at Fafo Institute for Labour and Social Research in Oslo. He has published extensively in the fields of comparative industrial relations, political economy, employment regulation, labour migration, and Nordic and European social models. He and Andrew Martin of Harvard University recently edited the book *European Social Models from Crisis to Crisis* (Oxford University Press, 2015).

**Ana M. Guillén** is full Professor of Sociology and director of research network PROMEBI at the University of Oviedo (Spain). She has published extensively on comparative social and labour policy, welfare state development in South Europe, Europeanization, and European integration. Her articles have been published in journals such as *Social Science & Medicine, Social Politics, Journal of European Social Policy, European Societies, International Journal of Health Services, West European Politics, Social Policy and Administration,* and *Comparative European Politics,* among others. She is founder of REPS (Red Española de Política Social, ESPAnet-Spain), member of the advisory boards of the Observatoire Social Européen (Brussels) and the International Social Security Association, and acts as consultant to the European Commission and the International Labour Organization.

**Agnar Freyr Helgason** is a Post-Doctoral Fellow in the Department of Political Science at the University of Iceland. He graduated with a PhD in Political Science from Ohio State University in 2015. His primary research is at the intersection of comparative political economy and political behaviour, with an emphasis on the politics of redistribution and taxation, on the one hand, and on the political consequences of economic context, on the other. His work has appeared in high-ranking academic journals, including *Journal of Politics, Comparative Political Studies, Socio-Economic Review,* and *Political Analysis.*

**Olli Kangas** was Director of the Research Department at the Social Insurance Institution of Finland, Kela, from 2008 to 2018. He is presently a Professor of Social Research at Turku University. Professor Kangas took his PhD in Sociology at the University of Helsinki (1991). He has worked as Olof Palme Visiting Professor at Uppsala University (2015), H. C. Andersen Professor at the University of Southern Denmark (2012), and at various other universities and research institutes. He is an invited member of the Finnish Academic Society for Letters and Sciences (2008–). He was the Chair of the Editorial Board of Kela Publishing (2008–15), and a member of the following editorial boards: *Social Politics* (2007–12), *Janus* (1991–4), *Sosiologia* (2001–2), *European Sociological Review* (2000–7), and *European Journal of Social Policy* (2001–8).

**Manos Matsaganis** is Professor of Public Finance at the Polytechnic University of Milan. He studied Economics in Athens, and Health Economics at the universities of York and Bristol. He has held posts at the London School of Economics, the Greek Prime Minister's Office, the universities of Crete and Thessaly, and the Athens University of Economics and Business, where he founded and directed the Policy Analysis

Research Unit. As an economist with an interest in public policy, he has published papers on the political economy of austerity, labour taxation, youth unemployment, health care, pensions, income support, poverty, European social policy, tax evasion, and other topics. He sits on the Board of ESPAnet. He has advised the European Commission, the Organisation for Economic Co-operation and Development, the United Nations Children's Fund, and the World Bank. He was recently Fulbright Scholar at Harvard and University of California Berkeley, and Visiting Scholar at Boston University.

**Stefán Ólafsson** is Professor of Sociology at the University of Iceland. He has a DPhil from Nuffield College, University of Oxford. Ólafsson was Director of the University of Iceland's Institute of Social Research (1985–99) and Chairman of the Board of Iceland's Social Security Administration (2007–16). He has written extensively on Icelandic society, particularly on welfare, work, and social change, including a recent book on the distribution of income and wealth in Iceland, from 1927 to 2015. Previous works deal with globalization, the Icelandic welfare model, social foundations of economic growth, and welfare developments. Stefán has, since 2008, been a member of the European Social Policy Network (ESPN) and previously the EU Social Inclusion Network and the Analytical Support on the Socio-Economic Impact of Social Protection Reforms Network, undertaking independent consultancy work and reporting for the European Commission.

**Johannes Oldervoll** is Research Fellow at Fafo Institute for Labour and Social Research in Oslo. Educated in the study of comparative politics, he is engaged in studies of labour market regulation, vocational education and training, collective action, and labour migration.

**Joakim Palme** is Professor of Political Science at the Department of Government, Uppsala University—a post he has held since 2009—and Chairman of the Migrations Studies Delegation (Delmi). Palme holds a PhD in Sociology from Stockholm University (1990). Throughout the 1980s and 1990s, he contributed to the Social Citizenship Indicator Program at the Swedish Institute for Social Research. In 1999–2001 he chaired the Swedish 'Welfare Commission'. From 2002 to 2011 he was Director of the Institute for Futures Studies in Stockholm. He has published extensively on the welfare state both in terms of its politics and as a strategy of equality. His publications also include studies of social policies in ageing societies and social investment. Currently he is directing a research project on the effects of the global financial crisis. He has edited three anthologies with international publishers.

**Kolbeinn Stefánsson** has a DPhil in Sociology from the University of Oxford and works as a Research Coordinator at Statistics Iceland. He is a Research Associate at EDDA—Centre of Excellence at the University of Iceland. His research interests include economic well-being, social policy, housing, gender issues, and research methods. Kolbeinn has published extensively on Iceland, often in a comparative perspective, in books, reports, and journals.

# 1

# Introduction

## Leading Themes and Explanatory Framework

*Stefán Ólafsson, Mary Daly, Olli Kangas, and Joakim Palme*

### 1.1 Leading Themes

The international financial crisis that took hold in 2008 has been described as the largest to hit the world since the Great Depression of the 1930s. It is usually referred to as the Great Recession in order to both underline its scale and compare it to the 1930s crisis. While the similarities are striking, the differences between the two are also evident and arguably more interesting.

Looking first at similarities, we can say that both crises caused significant economic and social disruptions. Growth slowed or reversed, unemployment and poverty increased, families were at risk of losing their homes, school leavers had difficulties entering the labour market, some firms and individuals went bankrupt, governmental finances were eroded, and debt levels escalated. Thus the crises involved significant setbacks for living standards beyond normal fluctuations.

Nevertheless, the impacts of both of these crises varied considerably among countries as well as between socio-economic groups within countries. Since financial crises are generally the consequences of financial bubbles—periods of unsustainable excesses associated with unrestrained markets and inadequate governance—it is only to be expected that countries sink to varying depths when the bubbles burst and the crisis begins.

The biggest difference between these two international crises is, however, in the institutional environment of these historical periods. In short, the key differentiating factor is the emergence of the modern welfare state. During the 1930s welfare states were still in their infancy, generally weak in terms of resources and incomplete in terms of coverage and functioning. They had but meagre means of protecting populations against disruptions in their living conditions. Governments also had limited knowledge and often limited understanding of how to react in a crisis situation. The Great Depression provided a hard but important lesson about possibilities for economic crisis management (Eichengreen, 2015; Keynes, 1936; Schumpeter, 1942). 'Hard times' were often a stimulus for the advancement of social protection systems, in addition to the influences of democratization and modernization (Flora & Heidenheimer, 1998; Weir, Orloff, & Skocpol, 1988).

The Western welfare state became a defining characteristic of societal development during the post-war period, providing new and more advanced institutional structures to secure and equalize nations' living standards. That is probably the main reason why the Great Recession did not have as serious a set of economic, political, or social consequences in many countries as the Great Depression. Modern welfare states have much greater capacity for smoothing economic cycles and softening the consequences of crises for population welfare (Starke, Kaasch, & van Hooren, 2013; van Kersbergen & Vis, 2014).

During the 1930s and 1940s the Great Depression was generally seen as a failure of unrestrained markets, especially financial markets. From that experience and World War II emerged a new social formation—the mixed economy or the Keynesian welfare state—with a greater role for governments and more embedded markets (Blyth, 2002; Polanyi, 1944; Ruggie, 1982).

While the negative consequences of the Great Recession were considerable in Europe and elsewhere, they have not yet led to a fundamental transformation of the social order in the Western Hemisphere, as happened after the Great Depression (Eichengreen, 2015; Gourevitch, 1986; Kahler & Lake, 2013). Some even fear another financial crisis may strike sooner than later (Streeck, 2017). Hence Western political economies are more or less on the same general tracks after the crisis, even if there is a somewhat stronger commitment to restrictive regulations than before the crisis.

In 2018, a decade after the onset of the Great Recession, we are in a position to systematically assess the consequences of the crisis. While the welfare state played a much larger role in averting negative crisis consequences than during the 1930s, its influence varied considerably between countries or welfare regimes. Other changes in the institutional environment of European countries also made a difference, such as the emergence of the European Union and the euro, as well as changes in politics and in the role of labour movements.

As the crisis unfolded, governments shifted from stimulus to austerity, and the worst-off countries had to cede some of their financial independence and live with strict constraints from external powers—which in turn jeopardized public support at home (Bermeo & Pontusson, 2012; Streeck & Schäfer, 2013). In this context welfare states became increasingly strained, even when and where they were most needed. Hence the Great Recession and higher public debt levels cast a long shadow on their future. The prevailing ideological environment is today somewhat negative towards the welfare state, as reflected in the shift from the post-war Keynesian social contract to a more neoliberal policy emphasis since the 1980s (Blyth, 2002, 2013; Farnsworth & Irving, 2015; Taylor-Gooby, Leruch, & Chung, 2017).

Globalization has no doubt contributed to increased political unrest and realignments in Western political systems since the 1980s. The Great Recession stimulated further political shifts. Political turmoil became more common, with loss of trust, new parties or movements, protests, and even revolts in some countries. Hence the political consequences of the crisis may linger or develop in new directions (Bartels & Bermeo, 2014; Funke, Schularick, & Trebesch, 2016). These political changes, as well as the erosion of trade union power in most Western countries, have to some extent weakened the social bases of modern welfare states. As we shall show, such political developments may appear as somewhat contradictory, given the important advantage that welfare states can provide in crisis situations for politicians as well as the public.

The particular type of welfare state in place when the crisis hit, as well as government responses, had crucial impacts on how the Great Recession unfolded and took effect, as will be revealed in this book. Many governments combatted the adverse conditions of the recession well, even some of the most financially constrained ones. Others did not. Thus there was considerable variation in the severity of the crisis as well as in the ways of handling it. This increased the variety of welfare outcomes. It is these varieties and variations that we map and analyse in this book.

The main focus of the studies that follow is on how individuals and households were affected by the Great Recession. We delineate a picture of Europe as a whole through comparative analyses, but we also paint sharper and more detailed portraits of country cases in individual chapters. The leading research question is how the burdens of the crisis were shared.[1] We pursue this question through within- and cross-country analyses of the relative position and well-being of households at varying levels of income and from different social classes. Ours is thus a household welfare perspective and Europe is the main setting for our studies.

Even though our primary focus is on households and individuals we relate our findings to macro conditions by seeking explanations for different welfare

[1] See a similar approach in Cantillon et al. (2017). While Cantillon and colleagues do focus on households/individuals, their primary concern is children's experience of poverty. Our book has a much broader focus—on populations in general—though it does compare major societal groups as well, including families with children.

outcomes, in the prevailing political economy, institutional structures and policy reactions. This puts welfare state institutions and politics at the forefront of our analyses.

## 1.2 Explanatory Framework

Figure 1.1 explains the general framework for the book. It is to be interpreted as a way of organizing our analyses and pinpointing key factors rather than as a finite and all-inclusive causal model.

We take our lead from the depth and persistence of the crisis in individual countries. Even if societal conditions and policy reactions vary greatly, the severity of the crisis could still be very important, possibly the most influential factor for the crisis experience and outcome.

The social protection system of the welfare regime in each country generally has the aim of sheltering members of society from adverse living conditions, including temporary crisis situations. So the strength, resources, and effectiveness of the system in place before the crisis can be of major importance for shaping or softening the crisis impact. The governmental debt situation before the crisis hit, as well as levels of affluence and unemployment, are also clearly of importance. We refer to these as the initial capacity position, seeing them as indicating strengths or weaknesses for responding to a deep crisis.

The reactions of governments are also of major importance, for better or worse. As is shown in Chapter 4 most governments significantly increased stimulus at the beginning of the crisis to avert a deeper slide into recession.

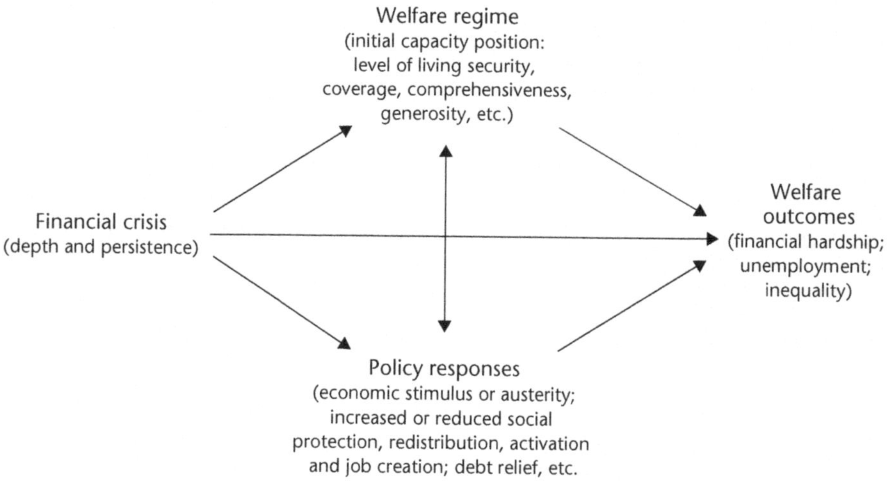


**Figure 1.1.** The explanatory framework: From financial crisis to welfare outcomes

However, as the crisis unfolded most shifted to austerity policies, either on the recommendations of the European Central Bank (ECB), European Commission, and International Monetary Fund (IMF), or in order to avoid more public debt accumulation. These reactions varied among countries and by stage of the crisis period. Most countries increased transfers, even beyond the automatic stabilizing effects of unemployment benefits. Some increased redistribution efforts and others let the burdens fall disproportionally on the lower income groups, thus contributing to increasing inequalities.

Most governments placed increased emphasis on activation and rehabilitation measures in the labour market and some promoted job creation. Another reaction was to place more emphasis on social investment expenditures while reducing traditional social protection measures in the context of constrained resources during the crisis (Ronchi, 2018). A common policy measure has been to increase conditionality (such as activation requirements) for the receipt of benefits and here the unemployment insurance programmes in Denmark and Finland serve as good examples. Some countries undertook considerable debt relief measures for households while others did little in that area.

The combined effects of the severity of the crisis, initial capacities for sheltering the population (including the characteristics and resources of the welfare states), and governmental priorities in dealing with the crisis all shaped the ensuing welfare outcomes for individuals and households, and conditioned the extent of unemployment and financial hardship experienced and how the burdens were shared amongst population groups.

We combine general comparative studies of some 30 European countries with a more in-depth analysis of nine countries, spanning differential crisis experiences. Thus we have four countries that experienced a very deep crisis (Greece, Iceland, Ireland, Spain), three that were not as severely affected (Denmark, Finland, the UK), and two that were only modestly affected (Norway and Sweden). The last two, along with Finland, did, however, experience very deep financial crises in the early 1990s from which we also draw lessons.

The broader comparative aim is to give a comprehensive picture of the crisis conditions and consequences for Europe as a whole, but also to provide a context for individual countries. This affords us the possibility of showing in considerable detail how the burdens of the crisis were shared by societal groups across Europe, by individual countries, and by societal groups within countries.

We base our analyses on classical indicators of welfare and well-being outcomes for households and individuals and relate these to various macro-level political economy indicators. In addition we develop a composite measure of financial hardship (based on income poverty, material deprivation, and difficulties in making ends meet) to survey the welfare impact on individual countries and on various societal groups. We show how this new measure of financial hardship relates to more traditional measures of crisis consequences (such as unemployment, poverty, and income levels) and assess its reliability in the appendix to the book.

## 1.3 Content and Structure of the Book

Part I develops the book's perspective and theoretical concerns and provides comparative material covering about 30 European countries.[2] It consists of three chapters. In Chapter 2 Stefán Ólafsson and Kolbeinn H. Stefánsson provide a general comparative overview of welfare consequences of the crisis, using the financial hardship indicator and a number of others, such as unemployment, income developments, and poverty indicators. They compare the outcomes between different welfare regimes and by depth of the crisis. They then go on to explore the development of financial hardship within socio-economic groups across Europe and indicate where this increased most. Hence the chapter provides an important insight into how the burdens were shared and which groups bore the brunt of the crisis.

Chapter 3, by Agnar Freyr Helgason, offers a review of political economy theories of crises responses. He starts by explaining the broad perspectives of the Keynesian and Austrian schools and then probes more deeply into recent work on government policy responses to economic crises, with a focus on the economic welfare of populations or households. The role of the welfare state and its importance during periods of crisis is considered, as well as the role of government policy more broadly, either that directed at the economy generally or at specific population groups. Key policy debates are covered, for example austerity versus stimulus, as well as mixed approaches.

In Chapter 4, also by Helgason, the focus is on statistical profiles of government policies and outcomes after the crisis hit. The Great Recession is placed in the context of longer-term developments of financial crises. The economic growth context is outlined, as well as, for example, current account balances and debt levels leading up to the crisis. The chapter focuses also on what governments did in terms of fiscal policy measures affecting population welfare (automatic stabilizers versus discretionary measures). The extent of stimulus, austerity, taxation, transfers, and other social protection efforts are considered in turn. These three chapters of Part I, along with the Introduction, set the scene for the more detailed country case studies in Part II, by providing

[2] This applies to most of our own analyses, but in a few cases, when using data from the Organisation for Economic Co-operation and Development (OECD), we have included a small number of other major Western countries for a wider comparison.

an understanding of the options available and comparative perspectives on what governments did and how populations were differentially affected.

In Part II, while working to a shared framework focused around leading research questions, each chapter is to some extent shaped by country-specific conditions and crisis developments. These chapters typically describe the political economy context prior to the crisis and relate that and other factors to the character and severity of the crisis in their respective countries. Each profiles the country-specific development of financial hardship from 2007 to 2015 overall and for the main socio-economic groups. The authors then reflect on the general reactions to the crisis and consider how the social protection system was used or not to soften the crisis impact and to facilitate a return to growth.

The selection of countries covered in these detailed studies is partly shaped by the origin of the project as a Nordic one, later extended to become a more fully European project, with the general comparative chapters covering about 30 European countries. The overall strategy was, however, to have representative countries from differing crisis severity levels in these more detailed studies. Thus we have four countries from the group that went deepest into crisis, three from an intermediate level, and two that were only modestly affected during the Great Recession. Altogether, however, we have seven cases of deep-crisis experiences to reflect on (by including three deep-crisis experiences from the early 1990s).

Manos Matsaganis starts in Chapter 5 with an account of the most severe crisis of the Great Recession—the case of Greece. He explains the conditions at the beginning of the crisis and how the situation developed over the following years. Greece was the first Euro area member to request a bailout, which was granted in return for massive fiscal consolidation and structural reforms. Matsaganis explains the bailout programme and its conditions, progress, and consequences, particularly the adverse effects of the austerity measures on levels of living and poverty. The Greek welfare state was weak before the crisis hit and lacked a resourceful minimum income protection scheme. Thus it was only capable of providing minimum shelter against the massive crisis impact, as reflected in the very large increase of financial hardship from 2007 to 2014 in most Greek socio-economic groups. Matsaganis lastly reflects on the politics of welfare and how the crisis has affected the Greek welfare state to date.

In Chapter 6 Ana M. Guillén and Sergio González Begega address the crisis management strategies of Spain's long-lasting recession and its associated protracted period of austerity. The Spanish economy enjoyed two decades of very intense expansion prior to the onset of the recession in 2008. That expansion was, nonetheless, unsustainable. Hence Spain went into a profound crisis with harsh social and employment consequences. Youth unemployment became excessive. The analysis of the overall policy responses to the recession and the reforms of the social protection system indicate a trajectory aimed unequivocally at regaining fiscal balance and appeasing the markets, while tending to growing social need remained a secondary objective. The outcome has been a substantive increase in financial hardship and socio-economic insecurity, borne most outstandingly in the lowest income quintile and in some active age population groups, such as single parents, immigrants, the unemployed, and, indirectly, children.

Mary Daly examines the crisis in Ireland in Chapter 7, which was severe by national and international standards and occasioned a major policy response. The analysis shows that while the crisis was preceded in Ireland by an extended period of rapid economic growth, the national financial situation had been deteriorating for at least five years prior to the recession. When it hit, a strong austerity approach was adopted, dictated especially by the terms of the financial bailout that Ireland secured from the international financial institutions in 2010. In return for this funding, Ireland undertook a very detailed programme of reforms in which social policy and changed taxation were prioritized. These reforms featured large reductions in social expenditure and significant cuts to all benefits (except old-age pensions) and services, with the major consequences of increasing poverty and hardship. Housing-related indebtedness increased quite widely as well. Reforms also institutionalized a much stronger activation approach. Apart from this though, there was little or no major restructuring of the Irish welfare state so we may conclude that this proved quite resilient in a period which saw the overshadowing if not demise of social partnership.

In Chapter 8 Stefán Ólafsson explains the characteristics of the bubble economy in Iceland, the magnitude of the financial collapse of 2008, and its economic and social consequences. The collapse was dramatic, leading to a rapid contraction of the economy, which bottomed out in 2010. Since then there has been relatively good growth. The governments of the crisis period applied various policy reactions that seem to have worked quite well, and included both macroeconomic stimulus measures and social protective efforts. Ólafsson describes what he terms Iceland's redistribution strategy, which aimed to protect the more vulnerable households. These included increased transfers aimed at lower income groups, job creation, activation and rehabilitation, debt relief, and changed taxation policy. Together these efforts succeeded in softening the worst crisis consequences and contributed to an equalization of income distribution. Financial hardship topped in 2010 and has come down since then, gradually and persistently. By 2017 the highest employment and income levels of the pre-crisis years had been regained.

In Chapter 9 Olli Kangas analyses crisis management strategies in two economic crises in Finland: the very deep crisis of the 1990s and the post-2008 recession. Causes of the 1990s crisis link to excessive lending during the economic boom of the late 1980s, to economic problems in Western markets in 1990, and to the collapse of the Soviet export market, which had amounted to 15–20 per cent of the export volume of Finland. These developments resulted in a serious depression, which lasted between 1990 and 1994, in which unemployment skyrocketed from 4 to 17 per cent. After that depression strong economic growth returned, fuelled by the information and communication technology (ICT) sector.

The overture to the post-2008 recession in Finland came in the form of the collapse of American banks, which had severe worldwide repercussions. Since 2008, gross domestic product (GDP) growth has been weak, unemployment has increased, and domestic demand is being held back by slow-income growth. Due to the EU embargo against Russia, Finnish exports to the East ceased, reinforcing the stagnation. For nine years, the national budget has been running a deficit and municipal finances have been in deficit for even longer. A series of austerity packages have made the Finnish welfare state leaner and meaner. Surprisingly, despite cuts in welfare provisions and the high level of unemployment, poverty and inequality of disposable incomes have been declining during the 2010s, due to the protective capacity of the Finnish welfare state. Financial hardship has not increased. However, the prolonged recession may have some long-standing consequences and expanding 'pockets' of poverty and social exclusion that may only become visible in the coming decades.

Fran Bennet shows how the UK tackled the crisis in Chapter 10. One of the first European countries to be affected by the crisis, the UK also implemented a post-crisis stimulus package early. But from 2010, with a new coalition government, austerity was the watchword, with cuts in public spending, in particular social security, prioritized over tax increases. Spending on education and health was shielded, and old-age pensioners' benefits were protected, but those of families with children were reduced. From 2015 a Conservative majority government continued on a similar path, though also implementing tax cuts and a higher minimum wage. Under the new prime minister in 2016, the aim of balancing the public finances was postponed. Initially the pain of the crisis was shared more broadly. But financial hardship increased after 2012, especially for lone parents and disabled people, and benefit cuts affected women in particular. Whilst employment increased, recovery was slow and wages were hit. Given the pressures of Brexit, it seems unlikely that positive welfare state developments can be expected in the near future.

In Chapter 11 Jørgen Goul Andersen focuses on Denmark, which entered the crisis with a strong economy, but also with a housing and credit bubble beginning to burst. This contributed to constraining private consumption for a long period, as home equity evaporated. When the government switched in

May 2010 to zero growth in public consumption and to a policy of significant cuts in social protection, this left exports as the only possible driver of growth. It took ten years for private consumption per capita to return to 2007 levels, while the number of public employees declined by 5 per cent from 2010 to 2016. Welfare and tax reforms since 2008 have contributed to an erosion of social citizenship, accompanied by strong rhetoric and administrative practices questioning the deservingness of people in a vulnerable position. Whereas the weakest groups are at risk of being excluded from social protection, the long-term decline in welfare services may 'crowd in' private welfare for the upper middle classes. Nevertheless, in a context of prosperity, there is resistance to retrenchment and greater support for damage repair of social protection.

Jon Erik Dølvik and Johannes Oldervoll review in Chapter 12 how recurrent crises since the 1980s have taught Norwegian policymakers to stabilize a crisis-prone petroleum economy through comprehensive macroeconomic policy coordination. While regaining monetary policy autonomy and establishing fiscal policy rules that enable countercyclical use of petroleum revenues, Norway has drawn on reinvigorated wage coordination and welfare state expansion to cushion joblessness and financial hardship in turbulent times. This coordination from the top has been successful in tackling economic volatility but has failed to stem widening wage and wealth gaps during recent years' affluence and rise in cross-border labour mobility and immigration. Although seemingly robust in the face of periodic shocks, the Norwegian policy regime appears to have lost some of its capacity to balance equity and efficiency.

Joakim Palme analyses two Swedish crisis experiences—the early 1990s and the Great Recession—in Chapter 13. The economic crisis of the 1990s was a tough challenge for the welfare state and for human conditions, but it was also a rehearsal for the Great Recession. In the 1990s GDP growth rates were negative for three years in a row and employment fell massively. At the same time Sweden experienced the most dramatic waves of refugee immigration since World War II. The deficit in public finances 'skyrocketed'. The Great Recession of 2008 and onwards was, in a number of important ways, different. It was caused by external factors and it was faster. Policy responses to the Great Recession were similar to those of the 1990s with regard to the financial sector but differed for social policies. In 2009, the fall in manufacturing was broad and deep but the domestic sector, both private and public, was unaffected. The recovery was fast and helped by the fact that Sweden had a floating currency.

There is ample evidence to suggest that the two crises examined in this chapter have left their imprint on the level of living conditions in Sweden. The effects of the 1990s crisis were broad ranging, but the data show the Great

Recession had a much more restricted effect on population hardship. The effects of the 1990s crisis were partially mediated by the retrenchment effects that the crisis had on social protection systems across the board. We can see this as an emerging institutional deficit in relation to the ideal type universalism that is often associated with the Swedish welfare state model. In contrast, there were no retrenchment effects during the Great Recession on social protection systems as such, but policy changes made before the crisis actually increased the universalism deficit further. This leaves the Swedish welfare state model at another crossroads, particularly in light of the massive refugee migration of 2015. It is not that the immediate effects have been massive for the welfare state as such, but that potentially far-reaching policy proposals have been placed on the table.

Chapter 14 in Part III, by Ólafsson, Helgason, and Stefánsson, assesses the overall effects of the institutional environment, societal conditions, and policy reactions on welfare outcomes, along with the direct effects of the economic contraction. This they do by undertaking a statistical analysis of associations between various background factors and financial hardship experiences in 30 European countries. The analyses demonstrate the importance of welfare state structures and varying policy priorities for differential welfare outcomes. Even though the depth of the crisis had a pivotal role in shaping welfare outcomes, the authors find that welfare state structures and policy priorities had significant independent effects on the financial hardship consequences of the Great Recession.

In the concluding chapter Stefán Ólafsson pulls the threads together and discusses lessons learned and prospects for welfare futures.

# Part I

# Comparative Profiles, Theories, and Policies

# 2

# Welfare Consequences of the Crisis in Europe

*Stefán Ólafsson and Kolbeinn Stefánsson*

In this chapter we show the variety of crisis experiences amongst European populations. We use a number of indicators, such as unemployment, income changes, and relative poverty rates, but our primary focus is on a new composite measure of financial hardship, which is based on income poverty, material deprivation, and difficulties in making ends meet. We examine these indicators in relation to the depth of the crisis for some 30 European countries and according to welfare regime landscapes of country groupings. In addition to surveying how countries were affected from 2007 to 2015, we also assess specifically how the crisis affected main socio-economic groups across Europe as a whole. We look at different age groups, single parents, the unemployed, immigrants, disability pensioners, low educational groups, and income groups in general. This is a good way to assess how the burdens of the Great Recession were differentially shared amongst population groups. Not only do we reveal the varying levels of financial hardship amongst these groups but we demonstrate how such hardship changed during the crisis. We also look at income developments by different income groups in various countries. The few cases of decreasing financial hardship and poverty during the crisis period are also discussed.

We find that consequences of the crisis were quite different, even amongst the countries that experienced the deepest crisis. On the whole, those on the lower rungs of the income ladder in European societies were particularly heavily affected, while the highest income groups barely experienced any increase in financial hardship.

## 2.1 Depth of the Crisis: Contraction and Unemployment

The Great Recession that started in 2007–8 was, for the most part, a typical financial crisis that came in the wake of an economic bubble that burst. There are many similarities between the Great Recession of the 2000s and the Great Depression of the 1930s (Aliber & Kindleberger, 2011; Eichengreen, 2015; Reinhart & Rogoff, 2009). The main difference is frequently conceived as one of degree: the Great Recession is typically branded as the deepest financial crisis after the Great Depression.

Images of the Great Depression of the 1930s are typically strongly connected to the poverty and widespread hardships of common people, such as bread and soup lines, the 'Hooverville' shacks of the homeless in the USA, and the legendary image of the 'migrant mother' with her children and a face of broken hopes, taken by Dorothea Lange during the Great Depression in the USA. Poverty and hardship greatly increased, suggesting that the poor or economically vulnerable were disproportionally affected.

But countries were differentially affected by the crisis of the 1930s. The USA was especially hard hit, with unemployment reaching 25 per cent and gross domestic product (GDP) contracting by some 30 per cent during a three-year period (Eichengreen, 2015; Gourevitch, 1986). The Nordic countries were not nearly as deeply affected as the USA at that time. However, the whole of the Western world was affected, with a significant slowdown of economic activities, growing unemployment, increased poverty levels, and social and political turmoil.

Countries were also differentially impacted by the contemporary Great Recession. The experience of Greece, the hardest-hit country at this time, in many ways resembles that of the USA of the 1930s as regards economic contraction and increased unemployment. Some other countries were also hard hit, but none to the extent of Greece. On the other hand, some countries in Europe were not strongly affected, such as Norway, Sweden, and those in the north-west of the Continent.

While Nordic countries seem to have had easy rides through both the Great Depression and the Great Recession, one should remember the very deep Nordic financial crises of the beginning of the 1990s, during which Finland and Sweden were particularly heavily impacted. The welfare consequences were quite extensive in these countries at the time, even though their strong welfare states significantly softened the impact on living standards (Palme et al., 2002; Uusitalo, 1996; see also Chapters 9 and 13). Norway was also significantly affected at the time but succeeded better than its neighbours at containing the crisis effect (see Chapter 12). For the Mediterranean countries the post-2008 crisis was generally very deep, as was the case for the Baltic States of Estonia, Latvia, and Lithuania.

In Figure 2.1 we present an overview of the contraction of real GDP from the pre-crisis peak to the trough after the onset of the crisis, as well as the recovery of GDP from the trough to 2015. This is a reasonable first indicator of how differently Western countries were affected by economic contraction and how differently growth resumed.

Of the 33 countries featured in Figure 2.1, 32 experienced some contraction of their GDP. Hence the recession experience was nearly universal, but at the same time countries were very differently impacted on the downward slide, but no less so on the upswing from the bottom of the recession towards 2015.

Apart from Greece, the hardest hit with economic contraction were the Baltic States (Latvia, Estonia, and Lithuania), other Mediterranean countries, and Iceland, Ireland, Slovenia, Slovakia, and Hungary.

Amongst those that were hardest hit with economic contraction, Greece, Slovenia, Cyprus, Finland, Italy, Spain, and Portugal progressed slowly from the depth of the crisis. Sluggish growth was also experienced on the upswing in Denmark, Austria, the Netherlands, France, and Belgium. At the same time a large number of countries that had experienced a relatively large economic contraction had a much stronger recovery of their GDP; these included the Baltic States, Ireland, Iceland, Slovakia, Luxembourg, and Sweden. For wider comparative purposes, it is interesting to note that the Anglo-Saxon countries outside Europe (USA, Canada, New Zealand, and Australia) were all only mildly impacted by economic contraction compared to most European countries. This is particularly interesting in the case of the USA, which by many is considered to be the main originator of the global financial crisis.

But GDP development is far from being the whole story. As we show in the rest of this chapter there is some divergence between the development of GDP during the crisis and various welfare outcome indicators. Thus we have countries that had a large contraction with severe consequences for the living standards of their populations (Greece and other Mediterranean countries). Some had large contractions with major negative welfare consequences but quick recoveries (the Baltic States, Iceland, and Ireland); others had significant contraction of their economy that did not significantly affect the living standards of their populations (Finland, Luxembourg, and Sweden).

There were also some countries that experienced only a modest contraction of their economy but saw significant decline in living standards or welfare (the UK and USA). In effect, a country's policy responses and the characteristics of their welfare state matter. Some countries with similar levels of economic contraction reacted very differently to the crisis, with varying impacts on the welfare of their population, as was the case with Ireland and Iceland. The point to underline again is the considerable variety of contraction and welfare outcomes in the crisis experience of Western nations in general and European ones in particular. In brief, institutions and politics mattered.

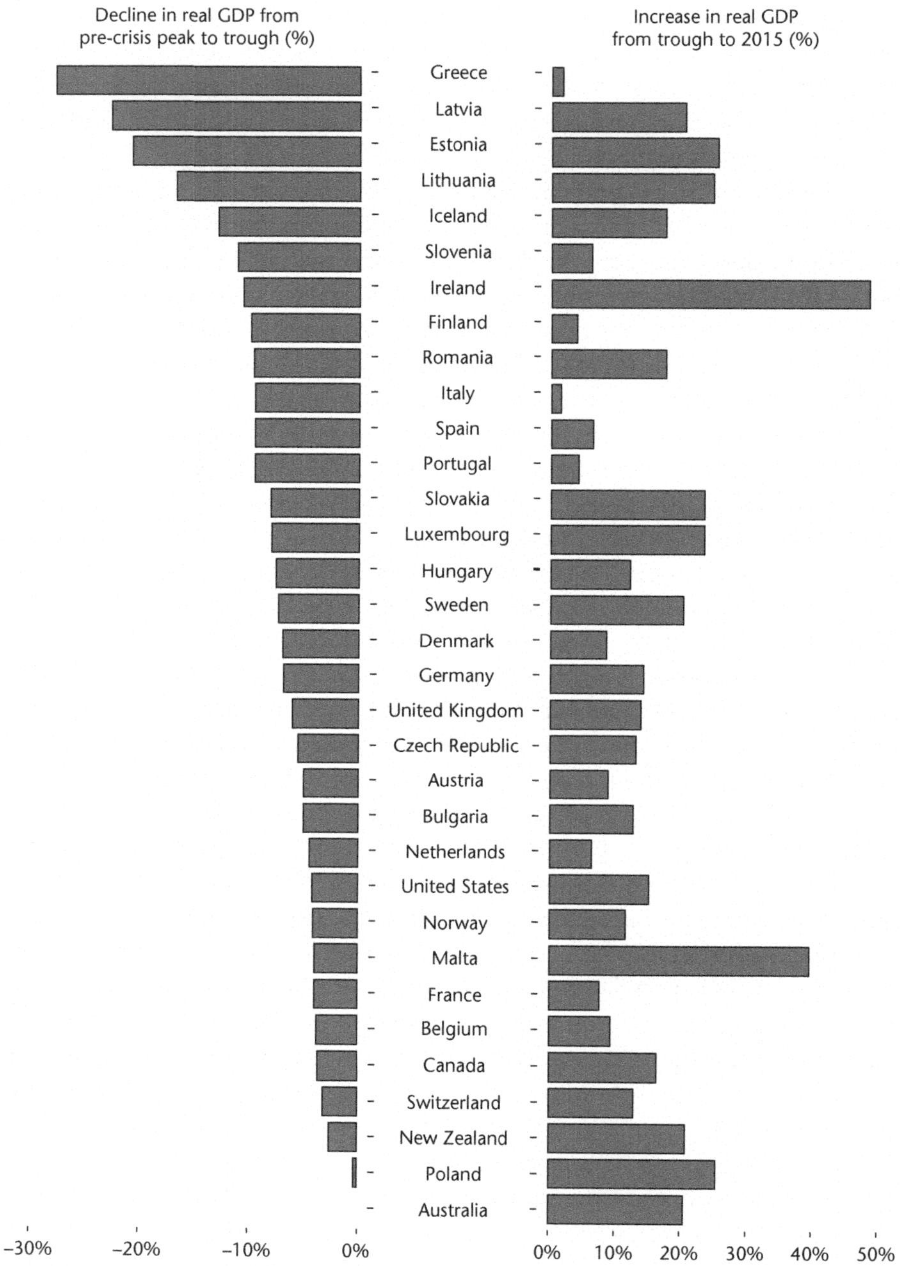


**Figure 2.1.** GDP developments during the Great Recession, from pre-crisis peak to crisis trough and up again to 2015

*Note*: Accumulated percentages. Main Western countries.

*Source*: OECD Quarterly National Accounts.

### 2.1.1 *Unemployment Levels*

Now we turn towards the factors that impacted on the welfare of populations, starting with unemployment developments through the crisis. Figure 2.2 shows the overall unemployment level through the crisis period for 33 countries, disaggregated for 13 deep-crisis countries and 20 countries that did not experience as deep a crisis (as measured by GDP developments).

Here we see how the deep-crisis countries were much more heavily impacted by unemployment, more than doubling their unemployment level from 5.7 per cent in 2007 to 13.2 per cent at the peak in 2012–13, while other countries went from 6.6 per cent on average to a peak of 8.5 per cent in 2013, before coming down again.

It is also of interest to note that by 2016 unemployment in the deep-crisis countries as a whole had still not come down to the level that prevailed before the crisis, remaining at 9.7 per cent on average (as against about 6 per cent in 2007–2008). Those countries that did not experience the crisis so deeply are as of 2016 much closer to regaining the low unemployment levels of the pre-crisis years.

In Figure 2.3 we profile the unemployment experience of 34 Western countries, showing the initial position in 2007 (grey column), the final

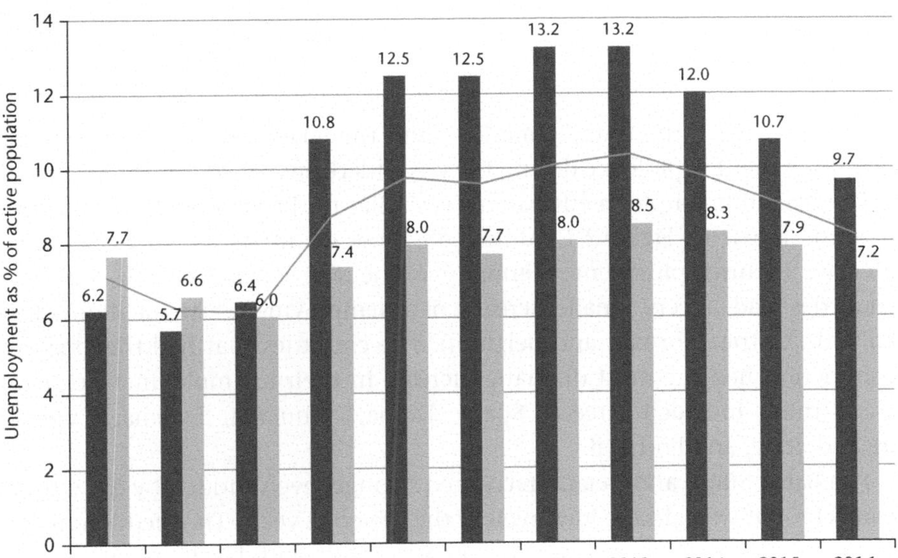


**Figure 2.2.** Overall profile of unemployment developments in deep-crisis and other countries, 2006–16

*Source*: Eurostat.

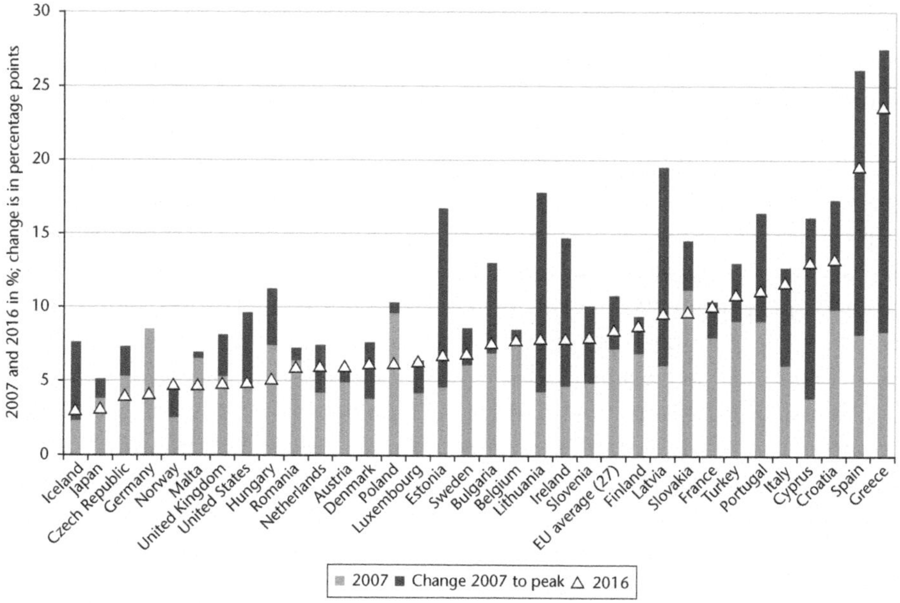


**Figure 2.3.** Country profiles of unemployment developments through the crisis

*Note*: Positions in 2007 and 2016 and accumulated change from 2007 to the highest level of unemployment reached in the crisis years (the dark parts of the columns). Ranked by position in 2016.

*Source*: Eurostat.

position in 2016 (the triangle marker), and the change to the peak of their unemployment experience during the crisis (dark area of columns).

The overall unemployment pattern is similar to the economic contraction pattern shown in Figure 2.1. Almost all these countries experienced some increase in unemployment (Germany is the sole exception and only six countries had a very small increase of unemployment—Malta, Romania, Poland, Austria, Norway, and Belgium). The countries that had the greatest contraction had the most dramatic increase in their unemployment experience; these included Greece, Spain, Latvia, Lithuania, Estonia, Cyprus, Ireland, Italy, and Portugal.

The Baltic States and Ireland recovered strongly even though by 2016 they had yet to fully regain the low levels of the pre-crisis years. The Mediterranean countries saw a slow recovery of their employment levels as well as of GDP. Iceland is an example of a country where the unemployment level increased significantly less than might have been expected from the size of the GDP contraction (and the collapse of about 90 per cent of its banking system), while unemployment in the UK and USA increased more than expected considering the scale of their GDP contraction. By 2016, however, all three countries (Iceland, UK, and USA) had regained their low pre-crisis level of unemployment.

On the whole most of these countries have improved their employment level from the lowest point of their crisis experience (only four have not done so). As of 2016 some countries (Germany, Hungary, Czech Republic, Malta, Poland, and Slovakia) had even lower unemployment levels than in 2007. The Mediterranean deep-crisis countries still had a very high level of unemployment in 2016, despite significant improvement. The Baltic States, which also suffered a big increase in unemployment, have recovered quite strongly.

It is interesting to examine more directly the relationship between maximum economic contraction and maximum increase in unemployment (i.e. to peak) (see Figure 2.4).

The correlation is very high (0.77), which indicates the depth of the crisis (economic contraction) has great importance as a source of negative welfare consequences. But as we show later in this chapter (see Figure 2.12) there is variation in the extent to which the contraction and increased unemployment experience was translated into financial hardship for populations. Figure 2.4 shows that increased unemployment was in rough proportion to the massive economic contraction in Greece, but that unemployment

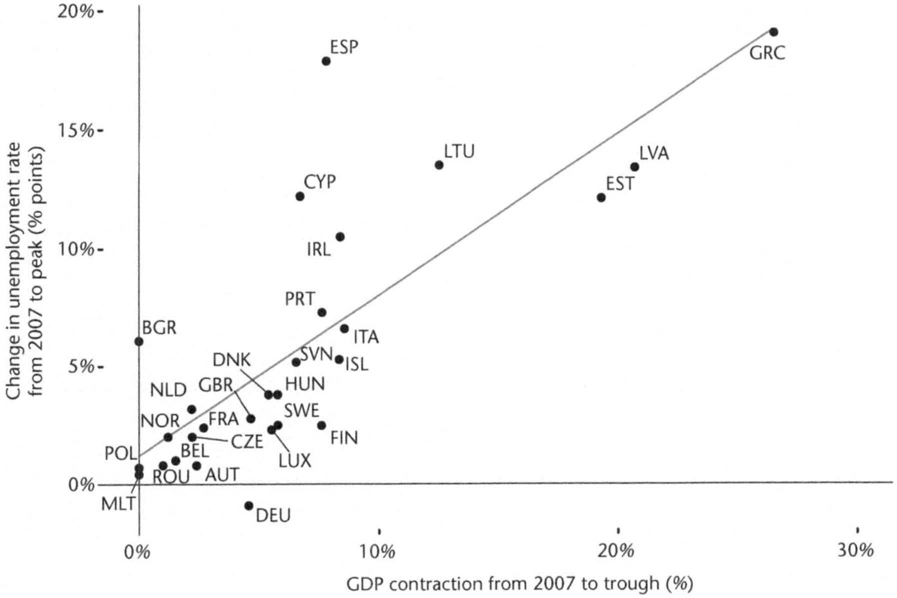


**Figure 2.4.** Change of GDP and unemployment from 2007 to trough (GDP) and peak (unemployment)

*Note*: Pearson's r = 0.77.

*Source*: Eurostat.

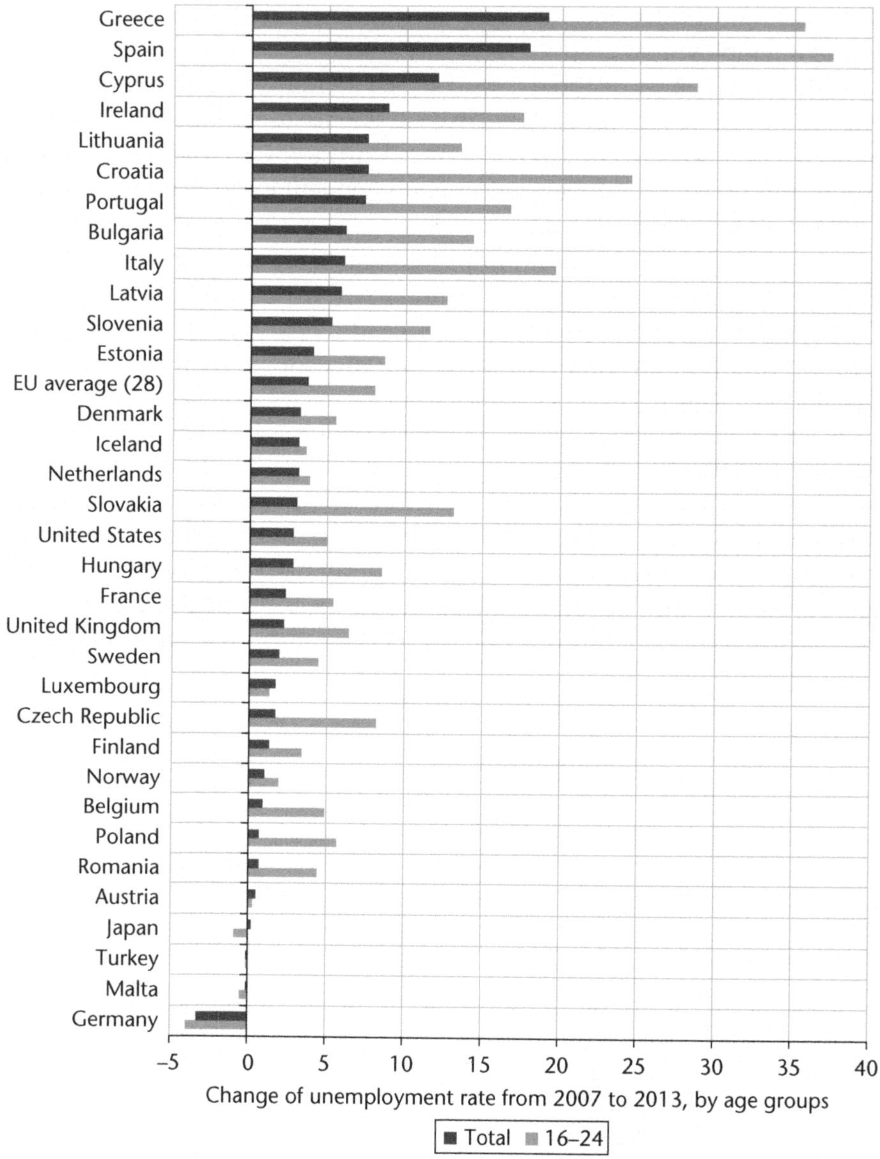


**Figure 2.5.** The special role of youth unemployment

*Note*: Increase of unemployment rates for 16–24 year olds compared to the total active labour force, 2007–13 (in percentage points).

*Source*: Eurostat.

increased proportionally more in Spain, Cyprus, Lithuania, and Ireland. On the other side of the regression line we have Finland, Sweden, Germany, Luxembourg, Austria, and Iceland, with a smaller increase of unemployment than might have been expected from the degree of economic contraction. The same also applies to Estonia and Latvia, which both, however, had a very large economic contraction. Bulgaria, which did not experience any economic contraction, saw an increase in its unemployment rate by some 6 percentage points.

Another very important aspect of the unemployment experience is how severely young people were impacted. On average the unemployment rate for 16–24 year olds was more than twice as high as the rate for the total active population in 2007, before the crisis hit. As shown in Figure 2.5, the youth unemployment rate increased on average just over twice as much as that for the labour force as a whole from 2007 to 2013, when the unemployment problem peaked for most countries.

Countries where this occurred include Greece, Spain, Cyprus, Ireland, Croatia, Portugal, Bulgaria, Italy, Slovakia, Hungary, the UK, and the Czech Republic. On the other hand, youth unemployment in Iceland and the Netherlands did not increase much more than the overall rate, and in Luxembourg and Austria the youth rate actually increased less than the overall rate. Germany is in a class of its own, with significant reduction of unemployment during the crisis, and more so for youth than the labour force as a whole.

It is logical, even in stable economic conditions, that new entrants to the labour market have a higher risk of becoming unemployed than other age groups (Müller & Gangl, 2003). During deep crises that risk can increase more than for other population sectors, as we have shown. In that scenario school leavers are likely to experience delays in their entry to a career. As such, the age group of 16–24 year olds is typically a victim of economic recessions. The degree to which that is translated into financial hardship for those individuals may be smoothed by options of pursuing further education and living longer in parents' households while the crisis lasts.

Taken as a whole, the data thus far show that the development of GDP and unemployment levels tell similar stories about the depth of the crisis experience, although there are some deviations, indicating the differing effects of policies, welfare regimes, and other conditions.

### 2.1.2 *Income developments during the crisis*

Next we profile real income changes from 2007 to 2014. This is an important addition to our analyses of unemployment and financial hardship developments and a good prologue to the assessments of changing inequality and poverty, which will be dealt with in section 2.4.

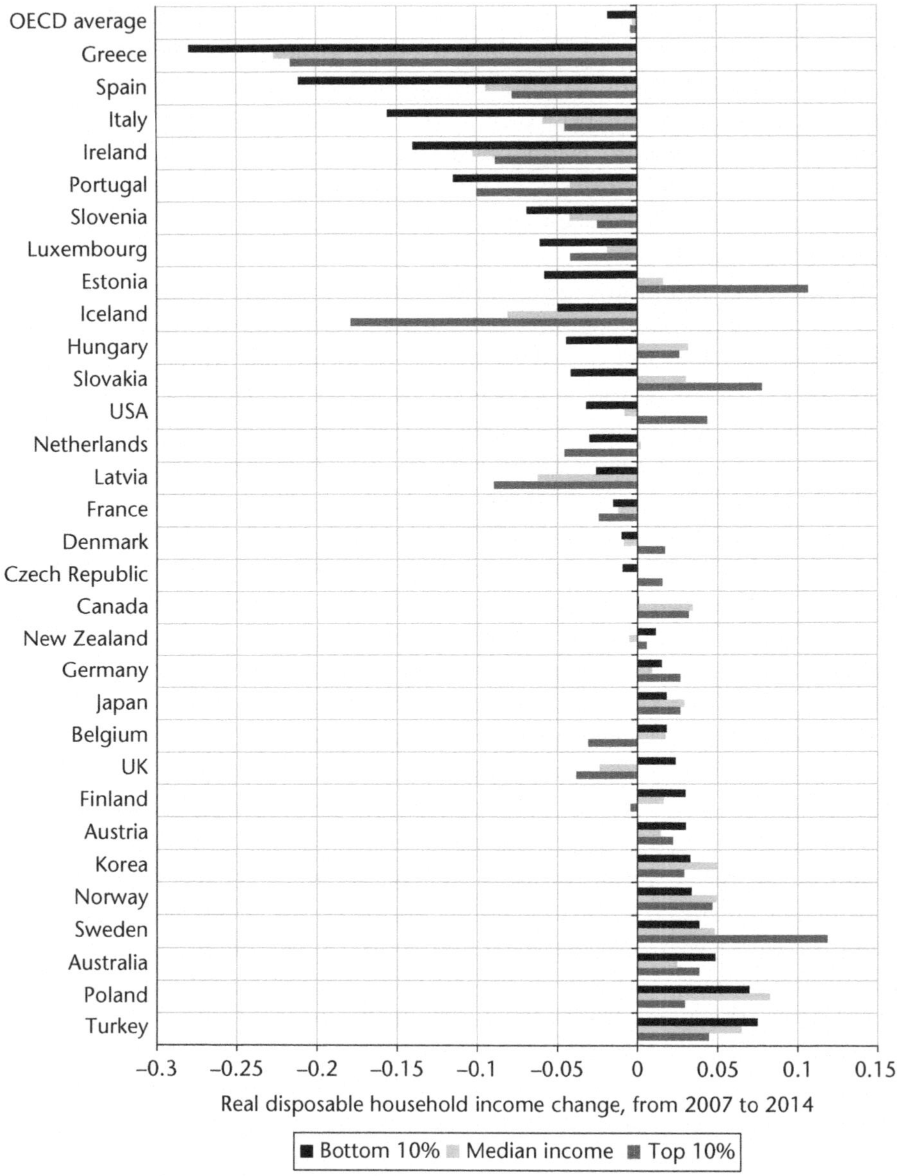


**Figure 2.6.** Change in real disposable income 2007–14, by income groups

*Note*: Countries are ranked by extent of changes for the lowest income group (the black columns).

*Source*: OECD (2016b).

Figure 2.6 shows the real income change at three levels of the income ladder in OECD countries: the lowest decile, the median, and the top decile. The countries are ranked by extent of income change in the lowest income group. Hence the countries at the top of the figure are the ones where low-income groups were hardest hit with income loss: Greece, Spain, Italy, Ireland, Portugal, Slovenia, Luxembourg, and Estonia. In all of these countries the real disposable incomes of low-income households contracted significantly more than those of the median- and top-income groups. Hence inequality increased in all of them, with the exception of Portugal and Luxembourg. These are all countries that also suffered relatively large increases in financial hardship.

Iceland comes next in rank, but with a very different pattern, in fact a completely opposite pattern. There the lowest incomes (the lowest decile) declined much less than higher incomes, particularly those at the top.[1] Latvia is the only other deep-crisis country that shares this pattern with Iceland, but to a significantly lesser degree. Portugal and Luxembourg experienced a decline both at the bottom and the top (more at the low end), but less so in the middle. The Netherlands and France, at a lower level of overall change, had a somewhat greater decline at the top than at the bottom and less so in the middle.

At the lower end of Figure 2.6 we have countries that primarily increased household incomes during the crisis period. Amongst those are some whose lowest incomes increased more than higher incomes (Belgium, UK, Finland, Austria, Australia, Poland, and Turkey). Sweden stands out in that grouping as the nation that increased the top incomes the most between 2007 and 2014.

Now we turn to an assessment of how the Great Recession affected the financial situation of European households.

## 2.2 Financial Hardship

In this section we use a new composite measure of financial hardship of populations in 30 European countries. The index is based on three variables in the European Union Statistics on Income and Living Conditions (EU-SILC) database of the EU's statistical office (Eurostat). These are measures of *income poverty*, *difficulties in making ends meet*, and an indicator of *material deprivation*

[1] Whelan et al. (2016) show a decisively larger income loss for Iceland in their comparison of Greece, Iceland, and Ireland, in the region of 40%. They use euros in that comparison. When using purchasing power parities (PPPs), as the OECD does in the data of Figure 2.6, the mean income loss was closer to 20%, which seems more realistic. It also chimes better with Icelandic currency figures of changing purchasing power of disposable incomes (see further details on this in Chapter 8). Our figures here cover 2007 to 2014 but Whelan et al. cover the 2008 to 2012 period. Iceland regained some of its income loss between 2012 and 2014 and by 2016 had almost fully regained this.

(not being able to afford three out of nine important consumption items). We apply a latent class analysis of the covariance of these three variables to determine whether an individual is classified as suffering financial hardship or not.[2]

All of these variables address the financial position of households or individuals, and even though they might be called composite measures of 'poverty' or 'economic vulnerability' it seems to us that they are best interpreted as reflecting the financial hardship experienced by individuals or households. As such they are particularly useful for monitoring the impact of the crisis on the finances of individuals or households, as well as for relating financial hardship to socio-economic position and to indicators of the institutional environment (strength of welfare states) and policy reactions of governments to the crisis (which are examined in the country case studies in Part II and in Chapter 14).

At the advent of the crisis the overall level of financial hardship of populations was generally on a downward trend in Europe, mainly due to a catch-up process amongst the less affluent countries in Eastern Europe. This can be seen in indicators of unemployment, anchored poverty rates, and proportions of populations experiencing great difficulties in making ends meet. A similar pattern is also revealed in our indicator of financial hardship. All these indicators also show that 2012–13 was the height of the financial hardship level for most countries, except for some Mediterranean countries that experienced stronger economic contraction. They peaked later.

As a composite measure the financial hardship indicator should reflect the financial burdens imposed on people by the crisis situation, taking account of unemployment and reduced work volumes, income loss, and tax increases, as well as the countervailing factors softening the crisis consequences, such as higher benefits and/or tax cuts, increased redistribution, and economic stimulus. Hence the measure should indicate the net effects of the crisis on financial hardship, as experienced by individuals or households.

### 2.2.1 *Which socio-economic groups were hardest hit?*

We start the survey of financial hardship developments throughout the crisis with a pan-European view on the collective population of these 30 countries (see Figure 2.7), calculating average financial hardship scores for the overall population in each year from 2007 to 2015, as well as for different socio-economic groups across Europe.[3] This is akin to calculating average poverty levels for all these countries, decomposed by socio-economic groups. There may,

[2] See the Appendix to this book for a more detailed explanation of the methodological issues relating to this composite measure of 'financial hardship' and its use.

[3] The 30 countries are those that take part in EU-SILC surveys and that have data for all the years. Numbers are unweighted country averages.

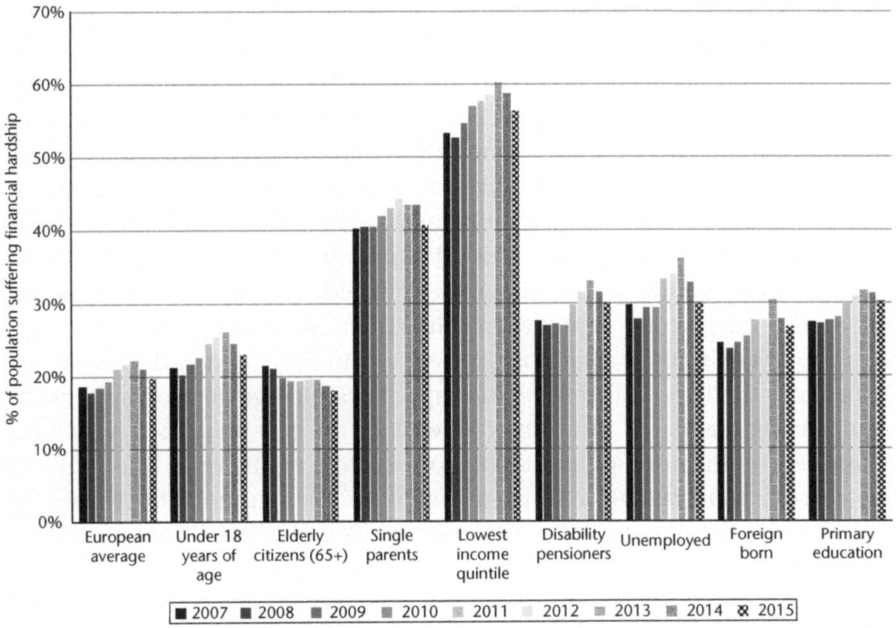


**Figure 2.7.** Financial hardship developments through the crisis, by main socio-economic groups

*Note*: Averages for 30 European countries, 2007–15.

*Source*: Author calculations from EU-SILC data.

of course, still be variation between countries, but we obtain the most common pattern, even though differences of degree will be evident (as will emerge in the country case chapters in Part II). We go on, later in the chapter (Figures 2.8 to 2.10), to assess to what extent different groups experienced increased financial hardship, allowing us to identify which groups were hardest hit.

The overall average financial hardship scores for the 30 European countries ranged from about 18 per cent in 2008 to 22 per cent at the peak in 2013. It came down to just under 20 per cent by 2015, which was still above the pre-crisis level. This, of course, includes both countries that were mildly or not affected as well as countries that were severely affected. The overall pattern is broadly reflected in most of the subgroups. Nevertheless, there are different levels and varying paths.[4]

[4] In the individual country case studies in Part II it is possible to see the financial hardship profile for each of the countries covered. While the overall pattern amongst the socio-economic groups is broadly similar, the levels of hardship in individual subgroups differ somewhat between countries, with some countries, of course, having steeper increases of hardship than others.

Before the crisis started the lowest income group (the lowest income quintile in this case) had the highest level of financial hardship, with about 52–3 per cent suffering financial hardship in 2007. They experienced increased hardship, up to 60 per cent in 2013, before coming down again towards 2015. At that time they were still significantly above the 2008 level.

Single parents had the second-highest financial hardship level in 2007, at about 40 per cent. Then came the unemployed, the lowest educational class (those with primary education or less), disability pensioners, immigrants, and then households with children under 18. The elderly generation (65+) stand out as the only group that lowered its financial hardship level through the crisis years, starting at almost 22 per cent in 2007 and ending at about 18 per cent in 2015. This reflects the capacity of old-age pension systems to secure living standards in a crisis, as well as the fact that each year new pensioners, with more accumulations of pension rights, enter the ranks of the elderly, thus raising average incomes for that group. The employed elderly were also less impacted by unemployment than younger workers (OECD, 2013).

Which socio-economic groups experienced the greatest increase of financial hardship during the crisis? Figure 2.8 presents two measures of increased financial hardship for ten income groups (deciles), first covering change from 2008 to what was the peak for most countries (2013) and then from

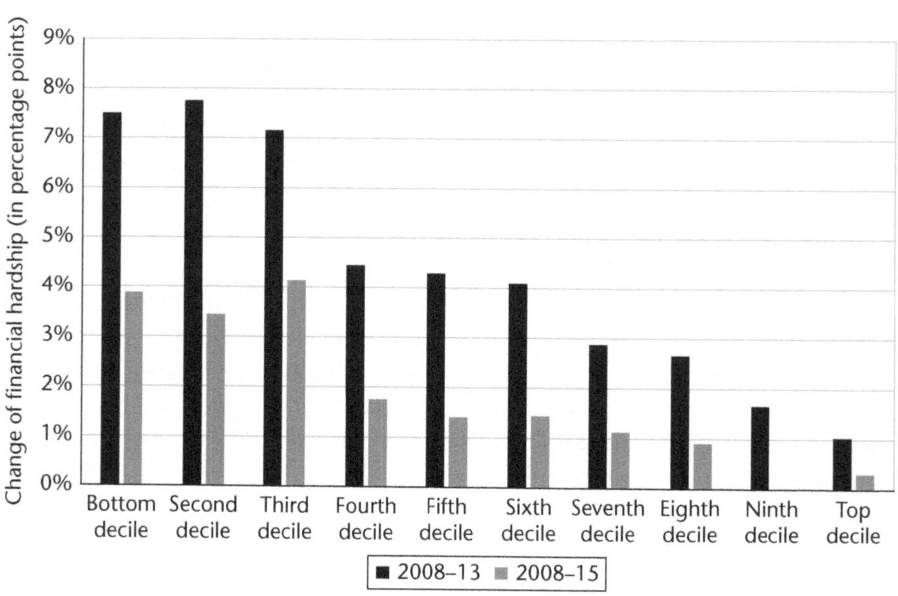


**Figure 2.8.** Changing financial hardship by income deciles, 2008–13 and 2008–15
*Note*: Change measured in percentage points.
*Source*: EU-SILC, authors' calculation.

2008 to 2015. These are unweighted averages for income groups in 30 European countries.

It is very clear from this data that the lowest income groups were by far most heavily affected by the crisis, while the highest income groups experienced only a minor change. The relationship is direct and quite strong. Not only did the lowest income groups have the highest level of financial hardship before the crisis, they also experienced the greatest increase in hardship during the crisis years. This applies particularly to the lowest three deciles, the 30 per cent of individuals with the lowest incomes. Their financial hardship level increased by 7–8 percentage points from 2008 to 2013, while the increase for the next three income groups was just above 4 percentage points. Income groups 7 and 8 increased their level by between 2.5 to 3 percentage points, while the top 10 per cent only saw an increase of around 1 percentage point, from a very low original level.

Another interesting feature of Figure 2.8 is the fact that the recovery from the initial impact was slower for the three very lowest income groups. This emerges when we examine the change from the beginning to the end of our period (i.e. from 2008 to 2015; the grey columns). The poorest individuals (deciles 1 to 3) still had a higher financial hardship level in 2015 of almost 4 per cent than they had in 2008. The top-income groups (deciles 9 and 10), on the other hand, had more or less fully recovered from their very modest increase of hardship by 2015. So recovery, as well as the initial effect of the crisis, was differentially shared.

In Figure 2.9 we disaggregate the changing financial hardship experiences further by socio-economic groups, again for the two periods of 2008 to 2013 and 2008 to 2015.

In this ranking the unemployed show the largest increase of hardship, slightly above the average for the lowest income quintile. Unemployment tends to hit lower- and medium-income groups disproportionally (OECD, 2013).

Single parents had the second-highest level of financial hardship before the crisis, but they were not amongst the groups that were particularly hard hit with additional financial hardship, as seen in Figure 2.9. Their hardship level increased less during the crisis than amongst other low-income groups, indicating that the welfare systems of European countries frequently sheltered that group more than some of the other most vulnerable groups. By 2015 single parents had more or less regained their pre-crisis level.

Foreign-born individuals, disability pensioners, and children under 18 were next in line as regards increased financial hardship towards 2013. Again, the elderly were in a class of their own, with decreasing hardships during the crisis. On the whole there was, however, a considerable improvement between 2013 and 2015 for all groups.

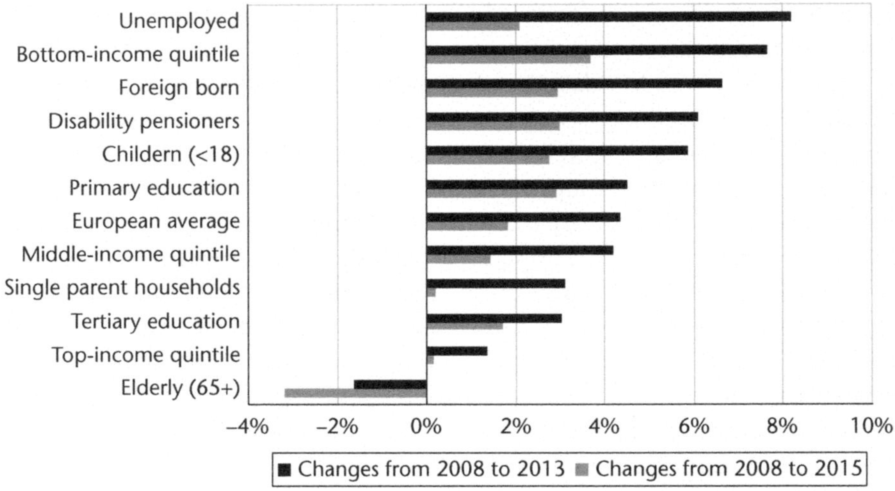


**Figure 2.9.** Changes in financial hardship during the crisis, by socio-economic groups

*Note*: Average hardship levels by socio-economic groups across Europe. Changes 2008–13 and to 2015 (in percentage points). Averages for 30 European countries.

*Source*: Author calculations from EU-SILC data.

In Figure 2.10 we further map the changes in financial hardship levels amongst different socio-economic groups, by comparing age groups and educational groups across all categories.

The experience of the 18–24 age groups was somewhat worse than for other prime age groups, both as regards the 2013 and 2015 outcomes. This is the age group with many school leavers who typically have difficulties entering the labour market during crisis years and it was indeed heavily impacted by unemployment, as we showed in Figure 2.5. While households with children under 18 years had a significant increase in their level of financial hardship during the crisis, their experience was not much more dramatic than that of the overall population average. Nevertheless, increased hardship and poverty amongst households with children was a significant burden in many countries (cf. Cantillon et al., 2017).

Individuals with the lowest education level, who often work in low-paid and insecure jobs, had both a high level of financial hardship before the crisis and a significant increase of hardship during it. But the intermediate educational level suffered an even larger increase of financial hardship, whereas those with university-level education were on the whole significantly less likely to experience increased financial hardship.

We can say clearly that it was the lowest income groups that bore the brunt of increased financial hardships during the Great Recession in Europe. In this context it should be kept in mind that the lower income groups in general

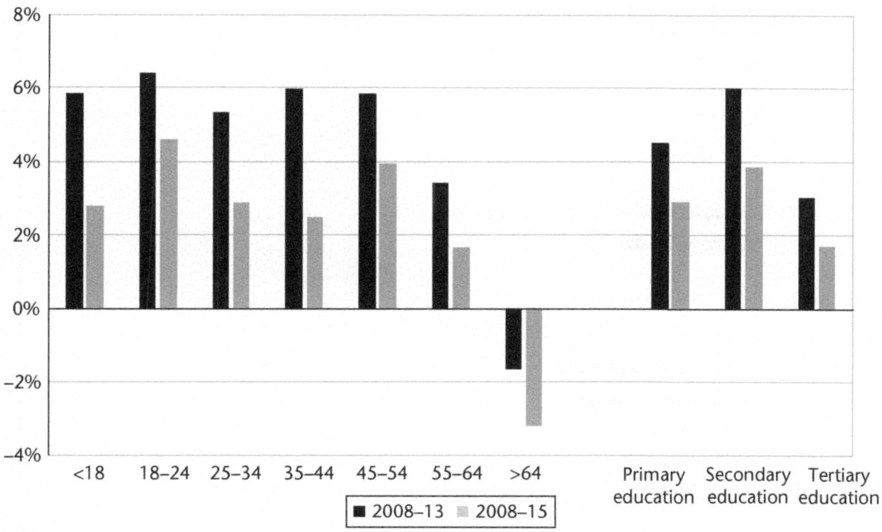


**Figure 2.10.** Changing financial hardship 2008–13 and 2008–15, by educational level, and age groups

*Note*: Averages for 30 European countries.

*Source*: Author calculations from EU-SILC data.

have less capacity for dealing with income loss and higher expenditures than other income groups. Those higher up the income ladder were either very modestly or not at all affected.

## 2.2.2 *Financial hardship in different welfare regimes*

It is now pertinent to examine how financial hardship progressed through the crisis in individual countries, reflecting at the same time differential welfare regimes or welfare clusters, which have differential capabilities for softening negative crisis consequences. This we aim to do in Figure 2.11.[5]

This is powerful material for outlining narratives of the crisis consequences in Europe. It shows at the same time differential original positions of these 30 nations before the crisis (in 2007), and how each progressed in 2010, 2013, and 2015. The groupings in the figure provide indications of differing capabilities of welfare states, as well as differing affluence and debt levels of governments and differing policy traditions (to which we turn more directly in Chapter 14).

[5] Our classification of countries here is not based on a detailed study of welfare state characteristics, although it partly resembles Esping-Andersen's 1990 and 1999 classifications of welfare regimes. In effect, our use here is closer to the 'families of nations' groupings of Francis G. Castles. See Castles (1993) and Castles and Obinger (2008).

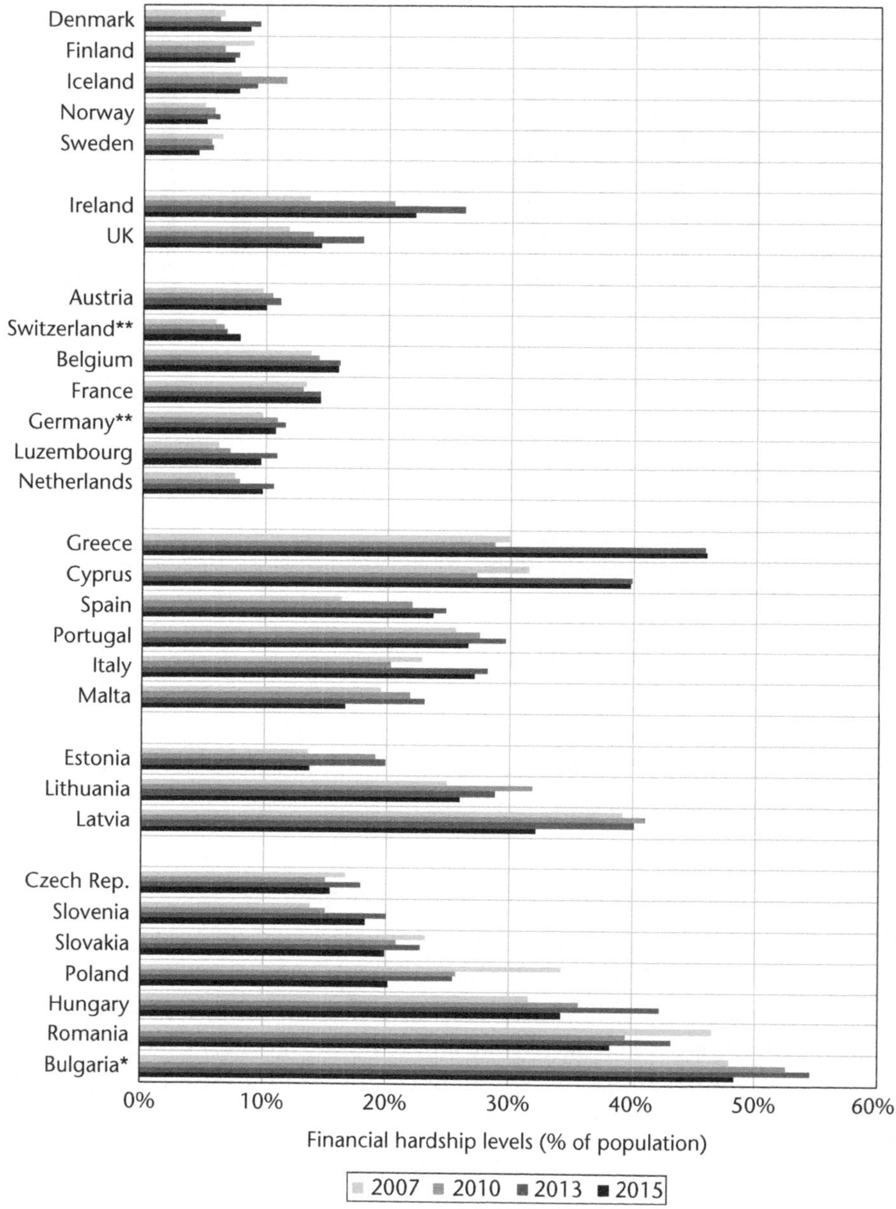


**Figure 2.11.** Financial hardship developments through the crisis, in different welfare regimes. Selected years, 2007–15

*Note*: The 2015 figures for Germany and Switzerland are for 2014; the 2007 figure for Bulgaria is for 2008.

*Source*: Author calculations from EU-SILC data.

If we start with the Nordic countries we generally find the lowest levels of financial hardship prevailing there before the crisis. Of the more advanced Continental countries, the only ones with comparably low hardship levels in 2007 were Switzerland, Luxembourg, and the Netherlands. Iceland, of course, stands out in the Nordic group for experiencing by far the deepest financial crisis. But in comparison to other deep-crisis countries, in Iceland the financial hardship level did not increase as drastically. Moreover, it bottomed out in 2010 and has been improving gradually since then. By 2016 Iceland had regained the lowest unemployment level amongst Western countries, as was shown in Figure 2.3.

Denmark is the only other Nordic country whose population has experienced significantly increased financial hardship during the crisis years, whereas Finland, Norway, and Sweden show very little change. Sweden in fact continually, albeit modestly, reduced its low hardship level during the crisis years.

The more liberal market-oriented countries, Ireland and the UK, have a different profile from the Nordic countries. At the outset they had significantly higher levels of financial hardship than the Nordics and this continually increased in both during the crisis years, up to 2013. The modest speed of recovery from hardship in the last two years means that both countries end the period at a significantly higher level than before the crisis hit, particularly Ireland. The fact that both Ireland and the UK increased their financial hardship levels more than Iceland indicates that there was more softening of the crisis consequences in Iceland.

The main Continental countries, as well as Switzerland, seem to have a pattern of their own, with generally little change in financial hardship during the crisis. Luxembourg, the Netherlands, and Switzerland increased their hardship levels modestly and continually, but from the lowest levels. The rest of that group saw a minor increase early in the crisis but some showed improvements again towards 2015. On the whole these Continental countries managed to counteract negative welfare consequences during the Great Recession quite well.

The Mediterranean countries also have their own distinctive, but more dismal, pattern. These countries have weaker welfare states than the more northern countries, which is, amongst other things, reflected in their relatively high levels of financial hardship before the crisis. Many of these countries experienced a very deep crisis, as shown, and their level of financial hardship continually increased up to around 2014. This applies particularly to Greece, Cyprus, Spain, and Italy, less so to Portugal and Malta. Our data show some improvement for Spain by 2015. All these Mediterranean countries (except Malta) had, however, a higher level of financial hardship in 2015 than before the crisis in 2007. It seems likely that these countries will lag further behind the main Continental and Northern countries in terms of living standards for the medium term as a consequence of the Great Recession.

The Baltic States revealed yet another pattern of financial hardship development during the crisis. They started from a relatively high level of hardship, like the Mediterranean countries, reflecting weaker welfare states and lower levels of affluence. They had, however, been on a firmly progressive path after their liberalization from the Soviet Union in the early 1990s. The characteristic pattern or trajectory of these countries is of a deep crisis (reflected in a very large increase of unemployment, cf. Figure 2.3), but a quick recovery after 2010–11. Latvia is now at lower financial hardship levels than it was before the crisis and Estonia (which was at a lower level than the other two throughout) and Lithuania are at a similar level as in the last pre-crisis years. The Baltic States may continue on their path from the pre-crisis years and thus emerge more strongly from the crisis experience than some of the worst-hit Mediterranean countries.

Lastly, the other former socialist countries have a different story to tell, and one that is not as harmonious as the countries in our other regime or family groups. Starting at the lower end we have a clear pattern for Romania, Poland, and Slovakia. They were all reducing their level of financial hardship before the advent of the crisis and that development generally continued through the crisis years to 2015. Even though they still have a long way to go to match the more affluent and welfare-oriented north-western European countries, they were on a convergence path towards improvement. Bulgaria and Hungary both experienced a high level of increased financial hardship towards 2013 but improved significantly after that, approaching their pre-crisis levels by 2015. Slovenia, with the lowest level of financial hardship in this group, increased its level up to 2013 but improved after that, while the Czech Republic and Slovakia remained at similar levels throughout, albeit with some variations.

There is thus not only considerable variety in the levels of hardship experienced among countries but also indications that welfare states had differing impacts. There are, of course, other conditions and policy contexts that may have mediated the consequences of the Great Recession with regard to the welfare of European populations, as we show in Parts II and III. Trends towards convergence and divergence also raise some interesting questions about future developments.

Next we examine this through a different window (Figure 2.12), by showing the relationship between economic contraction and maximum increase of financial hardship (using the composite measure) during the crisis amongst European countries.

The correlation between these variables is about 0.6, which indicates a considerable regularity. However, there are also significant deviations. Thus one can say that Ireland, Hungary, Cyprus, Spain, Bulgaria, Greece, Slovenia, and the UK saw increased financial hardship more than might have been

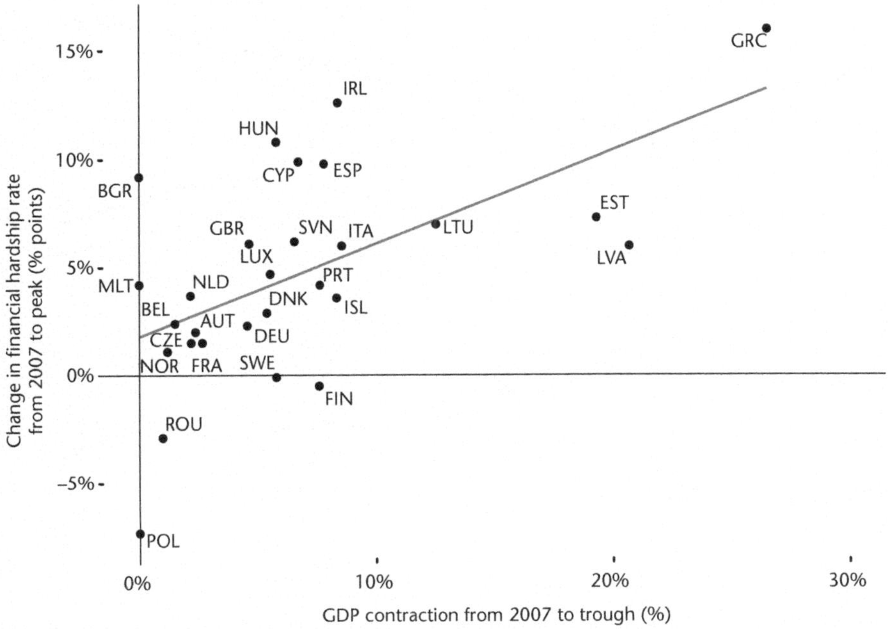


**Figure 2.12.** Association between economic contraction and increased financial hardship of European populations

*Note*: GDP contraction from peak to trough and financial hardship change from 2007 to peak value during the crisis years. Pearson's r = −0.61.

*Source*: OECD and author calculations from EU-SILC data.

expected given the extent their economies contracted. On the other hand, Latvia and Estonia, at the deep-crisis end, seem to have experienced increased financial hardship less than their contraction and increased unemployment might have dictated. The same applies to Iceland, Denmark, Portugal, Germany, and France. Amongst less affected countries, Finland and Sweden maintained or reduced financial hardship during the crisis despite significant contraction of their economies and increased unemployment. Germany, France, Romania, and Poland are also notable amongst the countries below the regression line. Economic contraction was evidently not the only driver of financial hardship.

Lastly, we compare the development of financial hardship throughout the crisis in six deep-crisis countries in Figure 2.13, focusing specifically on individuals in the lowest income quintile—the most vulnerable group. For interesting comparative purposes we include here two countries that did not experience such a deep crisis (Denmark and the Netherlands). This data shows, at the same time, differing levels of financial hardship to start with and differential impacts of the crisis over time for the most vulnerable groups in the most affected countries.

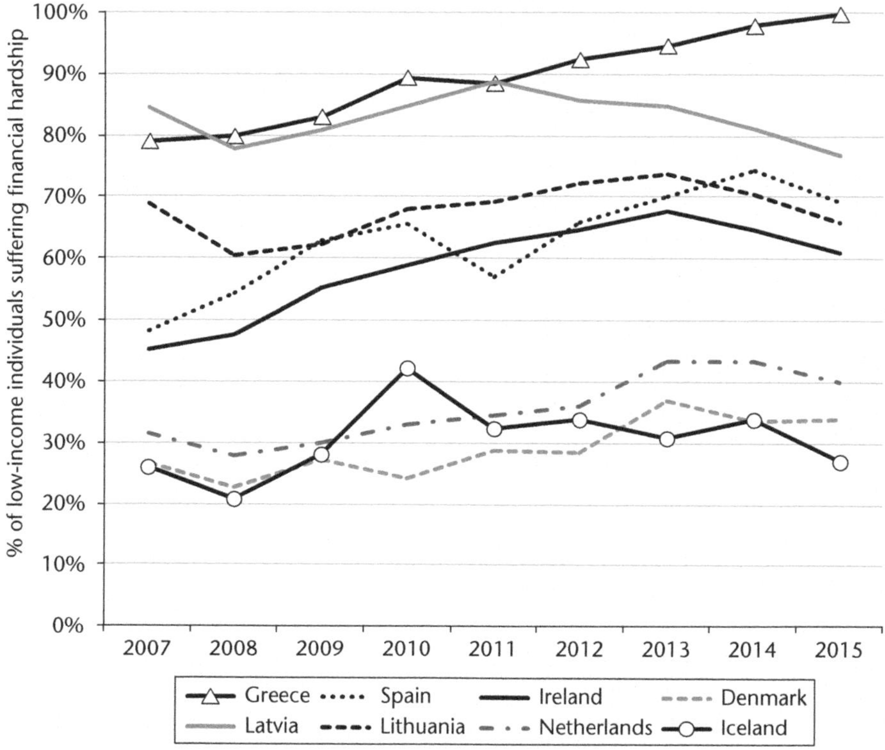


**Figure 2.13.** Financial hardship of low-income individuals in six deep-crisis countries, 2006–15

*Note*: Shows proportion of lowest income quintile suffering financial hardship.

*Source*: Author calculations from EU-SILC data.

Here we again see the convergence path of Latvia and Lithuania towards 2008 (which our source data show was even more forceful from 2005). In a way the Great Recession was a severe setback for that convergence development. However, these countries seem to have found their way again, Latvia after 2011 and Lithuania after 2013, improving continually towards 2015. Latvia dipped below Greece in 2012 and onwards. Lithuania went below Spain in 2014 and 2015. Greece and Spain, on the other hand, retained a dismal path of continued worsening; Greece all the way up to 2015 while Spain recorded only a modest change for the better in 2015.

While Iceland and Ireland were not so different as regards depth of their economic contraction they started at very different levels of financial hardship for low-income individuals, Iceland at just over 20 per cent in the pre-crisis stage while Ireland was in the range of 45–50 per cent. The increase was very steep in Iceland up to 2010, with a gradual improvement from then on. The increased financial hardship for low-income individuals in Ireland was also steep but primarily more prolonged than in Iceland, topping in 2013 and improving only modestly towards the end of our period. The different welfare outcomes in Ireland and Iceland clearly indicate a differing welfare state capacity and differing government policy environments (including the constraints of Eurozone membership for Ireland), since the extent and characteristics of the bubble economies of the pre-crisis period and the ensuing financial crises were not so different in these countries (cf. Blyth, 2013; Reinhart & Rogoff, 2010; see also Chapters 7 and 8). Both countries had to seek assistance, Iceland from the International Monetary Fund (IMF) and Ireland from the Troika, but the constraints imposed and the policy reactions were different, as were the welfare consequences.[6]

Looking beyond the deep-crisis countries, it is interesting that Iceland and Denmark show similar levels of financial hardship for low-income individuals in 2007–08. Both increased similarly in 2009 and then Iceland peaked in 2010, well above both Denmark and the Netherlands. Since then Iceland's figures have been similar to these two countries, neither of which experienced a particularly deep crisis. They were, however, impacted by the second dip, as was common amongst the EU countries, reaching their highest levels of financial hardship for low-income individuals between 2013 and 2015. Iceland was in fact doing better than both of them from 2013 to 2015.

On the whole, we can say that in 2015 there was still some way to go to fully redress the dismal consequences of the Great Recession in Europe. But more so for some countries than others.

## 2.3 How the Burdens were Shared: A Different Perspective

Lastly we examine how the burdens of the crisis were shared by comparing inequality and poverty developments through the main crisis years. Figure 2.14 shows the change of Gini inequality coefficients for equivalized disposable household incomes during two periods: the early crisis years and then for the whole period from 2007 to 2014.

As is to be expected from the data on income changes presented in Figure 2.6, Iceland stands out as the country that equalized its income distribution to the greatest extent after the onset of the crisis. This reflects the country's strategy of redistribution in dealing with the crisis, which emphasized sheltering lower income groups more than others, through redistributive tax and benefit policies and a strong emphasis on avoiding unemployment (see Ólafsson, 2016b; see also Chapter 8). The equalization process went even

[6] See also Whelan, Nolan, and Maitre (2016) for a comparison of economic stress in Greece, Iceland, and Ireland; see also Chapters 5–8.

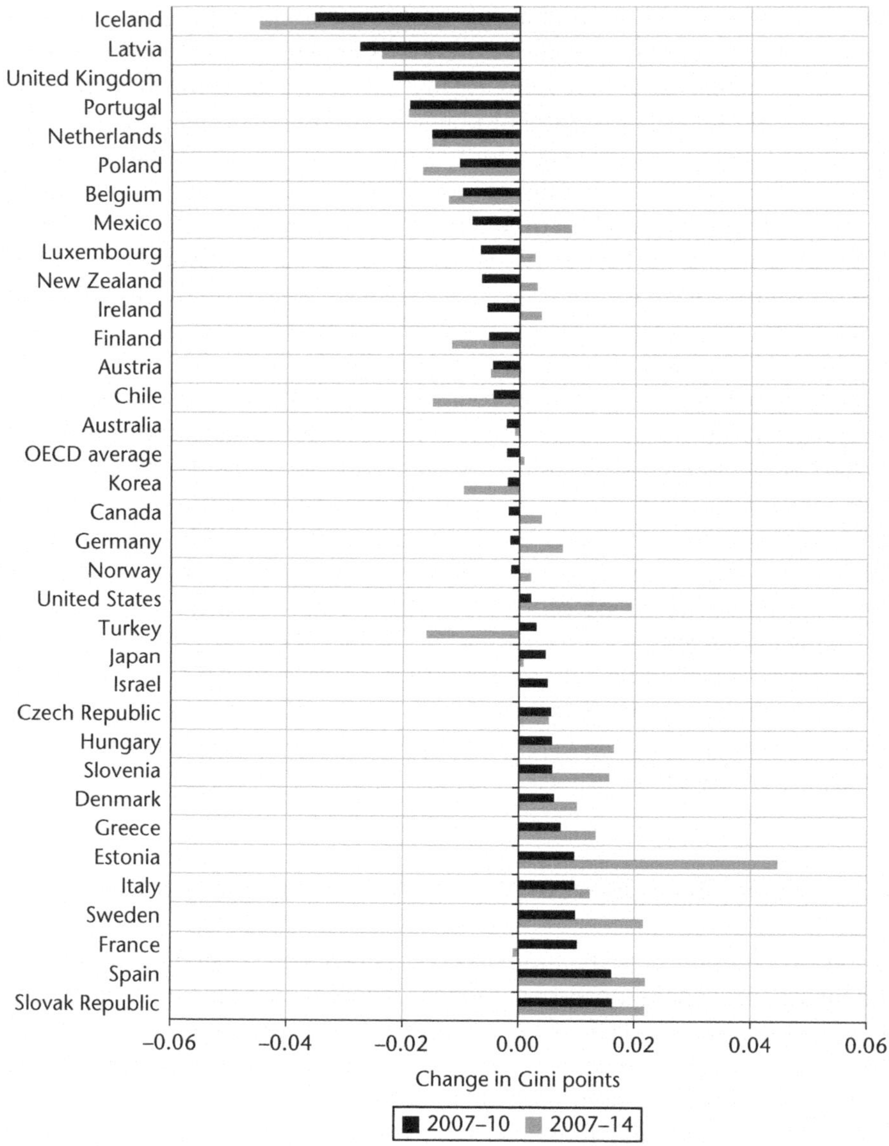


**Figure 2.14.** Inequality developments during the crisis

*Note*: Change of Gini coefficients (in Gini points) for equivalized disposable income, 2007–10 and 2007–14. Countries are ranked by change 2007–10 (the dark columns).

*Source*: OECD (2016b).

further after 2010 (see the grey column in Figure 2.14). Latvia, the United Kingdom, Portugal, and the Netherlands are next in line, but the first two reduced the degree of equalization after 2010, unlike the latter two. Poland and Belgium also equalized incomes during the crisis, more so when the whole period from 2007 to 2014 is considered, as did Finland. Ireland equalized a little in the first phase of the crisis but reversed that after 2010.

At the lower end of Figure 2.14 we have countries that increased inequality during the crisis. Most of the countries from Hungary down to the Slovak Republic increased inequality more in the whole of the period (2007 to 2014), except France, which increased inequality in the first phase but reversed that after 2010. Estonia stands out as the country that increased inequality to the greatest extent during the whole period, followed by Sweden, Spain, the Slovak Republic, the USA, Hungary, and Slovenia. The incomes of the higher income groups generally increased the most in these countries, with lower incomes lagging behind or declining.

Relative poverty rates (as measured by the proportion under 50 per cent of the median for equivalized disposable household income) have a limited role as measures of actual poverty experiences, especially in a crisis situation when the median itself falls (hence our preferred reliance on measures of financial hardship). Changes in relative poverty rates are, however, more useful indicators of how the burdens of the crisis were shared. They show whether the lowest income groups fared better or worse than the median. In Figure 2.15 we first show the relative poverty level before the crisis started (2007) and then the change in the poverty rates (increase or decline) from 2007 to 2014. The countries with column that change to dark grey on the left-hand side of the diagram are those that sheltered the lowest income groups, whereas those on the right-hand side could be said to have penalized the lowest income groups, placing heavier poverty burdens on them than on the median groups.

It was a more common pattern to increase the burdens of the low-income groups disproportionally (18 countries increased their burden while 13 sheltered them compared to the median). Iceland had one of the lowest relative poverty rates before the crisis and succeeded in reducing this significantly from 2007 to 2014. The UK was at a higher poverty level before the crisis but reduced it up to 2014; Latvia was at a much higher poverty level in 2007 but reduced it by almost 5 percentage points in the following seven years (mainly achieved by reducing middle and higher incomes more than the lowest incomes).

Other countries that sheltered the lowest groups to some extent are Australia, Mexico, Switzerland, New Zealand, Finland, and Ireland. The countries that increased the burdens of the poor disproportionally were Hungary, Estonia, Greece, Spain, the Netherlands, the Slovak Republic, Slovenia, and Italy.

In Figure 2.16 we examine poverty developments during the crisis differently, using a poverty line anchored in 2005, instead of the yearly nominal value poverty lines.

On this measure it is Greece, Cyprus, Spain, Ireland, and Italy that stand out, with relatively high pre-crisis poverty rates and large increases during the early

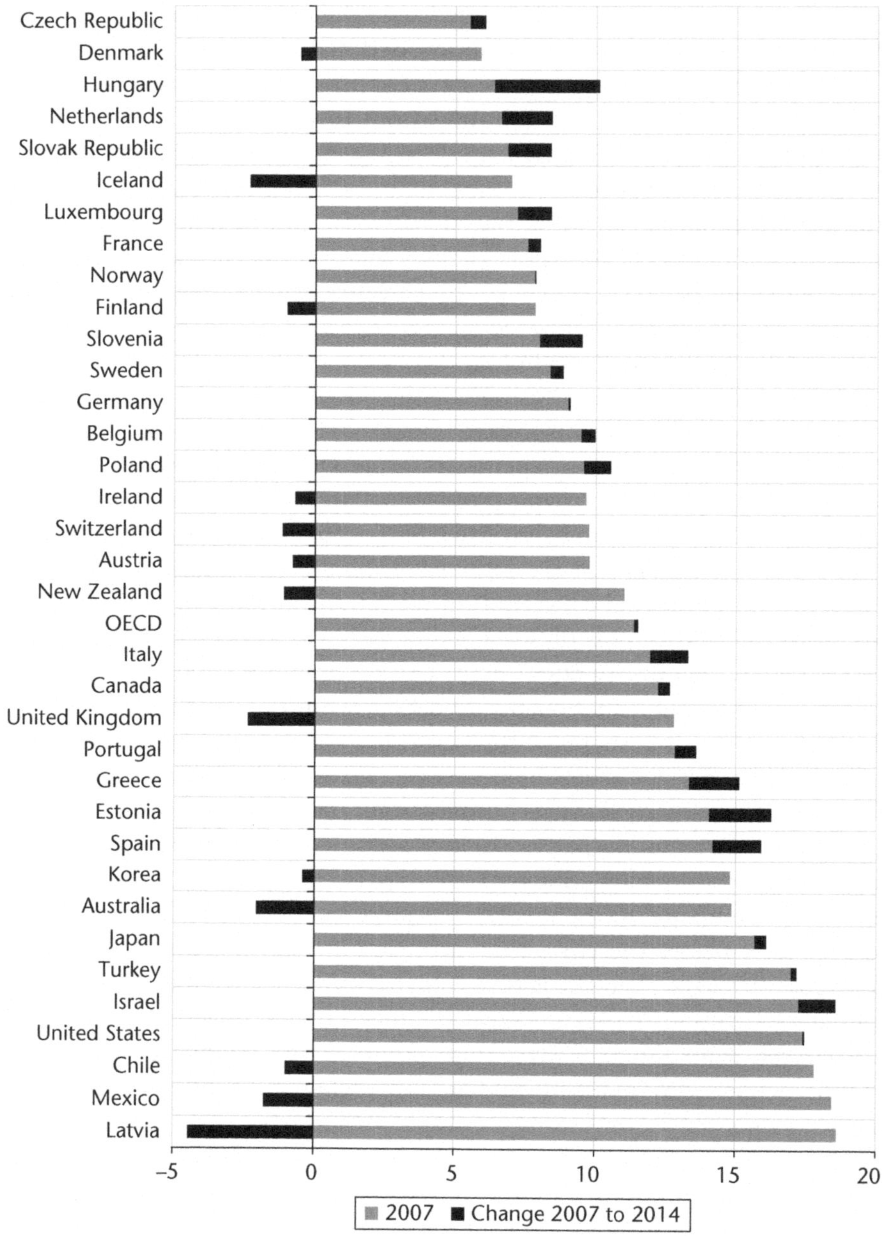


**Figure 2.15.** Relative poverty levels in 2007 and change 2007–14 (%)

*Note*: Poverty level is % of households under 50% of median. Ranked by poverty level in 2007.

*Source*: OECD (2016b).

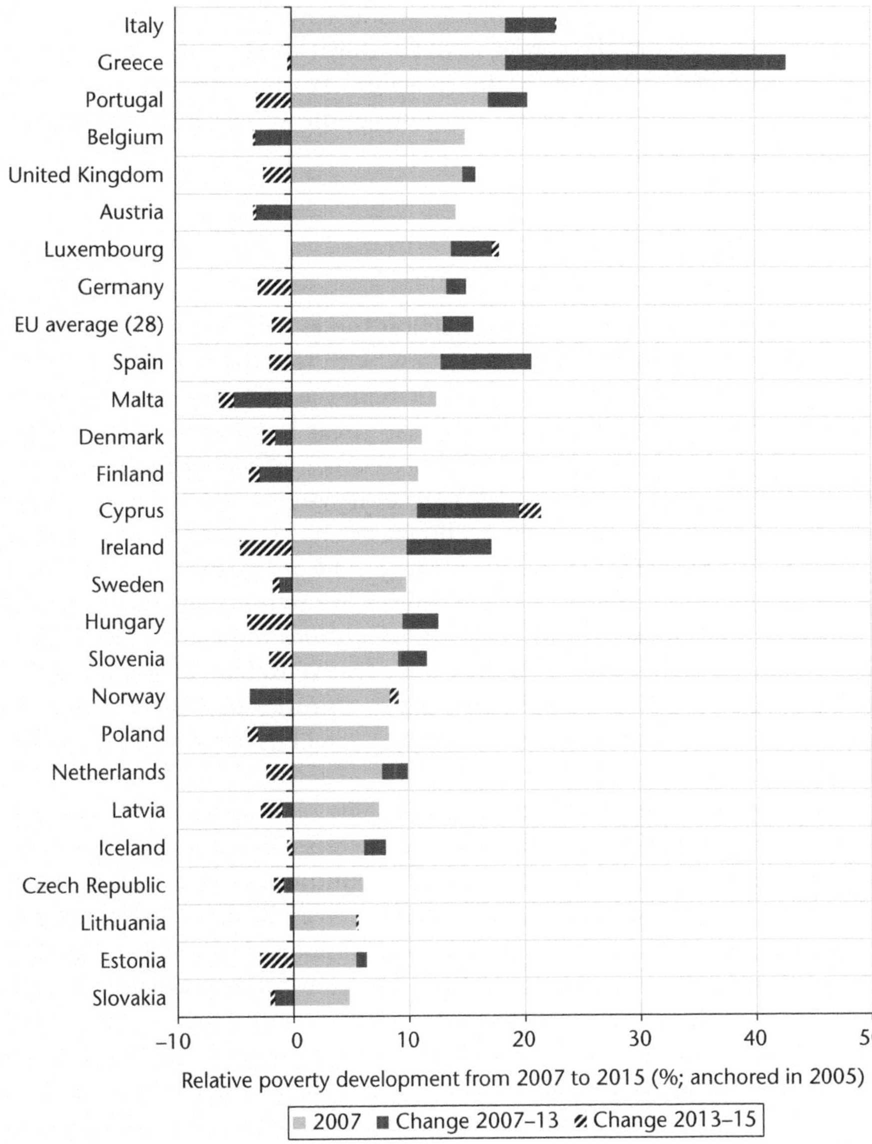


**Figure 2.16.** Relative poverty development 2007–15, anchored in 2005

*Note*: Based on 60% of median income. The numbers are % under poverty line (60% of median) in 2007; changes are in percentage points. Counties are ranked by poverty level in 2007.

*Source*: Eurostat.

part of the crisis years. In that grouping Ireland actually decreased its poverty rate in the latter part of the period, as did Portugal and the UK after a modest increase from 2007 to 2013. Malta, Belgium, Poland, Austria, and Latvia reduced their anchored poverty rate during the crisis, as did Denmark, Finland, and Sweden.

## 2.4 Summary

We have surveyed the economic contraction and welfare consequences of the Great Recession amongst European nations, with selective comparisons with other Western nations. There is great variety in the crisis experience of these nations, as indeed was the case during the Great Depression of the 1930s. Nowadays Western nations have the added benefit of modern welfare states that provide institutionalized social protection systems which aim to shelter the most vulnerable in society. There should also be the added benefit of more economic knowledge of how to prevent and react to financial crises (Eichengreen, 2015). Modern nations, however, use both of these potential benefits to differing degrees. It is already clear from the analysis that some welfare states cushioned more against the negative welfare consequences of the Great Recession than others—and most countries probably did significantly better than was the case in the 1930s. We will have more to say on this in later chapters.

Unemployment, financial hardship, inequality, and poverty increased significantly during the crisis, but to varying degrees, even amongst the deep-crisis countries. Some of the Mediterranean countries were particularly badly hit and have also had slow recoveries. Others, such as the Baltic States, Ireland, and Iceland, were also badly hit but recovered faster and better. Amongst less affluent Eastern European nations there are cases of continually reduced financial hardship during the crisis years, albeit from very high levels.

The Nordic nations, except for Iceland, had a fairly easy ride through the Great Recession, even though the Danes saw some real increase in their financial hardship levels. The main north-western Euro countries generally did not experience significantly increased financial hardships.

Therefore, there is a great variety of crisis experiences that signpost differing conditions and institutional environments, as well as differing policy reactions. We examine these in greater detail in the chapters that follow.

# 3

# The Political Economy of Crisis Responses

*Agnar Freyr Helgason*

In this chapter, we review the major political economy theories behind government policy responses to economic crises. We start by situating the scope of the Great Recession historically and then move on to discuss policymaking in crises and, in particular, how governments can employ fiscal and social policy to buffer the effects of crises on economic welfare. The chapter thus weaves together normative political economy theories of the appropriate and effective role of governments following a crisis and positive theories of how governments in advanced democracies have historically responded to large-scale economic disruptions. The chapter concludes by discussing the implications of political economy theories of policymaking for government policy responses and economic welfare during the Great Recession.

The discussion of normative political economy theories focuses on the two main theoretical perspectives that guide understanding of financial crises and the ways in which governments should respond to them. The theories come from classical political economy, not least from John Maynard Keynes' (1936) seminal work during the Great Depression and that of his followers. This is the perspective that emphasizes the active role of governments in combating economic crises, by applying stimulus measures to reactivate the economy and reduce unemployment. The main alternative stems from the Austrian perspective of laissez-faire economics and emphasizes the self-corrective powers of the market and futility of government intervention. From that viewpoint, governments should let the 'creative destruction' of market forces do their work, no matter how painful the cure may be in the short term (cf. Schumpeter, 1942). These two perspectives thus provide the basic theoretical rationales for the alternative policy responses of government intervention with debt-financed expenditure increases and laissez-faire with debt-reducing austerity measures.

Have governments historically followed either of these broad prescriptions? The discussion of positive theories of comparative political economy focuses on the broad contours of government intervention in the economy in advanced democracies in the post-World War II era. While a Keynesian perspective dominated in the decades following 1945, a number of factors contributed to the gradual erosion of Keynesianism in the 1970s, with more laissez-faire approaches gaining ground across advanced democracies (Hall, 1999). Such shifting trends were found not only in economic policymaking but also in the domain of the welfare state (Pierson, 2001). This was the political economy context in which the Great Recession unfolded.

While this chapter outlines contending theoretical perspectives, Chapter 4 builds on this and proceeds to survey how governments in Europe reacted to the Great Recession, with the help of various comparative statistical material. Collectively, these two chapters should provide a useful framework for reading and assessing the country-specific studies in Part II, as well as some lessons to build on in the comparative analyses of what shaped the welfare outcomes of the Great Recession, undertaken in Chapter 14.

## 3.1 Varieties of Economic Crises

Economic crises are characterized by 'a sudden, and often unexpected, deterioration of most, or all, macroeconomic indicators' (Starke, Kaasch, & van Hooren, 2013, p. 5). Their origins can be rooted in diverse economic mechanisms and their manifestations vary. With the onset of globalization from the 1970s, such crises have become increasingly common, as well as more intense in their effects on societies. They have also become more varied and complex, and more global in scale.

In their authoritative study on the topic, Reinhart and Rogoff (2009) outline four broad categories of economic crises. First are monetary crises, which are perhaps the oldest type of crises. Such crises are driven by abrupt changes in the value of the domestic currency and, as such, can be rooted in high inflation or hyperinflation, currency crashes, or currency debasement. While these are separate categories of crises, they are often interconnected—thus, sharp decreases in the exchange rate generally leads to higher inflation, while chronic inflation, or hyperinflation, often lead to currency debasement. International examples include periods of hyperinflation following World War I, the break-up of the Bretton Woods system of fixed exchange rates in the 1970s, and large increases in oil prices in the 1970s.

Secondly, there are asset price crises. Such crises are commonly associated with the bursting of an asset price bubble—that is, they involve large declines in asset prices following sharp, unsustainable increases in the prices of assets, such as stocks or real estate. The most famous example of such a crisis is no doubt the US stock market crash of 1929, which marked the onset of the Great Depression. More recently, the bursting of the dot-com bubble in the early 2000s had significant effects throughout the advanced economies.

Banking crises, which constitute the third type of crises, are usually characterized by bank runs, that is, a sudden withdrawal of deposits by a large number of customers or funds by a large number of lenders, or a protracted deterioration in asset quality, which undermines the long-term solvency of banking institutions. When such crises are systemic, affecting multiple banks in the same country or across countries, the consequences are likely to be especially dire. Major historical examples of such episodes include the Panic of 1907 and the Nordic and Japanese banking crises of the 1990s (see Figure 3.1).

Finally, sovereign debt crises involve instances whereby a country defaults on its debt obligations. Such defaults can either involve external or domestic debt, with the former typically involving debt held by foreign creditors and denominated in foreign currency, while the latter is generally held by local

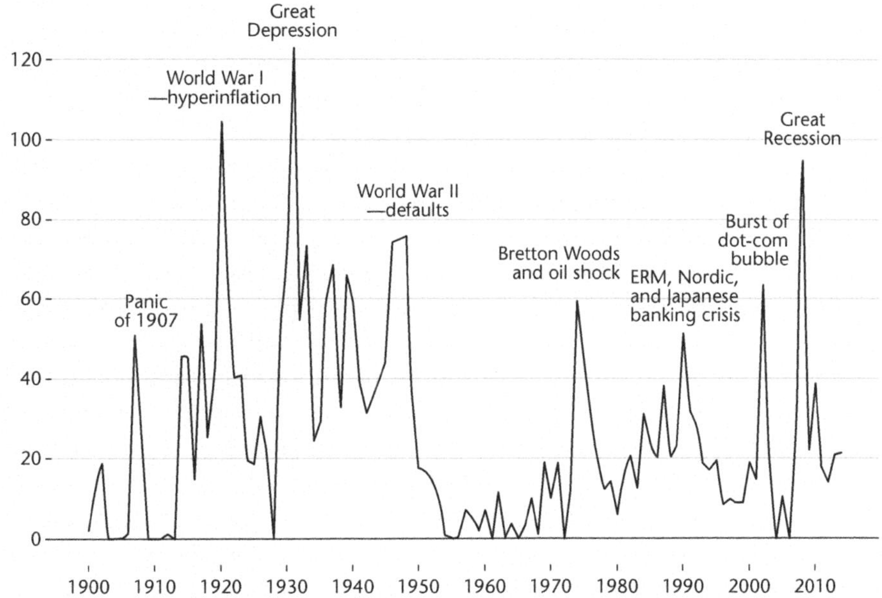


**Figure 3.1.** Reinhart and Rogoff's financial turbulence index for advanced economies, 1900–2014

*Note*: ERM = European Exchange Rate Mechanism.

*Source*: Reinhart and Rogoff (2009).

residents and denominated in the local currency. In the aftermath of World War II, several countries deeply affected by the war defaulted on their debt. Notwithstanding that episode, outright default on debt has been fairly rare in recent times in most advanced economies, though it remains common in less developed countries.

While each of the four broad types of crises can occur in isolation, they commonly occur in quick succession within the same country, as well as across multiple countries. Indeed, Reinhart and Rogoff (2009) identify such a scenario as a common theme among the many crises they consider: governments, banks, corporations, and/or individuals accumulate excessive debt during an economic boom; the economy as a whole becomes more vulnerable as a consequence, and any decline in economic confidence is likely to lead to a crisis spiral; asset prices plunge, economic output contracts, and government debt increases sharply, bringing about loss of trust in the soundness of banking institutions. Thus, conditions which might generally lead to minor recessions have the potential to cause major economic disruption in a high debt context and can, in severe cases, spread across multiple countries, plunging the global economy into a deep recession.

Figure 3.1 shows a composite index of financial turmoil among advanced economies (Reinhart & Rogoff, 2009). It takes account of the various types of economic crises and stock market crashes which occurred in the 18 advanced economies in its sample, weighing each economy with its share of world income. Higher values on the index signify more severe and widespread episodes of financial turmoil among the advanced economies.[1]

As can be seen from the figure, the Great Recession was the largest economic crisis in the post-World War II period, with only the Great Depression and the economic problems following World War I being more severe. All four varieties of crises more or less manifested themselves across multiple countries over the course of the Great Recession: asset prices plunged following unsustainable price increases and reckless borrowing by banks in the early 2000s, the balance sheets of banking institutions deteriorated causing widespread fears of the imminent collapse of multiple banks, and the sovereign debt burden of multiple advanced economies caused them to seek assistance from the International Monetary Fund (IMF). The Great Recession was truly a 'perfect storm' of multiple types of crises that spread across many countries and threatened to plunge the world economy into the depths of depression, the likes of which had not been seen since the 1930s.

[1] For a more detailed discussion of the methodology behind the index, as well as developments for a larger sample of countries, see Reinhart and Rogoff (2009, pp. 249–51).

## 3.2 Policymaking in crises

Policymaking during times of economic crises has long been understood to be qualitatively different from 'normal' times. While the latter are generally characterized by public policy theorists as times where only small-scale, incremental changes to policies are possible and feasible (e.g. Lindblom, 1959), many argue that crisis periods are more susceptible to radical reform. Kingdon (1984), for example, argues that crises open a 'window of opportunity' for policy reform, while Gourevitch (1986) contends that crises can instigate 'critical realignments', whereby existing political coalitions that sustain particular policies are broken up, making dramatic changes to policy possible. Yet another stream of research considers economic crises as fertile ground for so-called 'critical junctures', that is, brief phases of institutional flux when structural constraints on policymaking are temporarily relaxed and the range of possible policy changes becomes larger (Capoccia & Kelemen, 2007).

Keeler (1993) suggests three mechanisms by which crises can sweep away previous barriers to change and lead to radical reform: first, if presidential or parliamentary elections occur in the aftermath of a crisis, the public can lash out at the incumbent and endow the opposition with strong support. Such an electoral result can be interpreted as an electoral mandate and give legitimacy to sweeping policy change. Secondly, crises can create a sense of urgency, whereby particular policy decisions must be made under severe time constraints. Finally, crises can instil fear into policymakers—that is, a belief that if authorities do not act promptly, the situation will worsen. In each of these cases, the opposition is likely to be weaker than during normal times. Due to urgency and fear of inaction, the opposition might even reluctantly support sweeping reforms. Collectively, these mechanisms suggest that who governs—whether right-wing or left-wing parties, for example—might matter a great deal with regard to how the state acts upon the onset of economic crises.

Policymaking—even in times of crisis—does not, however, occur in a vacuum. Pre-existing policies form what Mettler (2015) calls a 'policyscape'—a mosaic of policies that generates feedback effects which influence political behaviour, policy agendas, and ultimately constrain subsequent policymaking. Importantly, the policyscape not only defines the status quo faced by policymakers during crises, but also forms the set of policies that are in effect at the onset of a crisis. This suggest that the extent to which states are 'prepared' for crises, that is, have in effect a set of policies which automatically ameliorate the effects of crisis on the general population, reduces the need for an explicit, discretionary reaction by the government (Starke et al., 2013).

While there are a variety of policies that can ameliorate the effects of economic crises on population welfare, they can broadly be classified according to their scope. On the one hand, there are general policies that affect the broader population throughout the crisis. Such policies are generally meant to support aggregate demand and stave off the loss of output, unemployment, and major economic disruptions. On the other hand, there are specific policies that directly affect those individuals who have been affected by the crises—such as unemployed persons, those who have been pushed into poverty, and those struggling to make ends meet. Those are ideal types of policies, as many policies will have elements of both aspects in their design.

Previous research on policy responses to economic crises has tended to focus on either one of these broad categories of policies. Gourevitch (1986), for example, focuses on economic policymaking, without considering social policy in particular, while Starke and colleagues (2013) and van Kersbergen, Vis, and Hemerijck (2014) give prominence to social policy, with economic policy playing a more limited role. In sections 3.3 and 3.4, we will discuss these separate literatures and shed light on major theories of economic and social policymaking, both during normal times and times of crisis. In particular, we will review the extent to which pre-existing policies may automatically buffer the effects of economic crises on the general population, but also cases in which economic crises are likely to induce fundamental policy change which impact upon the welfare of individuals and societies.

## 3.3 Fiscal Policy: Stimulus or Austerity?

When the Great Depression plunged societies into a deep economic crisis in the 1930s, the dominant view among economists and policymakers was that fiscal policy had no effect on economic output and unemployment, and, as such, the government should not actively use fiscal policy to stimulate aggregate demand and contain unemployment while the economy recovered from the downturn. The view, often referred to as the 'Treasury view' of fiscal policy, since it characterized the position of the British Chancellor of the Exchequer in the early 1930s, is based on the assumption that any government spending crowds out an equal amount of private spending, such that any increases in public spending are always matched by decreases in private spending. The premise of the assumption is that money has to be spent on something and that any borrowing (or tax increases) by the government to fund increased spending necessarily implies that there is less money to borrow (or spend) for other actors in the economy. As a consequence, government spending was assumed to have no effect on the macroeconomy.

As the Great Depression unfolded and governments were unable to recover from the crisis, John Maynard Keynes (1936) forcefully argued against the prevailing view, offering instead a theory of how activist government policies could raise aggregate demand and hasten economic recovery. At the core of Keynes' theory is the suggestion that the biggest problem of any economic crisis is involuntary unemployment caused by inadequate economic demand and that such a situation would not necessarily self-correct over time. Indeed, a destructive cycle could be set in motion. As individuals and firms prudentially start saving more of their income, aggregate demand falls even more since less is consumed, which in turn reduces the aggregate income of individuals and firms and, paradoxically, leads to less total saving (Krugman, 2012). Keynes argued that this cycle, sometimes referred to as the 'paradox of thrift', could entrap an economy in a permanent state of depression if the government did not react appropriately.

For Keynes the government could stimulate the economy through either monetary or fiscal policy or a combination of the two. On the one hand, by increasing the money supply ('printing money'), monetary policy could be used to hold back the drop in aggregate income, as well as reduce interest rates, making savings less attractive and stimulating investment (Krugman, 2012, p. 32). On the other hand, by increasing government spending (or decreasing government revenue) fiscal policy could be used to stimulate aggregate demand and counteract the effects of under-consumption by individuals and firms. Such fiscal policy measures could both be automatically induced by the state of the economy (that is, to let lower tax receipts from households and corporations and higher spending on unemployment benefits 'automatically' stabilize the economy) or determined at the discretion of the government in response to the state of the economy. In any case, Keynes' argument implies that the two broad policy tools of monetary and fiscal policy could collectively allow governments to break the cycle of more savings and less income and thus return the economy to normal functioning.

Keynes' theory revolutionized the field of political economy and was highly influential among economists and policymakers in establishing the political-economic institutional framework of advanced democracies following World War II. At the international level, a multilateral system of embedded liberalism was established, which involved the creation of a number of formal institutions, such as the IMF and the General Agreement on Tariffs and Trade (GATT) to regulate monetary and trade relations among advanced economies (Eichengreen, 2008; Ruggie, 1982). The defining feature of the system was that it was predicated upon interventionism at the domestic level, allowing governments to pursue expansive social and economic policies.

This was the environment in which the Keynesian welfare states blossomed. Economic policies were actively employed to stabilize economies and pursue the goal of full employment, while generous welfare policies were developed to provide income replacement to those needing further support (Blyth, 2002;

Esping-Andersen, 1985). In most advanced European countries, corporatism also played a key role, with unions accepting wage restraint and employers committed to reinvest profits in human and physical capital. While the extent to which such policies were followed differed across countries (cf. Hall & Soskice, 2001), this was on the whole a period in which policymakers across advanced economies subscribed to a similar set of views about the proper role of the state in the economy (Hall, 1989).

The Trentes Glorieuses, the golden years of the Keynesian welfare state, came to an end in the 1970s. Multiple factors caused the decline. At the domestic level, economic growth began to slow down, productivity growth stalled due to the increasing size of the service sector, and skill-biased technological change put pressure on collective wage bargaining. At the international level, the Bretton Woods system of fixed exchange rates came to an end, financial markets were becoming more open and integrated, and the price of oil increased sharply. With slowing economic growth, rising inflation, and growing budget deficits, Keynesianism was seen by critics to have failed and the consensus around the Keynesian welfare state weakened (Hall, 1999).

As Keynesianism lost credibility, monetarist economist theory gained ground and played an important role in changing beliefs about the proper role of the state in the economy at the beginning of the 1980s (Blyth, 2002; Hall, 1993). The primary goal of macroeconomic policymaking shifted from maintaining full employment to controlling inflation, with most advanced economies adopting an explicit inflation target and endowing an independent central bank with authority over setting monetary policy. For many countries of the EU, this culminated in the establishment of a common currency, which further limited the room to manoeuvre for national governments (McNamara, 1998). Importantly, the role of fiscal policy in stabilizing the economy was undermined and was mostly limited to automatic stabilizers rather than activist, discretionary stimulus spending (Hall, 1999). Indeed, from the mid-1980s right up until 2008, a period of 'Great Moderation' in advanced economies—that is, of stable, but modest, economic growth and low inflation—lent strong confidence to the belief that monetary policy was best suited to stabilize the economy (Blanchard, Dell'Ariccia, & Mauro, 2010). As such, activist fiscal policy was considered by mainstream economists to be ineffective and attempts at 'fine-tuning' the economy were seen as bound to fail (Auerbach, Gale, & Harris, 2010; Taylor, 2000). Thus, the overwhelming consensus within the economics profession and policymaking circles at the onset of the Great Recession was aligned with the view that governments should not use discretionary fiscal policy to ameliorate the effects of recessions on the economy. Several reasons justified such a strong position against activist fiscal policy.

First of all, policymaking occurs with a considerable lag. From the time policymakers become aware of an economic recession, they must formulate a policy response, enact legislation, and implement the policy, and there might be some lag from the time a policy is implemented until it has the desired effect. With such a long lag, critics argue that a recession might be over well before the fiscal policy response could become effective. This argument applies specifically to discretionary fiscal policy, rather than automatic stabilizers, since the latter come into play automatically as the state of the economy changes.

Secondly, as suggested by Lucas' (1976) critique, the rational expectations on the part of individuals, firms, and investors can undermine the effectiveness of any fiscal stimulus during a recession. Thus, for example, if the government implements a stimulus which is funded through government borrowing, rational actors should reduce their own spending, since they anticipate higher taxes and higher interest rates in the future, to repay the loans the government took out during the recession. The net effect of increases in government spending should therefore be minimal, since reactions by individuals, corporations, and investors to government actions would counteract the effects of the stimulus itself.

Thirdly, fiscal stimulus funded through government borrowing increases sovereign debt, which can bring the long-term solvency of the country into question and increase the interest rate premium charged by international financial markets (Garrett, 1998; Mosley, 2003). As such, stimulating the economy in the present might burden the future budget of the country with interest payments, which in turn might limit the country's potential for maintaining current spending and tax levels in the future, as well as reducing economic growth. At the extreme, countries which have a high risk of sovereign default might lose access to international funding markets and face sovereign default without external assistance.

In a series of influential papers, Alesina and colleagues (Alesina & Ardagna, 1998, 2010, 2013; Alesina & Perotti, 1997) warn of the dangers of unsustainable spending during recessions for future economic growth and even go on to argue that rather than use fiscal stimulus to recover from an economic recession, austerity—or fiscal consolidation—is more likely to renew economic growth. This strategy, generally referred to as 'expansionary austerity', suggests that the confidence of households and markets in the solvency of the government is critical for economic growth. By pursuing austere policies, authorities increase confidence in the future solvency of the government, which reduces expectations of high taxation and high interest rates in the future. As such, the theory implies that less public spending (austerity) leads to more private spending and, thus, actually causes an economic expansion. Alesina and colleagues also maintain that to be successful a fiscal consolidation must be expenditure based, or in other words, that governments should focus on reducing transfer payments to benefit recipients and the wages of public employees, rather than raising taxes on the general public.

Collectively, these points suggest that governments should either refrain from pursuing a plan of fiscal stimulus during downturns, as their actions would most likely have little or no effect, or actually pursue a plan of austerity in an effort to increase confidence in the solvency of the government. Therefore, rather than employing discretionary fiscal policy to stabilize the economy over the business cycle, authorities should primarily employ monetary policy to affect aggregate demand.

While this was the mainstream view prior to the crisis, many argued that this was wrongheaded in all recessions, but especially when countries were faced with major disruptions, such as the Great Recession. Harking back to the prescripts of Keynes himself, many forcefully argued for a policy of fiscal stimulus at the onset of the Great Recession, convincingly dismissing concerns from major adherents of austerity (Blyth, 2013; Krugman, 2012; Skidelsky, 2010). The case against austerity builds on multiple pillars. Certainly, Keynes' theoretical insight plays an important role, but so do concerns about the distributional fairness of austerity and the track record of austerity in the recent past.

On the one hand, austerity, especially the expenditure-based variety advocated by Alesina and Ardagna, is distributionally unfair (Blyth, 2013). In its simplest form, governments pursuing an austere fiscal policy aim to spend considerably less than they collect in revenues, accumulating a budget surplus and lowering government debt. There are, of course, many ways in which governments can go about pursuing such a goal. Governments can raise taxes on the general public or the wealthy, they can reduce spending on overhead or operational costs, or spending on infrastructure, defence, or on various other government programmes that do not directly contribute to maintaining the economic welfare of the national population. However, in the expenditure-based variety, the individuals who bear the weight of austerity on their shoulders are the members of society least likely to be able to do so, as such a policy is specifically aimed at reducing the costs of welfare policy programmes and the government wage bill. As such, benefit recipients and government employees are likely to suffer disproportionately under austerity. The effects are likely to be doubly harmful during economic recessions, when more individuals are likely to seek benefits due to unemployment and underemployment. Thus, austerity can have very specific distributional implications, especially for the most vulnerable members of society.

On the other hand, recent research suggests that austerity simply does not have the effects claimed by its advocates. A number of recent studies find that the short-term effects of austerity are in line with arguments made by

Keynesian economists, rather than the expansionary effects argued by Alesina and others. Romer and Romer (2010), for example, find that a tax increase of 1 per cent of gross domestic product (GDP) reduces output over three successive years by close to 3 per cent, while Guajardo, Leigh, and Pescatori (2014) find that fiscal consolidations reduce economic output and increase unemployment in the short term but that the short-term effects are contractionary regardless of whether a country is perceived to have a high sovereign default risk or not. In addition to these findings, the case against austerity has further been supported by the debunking of an influential paper by Reinhart and Rogoff (2010), which argued that when a country's external debt levels are in excess of 90 per cent of GDP, economic growth is considerably lower than at lower debt levels. Indeed, Herndon, Ash, and Pollin (2014) show that the findings are largely due to serious methodological errors by the authors and, once the errors are rectified, there does not appear to be a consistent relationship between debt levels and economic growth.

While the overall verdict on the macroeconomic effects of fiscal stimulus and austerity are becoming clearer, the distributional consequences are what matter most for the effects of economic crisis on welfare. By maintaining economic activity and containing unemployment, a plan of fiscal stimulus can limit the costs imposed by crises on individuals and societies. While it is important that such plans are fiscally responsible, that is, that they do not jeopardize the future solvency of the government, it should be noted that they limit other kinds of costs: most importantly, human capital is protected from erosion and suffering due to poverty and material deprivation is limited. In this regard, Keynesian fiscal stimulus is likely to play a particularly important role in maintaining economic welfare during crises.

## 3.4 Social Policy: Retrenchment or Resilience?

The welfare state is the primary policy mechanism through which governments protect populations from risks associated with the market economy. Unsurprisingly, the increasing economic insecurity caused by economic turmoil often brings about intense pressure for expanding the welfare state by those directly affected by crises as well as risk-averse individuals concerned for their economic security. Thus, as Polanyi (1944) famously argued, the vagaries of the self-regulating market can spontaneously bring about a movement towards increasing social protection (the 'double movement').

There is much evidence to suggest that major economic downturns played such a role in Western societies during the early 20th century (Rehm, 2016). Cutler and Johnson (2004), for example, attribute the introduction of major social insurance programmes in many countries to deep economic recessions while Miron and Weil (1998) argue that without the Great Depression, Roosevelt's landmark Social Security Act of 1935 might not have been introduced in the USA. Similarly, Castles (2010) suggests the Great Depression had a catalytic effect on social policy developments in Sweden and New Zealand. More generally, rising economic insecurity among the general public in the early 20th century is commonly thought to have played an important role in the development of generous welfare policies that protect individuals from a variety of social risks associated with the market economy (Baldwin, 1990).

The period following World War II marked what many consider to be the height of welfare state expansion. However, much like with Keynesian fiscal policy, the generous welfare state of advanced democracies came under increasing pressure from the 1970s onwards (Hall, 2013; Korpi, 2003; Scharpf, 2000). Some even went so far as to predict the ultimate collapse of the welfare state (cf. Offe, 1984; Svallfors & Taylor-Gooby, 1999). The implications were clear: in the period following the 1970s, the golden years of the Keynesian welfare state were over and a period of welfare state reconstruction or retrenchment was being visited upon advanced democracies.

Even so, there is considerable disagreement over the extent of retrenchment achieved. Writing about the governments of Margaret Thatcher in the UK and of Ronald Reagan in the USA—two most likely cases—Paul Pierson claims that 'the welfare state stands out as an island of relative stability' (1994, p. 5), compared to other policy areas. Pierson (1994, 1996) makes the central claim that welfare states themselves have changed the context in which they operate. Because of this, retrenchment is not simply expansion in reverse—there are entirely different factors at work. While the politics of expansion involve enacting popular policies in an underdeveloped interest group environment, causing only diffuse costs through taxation, retrenchment involves dismantling popular policies with concentrated benefits that enjoy the support of entrenched interest groups.

The path-dependent nature of the welfare state constrains policy changes that reform-minded politicians can pursue. Politicians, being both policy and office seekers, will have to take this into account when balancing those two objectives. Those wanting to retrench the welfare state due to ideological reasons, and stay in office, will try to minimize the associated political costs of retrenchment by manipulating the information available to possible opponents and voters about the policy changes. This can be achieved by lowering the visibility of unpopular policies, obscuring responsibility, hiding information about possible consequences of reform, making side payments to politically important groups for lost benefits, or achieving changes through decrementalism (Pierson, 1994, pp. 19–22). Whenever possible, governments will seek to gain broad support for their agenda and thus spread the blame. For governments that do not enjoy a wide electoral margin to 'buffer' unpopular decisions, such 'blame avoidance' will become even more important (Weaver, 1986).

Pierson argues that in this new environment it is justifiable to talk about an entirely 'new politics' of retrenchment, which is quite different from the 'old politics' of expansion. He thus challenges the relevance of the power resources approach in this new context, maintaining that labour unions, left-wing parties, and other social movements that expanded the state are no longer of central relevance to its sustainability. Instead, the welfare state has taken on a life of its own with the continuation of individual programmes depending on their popularity and associated interest groups. Retrenchment will thus only be possible when politicians can pursue the strategies outlined and 'hide' their success from the watchful eyes of the public and beneficiaries. More recent work by Huber and Stephens (2014) suggests that this is indeed the case for political partisanship—that is, while left-wing parties played an important role in the expansion of the welfare state, they are less important for its sustainability once it is in place.

Pierson's claim about the resilience of the welfare state to radical restructuring has, however, been met with considerable scepticism, with he himself acknowledging more recently that its resilience might have been overstated in his earlier work (Pierson, 2015). Three lines of arguments are especially salient in this context.

First, as Pierson focuses on the USA and the UK in his study, two liberal welfare states, he disregards potential differences in institutional dynamics under alternative welfare state regimes. Later studies critiqued Pierson for this and pointed out that his main conclusions did not hold in different settings (e.g. Anderson, 2001; Swank, 2001). This is especially the case regarding his treatment of 'old politics' and, thus, the distinctiveness of 'new politics'. While the liberal welfare states are dominated by narrow, fragmented interest groups, social democratic welfare states are characterized by encompassing, solidaristic labour market movements. In such an environment, the interests of those that depend on the social programmes in question will not be represented by client-based interest groups, but rather by the encompassing labour movement (Anderson, 2001, p. 1069). As Swank (2001, p. 208) shows, such encompassing interest groups are likely to constitute a major barrier to radical reform of the welfare state. Thus, Pierson's argument about the dominance of concentrated interest groups has limited relevance in social democratic regimes.

Secondly, Korpi and Palme (2003) argue that Pierson overstates the distinctiveness of politics in mature welfare states vis-à-vis politics during welfare state expansion. As they suggest, the expansion of the welfare state was not simply a popular credit claiming affair, welcomed by all voters. Indeed, concerns over high levels of taxation and the growth of 'big government' were highly salient throughout the golden years of the welfare state, suggesting that the politics of expansion are not qualitatively different from the politics of retrenchment. Furthermore, the primary beneficiaries of the welfare state are not necessarily client-based interest groups, but rather the mass of risk-averse citizens who benefit from the existence of social insurance schemes, whether or not they actually claim benefits over their lifetime. Again, the implication is that the two periods of welfare state developments are not as different as Pierson maintains.

Finally, a number of scholars critique Pierson's narrow conceptualization of the welfare state and his policy-based approach. By focusing only on observable changes in policy, Pierson overlooks the social context of those policies and the goals they are meant to achieve (Hacker, 2004). Thus, while the working class predominantly used its resources to protect male breadwinners from losing their ability to provide for their families due to unemployment, sickness, invalidity, or old age at the dawn of the modern welfare state, the risks facing citizens have changed substantially since the late 1980s (Bonoli, 2001; Taylor-Gooby, 2004). Furthermore, as Clayton and Pontusson (1998) point out, in the context of rising inequality and insecurity an unchanged welfare state will effectively have been retrenched. Ignoring these changes and focusing only on spending cuts or reforms of social programmes will thus overlook how the welfare state affects the labour market and vice versa.

In later work, Pierson (2001) offers a more nuanced analysis of welfare state change and how governments deal with pressures. Instead of focusing only on retrenchment per se, he accepts that reducing change to a single dimension is counterproductive. The resulting dimensions are three: (i) re-commodification, which entails dismantling social programmes and making individuals more reliant on the market; (ii) cost containment, which consists of those measures taken to make the welfare state more efficient and streamlined without sacrificing quality services; and (iii) recalibration, which entails modifying programmes to better achieve historical goals (rationalization) and adapting them to changing risks and norms (updating). These three dimensions do not play out in the same way in all welfare state regimes. Indeed, Pierson argues that 'there is not a single "new politics" of the welfare state, but different politics in different configurations' (2001, p. 455). Consequently, the welfare states of advanced industrial societies do not seem to be converging, as many have predicted, but rather growing apart (Swank, 2002).

What are the implications of these developments for welfare in times of economic turmoil? On the one hand, they suggest that pre-existing policies of social protection are likely to matter a great deal for the effects of economic crises on welfare. Generous social policies already in place will be difficult to retrench and are likely to enjoy support from a large part of the population. Moreover, since they will 'automatically' be triggered to meet growing needs at the onset of economic crises, they will buffer the effects of turmoil on welfare without any lags in time. On the other hand, however, they suggest that focusing solely on pre-existing policies might be misguided. As Hacker (2004) highlights, 'hidden' retrenchment can undermine pre-existing policies, making it critical to analyse not only what governments do, but also what they do not do in response to changes in social risks faced by the general population. Indeed, as Hacker and Pierson (2010) argue, such 'hidden' retrenchment has played a critical role in undermining welfare policy and economic equality in the USA.

## 3.5 Conclusions

The discussion in this chapter suggests that we can analyse policy responses to economic crises along two dimensions, each with implications for the welfare of the general population. First, we can analyse the extent to which governments expand, maintain, or retrench social policy programmes which provide income replacement or income support for economically vulnerable individuals and households. These can be individuals who are directly affected by the economic crises due to loss of employment, but also recipients of benefits due to old age, disability, and sickness, as well as receivers of social assistance and family benefits (such as children's allowance or parental leave). Secondly, we can analyse the extent to which governments seek to stimulate the economy to maintain aggregate demand while the private sector recovers, or alternatively, the extent to which they pursue austerity, with limited concern for stimulating demand. This latter dimension primarily affects the welfare of the general population indirectly and indiscriminately, that is, such policies are not targeted specifically at groups directly affected by the crisis condition.

The well-being consequences of policy responses along these two dimensions are likely to differ. On the one hand, changes in fiscal policy are likely to have larger consequences for the unemployment rate among the active population and household income for the average family. A policy of fiscal stimulus will halt increases in unemployment and support average household income, while a policy of austerity is likely to lead to rising levels of unemployment and a reduction in household income, either through higher taxes or lower benefits. On the other hand, changes in social policy will primarily affect already economically vulnerable households. More expansive social policies will reduce poverty, while retrenchment is likely to compound the effects of economic crises on poverty.

As should be evident, changes to both fiscal and social policy will affect redistribution and income inequality. Thus, policies designed to stimulate the economy or expand pre-existing social policies will lead to increased redistribution and a reduction in income inequality, while austere policies, especially when expenditure based, and retrenchment of social policy will decrease redistribution and increase income inequality. Thus, changes in redistribution and inequality will serve as important benchmarks against which the policies pursued by governments in the wake of economic crises can be evaluated.

# 4

# Government Responses to the Great Recession

## A Comparative Perspective

*Agnar Freyr Helgason*

The initial policy response by governments to the global financial crisis was focused on saving financial institutions and staving off a global recession, with the effects of the crisis on the economic well-being of individuals and households coming to the fore as developments unfolded. Unsurprisingly, such effects were particularly consequential in the countries that were hardest hit by the crisis, as painful and highly controversial austerity measures were disproportionally implemented there in efforts to consolidate governmental finances, often under the tutelage of international institutions (Cameron, 2012; Copelovitch, Frieden, & Walter, 2016).

In sections 4.1 and 4.2, we begin by outlining the macroeconomic environment that formed the backdrop to government policy responses in the aftermath of the global financial crisis.[1] We then describe the main contours of government policy responses, focusing on how various governments employed fiscal policy to ameliorate the effects of the crisis on the general population and, in particular, the extent to which policies of social protection were altered in response to the economic turmoil that ensued.

We find that there are broad similarities in how governments initially responded to the crisis, although the direct costs of refinancing financial institutions and the precarious fiscal position of the state limited the policy options available to those hardest hit by the crisis. The pre-crisis situation in

[1] For detailed discussions of the various causes of the crisis, see Reinhart and Rogoff (2009) and Baldwin et al. (2015). When available, we use data from the OECD, which includes data on non-European countries.

Greece was particularly dire, although several other economies, including other Mediterranean countries, the Baltic States, Iceland, and Ireland, were particularly vulnerable to the effects of sudden changes in the flow of international capital. At the same time, core EU countries were relatively well positioned financially to respond effectively to an economic contraction.

As the crisis developed, significant differences in fiscal policy choices across countries became apparent. The response in several countries, including Greece, Ireland, the UK, Spain, and Portugal, was characterized by harsh austerity measures, which relied primarily on significant cuts to government spending (see Chapters 5 to 7 and Chapter 10). Iceland stands out in this respect, as it was the only deep-crisis country that prioritized revenue increases over expenditure cuts in its fiscal policy response (see Chapter 8). Countries less affected by the crisis pursued a mixture of stimulating fiscal policies that were more conducive to maintaining aggregate demand and supporting economic well-being.

While fiscal policy choices differed significantly during the crisis, overall changes to social policy were characterized by continuity rather than change. Thus, the extent to which countries were prepared to deal with a deep recession at the outset mattered a great deal. While some, such as the Nordic countries, had forceful automatic stabilizers and generous unemployment benefit systems in place to cushion the most severe effects, others were neither fully prepared nor in a position to implement measures to adequately redistribute the costs of the crisis. Even so, Ireland and Greece stand out as cases of significant social policy retrenchment, while Iceland and Slovenia are exemplary cases where redistributive measures played a larger role as the crisis evolved. In any case, the social policy setting at the onset of the crisis played a crucial role in shaping the effects of the crisis on economic well-being.

## 4.1 The Great Recession and Beyond

Less than a year after the US subprime mortgage crisis erupted, the global economy teetered on the brink of collapse. Figure 4.1 traces the international scope of the crisis in 30 advanced economies from 2000 onwards, showing the number of countries experiencing recession in any given quarter. While only 3 of the economies were in recession in the final quarter of 2007, 22 were in recession in the autumn of 2008, and 26 out of the 30 were in recession at the peak of the crisis, in the first quarter of 2009. The global economy picked up steam later in 2009, with gross domestic product (GDP) recovering in most countries. However, as the Eurozone crisis unfolded another widespread downturn took place between 2011 and 2012, with just under half of the 30

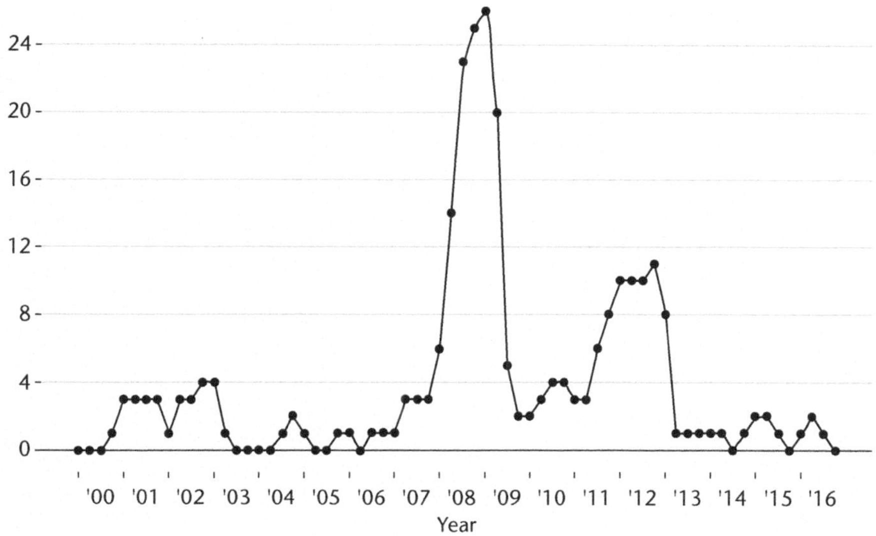


**Figure 4.1.** Number of advanced economies (n = 30) in recession, by quarters, 2000–16

*Note*: Recessions defined as periods of two (or more) consecutive quarters of declining real GDP, a commonly used indicator of recessions.

*Source*: OECD Quarterly National Accounts.

economies experiencing another deep recession. In 2013, economic recovery had resumed in most countries, albeit at differing speeds.

Long-lasting and deep economic contractions sparked by a financial crisis, such as the Great Recession, can have dire consequences for the economic welfare of the general population (Dao & Loungani, 2010). On the one hand, contractions generally reduce domestic economic activity, which leads to lower household income and increased unemployment. To maintain the economic welfare of the population, governments have to increase the resources dedicated to social protection and to supporting aggregate demand. On the other hand, however, financial crises can be costly for governments, especially as overall government revenues contract with the recession. These directly limit the resources available to pursue such policies of social protection. Moreover, governments must in many cases also dedicate considerable resources to bailing out ailing financial institutions or, alternatively, be forced to consolidate their finances due to the rising costs (or in the extreme, inability) of borrowing capital to fund their activities.

Indeed, the state of public finances differed considerably among advanced economies at the onset of the crisis, with the position of several countries such that there was limited room for government to respond effectively to the crisis that lay ahead. Figure 4.2 shows two important measures of such constraints: gross general government debt and the current account balance at the onset of

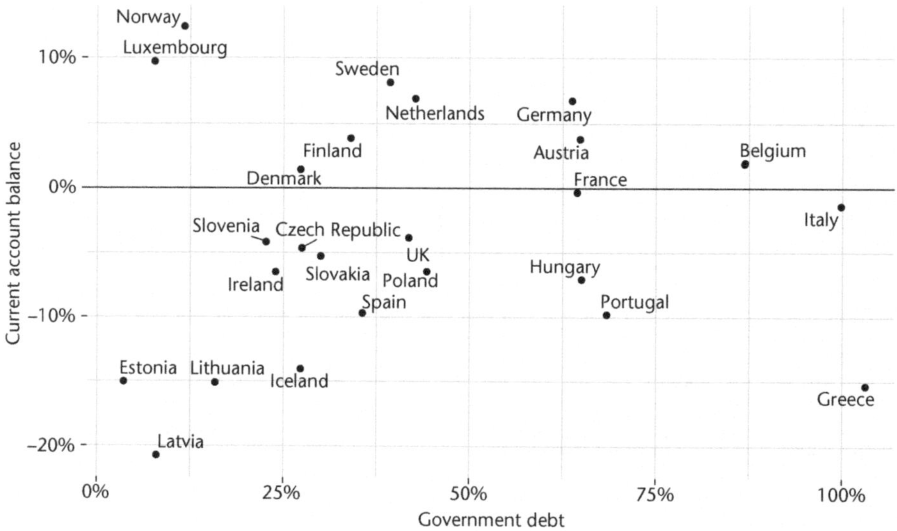


**Figure 4.2.** Gross general government debt and the current account balance in 2007 (% of GDP)

*Note*: Government debt as defined in the Maastricht Treaty. Data on Norway refers to central government debt.

*Source*: OECD National Accounts.

the crisis. The former measure can be taken as an indicator of the cumulative sustainability of government finances. To the extent that the Great Recession led to great demands on government resources, either directly due to the resurrection of financial institutions or due to the turmoil caused by a large economic contraction, governments faced quite different constraints based on debt levels. Consequently, countries with low levels of public debt were able to meet such demands to a greater degree than countries deep in debt, although low levels of debt in no way guaranteed acquiescence to such demands.

The second measure, the current account balance, can be seen as an indicator of the reliance of the domestic economy on foreign capital. After the establishment of the euro and in the lead-up to the crisis, such differences in current account balances became especially large within the EU, with capital flowing from core countries to countries on the periphery (Copelovitch et al., 2016). Rather than invest the inflow of credit in productive resources, it was generally used to fuel domestic consumption and asset bubbles, with governments doing little to counteract the growing imbalances (Lane, 2012). As the crisis unfolded and fears of defaults on debt increased, cross-border lending came to a sudden stop, causing a balance of payment crisis in peripheral countries, which would later develop into a full-blown sovereign debt crisis (Baldwin et al., 2015).

As Figure 4.2 shows, Greece was unique in its precarious position on both indicators, having accumulated large public debt as well as being reliant on capital inflows before the crisis began. Italy and Belgium also had extremely high levels of public debt, although they were not as reliant on foreign capital. Several other countries, however, entered the crisis with a large exposure to cross-border lending, including the Baltic States, Iceland, Spain, Hungary, and Portugal.

As it turned out, the countries in the most precarious position at the onset of the crisis also incurred the largest direct costs due to the failure of financial institutions. The biggest direct costs were suffered by Iceland and Ireland, which each contributed over 40 per cent of GDP from 2008 to 2011 to recapitalize financial institutions, with Greece already suffering the third largest costs, at just under 30 per cent of GDP (Laeven & Valencia, 2013). The cost of the crisis increased even further for Greece as the crisis lingered on (see Chapter 5). The Netherlands and the United Kingdom also had considerable losses, with Denmark being the only other Nordic country (apart from Iceland) to bear considerable direct costs due to the restructuring of financial institutions. Most advanced economies, however, suffered negligible direct fiscal costs caused by a banking crisis.

Even though an outright banking crisis only occurred in a couple of countries, their effects were felt throughout the global economy. Figure 4.3 shows the decline in quarterly real GDP from pre-crisis peak to post-crisis trough in 30 OECD/EU economies. The effects of the crisis on Greece stand out as particularly dire, with its GDP contracting by well over 25 per cent over the course of the crisis. The contraction in the other two countries most affected by banking crises, Iceland and Ireland, were considerably smaller at just over 15 per cent and 10 per cent respectively.

Several other countries experienced a similar or greater downturn during the Great Recession, even though their direct exposure to the fiscal costs of the global financial crisis were limited. Thus, the economies of the three Baltic countries, Latvia, Estonia, and Lithuania, contracted by 23 per cent, 21 per cent, and 17 per cent respectively, while the economies of Italy, Portugal, and Spain each contracted by about 10 per cent. Of the Nordic countries, Finland suffered the second largest drop in GDP after Iceland, at about 10 per cent, while the contraction in Sweden, Denmark, and Norway amounted to 7 per cent, 7 per cent, and 4 per cent respectively.

In addition to varying in depth, the duration of the contraction differed considerably across countries, as well as the extent to which economies recovered from the drop in GDP. This was especially the case for peripheral Eurozone countries. While Greece was already in a precarious situation following the financial crisis, the announcement by Greek authorities in late 2009 that their budget deficit was much higher than previously

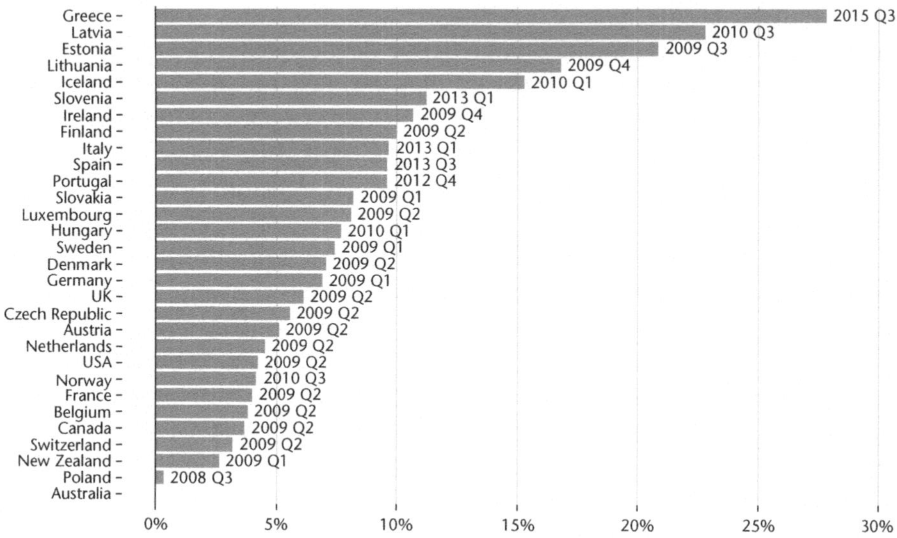


**Figure 4.3.** Decline in quarterly real GDP, seasonally adjusted, from pre-crisis peak to post-crisis trough

*Note*: Labels show the quarter in which trough was reached.

*Source*: OECD Quarterly National Accounts.

believed fuelled concerns about the sustainability of the government finances in Greece, as well as in Italy, Ireland, Portugal, and Spain (or the 'GIIPS' countries, as they came to be collectively known at the time) (Copelovitch et al., 2016).

Figure 4.4 shows how quarterly real GDP developed in our sample of 30 countries from 2007 to 2016, with periods of recession highlighted in grey. Comparing and contrasting the timelines of each case reveals several features which deserve emphasis. First, the toll of the crisis in Greece is without parallel in terms of depth, duration, and lack of recovery. After a long period of continuous contraction, GDP had settled at about a fifth lower value in 2015 as compared with before the crisis. Secondly, Iceland and Ireland had both regained their pre-crisis peak GDP in 2015, with growth in Ireland being especially fast in 2014 and 2015 (see Chapter 7).[2] Thirdly, the Baltic States enjoyed continuous growth for multiple years after sharp declines in economic output during 2008–9. Fourthly, the Southern European neighbours of Greece—Italy, Portugal, and Spain—all experienced a sizable recession around 2012, amid fears of a default on sovereign debt. Both Italy and Portugal

[2] Note that in the first quarter of 2015, the Irish economy grew by over 20%. This phenomenal growth rate is largely attributable to the relocation of large multinational companies to Ireland in the period, rather than changes in the underlying economy. See European Commission (2016b) for further details.

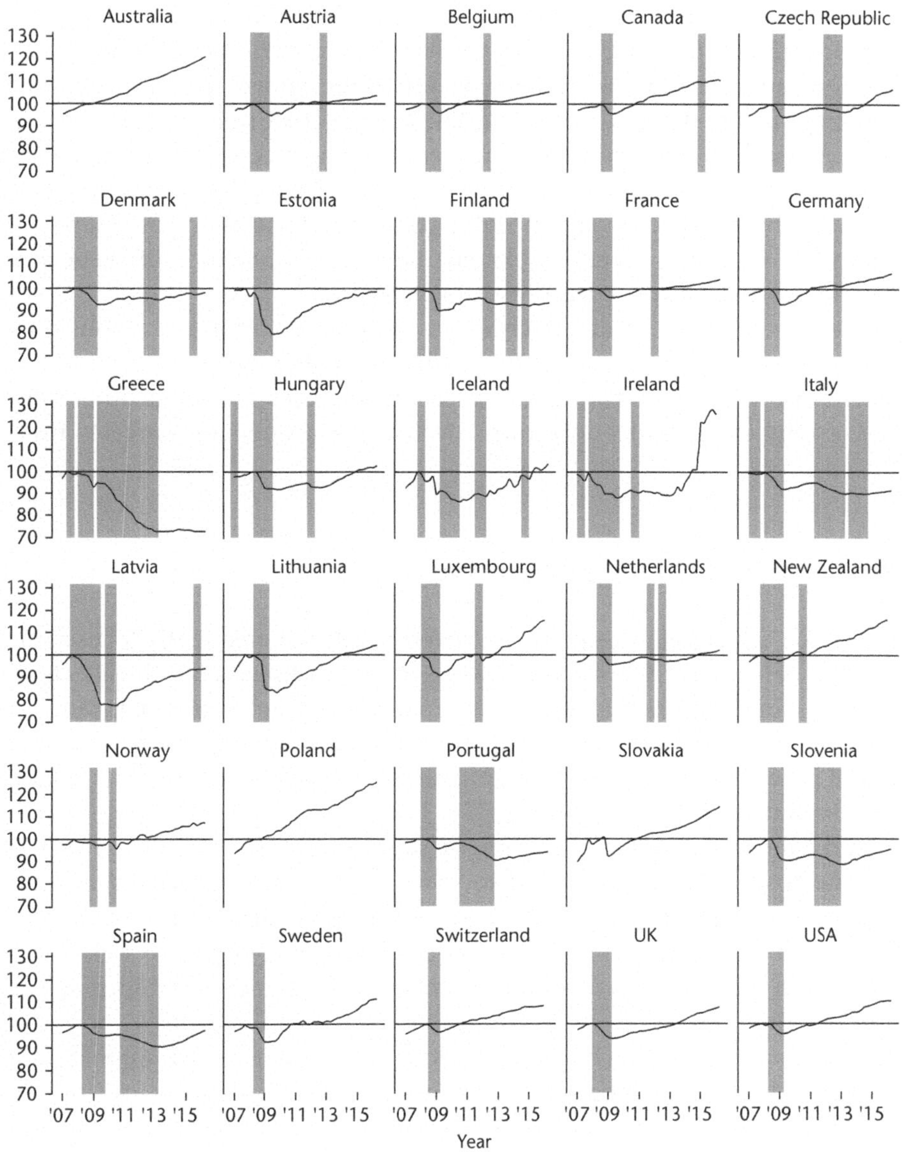


**Figure 4.4.** Quarterly real GDP, seasonally adjusted, 2007–15

*Note*: Index, pre-crisis peak = 100. Shaded areas show periods of two (or more) consecutive quarters of declining real GDP, a commonly used indicator of recessions.

*Source*: OECD Quarterly National Accounts.

remain well below their pre-crisis peak GDP. The Nordic countries fared quite differently over the course of the six years to 2016. While Norway and Sweden (and Iceland) are recovering, economic growth in Denmark and Finland remains sluggish and still below the pre-crisis peak in 2016. This is the case even though these countries entered the recession with relatively low public debt and suffered limited costs associated with restructuring of financial institutions. Finally, the crisis had limited effects on core Eurozone countries, including Germany, France, and Austria, with GDP generally having surpassed its pre-crisis peak value in 2015.

The overall picture of the effects of the crisis on economic conditions thus varies considerably across countries, with seemingly little connection to the extent of the initial costs of the Great Recession. Clearly, factors other than the severity of the initial downturn affected how economies recovered from the crisis.

## 4.2 Government Policy Responses

While the initial policy response by governments was frequently focused on saving financial institutions and staving off a global recession, the effects of the crisis on the economic well-being of individuals and households came to the fore as the crisis unfolded. How governments subsequently acted was heavily characterized by the two dimensions of 'rebalancing', internationally and domestically (Frieden, 2015).

Internationally, countries running a large current account deficit in the lead-up to the crisis were forced to swiftly reduce aggregate consumption and increase exports to regain their current account balance. As cross-border lending came to a sudden halt, this required several countries to seek assistance from international institutions to buffer the speed of the required adjustment.

Iceland was the first such country to do so when it entered an International Monetary Fund (IMF) programme in November 2008. Latvia entered into an agreement with the IMF and EU in December 2008, while Greece, Ireland, Portugal, and Cyprus each entered macroeconomic adjustment programmes with the 'Troika' of the IMF, the European Commission, and the European Central Bank (ECB). Greece agreed to its first bailout in May 2010, a second bailout in February 2012, and a third bailout in July 2015; Ireland entered into an agreement with the Troika in November 2010, Portugal in May 2011, and Cyprus in March 2013. Furthermore, Spain sought assistance from the Troika in June 2012 to recapitalize its banking system, but did not enter a macroeconomic adjustment programme as had the other six countries. The adjustment programmes all involved conditions requiring the countries to take defined steps to reduce the budget deficit, effectively forcing them to give up their policy autonomy and eroding their ability to provide social protection to the general population (Baldwin et al., 2015). The required austerity measures caused a heated conflict between creditor and debtor countries, with creditors demanding swift domestic adjustment from debtors and debtors requesting a longer adjustment period (Baldwin et al., 2015).

Domestically, governments sought to minimize the effects of the crisis on aggregate demand. Their ability to do so, however, was constrained by the state of public finances at the onset of the crisis, the direct fiscal costs of the crisis, as well as the extent to which international rebalancing was required. For current account deficit countries with an independent currency, for example Iceland, an exchange rate depreciation could shoulder part of the necessary adjustment. For other countries, however, much of the adjustment was accomplished internally, through painful macroeconomic austerity measures (Copelovitch et al., 2016).

In what follows, we outline changes and continuity in government policies aimed directly at ameliorating the effects of the crisis on economic well-being of populations. As argued by Pontusson and Raess (2012), the policy menu available to governments was much narrower than in earlier crises. Thus, protectionism, currency devaluations, nationalizations, and industrial policies were mostly off the table, and although monetary policy played a crucial role in stimulating economies throughout the crisis it was no longer directly under the control of elected national officials, making for a more uniform situation across countries (see, for example, Mandelkern, 2016). Thus, fiscal policy came to play a central role in the crisis responses of governments.

We begin by outlining whether governments employed fiscal policy to maintain aggregate demand throughout the crisis by way of a fiscal stimulus or whether they focused on austerity measures to balance the budget and current account. We go on to delineate the relative effects of automatic stabilizers and discretionary policymaking, focusing separately on changes in government taxation and expenditures. Finally, we outline the extent to which tax and benefit systems were changed in response to the crisis. Ultimately, government policy reactions along these dimensions had much to do with how well or poorly the economic welfare of the general population was shielded from the effects of the crisis.

## 4.3 Fiscal Policy

The Great Recession led to a decline in the budget balance for almost all advanced economies. While the shift was mild for most countries, several amassed significant amounts of new debt. Figure 4.5 shows the cumulative budget balance for OECD countries over the first four years of the crisis. The countries in the figure are ordered from those with the most negative to the most positive cumulative budget balance, while the balance itself is decomposed into four main components, which are further discussed in this section.

Looking at the total cumulative budget balance reveals that the countries hit hardest generally accumulated the most debt in the years following the onset of the crisis. Ireland amassed over 70 per cent of GDP in new debt, with Greece, the USA, Spain, the UK, Portugal, and Iceland also accumulating significant new debt. For the aforementioned countries in the EU (all but Iceland), as well as 21 other EU countries, the deficits triggered the excessive deficit procedure (EDP) of the EU's Stability and Growth Pact, which stipulates that yearly deficits should not exceed 3 per cent of GDP unless they are 'exceptional and temporary' (European Commission, 2016a). With the EDP triggered, governments were expected to restore fiscal balance rapidly by pursuing austere policies in the succeeding two to three years (Cameron, 2012, p. 102).

However, not all deficit components are created equal in terms of their impact on the economy and economic welfare of populations. In particular, the cumulative budget balance combines the results of discretionary policymaking following the crisis, the workings of automatic stabilizers, net interest payments, and direct fiscal costs due to the crisis. Thus, it does not allow one to easily gauge the overall fiscal policy choices made by the authorities, nor their incidence over the course of the crisis.

The decomposition of the budget balance in Figure 4.5 shows, in admittedly crude fashion, the relative shares of the four constituent parts. While interpretations based on such a decomposition can be problematic (e.g. Devries et al., 2011), it allows one to compare rough estimates of the different components for each country, as well as across countries.

Two components—one-offs and net interest payments—reflect constraints on fiscal policymakers, rather than polices enacted to affect the macroeconomy directly. The former includes bank recapitalizations, while the latter includes interest payments on accumulated loans, which often accrue to actors outside of the economy. However, the other two components—automatic stabilizers and the underlying primary balance—come closer to capturing the parts of fiscal policy which impact more directly upon current economic well-being.

Automatic stabilizers consist of automatic changes to revenues from taxes and expenditure on social benefits due to the position of the business cycle. In downturns, when economic activity contracts, automatic stabilizers will automatically inject a fiscal stimulus into the economy, as less revenue will be collected from taxes (due to lower income and less profit) and more will be spent on social benefits (due to more unemployment). The size of automatic

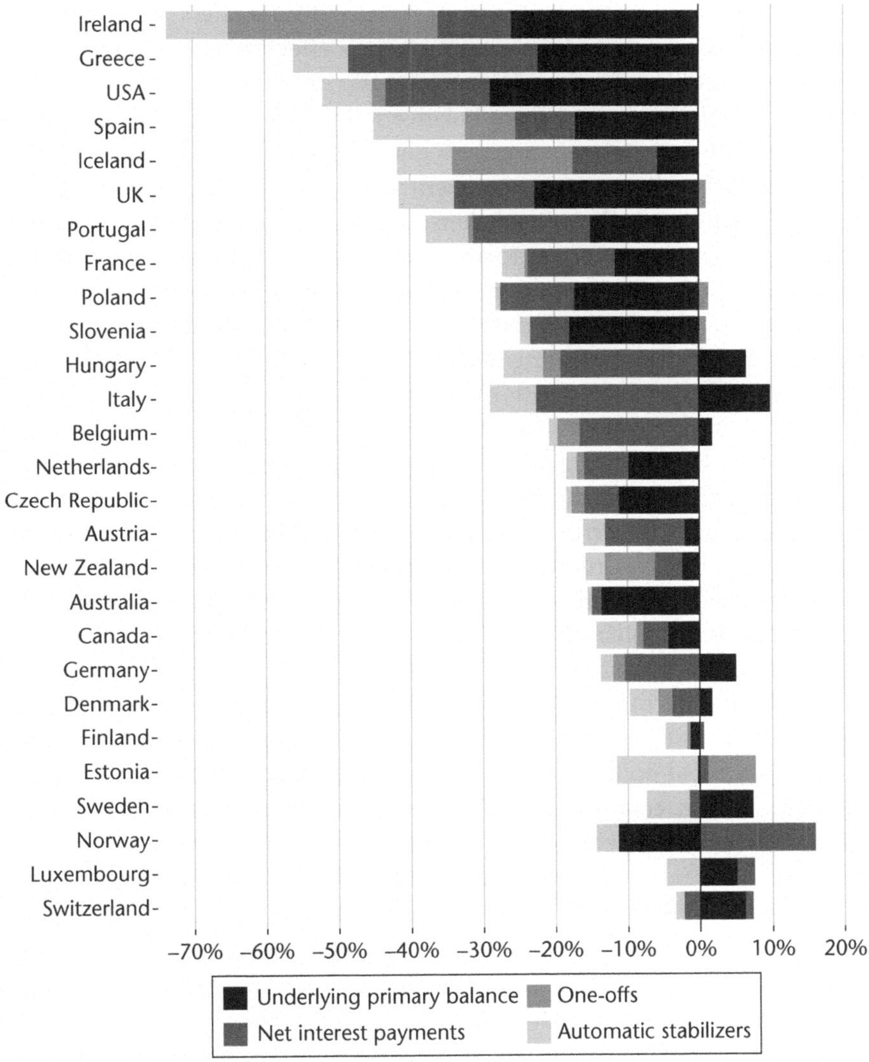


**Figure 4.5.** Decomposed general government cumulative budget balance, 2008–12 (% of GDP)

*Note*: Countries ordered from largest to smallest cumulative budget deficit. Positive (negative) values indicate a budget surplus (deficit). Norwegian data is for mainland Norway, i.e. excluding the oil fund.

*Source*: Author calculations based on OECD Economic Outlook No. 98.

stabilizers—that is, the sensitivity of taxes and transfers to changes in GDP—differs across countries and as such their effects will vary due to policy differences, as well as the size of the economic contraction.[3]

Finally, the underlying primary balance reflects the budget balance net of the effects of the previous three components. It is often taken as an indicator of discretionary policymaking by governments, that is, the budgetary policy changes actually made by policymakers.[4] As such, a more negative underlying primary balance from one year to another is associated with a fiscal stimulus, while a more positive balance is associated with austerity measures.

Figure 4.5 shows the cumulative size of these four components over the first four years of the crisis, revealing several patterns of interest. First, the decomposition reveals the massive costs of one-offs and net interest payments for the deep-crisis countries, especially Ireland, Greece, and Iceland. These reflect the costs associated with bailing out and/or recapitalizing financial institutions as well as interest payments due to loans granted by the IMF and EU institutions. Countries entering the crisis with high levels of public debt, such as Italy and Belgium, similarly contributed a significant share of their budget towards interest payments. Importantly, when analysing the implications of policy responses for economic welfare of populations it is necessary to look beyond the costs of one-offs and net interest payments.

Secondly, the decomposition reveals that almost all 27 countries accumulated significant deficits due to the workings of automatic stabilizers and/or discretionary fiscal policy over the period from 2008 to 2012. In this regard, the liberal market economies (LMEs) (the USA, UK, and Ireland) stand out, accumulating over 30 per cent in new debt due to these two factors, with deep-crisis countries in Southern Europe (Greece, Spain, and Portugal) following suit with over 20 per cent accumulated. Interestingly, discretionary spending seems to have played the most significant role in countries with weak automatic stabilizers, such as the LMEs, which underlines how each of the two components can partly substitute for the other.

While Figure 4.5 highlights the cumulative build-up of budget deficits, it does not reveal the extent to which countries pursued a policy of fiscal stimulus or austerity. Figure 4.6 addresses this task by showing year-on-year changes in spending due to automatic stabilizers and discretionary fiscal policy, with positive values indicating fiscal tightening and negative values indicating a fiscal stimulus. Trends in these factors are shown for 27 OECD

[3] Price, Dang, and Botev (2015) provide further information on the methodology used by the OECD in calculating the size of the automatic stabilizers.

[4] See, for example, Raess and Pontusson (2015) and Armingeon (2012). For a critique of the measure, see Guajardo et al. (2014).

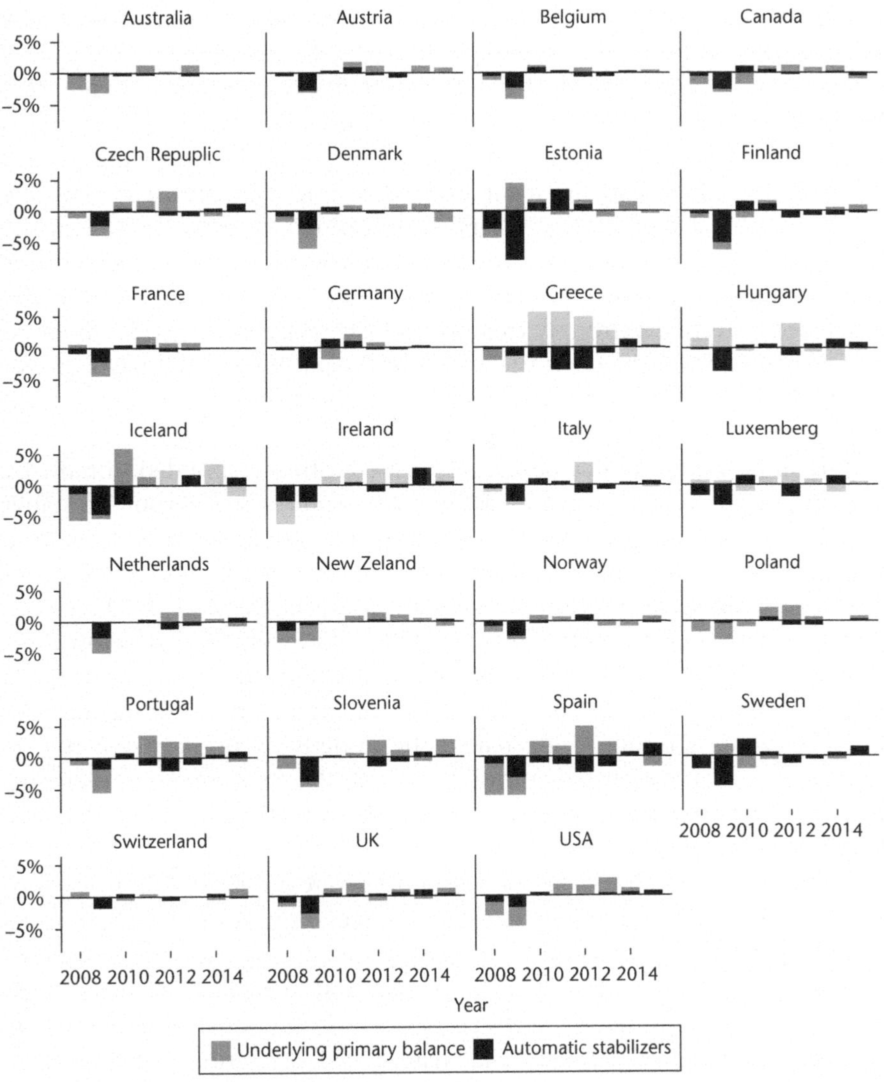


**Figure 4.6.** Year-on-year changes in components of the budget balance, 2008–15 (% of GDP)

*Note*: Positive (negative) values indicate that the component decreases (increases) the budget deficit. Norwegian data is for mainland Norway.

*Source*: Author calculations based on OECD Economic Outlook No. 98.

countries, although most of the variance in the measures can be attributed to the countries hardest hit by the crisis.

Several interesting factors emerge from Figure 4.6. For one thing, automatic stabilizers played a crucial role in stimulating the economy at the onset of the crisis. Since they respond automatically to downturns, they are more likely to provide a timely response than any discretionary measures passed by policymakers, as the latter have to go through all parts of the policymaking process before being felt in the real economy (Baunsgaard & Symansky, 2009). Unsurprisingly, automatic stabilizers provided the largest stimulus in countries most affected by the crisis. However, they also provided a relatively large buffer in the most-affected Nordic countries. This was due to the fact the size of the stabilizers is determined by both the size of the economic contraction as well as the overall sensitivity of the budget balance to the business cycle, with tax and transfer policies in the Nordic countries structured to respond strongly to drops in GDP (Price et al., 2015). As countries recovered from the crisis the effects of the automatic stabilizers diminished, although they continued to have a sizable impact in the hardest-hit countries: Greece, Portugal, and Spain.

More importantly, policymakers in most countries responded initially by enacting discretionary measures designed to support the automatic stabilizers in stimulating the economy (Armingeon, 2012; see also Cameron, 2012). Such forceful Keynesian policies were strongly supported by mainstream economists and international institutions at the time, to stave off a global recession (cf. Spilimbergo et al., 2008). However, from 2010 onwards there was a decisive shift towards balancing the budget. Thus, governments of the countries most affected by the crisis all implemented strong austerity measures and, by doing so, decreased the underlying primary deficit. The reversal in Greece is especially prominent, with the government implementing a multiyear package, greatly reducing the underlying primary balance deficit (see Chapter 5).

Overall, government fiscal policy responses were quite varied across countries and through the different stages of the recession. Automatic stabilizers played a particularly important stimulating role during the earlier stages of the Great Recession, especially in deep-crisis and in Nordic countries. Such automatic policies buffered the effects of the crisis on household income. As time passed and the global financial crisis abated, discretionary fiscal policy measures began to play a larger role. In all deep-crisis countries, governments pursued a variety of austerity measures designed to rapidly reduce the budget deficit, exactly at a time when further stimulus spending would have provided a larger buffer for the economic welfare of households, which were still greatly affected by the crisis. Greek authorities implemented the most severe austerity measures, although Iceland, Ireland, Portugal, and Spain each reduced the budget deficit significantly in the years following 2009. During this time, all these countries were participants in IMF or Troika programmes.

## 4.4 Social Protection

A great deal has been written about the effects of austerity on economic growth, with the emerging view suggesting that episodes of fiscal consolidation reduce aggregate output (Guajardo et al., 2014). Furthermore, these negative effects seem to be more consequential when they are tax based, rather than expenditure based, according to Alesina and colleagues (2015). That is to say, fiscal consolidation plans driven by tax increases seem to be more damaging to economic growth than those driven by expenditure cuts.

When analysing the effects of austerity on the welfare of populations, however, the reverse association seems to hold true. Tax-based fiscal consolidation episodes reduce income inequality, but expenditure-based episodes are associated with sharp increases in inequality (Agnello & Sousa, 2014; Ball et al., 2013). This is as expected, since expenditure-based austerity measures are generally focused on reducing benefit generosity and the government wage bill, which hit lower and middle-income groups the hardest, while tax-based measures are more likely to fall on the better off. The composition of austerity measures thus has a great impact on the effects of austerity on economic welfare.

Figure 4.7 decomposes the cumulative underlying primary balance for the period 2009 to 2013 (the main years of fiscal consolidation) into its revenue and expenditure parts, thus allowing for the comparison of the relative sizes of tax-based and expenditure-based austerity measures. Positive values on the measures indicate fiscal tightening, that is, that higher revenues are collected or that expenditures are lower in 2013 as compared to 2009, while negative values indicate fiscal stimulus, that is, that lower revenues are collected or that spending has increased.

Again, the figure demonstrates the severity of the crisis and policy response in Greece, with the authorities implementing both large revenue increases as well as expenditure cuts. Trailing Greece by some margin come the other four countries most affected by the crisis: Spain, Iceland, Portugal, and Ireland. Interestingly, while the balance of tax-based and expenditure-based austerity measures in Spain and Portugal are similar to that of Greece, Iceland and Ireland pursued considerably different compositions. Thus, relatively large shares of the Icelandic measures were based on revenue increases, primarily affecting the higher income groups, with more limited expenditure cuts (see Chapter 8). Meanwhile, the bulk of the Irish measures were based on expenditure cuts. In terms of their effects on population welfare, these compositional differences should have quite different distributional implications (Blyth, 2013; see also Chapter 7).

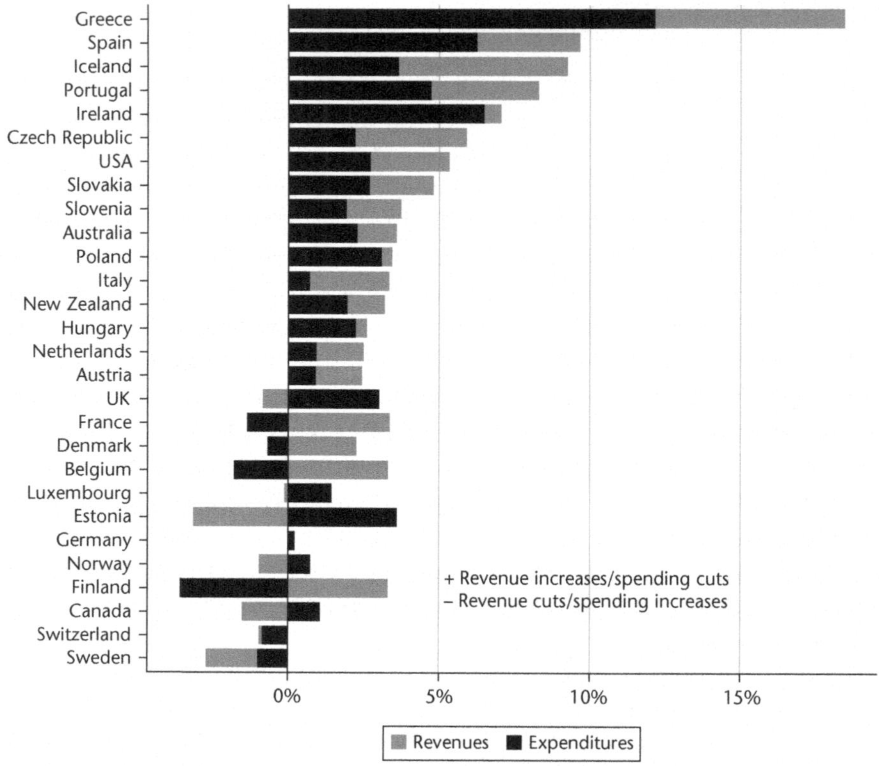


**Figure 4.7.** Cumulative changes to underlying primary revenues and expenditures, 2009–13 (% of potential GDP)

*Note*: The bars show cumulative changes to underlying primary revenues and spending from 2009 to 2013. Positive (negative) values indicate an austere (stimulating) budget position. The countries are ordered by the sum of the two bars.

*Source*: OECD Economic Outlook No. 98.

Figure 4.8 attempts to shed some light on these policy differences with the help of the OECD Tax-Benefit Model (OECD, 2016d). The model includes yearly national policy profiles on various redistributive policies and allows for a rough and ready analysis of how cumulative changes to these policies affect the disposable income of selected household types. While such a model necessarily involves the comparison of a restricted set of household types, it gives insight into the broad contours of policy changes over the period in question (for an early application of this approach to comparative policy analysis, see Bradshaw et al. (1993)).

Developments in the net effects of taxes and transfers on household income are shown in the figure. Transfers consist of family benefits, housing benefits, in-work benefits, and social assistance, while taxes consist of income taxes and employee social security contributions. The examples in the figure are based on a

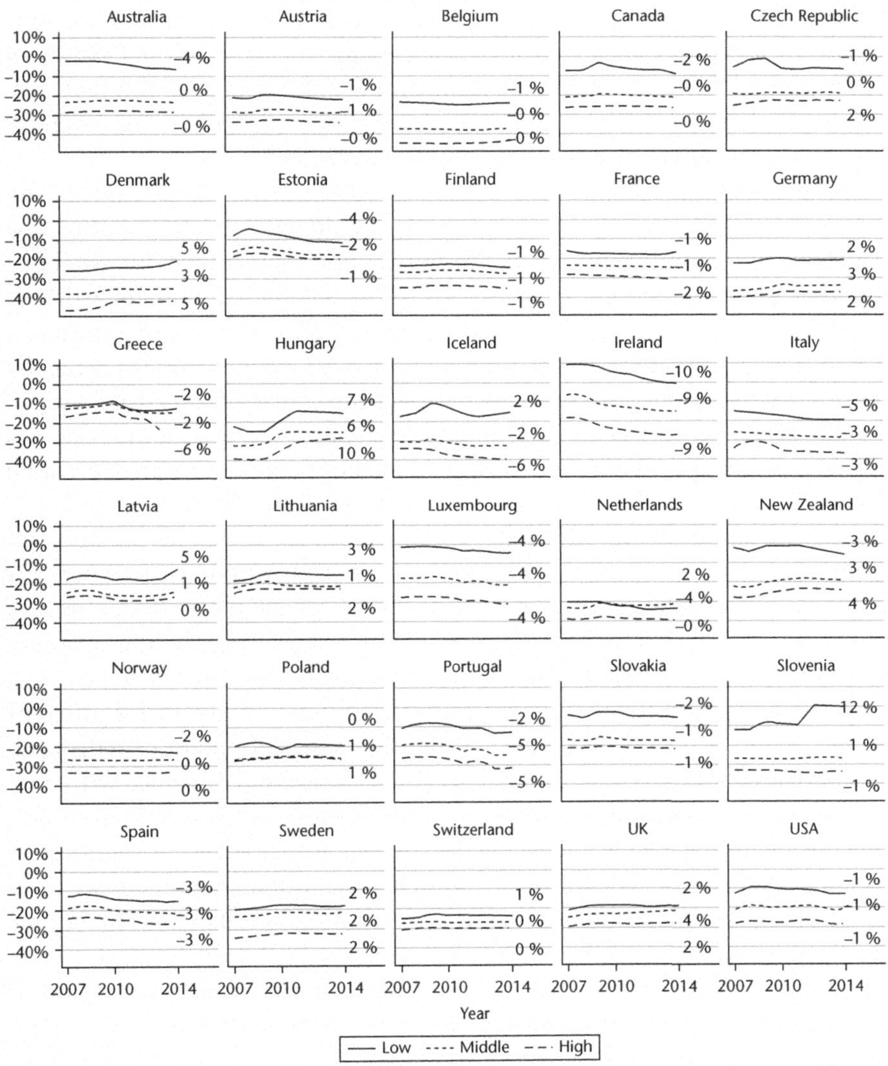


**Figure 4.8.** Net effects of taxes and transfers, by household income, 2007–14 (% of market income)

*Note*: Numbers shown to the right of each line show the cumulative change (in percentage points) from 2007 to 2014 for each income group. Earnings for the reference worker in Ireland are based on an 'average production worker', rather than an 'AW', which inflates the net effect. For additional details, see section 4.4 and OECD (2016d).

*Source*: OECD (2016d).

model of two-earner families with two children at three levels of market income: (i) low: 100 per cent of average worker (AW) market income and non-working spouse; (ii) middle: couple each with 100 per cent AW income; and (iii) high: 200 per cent of AW income and spouse with 100 per cent of AW income. Since the only factor varying among the three model families is market income, it allows for a direct comparison of changes in the distributional effects of redistributive policies. Finally, by standardizing income with current AW income, the comparison is focused squarely on how policies change over the time period and affect identical households differently.[5]

Overall, the figure reveals considerable stability in the overall effect of the main redistributive policies on households not directly affected by the crisis (e.g. due to unemployment). Thus, the global financial crisis did not usher in a period of great retrenchment or expansion of income support for working families. Similarly, in most cases the developments for the three income levels within each country are parallel, suggesting that tax-benefit systems generally did not become more or less progressive over the course of the crisis.

There are, however, a couple of notable exceptions. Ireland stands out as a case of considerable change, with the net effect of taxes and transfers for all household types declining by 9–10 percentage points from 2007 to 2014. Thus, for example, while the net effect for families with low income was about +10 per cent of their market income in 2007, it was down to 0 per cent in 2014 (i.e. they paid as much in taxes as they received in benefits). This is in line with the data shown in Figure 4.7, which suggests that the austerity measures enacted by Irish authorities were mostly expenditure based.

Similarly, developments in Iceland are exceptional, although for different reasons than in Ireland. As Figure 4.8 highlights, development of redistributive policies differed considerably based on household income, with tax-benefit policies becoming slightly more generous for low-income households, but considerably less so for high-income households. The data thus underline how the 'strategy of redistribution' shifted the burden of adjustment from low- to high-income households in the Icelandic case (Ólafsson, 2016b; see also Chapter 8).

In addition to Iceland, Slovenia stands out as exceptional with regard to increasing the redistributive effects of taxes and benefits during the crisis. Besides Ireland, other notable regressive cases include Estonia, Greece, Italy, Portugal, and Spain. For most countries, however, the overall effects of taxes and transfers on household income for working families remained roughly constant over the crisis period.

A similar story of stability can be told about unemployment benefits, which are the primary tool for income replacement for those directly affected by the crisis through loss of employment.[6] Figure 4.9 shows the initial net

[5] For additional details, see OECD (2016d).

[6] It should be noted that initial replacement rates for particular household types are only one of many relevant dimensions of unemployment benefit generosity. Other important dimensions include benefit duration, as well as the extent to which benefits are earnings related (Esser et al., 2013). Furthermore, for those not eligible for unemployment benefits, the development of

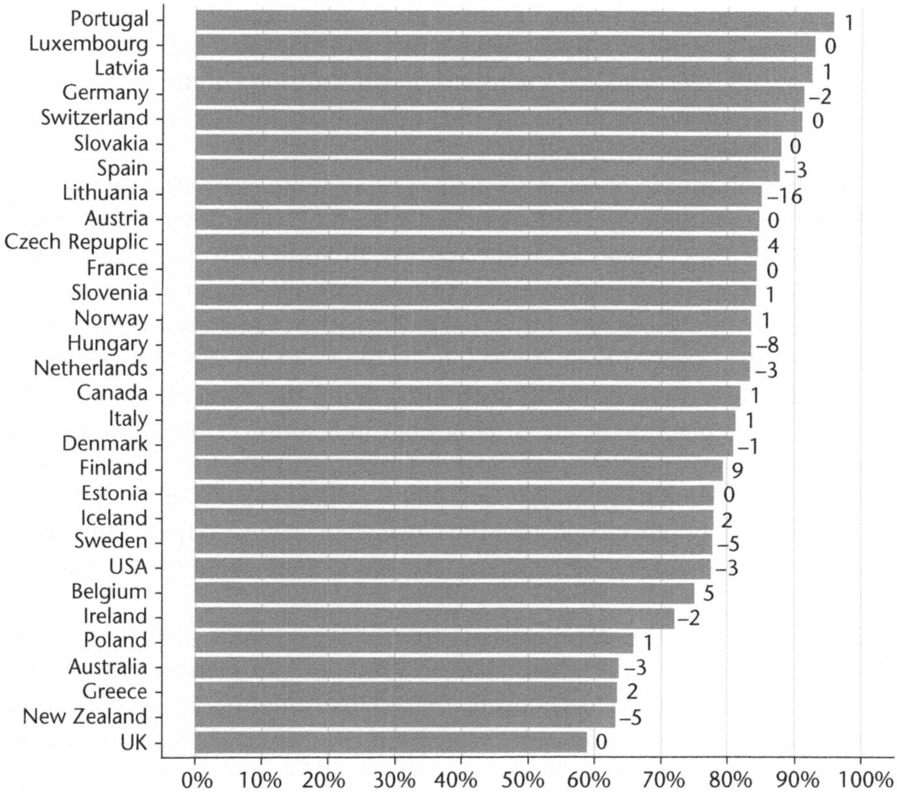


**Figure 4.9.** Initial net unemployment replacement rates in 2007 (% of previous earnings) and change during the crisis

*Note*: The numbers to the right of each bar show the change 2007–14, in percentage points.

*Source*: OECD (2007).

unemployment replacement rate (NURR) in 2007 as a share of previous earnings for a two-earner family (one spouse unemployed) with two children, each earning 100 per cent of AW market income prior to the unemployment spell. The figure also shows the change in the rate (in percentage points) from 2007 to 2014.[7]

For most countries, the rate was next to constant over the time period. Lithuania, though, stands out as a case of significant retrenchment, with a

minimum income protection is more important. These dimensions are not further examined here (see Marchal, Marx, & van Mechelen (2016) for a survey of minimum income protection in the crisis and Palme (2017b) for a more comprehensive analysis of how different dimensions of unemployment insurance were affected over the crisis period).

[7] Supplements are included. For additional details, see OECD (2016d).

16-point drop in the replacement rate, from 85 per cent in 2007 to 69 per cent in 2014. The rate also dropped significantly in Hungary (8 points), Sweden (5 points), and New Zealand (5 points), countries affected quite differently by the crisis. In only two countries did the rate increase significantly: Finland by 9 points and Belgium by 5 points.

While the aftermath of the crisis did not bring about significant changes in the rate, the absolute level of income replacement did differ significantly between countries. Therefore, while the AW in Portugal would receive over 90 per cent of his/her previous earnings during the initial phases of unemployment, an identically situated individual in the United Kingdom would receive less than 60 per cent of his/her previous income. In fact, the countries most affected by the crisis are widely distributed along this measure. Along with Portugal, the replacement rate is fairly high in Spain, Iceland is around the middle, while it is quite low in Ireland, Greece, and the UK. Clearly, these differences in national unemployment policy profiles suggest that individuals who lost their jobs during and after the Great Recession fared quite differently based on their country of residence. Hence welfare regimes did make a difference.

Overall, social policy developments from 2008 onwards have been more characterized by continuity than change. While specific elements of tax and benefit systems may have changed, the relative importance of taxes and transfers have remained constant throughout the crisis and post-crisis period for different income groups in most countries. This further highlights the importance of the institutional and policy setting at the onset of the crisis. However, there are notable exceptions to this trend, which can be seen as more representative of fundamental changes. In that regard, Ireland stands out as a particularly regressive case, with the net effects of taxes and transfers being reduced for low-, middle-, and high-income groups alike. At the other end of the spectrum, Iceland stands as a progressive case, with taxes and benefits becoming more generous for low-income households, while less so for high-income households. These differences in social policy developments are likely to have divergent outcomes for the economic welfare of households in the two countries.

## 4.5 Discussion

The global financial crisis was at its height in the winter of 2008–9 as financial institutions around the world teetered on the brink of collapse. The crisis brought the largest economic contraction in advanced economies in the post-war era. While the effects of the crisis were particularly devastating in Greece, multiple countries experienced severe domestic recessions in the years following the peak of the crisis. This was especially so for countries that entered the crisis in a precarious fiscal position, as they were highly vulnerable to the sudden stop in cross-border lending that developed amidst fears of banking and sovereign defaults. The other countries most affected, including Ireland, Iceland, Portugal, Spain, and Latvia, were forced to seek the assistance of international lenders of last resort to stave off an economic collapse. Although the effects of the Great Recession were most pronounced in these deep-crisis countries, almost all OECD countries experienced a recessionary period in the aftermath of the crisis.

The crisis undermined the budget balance of most countries in the first years after the crisis hit and led to higher public debt levels (Streeck, 2017). While the restoration of financial institutions and interest payments due to debt obligations were particularly costly for the deep-crisis countries, all governments provided some form of fiscal stimulus in the initial stages of the Great Recession. Automatic stabilizers played a particularly large role in buffering the initial effects of the crisis on aggregate demand, while discretionary stimulus measures were also employed to support their operation at the height of the crisis. However, from 2010 onwards harsh austerity measures were generally introduced, most markedly in deep-crisis countries.

Even so, not all austerity measures were designed in a similar fashion. Governments in several countries, including Greece, Spain, Ireland, and the UK, focused on spending cuts, which were likely to have dire consequences for individuals and households most in need of social support during the crisis. Meanwhile Iceland stands out as a deep-crisis country that took the opposite route, prioritizing revenue increases over spending cuts in its fiscal consolidation plans. Although not hit as hard by the crisis, a similar pattern can be seen in the other Nordic countries.

Although these policy differences are likely to be consequential for the economic welfare of populations, the overall story for tax and benefit policies in the crisis is one of continuity rather than change. This suggests that the institutional and policy setting at the onset of the crisis was substantially more important for the welfare of those affected by the crisis than most discretionary policy changes made during the crisis years. On balance, countries with more generous welfare states at the onset of the crisis were therefore better positioned to protect the welfare of the general population.

# Part II

# Country Case Studies

# 5

# Greece

## The Crisis, Austerity, and the Transformation of Welfare

*Manos Matsaganis*

The aim of this chapter is to discuss how the Greek welfare state responded to the economic crisis, and how it was shaped by austerity.[1] The structure is as follows. The first section presents a brief overview of the origins of the Greek crisis, the way it unfolded, and its aftermath. Section 5.2 traces the social impact of the crisis in terms of jobs, earnings, and family incomes. Section 5.3 details the policy response to the crisis, as well as the effects of austerity policy on the welfare state. Section 5.4 examines the profound changes in the distribution of jobs, earnings, and other market income, as brought about by the crisis, and their interaction with policy changes. Section 5.5 focuses on financial hardship. Section 5.6 concludes by summarizing the main findings and drawing out the main policy implications.

### 5.1 The Crisis

It is difficult to escape the thought that Greece's current predicament is largely rooted in its unsustainable growth prior to the crisis. In 2000–7, the Greek

[1] A previous version of this chapter was presented at a workshop in Reykjavik (30 September 2016). I am grateful to discussants and participants for their remarks. Chrysa Leventi made extensive comments on earlier drafts, while Sophia Tsaroucha compiled a timeline of policy developments during the crisis in Greece which was used in the writing of this chapter. I am indebted to both. Financial support under the Reconciling Economic and Social Europe project (www.resceu.eu), funded by the European Research Council (Advanced Grant no. 340534) is gratefully acknowledged. The usual disclaimer applies.

economy grew twice as fast as that of the rest of Europe (+32.4 per cent in real terms, compared to +17.1 per cent in the EU28 and +14.2 per cent in the Euro area). However, behind the façade of prosperity, fuelled by strong consumer demand and boosted by cheap credit, lay a largely uncompetitive economy, its many weaknesses revealed in the gradual deterioration of the balance of payments (BoP), with the account deficit reaching 14.9 per cent of gross domestic product (GDP) in 2008.[2]

The Greek crisis hit the headlines in October 2009, when the socialist government, fresh from its electoral triumph earlier that month, announced that earlier fiscal data had been misreported. The general government deficit as a share of GDP for 2008 was corrected from 5 per cent to 7.7 per cent (later revised to 9.4 per cent and then to 9.9 per cent), while the estimate for 2009 was raised from 3.7 per cent to 12.5 per cent (finally settled at 15.6 per cent).

The figures stunned public opinion in Europe and shocked markets worldwide. Coming not long after the onset of the international financial crisis, and coinciding with sluggish growth everywhere, the realities of the Greek case assumed unanticipated dimensions. Markets, until then oblivious to country risk, treating the entire Eurozone as a single undifferentiated entity, overreacted by increasing spreads (that is, interest rate differentials from German government bonds) and lowering credit ratings. This turned a fiscal crisis into a sovereign debt crisis, threatening to bring down the entire edifice of Europe's Economic and Monetary Union (EMU). Almost at a stroke, Greece effectively lost access to the international financial markets and was no longer able to service its debt except at prohibitive costs.

The Greek saga was decisive in reinforcing the perception that the Eurozone crisis really was the fault of irresponsible governments violating the pacts they had vowed to respect (in the case of public deficit 3 per cent of GDP, as enshrined in the 1992 Maastricht Treaty, which led to the creation of the common currency, and later in the Growth and Stability Pact). And yet the fiscal woes of Ireland only started when the government decided to issue a broad guarantee to Irish banks, while in both Ireland and Spain public debt as a proportion of GDP was below 40 per cent (against the 60 per cent ceiling agreed first at Maastricht then under the Stability and Growth Pact). Furthermore, the standard view among mainstream economists has now shifted towards a more nuanced understanding that the Eurozone crisis was primarily due to external rather than fiscal imbalances (Baldwin et al., 2015; also Baldwin & Gros, 2015). In spring 2010, as Greece's EU partners debated whether to circumvent the Maastricht Treaty's 'no bailout' clause and on

[2] On the origins of the Greek crisis, see also Katsimi and Moutos (2010), Featherstone (2011), Mitsopoulos and Pelagidis (2011), Galenianos (2014), Christodoulakis (2015), and Matsaganis (2018b).

exactly what terms, the conviction set in almost everywhere in Europe (and beyond) that Greece was not to be trusted and should never have been allowed to join the Eurozone in the first place.

As it turned out, Greece was the first Euro area member (May 2010) to request a bailout, which was granted in return for massive fiscal consolidation and structural reforms supervised by the European Commission, the International Monetary Fund (IMF), and the European Central Bank (ECB), collectively known as 'the Troika'. Ireland (December 2010) and Portugal (May 2011) were to follow. Other EU countries, in the Eastern fringe, having run early into BoP difficulties, had to apply for more limited financial assistance, which also came with close surveillance and austerity. Involved were Hungary (October 2008), Latvia (December 2008), and Romania (May 2009). As for the more robust economies of larger member states, such as Spain and Italy, they were subject to softer forms of conditionality.

In the narrow terms of fiscal consolidation, the 'Greek Programme' was a triumph. Pre-crisis, fiscal chronic imbalances had grown enormously, public deficits reaching 15.6 per cent and public debt 126.7 per cent of GDP in 2009. The magnitude of the deficit reduction in 2010 (almost 5 per cent of GDP) was the biggest in a single year in any developed country.[3] Over a longer period, the 'general government primary balance' (a budget deficit metric excluding net interest payments, that is, debt servicing costs, that lie beyond the control of current governments) went from a 10.1 per cent of GDP deficit in 2009 to a 1.1 per cent surplus in 2013. All this at the depth of the recession, at a time when both Ireland and Portugal still ran primary deficits (cf. IMF, 2015, table A2).

Nevertheless, the effects of the austerity policy and the recession were severe. In the 2008–13 period, the size of the Greek economy shrank by as much as 26.3 per cent. In the other Southern European countries, the size of the contraction was considerably lower: −8.9 per cent in Spain,−7.8 per cent in Portugal,−7.6 per cent in Italy.[4] To find another example of such a deep and drawn-out recession in the peacetime economic history of advanced economies, one would have to go back to the US Great Depression (−30 per cent of GDP in 1929–32).

As domestic demand collapsed, the BoP improved, registering a small surplus (0.7 per cent of GDP) in 2013. Nevertheless, this was exclusively driven by a precipitous fall in imports. Exports were below their 2008 level until 2013 and have remained sluggish ever since. In other words, many Greek firms proved incapable of switching to international markets, whether because their products were of poor quality, or were sold at high prices, or both. The poor

[3] 'No other OECD country has achieved such a fiscal improvement in a single year over the past three decades' (OECD, 2011b, p. 12).

[4] See Eurostat data, http://ec.europa.eu/eurostat/data/database.

performance of exports revealed the structural flaws of Greece's growth model (Arkolakis, Doxiadis, & Gelanianos, 2017; Ioannides & Pissarides, 2015).

In the meantime, both Ireland (December 2013) and Portugal (June 2014) had successfully exited their 'Economic Adjustment Programme',[5] while Greece's desperate attempts at an early exit (October 2014) and renegotiation (February to July 2015) backfired, culminating in the bailout agreement of summer 2015, the third since the crisis began. This time, the 'Greek Programme' (guaranteeing financial assistance, conditional on fiscal consolidation and structural reforms) was signed by a government that had come to power earlier that year (January 2015) with the explicit promise to end austerity.

In the period between 2013 and 2016, when the European economy returned to growth (+6.2 per cent in the EU as a whole), Greece was still mired in stagnation (+0.2 per cent cumulatively over three years). In contrast, over the same period the economy grew by 8.3 per cent in Spain, 4.3 per cent in Portugal, and 2 per cent in Italy.[6]

In effect, the Greek crisis put in reverse the process of convergence with the rest of Western Europe that had finally seemed to gather speed with the introduction of the common currency in 2001. Because of the deep recession and the anaemic recovery, relative living standards, having peaked at 85.4 per cent of the EU15 average in 2009, plummeted to 61.3 per cent in 2016, a level last seen in the early 1960s.[7]

## 5.2 The Social Impact of the Crisis

The Troika's main solution for engineering an export-led recovery was 'internal devaluation' (i.e. a policy-driven compression of wages via labour market deregulation, including a drastic cut in the minimum wage). This was duly implemented, especially in 2012–13. Nevertheless, the reduction in labour costs (including wages) put forward as the key to reversing the decline in employment has so far produced decidedly unimpressive results. In March 2017 the number of workers remained 2 per cent below the March 2012 level (when the minimum wage was cut by 22 per cent in nominal terms) and a full 21 per cent below its pre-crisis peak of May 2008.[8] It seemed clear that massive fiscal consolidation had been achieved in spite of a low-performing economy, rather than on the back of a new dynamism. Eliminating the twin deficits,

[5] Hungary (November 2010), Latvia (January 2012), and Romania (June 2011) also exited their BoP financial assistance programmes.

[6] See Eurostat data, http://ec.europa.eu/eurostat/data/database.

[7] See AMECO database, https://ec.europa.eu/info/business-economy-euro/indicators-statistics/economic-databases/macro-economic-database-ameco/ameco-database_en.

[8] See Hellenic Statistical Authority, Elstat Database, table 1A, http://www.statistics.gr/en/home/.

fiscal and external, had been accomplished by simply moving the economy to a much lower equilibrium.

More generally, as a result of the recession and the austerity, labour market conditions deteriorated rapidly. Unemployment rose precipitously (from 7.8 per cent in 2008 to 23.6 per cent in 2016, having peaked at 28.7 per cent in November 2013; cf. footnote 4). The employment rate fell from 61.4 per cent in 2008 to 48.8 per cent in 2013 and still stood at no more than 52 per cent in 2016, that is, below its level two decades earlier (it was 54.7 per cent in 1996). Part-time employment grew (to 9.8 per cent of all jobs in 2016, from 5.4 per cent in 2008), but remained well below the EU average (19.5 per cent in 2014). Moreover, part-time work was largely involuntary—that is, taken up not by choice, but because no full-time jobs were available (72 per cent of all part-time workers in 2016, versus 27.7 per cent in the EU28, according to Eurostat data). In other respects, the effect of the crisis was asymmetrical: more jobs were lost in private enterprises than in the public sector, in micro firms (employing zero to nine workers) than in larger ones, in construction and manufacture than in services. Moreover, men were worse affected than women, foreign workers than nationals, and temporary workers than permanent workers.

Given the length of the recession, as of 2018 the majority of jobless workers have been out of work for over a year: the long-term unemployment rate went from 3.7 per cent in 2008 to 19.5 per cent in 2014 and was still as high as 17 per cent in 2016 (relative to an EU average of 4 per cent).[9] New entrants to the labour market faced unfavourable prospects, often choosing to prolong full-time education. Thus the proportion of those aged 15–24 years who were not in employment, education, or training increased less than might have been expected (from 11.4 per cent in 2008 to 20.4 per cent in 2013), then fell back to some extent (to 15.8 per cent in 2016, compared to 11.5 per cent in the EU28).

For those still in employment, real earnings fell as a result both of the recession (i.e. lower demand for labour) and of 'internal devaluation' (i.e. policy-driven compression of wages via labour market deregulation). The relevant changes disproportionately affected the overlapping categories of newly hired and young workers. Administrative data from IKA (the social insurance agency for private sector employees) indicate that the median reported earnings of newly hired workers declined by 34.2 per cent, and of workers aged below 30 by 34.8 per cent, in real terms in the 2010–14 period. In contrast, the median earnings of those who kept their job with the same employer were cut by 9.6 per cent (see Dimakakos & Skiadas, 2016).

[9] See Eurostat database. Long-term unemployment by sex; annual average, http://appsso.eurostat.ec.europa.eu/nui/show.do?dataset=une_ltu_a&lang=en.

On the whole, Bank of Greece estimates show that average gross earnings of all employees in 2014 were 25.4 per cent below their pre-crisis peak (in 2009) and as much as 8.4 per cent below their 2000 level.[10] In the 'informal sector' (typically in construction, agriculture, tourism, and other services), where employers are often subject to no legal or other constraints, except those implicit in the free play of unregulated market forces, earnings fell even more. Because of the rising tax pressure, earnings losses were more pronounced in net terms.

More recent evidence confirms that earnings losses were pervasive and persistent. As the Institute of the General Confederation of Greek Workers has noted in its latest annual report, in 2016 the share of employees in private firms who earned less than €700 per month was 38.8 per cent, whereas in 2009 it had been 13.1 per cent (see INE, 2017, graph 3.16).

Because of the austerity, changes in taxes and benefits were cyclical rather than countercyclical. The tax burden, in particular, increased sharply. As a result, disposable incomes declined more abruptly than GDP and earnings. Specifically, mean (median) incomes fell by some 38 per cent in real terms in 2010–16 (see footnote 4).

## 5.3 Policy Responses to the Crisis

In spite of rising social spending pre-crisis, the Greek welfare state was particularly unfit for the challenge posed by the crisis (Matsaganis, 2011). It has always fitted the characterization of the Southern European model of welfare as a combination of 'unparalleled peaks of generosity reserved for the protected core of the labour market' and serious gaps in the social safety net quite well (Ferrera, 1996, p. 21). When the crisis hit, there was little to prevent hundreds of thousands of families suffering losses in terms of jobs and/or earnings from falling into poverty. The social protection system generally failed to support the living standards of vulnerable groups.

In the 2010–14 period, the Greek welfare state itself, just like every other policy area, became subject to fiscal consolidation. The extent of waste and inefficiency in resource use, ineffectiveness in terms of social objectives, poor administration, outright fraud in some cases, overlaps or duplication between schemes, as well as coverage gaps, suggested that the scope for strengthening social protection while cutting social expenditure was considerable, although political and technical constraints limited what could realistically be achieved. As it turned out, welfare state 'recalibration' was not

[10] Author calculations based on Bank of Greece figures for 2015 and earlier (Bank of Greece, 2015, table V10).

pursued at all until 2013.[11] In the meantime, the supply of social protection was reduced, just as demand for it reached unprecedented heights.

In absolute terms (per inhabitant, at constant prices), expenditure on social benefits peaked in 2009, that is, the last pre-crisis year. Thereafter, as the recession deepened, social spending declined. By 2014, the size of the Greek welfare state (proxied by social expenditure per capita in real terms) had shrunk by over 20 per cent relative to what it had been in 2009.[12] In relative terms, as a share of GDP, expenditure on social protection continued to grow from 24.8 per cent in 2009 to 28 per cent in 2012, coming close to the EU28 average (28.7 per cent). Between 2012 and 2014, as the cuts in social protection under fiscal consolidation took effect, social spending fell faster than GDP (to 26.1 per cent in 2014).[13] However, it seems to have picked up again in more recent years.[14]

Not all policy areas were treated equally. Pensions expenditure, driven by the opposing forces of nominal benefit cuts and rising pensioner numbers, continued its upward trend, temporary setbacks notwithstanding, to reach 18.3 per cent of GDP in 2016 (from 14.6 per cent in 2009), according to Greek government estimates. Predictably, the growth in pensions spending crowded out other components of Greek welfare to a greater extent than had hitherto been the case.

Pension reform had been high on the agenda since the early 1990s, when it first became evident that Greek pensions were neither sustainable nor equitable. In 2010, pension reform returned to the top of the political agenda, as the Memorandum of Economic and Financial Policies signed in May 2010 contained the blueprint of a drastic pension reform. The 2010 reform had established a new structure, combining a tax-funded basic pension with a contributory proportional pension. The new system was due to come into force in January 2015, but the general election of that month disrupted its introduction. The incoming government repealed the 2010 law and a year later brought a new one to parliament. The 2016 reform accelerated the consolidation of Greek pensions, unifying entitlements across categories, and between future retirees and those already retired. It also further reduced

[11] See Pierson (2001) and Ferrera and Hemerijck (2003) for a fuller analysis of 'recalibration' as a strategy to expand coverage for new social risks (e.g. child care) while 'retrenching' spending on old social risks (e.g. retirement benefits) under conditions of 'permanent austerity'.

[12] Social expenditure per capita decreased from €5,495 in 2009 to €4,374 in 2014 (at 2010 prices), a fall of 20.4%. In Spain social spending fell by 6.3% over the period, in Italy by 2.6%, in Portugal by 0.1%. In the EU28 as a whole, social spending increased by 2.4%. See footnote 4.

[13] See footnote 4. Note that earlier Eurostat estimates (updated on 26 January 2016) had put social expenditure in Greece at 31.6% in 2012.

[14] From 26.1% of GDP in 2014 to 26.5% in 2015, or from €4,374 in 2014 to €4,510 in 2015 (per capita at 2010 prices), according to Eurostat. OECD estimates show social expenditure to have increased further to 27% of GDP in 2016. See OECD, Social Expenditure Update, https://www.oecd.org/els/soc/OECD2014-SocialExpenditure_Update19Nov_Rev.pdf.

accrual rates, especially for those with a long contributory record. At the same time, it reinstated the sharp division between those with an adequate contributory record (of at least 15 years) and those without. The latter may only be eligible for a means-tested national pension of €384 per month, with their contributions counting for nothing. Furthermore, Greek pensions were made subject to a higher retirement age and various benefit cuts. Nominal reductions varied with benefit level and sometimes pensioner age. Their cumulative effect was considerable, ranging from 15 to 45 per cent in real terms.[15]

The diminished capacity of the welfare state to respond to the increased need for social protection can be seen most clearly in the area of income support for the unemployed. Between 2010 and 2014, unemployment protection became subject to a flurry of legislative or administrative changes. On the one hand, the benefit rate of contributory unemployment insurance was cut (from €454 to €360 per month) and the duration of repeat spells over a period of four years was limited. On the other hand, access to means-tested unemployment assistance was relaxed (with the benefit rate left unchanged), while a benefit for formerly self-employed workers was also introduced (Matsaganis, 2018a).

Yet the combined result of these changes was reduced coverage. As unemployment soared and unemployment spells grew longer, the coverage of unemployment benefits declined. Between 2010 and 2014, as the number of jobless workers doubled (from 624,000 to 1.27 million), the number of recipients of any of the three unemployment benefits mentioned fell considerably (from 226,000 to 155,000). In view of that, the coverage rate over the same period decreased steeply, from 36.2 to 12.7 per cent of all jobless workers. It is hard to reconcile this evidence with the claim that, under IMF advice, unemployment benefit coverage in Greece 'expanded' (Blanchard, Jaumotte, & Loungani, 2014, p. 20).

The low coverage of unemployment benefits (and the cut in the level of unemployment insurance benefit), together with the lack of a broad-based social assistance scheme of last resort, condemned most families where no adult worked to extreme poverty. According to a recent micro-simulation study, the extreme poverty rate of workless households had risen to 71.2 per cent in 2013.[16]

[15] For more detail, see Leventi and Matsaganis (2018). For the pre-history of pension reform, see Featherstone (2005), Tinios (2005), and Matsaganis and Leventi (2011).

[16] The study set the extreme poverty threshold at the cost of purchasing a basket of basic necessities, excluding health care, adequate to sustain a family just above destitution level, without dissaving or running into debt. In 2013, the extreme poverty rate for the population as a whole, i.e. the proportion of persons living in families with an income below that threshold, was estimated at 17.1%. See Matsaganis et al. (2017).

This is not to say that policy initiatives to strengthen the social safety net were completely absent. In fact, some 'recalibration' did take place from 2013 onwards. The introduction of a non-categorical means-tested unified child benefit in 2013, the payment of a lump sum social dividend in 2014, and the launch of a guaranteed minimum income (GMI) pilot in a number of local areas in 2014–15 were the main policy changes concerning improvements to income support under the conservative–socialist coalition ruling the country from June 2012 to January 2015. Other measures, discussed earlier in this section, included the broadening of eligibility conditions for unemployment assistance and the extension of unemployment protection to the self-employed. These changes made a welcome contribution to coping with the social effects of the economic crisis. Nevertheless, their size was modest: their combined cost was 0.36 per cent of GDP in 2013 and 0.64 per cent in 2014. All in all, the balance of 'retrenchment' versus 'expansion' remained overwhelmingly tilted towards the former: for each €100 saved as a result of cutbacks in social expenditure under the 2013–14 spending review, only about €7 was 'reinvested' in policies strengthening the social safety net.

The anti-austerity coalition of the radical left and the nationalist right that won the January 2015 general election had amassed considerable political capital when in opposition by denouncing the country's 'humanitarian crisis' (its preferred term for the social situation in Greece). Nevertheless, once in government, its much-awaited social programme proved something of an anti-climax. Legislation on 'immediate measures to fight the humanitarian crisis' actually boiled down to three income- and asset-tested schemes: an electricity allowance for poor families, some of which had had their homes disconnected because of unpaid bills; a rent benefit paid directly to landlord home owners on behalf of their tenants; and a food subsidy in the form of a smart card accepted at supermarkets and other grocers. The total cost of these policies amounted to a mere 0.06 per cent of GDP in 2015 and 0.14 per cent in 2016, that is, considerably less than the previous government's discretionary measures, rightly criticized as inadequate.

More recently, the Greek government reluctantly abandoned its preferred policies 'to fight the humanitarian crisis' in favour of joining the European mainstream by introducing a nationwide GMI scheme, under the name Social Solidarity Income. This was certainly a major policy development and a long overdue addition to the country's social protection system. The road to a GMI was opened by the ignominious end of the government's confrontation with the EU in July 2015. The Memorandum of Understanding (MoU), signed in August 2015, explicitly stipulated that financial aid to Greece would be conditional on the government introducing a nationwide minimum income scheme. Thereafter, implementation proceeded relatively smoothly. After a brief 'phase I' from July 2016 in 30 municipalities, accounting for 15 per cent of the country's total population, Social Solidarity Income was launched nationwide on 1 February 2017. The number of recipients was expected gradually to reach 6.5 per cent of population, at an estimated cost of 0.42 per cent of GDP. Political pressure from the European Commission and the IMF, technical assistance by the World Bank, and the active support of pro-GMI enclaves within public administration at ministry and municipal level, more than compensated for the distinct lack of enthusiasm for the programme on the part of Greece's anti-austerity government.[17]

## 5.4 Outcomes

The implications of the crisis in terms of jobs and earnings (discussed in section 5.2), mediated by policy changes under austerity (analysed in section 5.3), profoundly affected the distribution of incomes, whether in cash or in kind, including access to publicly funded services.

The available evidence shows that while attempts were made to limit the impact of austerity on inequality, by designing spending cuts and tax increases in a more progressive manner, this was not always the case. In any case, austerity had pernicious effects on demand, depressing economic activity, causing business closures and job losses. These second-order effects increased inequality and poverty and more than offset the first-order effects of tax-benefit policies, even when the latter were progressive (Perez & Matsaganis, 2018; also Matsaganis & Leventi, 2014).

Inequality increased, though less spectacularly. The Gini index, more sensitive to changes near the middle of the income distribution than to those affecting the poor (or the rich), rose from 0.335 in 2010 to 0.345 in 2014 (0.343 in 2016). The S80/S20 income quintile share ratio, by definition more sensitive to changes at the two ends of the distribution, went up from 5.6 in 2010 to 6.6 in 2016 (relative to 5.2 in the EU28 as a whole, according to Eurostat; see footnote 4).

With respect to poverty, it is too early for the effect of the Social Solidarity Income to show up in official statistics. However, there is evidence that it might contribute to closing the extreme poverty rate and the relative poverty gap (see European Commission, 2017c, p. 80; also Matsaganis et al., 2017).

As for the standard poverty rate (i.e. the share of population with incomes below 60 per cent of median), it went up by 3 percentage points between 2010 and 2012 (from 20.1 per cent to 23.1 per cent), falling by 2 percentage points

[17] See Matsaganis (2017) for an extensive account of the long and winding road to a GMI in Greece.

in later years (to 21.2 per cent in 2016). The share of population with incomes below a lower threshold of 40 per cent of median income increased by a great deal more (from 6.6 per cent in 2009 to 11.1 per cent in 2013) and remained high after the worst of the crisis had passed (to 10.2 per cent in 2016, relative to the EU28 average of 6.4 per cent; cf. footnote 4).

On the other hand, when income change is rapid, people tend to compare their situation not only to that of others in society (the rationale behind relative poverty), but also to their own situation before the rapid income change occurred. 'Anchoring' the poverty threshold at the start of the crisis might give us a better sense of the actual deterioration in living standards. In Greece, the 'anchored' poverty rate (i.e. the share of population with incomes below the 2008 poverty threshold, adjusted for inflation) rose vertiginously, from 18 per cent in 2010 to 48 per cent in 2014 and then to 47.8 per cent in 2016, according to Eurostat data.

Interestingly, the composition of the population in poverty changed rapidly during the crisis. While pensioners suffered significant income losses (and were adversely affected by funding cuts in health care), the unemployed and their families lost even more income and were offered less protection. As a result, the poverty rate of the elderly (and that of other categories traditionally seen as poor, e.g. farmers) fell, while child poverty (and that of residents in urban centres) rose significantly (see European Commission, 2017c; also Matsaganis et al., 2017).

Furthermore, Eurostat's measure of severe material deprivation also increased, steeply and steadily, from 11 per cent in 2009 to 22.4 per cent in 2016 (relative to the EU28 average of 7.5 per cent).

Finally, in health care, where the scope for efficient savings was considerable, funding cuts and organizational reforms, even when well meant, often ended up disrupting service provision (Matsaganis, 2013; also Petmesidou & Guillén, 2014). As a result, the population share of those who reported unmet need for health care (specifically, they did not seek care because they could not afford it) almost trebled during the crisis, from 4 per cent in 2009 to 10.9 per cent in 2015 (relative to 2 per cent in the EU28 as a whole; cf. footnote 4).

## 5.5 Financial Hardship during the Crisis

The combination of falling household incomes, low benefit coverage, rising prices (albeit at a low inflation rate), and significantly increased user charges in health care and other public services, has brought extensive financial hardship, reaching higher levels than is implied by the rise in income poverty alone.

As a result, economic strain has become more pervasive, with 40.6 per cent of households making ends meet 'with great difficulty' in 2016 (compared to 9.1 per cent in the EU28 as a whole), up from 20 per cent in 2008.[18]

The financial hardship indicator used throughout this volume is even more revealing. As Figure 5.1 shows, our composite measure continued to increase even after the peak of the crisis, affecting about 45 per cent of the population in 2014 and 2015 (compared to about 20 per cent in the EU as a whole).

Financial hardship is always likely to be highest among low-income groups. Still, it seems alarming that in Greece among households in the bottom quintile of the income distribution its level has now risen to more than 95 per cent. Single parent families and foreign-born individuals experienced particularly high levels of financial hardship (exceeding 60 per cent and

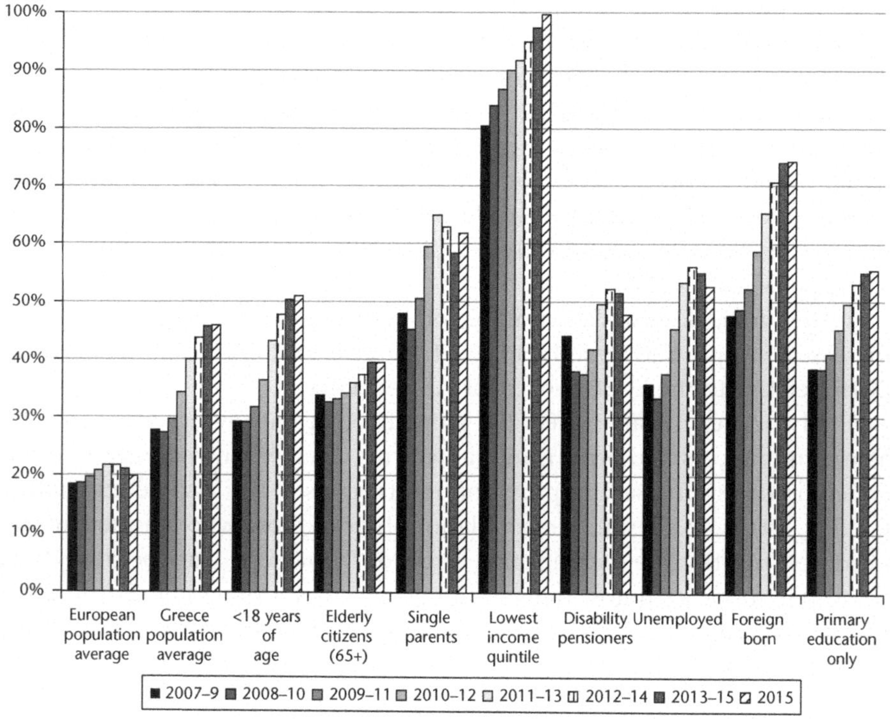


**Figure 5.1.** Financial hardship profiles through the crisis in Greece, 2007–15

*Note*: This shows Greece compared to the European average and disaggregated by main socio-economic groups. It is a composite measure based on income poverty, difficulties in making ends meet, and material deprivation (see the Appendix for explanation of the methodology) and shows the proportion suffering financial hardship over three-year moving averages to 2015.

[18] See Eurostat European Union Statistics on Income and Living Conditions (EU-SILC) survey, 'Inability to Make Ends Meet', http://appsso.eurostat.ec.europa.eu/nui/show.do?dataset=ilc_mdes09.

70 per cent respectively). Financial hardship is also above average among low educated persons (over 50 per cent in 2014 and 2015), the unemployed, and disability pensioners (over 50 per cent in 2013 and 2014).

The case of the elderly merits attention. In terms of relative (monetary) poverty, the elderly have paradoxically done rather well in recent years, as their incomes (chiefly pensions) have been cut less than wages and other earnings, while those on low incomes were protected, albeit to a limited extent (in the sense that pension cuts have been progressive, with higher pensions being reduced by a higher proportion). Moreover, pensions continued to be paid every month, which was not the case with wages in the event of job loss. In view of this, poverty rates have fallen for the over-65 age group while those of children and other age groups have risen.

Nevertheless, we know that the elderly are particularly vulnerable to changes in the funding and delivery of health care, as they have more medical needs than younger groups. In Greece, the proportion of those aged 65 and over who reported unmet need for health care (specifically because they could not afford it) went up in recent years, reaching 15 per cent in 2015 (relative to 10.9 per cent for the population as a whole). That figure was higher among even older groups (19.5 per cent among those aged 85 and over in 2016) and especially those on lower incomes (48.5 per cent among those aged 65 and over *and* in the lowest 20 per cent of the income distribution in 2016, according to Eurostat; see footnote 4).

The plight of the elderly in Greece is clearly borne out by our composite indicator, which shows that their share facing financial hardship continued to rise even after the country's economic situation stabilized, exceeding 40 per cent in 2014 and 2015.

## 5.6 Conclusions

Greece has faced an acute economic crisis in the 2010s, more so than any other country since the USA during the Great Depression. In retrospect, its depth and duration, including mass joblessness, would have probably posed stark challenges to the most advanced of welfare states, which Greece certainly is not. Yet the performance of the country's system of social protection was particularly disappointing. As a result, and as the preceding analysis in sections 5.4 and 5.5 illustrates, the social costs of the crisis for vulnerable groups in the country have been unnecessarily high.

Prior to 2009, Greek welfare was particularly unfit for the challenge in spite of high and rising social expenditure. Under austerity, social spending was significantly retrenched. The social policies urged by the EU–ECB–IMF Troika and pursued by national governments of all political hues failed to compensate for the adverse effects of the recession.

Moreover, a policy shift has taken place from income replacement to poverty relief. Excesses in pension policy were curbed, probably going all the way to the other extreme of failing to provide adequate incomes in old age. The introduction of a consolidated child benefit in 2013 and of a nationwide GMI programme in 2017 were the high points of efforts to improve the anti-poverty effectiveness of Greek welfare. While their impact has so far been limited, there can be no doubt that they represent important though belated moves towards strengthening the social safety net.

On the whole, the crisis has undoubtedly transformed Greek welfare. The system of social protection emerging from the recession and the austerity period differs significantly from the one that preceded it. It is certainly leaner, probably less robust in core policy areas (pensions, health), but also quite likely more effective in fighting extreme poverty than at any time in history.

Even so, dealing with the social implications of the Greek crisis will not be a matter for the welfare state alone: it will crucially hinge on job creation and wage growth, of which there is little evidence at present.

# 6

# Spain

## Economic Crisis and the Politics of Welfare under Austerity

*Ana M. Guillén and Sergio González Begega*

Spain enjoyed a rapid and steady economic expansion during the two decades prior to the onset of the global recession in 2008, when it entered a profound financial, fiscal, and economic crisis, posing exceptional challenges to the social protection system and the labour market. This chapter addresses the crisis management strategies implemented during the long-lasting recession and their ability to tackle the impact of the economic shock and related social risks. The focus is on the overall policy response to the recession as well as the changes introduced to social policies, including protracted austerity measures. We also show how social groups were differentially affected by the massive growth of unemployment, inequality, and socio-economic insecurity.

### 6.1 Growth Model with Feet of Clay: The Political Economy Context in Spain before the Crisis

Contrary to other large Continental European economies, Spain experienced a golden age of economic expansion and rising living standards during the 1990s and early 2000s. From 1985 to 2007 the annual economic growth averaged 3.4 per cent and the real household disposable income per capita peaked at US$24,740 in the year the global financial crisis started to spread.[1] This long-lasting period of economic growth was interrupted only once,

[1] See OECD, National Accounts Data Files, http://www.oecd.org/std/na.

between 1992 and 1994, when the Spanish gross domestic product (GDP) contracted by 1.5 per cent and the unemployment rate increased from 16 per cent to 24 per cent (Horwitz & Myant, 2015). This was but a short-term shock and the economy recovered quickly after the government announced several stabilization measures, including four devaluations of the national currency in order to regain external competitiveness. The government remained committed to maintaining fiscal and price stability on the road to accession to the European Economic and Monetary Union (EMU).

During the early 2000s, the Spanish economy was booming and like Ireland it was widely recognized for its liberalization and openness to international markets, with new emerging corporate players in the financial, public works, and civil engineering sectors. One of the most prominent features associated with this Spanish economic miracle was employment recovery. The labour market was able to absorb more than 4 million economic immigrants over a decade. Unemployment dropped to its lowest rate of 8 per cent in 2007-Q2, although still above the Organisation for Economic Co-operation and Development (OECD) average of 5.6 per cent (see footnote 1). The housing market was very dynamic and prices surged at a record-breaking pace. In early 2007, Spain had overcome Italy in GDP per capita and the government confidently announced that Spain would catch up with the other large EU economies in only a few years (*El País*, 25 September 2007).

This long-lasting period of expansion was not the result of an economic miracle nor did it imply a fruitful renewal of the Spanish growth model. Steady economic development was made possible under a favourable international conjunction and easy access to external credit (Cancela Outeda & González Cacheda, 2017). Spain entered the European Economic Community (EEC) in 1986 with a growth mix based on low labour costs, low technological development, and meagre productivity. Although the country became a market of interest for European producers, the external competitiveness of the Spanish economy quickly deteriorated in the face of increasing international competition (Fernández-Otheo, Barroso, & Sánchez, 2004). Some industries expanded (i.e. car production and tourism) but other industrial sectors soon lagged behind and the negative performance of exports led to a large current account deficit. Before the crisis, Spain's external debt (as a percentage of GDP) was one of the highest of the developed economies, while amongst the OECD countries the size of its external debt was second only to the USA in its absolute value (Sánchez, 2011). Accession to the EMU facilitated cheap credit and permitted Spain to maintain a high external trade deficit, as was the case in Greece (see Chapter 5). Deindustrialization and the loss of international foreign direct investment (FDI) flows in the process of eastward enlargement of the EU prompted national investors to concentrate on banking and financial operations, semi-oligopolistic companies that were being privatized (i.e. communications and energy), and other non-tradable low competitive sectors (i.e. civil works building and retail) (Myro & Gandoy, 2009). The abundance of cheap external credit led to a real estate boom, which started to turn into a bubble in the late 1990s. The price of housing in Spain rose about 150 per cent in nominal terms during the decade from 1997 to 2007 (Sureda-Gomila, 2011).

The key features of the Spanish economic policy approach over the long run are consistent with the dual political objective of attaining first-class EU membership and reaching a European equivalent level of household economic well-being and consumption. The centre-left and conservative governments, alternating in power from the 1980s, shared a common (rather uncritical) understanding of EU membership as a crucial modernization force (Moreno, 2013). Europe has in fact been a powerful discursive tool to legitimate the transformation of the Spanish productive model, the labour market, and the social protection system (González Begega & Del Pino, 2017).

Spanish politics have been characterized by a near absence of confrontation on fundamental economic policy principles. No fundamental ideological cleavage has separated left-wing and conservative governments as regards the long-term modernization effort (Royo, 2009). Reform has been markedly state led but governments have also retained wide support from civil society. Decline in industrial conflict and a wide-ranging recourse to social dialogue have been core features of the process of public policy formulation in Spain since the 1980s (González Begega & Luque Balbona, 2014). A further aiding factor was an increasingly flexible labour supply that was burdened with reduced job security and squeezed real wages in the effort to meet EEC and EMU accession criteria (Fernández Rodríguez, 2014).

Social policy reform has also played a highly relevant role in the far-reaching modernization of Spanish social, economic, and political structures. The establishment of a democratic welfare state came after a long period of dictatorship which set the ground for a Bismarckian social security system in 1960s, against the backdrop of a late and abrupt Fordist industrialization (Guillén & González Begega, 2016). Spain achieved substantial welfare developments between the 1980s and the 2000s. From the late 1970s, the country pursued an intensive catch-up process in social spending, which in 1975 represented around 10 per cent of the GDP. The pillars of the Spanish welfare state were expanded; the social security system, comprising principally contributory pensions, was thoroughly redesigned at the end of the decade; unemployment benefits were put in place in 1980; a national universal health system, funded by general taxes, was introduced in 1986; and access to tertiary education became more widespread (Muñoz del Bustillo & Antón, 2015).

Public social spending peaked in the mid-1990s at around a quarter of GDP. The Spanish welfare system went through both an expansion and a contraction due to the imperatives of fiscal consolidation on the course to EMU membership. In the 2000s, welfare expansion into other areas, namely long-term care, gender equality, and reconciliation of work and family life, was attained under tight cost-containment constraints (Rodríguez Cabrero, 2011). Notwithstanding persistent problems with the coordination of financing and managing associated with the devolution of social policy competences to subnational governments, reforms in the Spanish social policy realm aimed to ensure the consolidation of a fully fledged European welfare state. Furthermore, before 2007, Spain had embarked on post-industrial welfare reform by exploring recalibration of the social protection system. Arguably, the country was in a position to close the social gap with the European core but also to become an innovator as regards welfare state development (Guillén, 2007).

## 6.2 The Economic Crisis: Austerity and the Political Effort to Avoid Bailout

As it turned out the Spanish growth model was built on sand. That became evident with the onset of the global financial crisis by the end of 2007. Similar to other EMU periphery countries, the Spanish economy had benefited a great deal from Euro membership. The surge of the real estate sector in the 2000s had hidden the impact of deindustrialization and delocation of productive activity and employment. Household debt levels were above 200 per cent of GDP in 2007, the external deficit was close to 10 per cent of GDP (dropping to 4.7 per cent in 2010) and other indicators related to technological development, productivity, and external competitiveness were equally worrisome (Ortega & Peñalosa, 2012).

The collapse of the real estate sector is an essential factor for understanding the dynamics, duration, and intensity of the crisis in Spain. Investment in housing had expanded sharply in the 2000s, exceeding 12 per cent of GDP in 2007 (compared to less than 7 per cent in 2011). The global financial crisis precipitated a near collapse of activity in the construction sector, which amounted to 2.7 million jobs in 2007-Q3. The worsening of macroeconomic conditions hit employment hard while the position of financial institutions also started to deteriorate, on account of greater exposure to real estate risk. Spain went into recession in 2008-Q2 and remained in negative GDP growth until 2010-Q1. The contractionary cycle of 2008–9 meant a decline of output of around 5 percentage points. After a modest recovery, the Spanish macroeconomic scenario was again hit by the Euro sovereign debt crisis, which endangered public finance stability of EMU periphery countries. Against the background of a double-dip multilayered crisis, Spain did not return to GDP growth until 2013-Q3.

Although the magnitude of economic recession did not differ significantly from that of other European economies, Spain stood out as the country that experienced the heaviest fall in national demand and employment. Employment adjustment has been protracted and virulent, starting in early 2008 and continuing apace for a period of five years. The unemployment rate reached a staggering 26.9 per cent in 2013-Q1, after increasing by 19 percentage points since 2007-Q2. In mid-2015, households with nobody at work still amounted to 721.900 (1.57 million people) according to Instituto Nacional de Estadística (INE) data.[2] Labour productivity showed a similar countercyclical pattern as in previous employment crises.

The breakdown of entire portions of the private sector was followed by a mutation of the crisis after mid-2010. As in other EMU periphery countries, notably Ireland, difficulties in the real estate, civil works, and banking sectors spread to public finances, thus opening a new phase in the crisis (see Chapter 7). Spanish public debt was in fairly good condition at the onset of the global crisis compared to other large EMU economies, amounting to only 35.5 per cent of GDP in 2007. In contrast to private debt, the situation of public finances was healthy. As regards fiscal balances, revenues and expenses had shown a parallel evolution coupled with a slight increase of revenues during the 2000s, which allowed for fiscal surpluses in the 2005–7 period.

As in other OECD countries, the initial response of the Spanish government to the drop in economic activity combined with rapidly rising unemployment was a wide-ranging neo-Keynesian stimulus package, which was implemented in late 2008, upon recommendations from international institutions. The so-called Plan E (Spanish Plan for Stimulating the Economy and Employment) received broad support from trade unions and employers. Despite this major injection of funds, amounting to €12.8 billion mainly aimed at reviving economic activity and employment in the civil works and housing sector, unemployment kept growing at a rapid pace.

An unintended consequence of the stimulus package was the sharp deterioration of public fiscal balances. Public revenues had contracted since the beginning of the crisis while expenditures were on an upward trend, even before the introduction of Plan E. As a result, a public deficit of almost €50 billion was registered in 2008. The fall in revenues was even more pronounced in 2009, thus causing public deficit to rise to −11.2 per cent. It remained well above −9 per cent until 2013. Fiscal balances remain negative to date (2018) despite the drastic austerity measures implemented after 2010. The Spanish

[2] See http://www.ine.es/en/welcome.shtml.

public deficit reached −4.6 per cent in 2016, still above European Central Bank (ECB) requirements, while public debt escalated to 100 per cent of GDP.

The turn to austerity in the EMU was a response to the outbreak of the sovereign debt crisis in Greece, Ireland, and Portugal. Spain was also affected after spring 2010, when the first expenditure adjustment measures were taken by the centre-left government. Starting in 2010, the Spanish prime minister and economy and finance ministers engaged in a desperate race to regain the trust of international investors and to avoid a European bailout (Rodríguez Zapatero, 2013). This holds for the Spanish Socialist Workers' Party (PSOE) government in office until November 2011 but also for the subsequent conservative cabinet led by Mariano Rajoy (Magone, 2016). Nevertheless, the loss of investor confidence in Spanish bonds was not exactly exogenous with respect to the lending policies of the finance sector. An important contributory factor to the crisis was inadequate regulation and supervision of Spanish banking institutions (as in Ireland). Most were overexposed to the real estate risks that ultimately caused the bailout of a considerable portion of the finance sector in 2012 (de Guindos, 2016).

A process of internal devaluation coupled with budgetary cuts was initiated in May 2010. The government approved a €15 billion austerity plan to rein in the public deficit and ease fears of a contagion of the sovereign debt crisis to Spain. Prime Minister Rodríguez Zapatero announced a tough adjustment programme that included freezing pensions and reducing civil servants' wages by 5 per cent. While the media sided with the government (*El País*, 13 May 2010), the trade unions reacted with a call for a public sector strike that was held on 8 June 2010.

A second general strike was called on 29 September 2010 against the first labour market reform implemented during the austerity years. The regulation of the Spanish labour market changed once again in 2012. The climate of social dialogue was severely impaired after spring 2010. The PSOE government was able to agree on a pension reform with its social partners in July 2011, aimed at improving the sustainability of the system. Nevertheless, as in other EMU periphery countries, austerity soon led to the concentration of power in the hands of executives coupled with the deactivation of social dialogue under the pressure of fiscal consolidation objectives (Pavolini et al., 2015).

The situation continued to deteriorate. At the time of the first rescue of Greece, the yield of the Spanish ten-year bond was 4.149 per cent, with the spread to the German bond reaching 99 basis points. On 2 August 2011, it had reached 6.323 per cent and a spread to the German bond of 390.5 points. Both figures were unparalleled since the creation of the EMU. They peaked at a maximum of 7.7 per cent and 650 points, respectively, on 25 July 2012. Further, Spanish bonds were downgraded several times during the 2010–12 period (Ferreiro & Serrano, 2012).

The political cost of austerity was high for the centre-left government in office. In August 2011, article 135 of the Spanish Constitution was reformed to guarantee the principle of budgetary stability for all levels of public administration, in an attempt to ease bond market instability and pressure coming from the ECB. A general election had to be called in advance. This was held in November 2011 and won by the Conservative Party with an absolute majority. The new government in office decided to dive deeper into austerity. The voices in favour of a complete bailout of the Spanish economy were roaring in autumn 2011 (*El País*, 20 November 2011).

The new conservative government approved a second broad austerity package of €65 billion for the 2012–14 period, which included raising the main VAT rate from 18 per cent to 21 per cent, a scrapping of one month's pay for public employees, lengthening of working hours, discontinuing of contributions to pension plans of civil servants, no hiring of new public personnel, and limited replacement rate for retirements in the public sector. Moreover, taxes on income, housing, and capital investments were increased. The minimum wage was frozen at €641.4 per month (14 annual payments) and public transfers to trade unions and employers associations were reduced by 20 per cent. Budget cuts were accompanied by further structural reform of the labour market in early 2012 and the pension system in mid-2013. Two general strikes were called on 29 March and 14 November 2012. Despite these efforts, the government was forced to request assistance to prevent the collapse of the banking sector in June 2012. The funds from the newly created European Stability Mechanism (ESM) amounted to €100 billion, although only €41.3 billion were disbursed. The Memorandum of Understanding (MoU) granted financial aid to Spain subject to conditions, which implied higher political intrusiveness of the EU (de la Porte & Heins, 2015). Spain's implementation of the ESM assistance programme was monitored until December 2013.

The return to GDP growth and the fall of unemployment after 2014 alleviated austerity measures, although the government continues to pursue efforts to further reduce public deficit. GDP growth rose to 3.4 per cent in 2015 and 3.2 per cent in 2016, well above other large EMU economies. The unemployment rate still stood at a high of 17.1 per cent in 2017-Q3. The struggle to attain market credibility on terms acceptable to the domestic electorate has proved difficult. The governments have been punished at the polls. The challenge to bipartisanship has been gaining pace since the European elections of May 2014, when two new parties made their appearance, in the populist far-left Podemos and centre-right Ciudadanos (Vidal, 2018). Austerity policies have also led to the rise of important territorial tensions in Spain, as for example in Catalonia (Dellepiane-Avellaneda & Hardiman, 2015).

## 6.3 Financial Hardship through the Crisis

The crisis hit Spain after 2008. As is shown in Figure 6.1, financial hardship in the country was, on the whole, close to the European average before the crisis hit. It increased in the early phase of the crisis and then again after 2011. The expansionary measures adopted during the early phase of the crisis helped to ease the situation of the population as a whole. Hardship levels dropped in 2011, before rising again to around 25 per cent by 2014, thus reflecting the forceful double dip recession of the Spanish economy. Financial hardship only started to fall again in 2015.

The impact of hardship was quite dissimilar for different groups of the Spanish population though. As indicated by Figure 6.1, the lowest income quintile had the greatest difficulties, with more than 70 per cent of this group living in financial hardship by 2014. Immigrants and single parents also reached hardship levels over 40 per cent during the crisis. The situation of

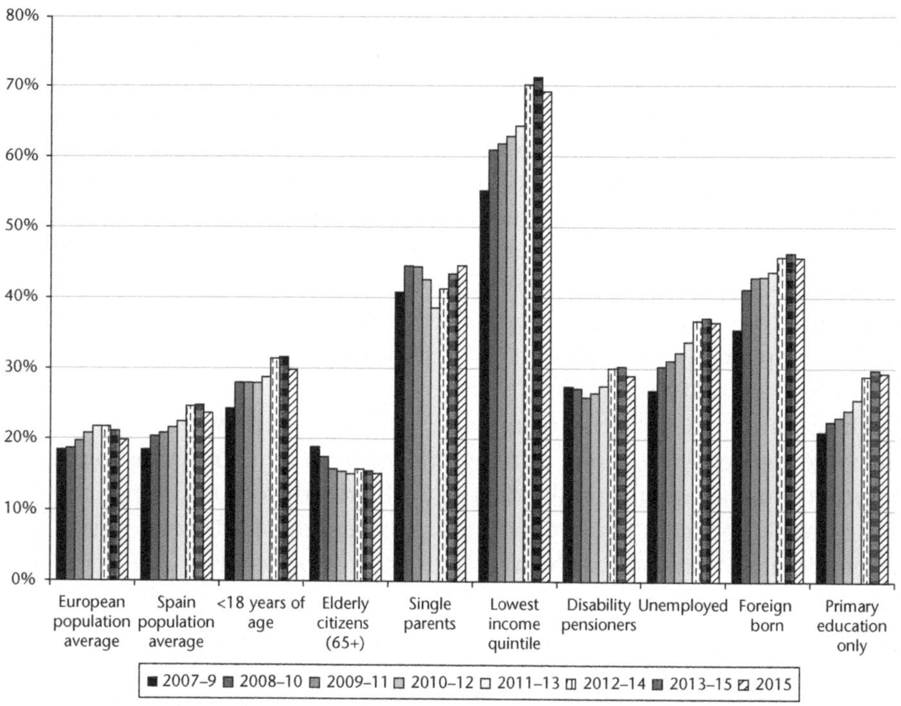


**Figure 6.1.** Financial hardship profiles through the crisis in Spain, 2007–15

*Note*: This shows Spain compared to the European average and disaggregated by main socio-economic groups. It is a composite measure based on income poverty, difficulties in making ends meet, and material deprivation (see Appendix for explanation of the methodology) and shows the proportion suffering financial hardship over three-year moving averages.

single parents was particularly rough in 2010 and 2014, with an in-between period of slight easing in financial conditions for them. Immigrants, however, had a significant increase at the start of the crisis and then a gradual further increase up to 2014.

The data also reveal the comparatively well-protected situation of those aged 65 and over. Their level of financial hardship decreased during the crisis period, uniquely among the main socio-economic groups. Finally, it is notable that those affected by unemployment experienced a steep increase of hardship during the crisis, as did families with children under 18. Disability pensioners improved at first and then were impacted with increased hardship during the latter dip after 2011.

The breakdown of the labour market after 2009 was cushioned by unemployment benefits, whose coverage started to decline after 2012. The protection of the unemployed and pensioners against financial hardship, particularly the latter, is connected with the uneven and imbalanced responses of the social protection system to the crisis and differing political priorities, as reflected in varying social budgets of different governments.

## 6.4 Role of the Welfare State in Tackling the Crisis

The government led by Rodríguez Zapatero made a noteworthy effort to cushion the initial effects of the crisis through social protection. Parallel to the introduction of the economic stimulus package in 2009, the centre-left government—in office until autumn 2011—repeatedly declared its intention to use social protection as an instrument to ease the impact of recession and even to expand it whenever possible (del Pino, 2013). Still, the PSOE government was at first reluctant to acknowledge the presence and severity of the crisis itself and then prone to put the blame mainly on external financial factors (Rodríguez Zapatero, 2013). This may partially explain why restrictive structural reforms in the realm of social protection (i.e. pensions), the labour market, and the supervision of the banking sector were not enacted until late 2010 and 2011 when they were to all intents and purposes externally imposed under mounting pressures by international investors and EMU institutions (Guillén & Pavolini, 2017).

The trajectory of Spanish welfare state reform during the crisis demonstrates an absence of paradigmatic path departures. Still, some salient reforms have taken place together with drastic budget cuts. This has led to a moderate dose of recalibration but also to a general weakening of the social protection system (Petmesidou & Guillén, 2014). Hereafter, we detail the main initiatives of welfare reform and the magnitude of budget adjustment in pensions, unemployment protection schemes, health care, education, long-term care, reconciliation of work and family life, and social services.

The Spanish pension system was in a good condition right up to 2007. Social security accounts had enjoyed surpluses since 1998 due to the creation of over 8 million jobs since the mid-1990s and the very positive evolution of the contributor–pensioner ratio. The Social Security Reserve Fund, established in 2000 with the aim of investing social security surpluses to finance future public pension scheme shortfalls, had accumulated to €47.716 billion (4.7 per cent of the GDP) by 2007. The breakdown of the labour market and the fall in payroll taxes led to a social security deficit, after reserve funds had reached a peak of €66.815 billion (6.2 per cent of the GDP) in 2011.

The Spanish government has been tapping the fund since 2012 in an attempt to pay contributory pensions while meeting EMU fiscal consolidation targets. As a result, public pension financial reserves amounted to only €8.095 billion (0.6 per cent of the GDP) in 2017.

Structural reform of the pension system gathered momentum in mid-2010, when the first retrenchment measures were announced by Prime Minister Rodríguez Zapatero. Pensions were frozen for 2011. A social pact on the long-term sustainability of the pension system was reached under intense international pressure, after a heated public debate. The 2011 pension reform entailed a gradual postponement of the official retirement age from 65 to 67 and an expansion of ten years (from 15 to 25) in the number of salaried years used to calculate the initial pension, to be phased in between 2013 and 2027, thus lowering the replacement rate. A second pension reform was adopted unilaterally by the conservative government which assumed office in 2013, after informal consultation with social partners and independent experts. The reform introduced further restrictions to early retirement and also a sustainability factor, the latter including corrections to expenditure according to the evolution of life expectancy and making revaluation of pensions dependent on the situation of social security accounts. When fully implemented, the effect of pension reform will mean higher poverty risks for pensioners. Implementation of legislation on integration of the self-employed and other salaried workers (i.e. domestic service workers and salaried agrarian workers) into the general social security scheme has been pursued by governments since mid-2010. Thus far, the Spanish welfare system has been particularly effective in preserving the living conditions of current pensioners. As already shown in section 6.3, this population group was among the least affected by deterioration of disposable income and financial hardship.

Unemployment benefits were subject to minimal cutbacks during the crisis (Muñoz del Bustillo & Antón, 2015). The centre-left and the conservative governments struggled to control the economic impact of the job crisis through new unemployment assistance schemes. Unemployment insurance was extended to the self-employed, although only on a voluntary basis. Further, a non-contributory unemployment benefit of €426 per month was established in 2009 for those unemployed receiving training who had used up their contributory benefits. The measure was repeatedly renewed after 2011 under different denominations (i.e. Temporary Programme for Unemployment Protection and Insertion (PRODI), Professional Retraining Programme for People who Exhaust their Unemployment Protection Rights (PREPARA), and Employment Activation Programme (PAE)), but it has had meagre effects on retraining and job activation (Jansen, 2016). In addition, the increase in long-term unemployment reduced the coverage rate of unemployment benefits from 70 per cent of unemployed workers in 2008 to 54 per cent in 2017-Q2.

Health care and education are the main social protection policies in the hands of subnational governments. Together, they amount to almost 75 per cent of public regional budgets. Legislation was issued on a new expansionary model of regional financing in December 2009. The reform allowed for adjustments to new needs related to changes in key variables such as variations in volume and distribution of population. The model was a precondition for territorial cohesion gains but it also produced higher expenditure. After 2010, measures to promote fiscal consolidation were adopted within the National Health Service (NHS). Pharmacy expenditure was rationalized by reforming the reference price system, reducing the industrial price of generic drugs, and promoting cuts in the profit margins of pharmacy distributors.

The most controversial decision with regard to public health-care coverage was taken in 2012 when the government decided to exclude non-legal immigrants from the NHS, with the exception of emergencies, minors, pregnancy, and post-birth care. Contestation by regional authorities has been high and the measure remains largely unimplemented. Also in 2012 co-payments on over-the-counter drugs were applied to previously exempted groups (i.e. pensioners) and graded according to income for the whole population. Even though the basic institutional infrastructure of the NHS remains in place, budget cuts have had negative effects on quality and access (as reflected, for instance, in longer waiting lists).

Long-term care, work–life balance, and social services suffered important cuts during the recession, thus causing the discontinuation of the important welfare recalibration effort made in the 2000s. A universal right to long-term care was introduced in Spain in December 2006, with a time span of eight years initially envisaged for the implementation of service provision and/or economic transfers. However, the development of this system in Spain was seriously delayed after the arrival of the crisis. In 2010, the arrears of long-term term care benefits of those with recognized rights were suppressed. The conservative government in office after November 2011 extended the waiting period before the provision of the benefit and reduced cash benefits for in-home care by 15 per cent. Further, the system failed to provide full coverage of dependants as initially planned, thus creating a 'dependency limbo' (i.e. a large number of people eligible for benefits but not receiving them). In 2013, the central government reduced its contribution to the maintenance of the system, which is operated by regional governments, by 20 per cent. The regions have striven to cover budget gaps in a context of serious financial hardship, although with very different geographical levels of generosity and benefit uptake.

Family protection policies have remained comparatively weak in Spain, including family allowances, fiscal deduction policies, and reconciliation of work and family life policies. Up to 1990, family allowances were contributory and low, thus producing coverage gaps for those without a sufficient record of employment. At this point in time, family allowances were universalized but remained at low levels. The most ambitious piece of legislation regarding reconciliation measures was passed in 2007. It included flexibilization of working hours, expansion of public childcare services, and parental leave, among other measures. The advent of the crisis impeded the implementation of many aspects of the 2007 legislation, including the extension of parental leave. In 2010 the government announced the elimination of the one-off payment of €2,500 for the birth or adoption of a child, the so-called 'baby-cheque'. Maternity leave in Spain is currently 16 weeks, in line with European directives: 6 compulsory weeks to be taken after childbirth by the mother and 10 non-mandatory weeks which can be shared between the parents. Leave is provided at 100 per cent of covered pay. A recent law, passed in early 2017, increased compulsory parental leave from 13 calendar days to 4 weeks. The crisis has also slowed down extension of public childcare facilities for under-3s run by subnational governments.

Resort to cost containment has also affected minimum income schemes run by regional and local governments. Amounting to an average of €400 per month, these constitute the last resort of welfare protection when no other public transfers are available. Minimum income policies, which are means-tested on household income, have traditionally been a poorly developed part of the Spanish social protection system. Further, there are important geographical differences in access requirements, forms of protection, and rates of success in reducing poverty, which have so far proven to be limited in a context of budgetary constraints and increasing need (Natili, 2016).

As regards housing, 77.8 per cent of the Spanish population lived in an owner-occupied dwelling in 2016, according to European Union Statistics on Income and Living Conditions (EU-SILC) data. The figure was 80.2 per cent in 2008. Almost a third (30.9 per cent) of them have a mortgage while 13.8 per cent were tenants with a market price rent, and 8.4 per cent tenants in reduced-rent or free accommodation. Many of those having to pay a mortgage have experienced increased financial hardship. One out of ten households is under strain because of mortgage payments and the proportion rises to almost four out of ten among households with an income below the poverty level. In March 2012, an agreement with the banking sector was reached to exempt from eviction those households with nobody at work with mortgage payments above 60 per cent of their income. However, adherence by banks is voluntary.

Budget adjustment has been widespread in all areas of social protection with the exception of the pension system, the reform of which did not affect pensioners during the crisis but will impact them in the near future. Estimations by Lago Peñas (2016) calculate the total financial adjustment made by governments in the 2009–14 period at €30.8 billion, which accounts for roughly 3 per cent of Spanish GDP. According to State Public Accounts Department (IGAE) data, total consolidated public expenditure amounted to €493.865 billion in 2009. When Spain returned to steady GDP growth in 2014, total public expenditure had dropped to €463.041 billion, thus implying a 6.2 per cent reduction in nominal terms in this five-year period and, accounting for inflation, a reduction of 15 per cent in real terms.

Table 6.1 summarizes social protection expenditure developments during the recession. We focus on expenditure trends in volumes and on the distributional impact of austerity measures by social policy functions. The data should be interpreted carefully due to the devolution of major welfare powers to the subnational level, including policy design and supply in health care, education, and social care, and social exclusion policies (Gallego Calderón & Subirats, 2011). The scale of the budget cuts in health care and education is striking. Aggregate expenditure reduction for these universal welfare services amounted to €18.400 billion in the 2009–14 period. Health-care expenditure was reduced by 13.2 per cent in nominal terms (−22 per cent in real terms), amounting to €9.600 billion. Pharmacy expenditure and economic transfers to private health care were also reduced by €3.402 billion. Education expenditure fell by €7.394 billion, equivalent to 14.9 per cent in nominal terms and 23.7 per cent in real terms.

Public expenditure in social protection grew by 6.2 percentage points over the five-year period. Nevertheless, the evolution of public expenditure among sub-areas is quite disparate. Old age and survivor pensions grew by €23.577 billion. The reforms introduced to ensure long-term financial sustainability in the pension system have not been capable of counteracting demographic trends. Mounting pressure on pensions is also connected to the fragile financial foundations of the system. Meanwhile, unemployment expenditure decreased by 20 per cent, due mainly to the drop in the overall coverage rate. Expenditure on social housing policies and, even more distressing, of

**Table 6.1.** Total consolidated public expenditure developments in Spain (fiscal years 2009–14; in billion euros)

| | 2009 | 2014 | Change 2009–14 | Change in % |
|---|---|---|---|---|
| Total consolidated public expenditure | 493.865 | 463.041 | −30.824 | −6.2 |
| Health care | 72.939 (6.8% of GDP) | 63.339 (6.1% of GDP) | −9.600 | −13.2 |
| Education | 49.692 (4.6% of GDP) | 42.298 (4.1% of GDP) | −7.394 | −14.9 |
| Social protection* | 172.693 (16% of GDP) | 184.443 (17.7% of GDP) | 10.750 | +6.2 |
| *Old-age (retirement) pensions* | *75.330* | *95.562* | *+20.232* | *+26.9* |
| *Survivor pensions* | *21.616* | *24.961* | *+3.345* | *+15.5* |
| *Sickness and disability allowances* | *25.627* | *24.528* | *−1.099* | *−4.3* |
| *Unemployment benefits* | *33.044* | *25.813* | *−7.231* | *−21.9* |
| *Child and family benefits* | *8.832* | *6.140* | *−2.692* | *−30.5* |
| *Housing social policy* | *1.048* | *0.415* | *−0.533* | *−60.5* |
| *Social exclusion NCE*** | *2.572* | *2.900* | *+0.328* | *+12.8* |
| *Other forms of social protection* | *4.624* | *3.124* | *−1.500* | *−32.43* |

*Note*: Shows social expenditure by social policy area. *Includes public social expenditure on pensions, unemployment, work disability, child and family protection, social exclusion, and social housing policy. **NCE = not classified elsewhere.

*Source*: Adapted from Lago Peñas (2016). Based on IGAE and Eurostat.

child and family benefits were also cut by roughly 60 per cent and 30 per cent respectively. Social exclusion and other Not Classified Elsewhere (NCE) programmes expenditure grew by 12.8 per cent, although the financial effort was below €3 billion in 2014. Overall, social expenditure grew by €10.750 billion in the period but this only reflects the internal dynamics of the pension system, with more recipients and higher benefit levels—this latter connected to higher salaries of the newly incorporated.

## 6.5 Social Impact of the Crisis: Unemployment, Inequality, and Poverty

After 2008 Spain experienced the third highest rise of the unemployment rate amongst EMU countries, below only Cyprus and Greece. Unemployment levels peaked at 26.9 per cent in 2013-Q1, rising from 7.9 per cent in 2007-Q2. This followed previous major increases in unemployment during recessions of the 1980s and 1990s, when unemployment had likewise approached 25 per cent (Horwitz & Myant, 2015). Job destruction also outpaced the decrease in GDP. In fact, the Spanish employment rate dropped by 4.5 per cent, thus outpacing the 3.8 per cent contraction in GDP when the recession hit Spain in 2009. Employment continued to fall in the two following years, even though the economy showed a slight recovery. Job losses accelerated again after 2011-Q3 and employment did not start to grow until 2013-Q2.

Table 6.2 shows the impact of the recession on unemployment outcomes (total unemployment, long-term unemployment, and youth unemployment) together with the evolution of unemployment coverage rates in the 2007–17 period. Long-term unemployment as a share of active population has risen since 2007, increasing by roughly 750 per cent between 2007 and 2013. The crisis of the Spanish labour market has been particularly harmful for people aged under 25 years. The youth unemployment ratio has remained the highest of all EMU countries through the whole 2007–17 period—higher than in Greece.

Unemployment-related benefits coverage rate peaked at 81.2 per cent of unemployed workers in 2009. The increase in long-term unemployment reduced the unemployment coverage rate after 2010, as unemployed workers exhausted their regular benefits. The net coverage rate has remained below 60 per cent since 2014 (Muñoz del Bustillo & Antón, 2015). The share of temporary work has been on the rise after 2012. It reached 27.4 per cent in 2017-Q3, the second highest share in the EU28.

Increases in poverty and inequality have been fuelled by the recession and the labour market crisis. The policy of austerity promoted by European authorities and zealously applied by Spanish governments after 2010 has been detrimental to the ability of the social protection system to cope with increasing welfare needs. In this respect, the most important trends have been the rise of relative poverty after taxes and transfers by roughly 10 per cent between 2007 and 2015, based on OECD data (see Table 6.3). According to the more comprehensive 'at risk of poverty and social exclusion' (AROPE) criteria, as of 2016, 27.9 per cent of the population in Spain live below the poverty line or are socially excluded. It was 23.8 per cent in 2008, before the recession had begun and peaked at 29.2 per cent in 2014. The increase of the poverty rate by 4 percentage points between 2008 and 2016 is amongst the highest in the EU28. Just over 6 per cent of the Spanish population was experiencing severe material deprivation in 2015, up from 3.6 per cent in 2008. Further, the child poverty rate has increased above average. Spain had the third-highest relative child poverty rate among EU countries in 2015, with only Romania and Greece having higher rates. In 2016, 13.1 per cent of employees in Spain were at risk of poverty (see footnote 2). By contrast, poverty for those aged 65 and over has fallen substantially.

The increase in income inequality in Spain after 2010 is significant. The deterioration in living standards has indeed been widespread in Southern European countries (see Chapter 5 on Greece). But it is in Spain where

**Table 6.2.** Total unemployment, long-term unemployment, youth unemployment, and unemployment benefits coverage (net rate in Spain, 2007–17)

| | 2007 | 2008 | 2009 | 2010 | 2011 | 2012 | 2013 | 2014 | 2015 | 2016 | 2017 |
|---|---|---|---|---|---|---|---|---|---|---|---|
| Total unemployment* | 8.5 | 13.7 | 18.6 | 20.1 | 22.5 | 25.7 | 25.7 | 23.7 | 20.9 | 18.6 | 16.3 |
| Long-term unemployment | 1.7 | 2.0 | 4.3 | 7.4 | 8.9 | 11 | 13 | 12.9 | 11.4 | 9.5 | |
| Youth unemployment** | 18.6 | 28.9 | 38.8 | 42.7 | 48.1 | 54.8 | 54.8 | 51.8 | 46.2 | 42.9 | 35.9 |
| Unemployment coverage rates*** | 73.7 | 77.7 | 81.2 | 78.8 | 70.8 | 65 | 62.5 | 58.9 | 56.2 | 55.6 | 57.9 |

*Note*: *Q4 of each year, except Q3, 2017. **As a share of active population. ***M12 of each year, except M11, 2017. Includes contributory and non-contributory benefits.

*Source*: National Statistical Institute Labour Force Survey (NSI-LFS) and Ministry of Employment and Social Security.

**Table 6.3.** Evolution of relative poverty and inequality in Spain, 2007–16

| | 2007 | 2008 | 2009 | 2010 | 2011 | 2012 | 2013 | 2014 | 2015 | 2016 |
|---|---|---|---|---|---|---|---|---|---|---|
| Poverty rate before taxes and transfers* | 0.326 | 0.350 | 0.381 | 0.390 | 0.392 | 0.410 | 0.430 | 0.423 | 0.420 | |
| Poverty rate after taxes and transfers* | 0.202 | 0.209 | 0.214 | 0.212 | 0.214 | 0.209 | 0.276 | 0.218 | 0.227 | |
| Age group 66–75, poverty rate after taxes and transfers* | 0.174 | 0.158 | 0.153 | 0.113 | 0.088 | 0.064 | 0.046 | 0.047 | 0.053 | |
| Poverty rate (AROPE index) | | 23.8 | 24.7 | 26.1 | 26.7 | 27.2 | 27.3 | 29.2 | 28.6 | 27.9 |
| Gini, disposable income post-taxes and transfers | 0.324 | 0.327 | 0.333 | 0.339 | 0.341 | 0.334 | 0.345 | 0.334 | 0.345 | |

*Note*: * Poverty line is 60 per cent of the median household equivalent income. ** AROPE: at risk of poverty or social exclusion.

*Source*: Authors' elaboration from OECD Income Distribution Database and National Statistical Institute Survey on Living Conditions, 2007–16.

inequality has increased the most (Pérez & Matsaganis, 2017). The rise in unemployment, the limited impact of social spending and taxes on redistribution of income, and the double effect of austerity and internal devaluation have combined to increase inequality and the economic vulnerability of the least well off. The 2017 European Semester Country Report for Spain (European Commission, 2017b) confirms that income inequality widened during the crisis and is one of the highest in the EU28, being below only Bulgaria, Greece, and Romania. The overall inequality-reducing impact of the tax and benefit system as measured by the difference between Gini coefficients before and after taxes and transfers is still well below the EU average despite a slight increase since 2007. In late 2017, the government agreed with its social partners to increase the minimum wage substantially, namely by 8 per cent. The new minimum wage is set at €707.60 a month, with 14 payments a year.

## 6.6 Conclusions: The Condition of the Spanish Welfare State after Austerity

The overall trajectory of welfare reform in Spain since the onset of the crisis shows that efforts at keeping up with the implementation of expansionary social programmes were enacted just before the crisis started, as well as efforts at cushioning the social impact of recession and austerity for some population sectors. Still, the period from 2010 to 2014 meant harsh adjustment and significant internal devaluation, in the service of an overarching objective of fiscal rebalancing.

In the Spanish case, the burden was disproportionally borne by the lowest income quintile. Furthermore, the crisis has proven that, despite considerable effort with regard to adjusting unemployment transfers, the Spanish social protection system has not been able to provide adequate protection for the working-age population. While it could be claimed that hardly any welfare state would be able to fully meet increasing social needs during such a deep and protracted recession, with staggering unemployment rates, it is also evident that the effort carried out during the 2000s and subsequently to improve social protection within active ages, and indirectly for children, was far from sufficient.

Fiscal consolidation was adopted as a mantra by the different governments that held office after 2010. Wide-ranging decisions in the area of social policy were taken without political or social dialogue, thus undermining the overall consensus-seeking approach that had supported the Spanish welfare state since the early 1980s. Austerity put on hold the efforts at recalibration, at enhanced coverage of new social risks, and the tentative steps towards social investment made in the 2000s. To a large extent, responding to the crisis has, in Spain, meant turning to a feebler and more imbalanced kind of welfare state. The negative consequences of austerity measures in Spain have also affected universal in-kind transfers, such as health care and education. However, social security contributory benefits were broadly preserved, particularly those relating to unemployment and pensions. The Spanish welfare state proved quite effective in providing income security for old-age pensioners. Hence, the outcome leans to a combination of social policy resilience on the one hand and retrenchment on the other.

Strategic options in the post-austerity scenario are difficult to identify. The analysis of the social policy responses to the crisis in Spain tells us that welfare state reform has barely followed the projected strategy since fiscal rebalancing became a sustained focus from 2010. The picture is rather one of last-minute-approved changes aimed at easing international pressure on public finances and debt sustainability. Loosening of austerity after 2015 and the near achievement of the fiscal consolidation target can help to regain lost strategic welfare planning and social dialogue. This is essential for the attainment of renewed post-crisis social agreements allowing for a redefinition of the future path of reform of social protection policies and income security policies in Spain.

Recently, political parties have engaged in heated debate over how to broaden minimum income policies and what model to introduce towards that end, which is a promising proof of growing concern about the protection of the working-age population. After two failed electoral attempts at forming a government in 2015, the newly appointed conservative cabinet in November 2016 has so far promised to be less stringent with deficit reduction, thus facilitating a potential recovery of the resources available for health-care and education policies if carried out. Current vigorous economic growth should contribute to this end.

# 7

# Ireland

## The Welfare State and the Crisis

*Mary Daly*

Having experienced nearly two decades of strong economic growth, Ireland entered a deep—and multifaceted—crisis in 2008. This chapter analyses the nature of the crisis and the social policies adopted to address it. The main policy responses and approaches undertaken are considered in context along with their consequences, especially from the perspectives of poverty, indebtedness, and inequality. The main focus of critical enquiry is the role of the welfare state in tackling the crisis and how it was itself affected by the crisis. A second and related analytic thread is how the burdens of the crisis were shared.

### 7.1 Political Economy Context at the Onset of the Crisis

Economic growth in Ireland averaged 6.3 per cent per year from 1987 to 2007 (Whelan, 2014, p. 424). One of the most remarkable features of developments associated with the so-called 'Celtic Tiger' was the job-intensive nature of growth. Whelan (2014, p. 426) likens the Irish economy at that period to 'an employment creating machine', with the numbers employed almost doubling between 1988 and 2008 (O'Riain, 2014, p. 4). How was this brought about?

It is my view that this period of Irish development was not an example of a miracle but the outcome of a conjuncture of economic and political circumstances that saw Ireland's plans to benefit from foreign direct investment (FDI) bear fruit when globalization started to intensify.

The policy followed prior to and during the growth period, known colloquially as the 'Celtic Tiger', is best thought of as an economy-oriented, carefully managed model of national modernization (Daly, 2005). The key features of the long-term Irish policy approach centred around an economic policy that was strongly focused on attracting (foreign) capital, a political culture oriented to consensus, and an understanding of 'social' development as secondary to and following from economic growth. Ireland benefited disproportionately from adopting the euro while the country's low corporation tax regime made it an attractive European location for foreign investment (particularly the US high-technology sectors) (Hick, 2014, p. 396). In tandem with exponential economic growth and the inflow of cheap capital, there was a housing (and construction) boom, which, from the early 2000s on, became a bubble. With credit widely available and low mortgage rates, housing prices quadrupled in value between 1996 and 2007 (Whelan, 2014, p. 424).

The Celtic Tiger was underwritten as much by political as economic factors. As O'Riain (2014, p. 37) points out, in this period (and before) the Irish state undertook a strong developmental leadership role, not just in driving industrial and innovation policy but also in creating a facilitating political environment. The wide-ranging recourse to social partnership from the mid-1980s on—which delivered six successive 'national agreements' between 1987 and 2008—is rooted in a development-supportive and consensus-seeking state. The Irish political context—marked by a relative absence of a left–right political cleavage and no great ideological divides—also facilitated pragmatic responses to problems or challenges. It depoliticizes how policy choices are framed (Hardiman & MacCarthaigh, 2016, p. 2). A further facilitating factor was more historical. Ireland's population had been underemployed for many years and the availability of a large labour supply contributed significantly to the period of rapid growth. Larragy, O'Cinnéide, and O'Riain (2006) speak of a 'social bonus'—referring not just to the untapped labour supply from a young population, many home-based married women, emigrant Irish abroad, and a mix of skill and labour supply among the unemployed, but also the plentiful resources around informal care-giving which facilitated labour market entry on the part of many women (O'Riain, 2014, p. 57).

In terms of policy approach, it is now widely accepted that the Celtic Tiger phenomenon was more complex and multifaceted than might otherwise be assumed. O'Riain (2014) differentiates between (at least) 3 periods over the 20 years. From 1987 to 1994 the main focus was on macroeconomic stabilization (facilitated by the social partnership process) with some cuts in welfare entitlements early in the period but stabilization thereafter. From 1994 to the early 2000s, there was a concentration on building human capital capacity—in employment placement and training for example (not least through the facilitation of state-funded community development programmes and a network of local area partnerships), in research and development (R&D) and other aspects of innovation, as well as in the social partnership process (in this period participation was partially extended to the social pillar).[1] The third period—from 2003 to the crisis of 2008—was characterized by high economic growth that was driven by a credit and property bubble rather than by export and output growth.

A significant amount of social policy reform was pursued during the Celtic Tiger period. Against a backdrop of significant welfare state underdevelopment, especially of social services, and a tradition of low-paying social benefits, programmes were streamlined and the value of all welfare payments was significantly increased (especially those for the unemployed, pensioners, and families with children) from the 1990s. The effect was to make Irish benefits much more generous, by national and also international standards. A comparative analysis of Irish social security (Employee Assistance Programme, 2009, cited in Murphy, 2012, p. 348) showed the annual value of the benefit paid to a single unemployed claimant in 2007 to be €9,962 in Ireland compared to €3,631 in the UK.[2] Moreover, the period of entitlement for jobseeker's benefit remained over twice as long in Ireland (13 months) as the UK (6 months). To take another example, the non-contributory old-age pension received by a qualifying individual in Ireland in 2007 was €805 per month compared to €693 in the UK. Supporting families with children was a policy priority—the universal child benefit was increased fourfold in value between 1997 and 2007—from €40 to €160 per month per child. In addition, a minimum wage was introduced (in 2000) and sustained attention was given to making employment more attractive (especially for those on low incomes) through tax and welfare reform and significant investment in active labour market policies (ALMPs) (especially in the 1990s). Furthermore, Ireland was the first EU member state to introduce a wide-ranging programme to combat and prevent poverty (in 1997).

These developments have to be contextualized, however; doing so helps to reveal other less obvious underpinnings of the emergent Irish welfare state. Essentially, moderate wage and welfare increases were traded for significant tax privileging of those on middle and high incomes (the quite erratic nature of tax reform from year to year of the Celtic Tiger notwithstanding). Persistent cuts in the personal income tax from 1997 onwards reduced the tax burden to the extent that by 2007 Ireland had the lowest effective tax on labour in Western Europe and a half of all earners were paying no personal income tax (Christensen, 2010). This suggests dualism in the Irish welfare state—the

[1] This saw the inclusion of representatives of the unemployed, some religious organizations, women's groups, and community development organizations.

[2] See also comparative data on relative compensation levels in Chapter 4, Figure 4.9.

Celtic Tiger period deepened the gap between those maintained by the state through the benefit system and those earners who received significant subsidies and top-ups to purchase or otherwise avail themselves of benefits and services (especially pensions, health insurance, housing, and education) from private or quasi-private providers (O'Riain, 2014, p. 209). In effect, the successive national agreements that were produced over the course of the Celtic Tiger years institutionalized trade-offs between wage moderation, fiscal restraint, and tax concessions as well as a preference for tax cuts over service improvements (Christensen, 2010).

## 7.2 The Characteristics and Severity of the Crisis

There are different interpretations of how to analyse Ireland's crisis but all generally agree that it was a relatively complex set of events, occasioned nationally by a policy approach that had started to come undone before the crisis in the international economy hit in 2008.[3] It is helpful to focus on the key dimensions separately, considering in turn the banking crisis, the fiscal crisis, the financial crisis, and the social policy crisis (Donovan & Murphy, 2013).

The banking crisis was in effect two crises. First, as mentioned, much of the later period of the Celtic Tiger boom was fuelled by activity in the construction sector—so much so that, from around 2001 on, the country shifted from export-led growth to construction-driven growth. Underwritten by money sourced cheaply by financial institutions on international markets and by the structure of tax incentives, construction peaked at 24.5 per cent of gross national product (GNP) in 2006, by which time, according to the NESC (2009, p. 18), the level of Irish house building was as remarkable internationally as the growth rate of Irish manufacturing exports had been in the late 1990s. A second contributory factor was ineffectual regulation and supervision of Irish financial institutions. The preference to operate a principles-based rather than a rules-based regulatory regime left the way open for poor practices in a number of financial institutions and an environment in which the banks and other lending agencies overlent and operated a culture of paying little heed to liquidity issues and portfolio diversification (Donovan & Murphy, 2013, p. 7).

In the event, the Irish banking system would undergo a near collapse, necessitating a bailout, first via a more or less blanket government guarantee

[3] Donovan and Murphy (2013) speak of a four-part crisis, comprising a property market crisis, a banking crisis, a fiscal crisis, and a financial crisis. For the governmental think tank—the National Economic and Social Council (NESC, 2009, 2013)—Ireland's was a five-part crisis, spanning banking, public finances, economic, social, and reputational elements.

in September 2008 and, later, by way of massive capital injections to be paid for by tax payers. Recourse also had to be made to large-scale liquidity assistance from the European Central Bank (ECB). It should also be noted that the wide availability of credit led to high private debt, as in Greece and Spain. When the crisis hit, rapidly falling house prices and incomes left large numbers of households falling behind on their mortgage payments—as of September 2013, one in eight private residential mortgages were in arrears of 90 days or more. By the second quarter of 2015 that proportion was falling but by international standards continued to be high, with some 8 per cent of all mortgages in arrears of over 90 days (Central Bank of Ireland, 2016).

The crisis in public finance was occasioned in part by the banking crisis, but fiscal problems were so profound that it is now generally agreed that Ireland would have needed outside intervention even if the banking crisis had not happened and the blanket guarantee not been given. A largely unnoticed fiscal crisis preceded the international economic crisis. The tax base had been altered over time to exclude more and more tax revenue from the construction and housing sector, while Ireland's international competitiveness had become undermined by rising wage and other costs and stable if not declining productivity. For the economy as a whole, unit wage costs in common currency terms relative to Ireland's main trading partners were 32.4 per cent higher in 2007 than at the start of the decade (NESC, 2009, p. 20). Moreover, the government largely abandoned a countercyclical fiscal policy throughout most of the period between 2000 and 2008, making for a structural deficit in the public finances such that, as revenues soared, expenditure was boosted simultaneously (Donovan & Murphy, 2013, p. 105). The creation of the National Pension Reserve Fund, financed by an annual budgetary transfer equal to 1 per cent of GNP, was insufficient to stem a major ramping up of public expenditure.

So when the property bubble burst, it left a hole in Exchequer revenue. With domestic construction activity collapsing and the world economy entering a severe recession, Irish real gross domestic product (GDP) declined by 10 per cent over 2008 and 2009 (Donovan & Murphy, 2013, p. 105). As the deterioration accelerated, the budget deficit jumped to 31 per cent of GDP in 2010 and the debt/GDP ratio quadrupled, rising to almost 110 per cent by the end of 2011 (Donovan & Murphy, 2013, p. 105).

Policy was active, although to a large extent in crisis mode. Between July 2008 and end 2012, Ireland had seven episodes of fiscal adjustment (see Table 7.1). In the most decisive event of all, in November 2010, the Irish government accepted the terms of a bailout or rescue package from the international institutions, and drew up a four-year austerity plan. The programme agreed with the so-called 'Troika' (EU, International Monetary Fund (IMF), and ECB) provided funding commitments of €67.5 billion, two-thirds

Table 7.1. Main government responses to the crisis, 2008–12

| Date/intervention | Key budgetary measures | Size of fiscal effort |
|---|---|---|
| July 2008: expenditure adjustments | Efficiency cuts | €1 bn |
| October 2008: budget for 2009 | Income levy, spending cuts, including welfare | €2 bn |
| February 2009: expenditure adjustment | Cuts to public sector pay as a pension levy; public sector pay increase stopped | €2.1 bn |
| April 2009: supplementary budget | Tax increases especially levy; €1.2 bn current, €600 m capital | €5.4 bn |
| December 2009: budget for 2010 | Spending cuts on all welfare, public sector pay and numbers; capital cuts, tax increases | €4.4 bn |
| December 2010: budget for 2011 | Current cuts €2.1 bn; capital cuts, €1.9 bn. Other €0.7 bn, tax increases €1.4bn | National Recovery Plan 2011–14 projects 10 bn cuts, €5 bn tax |
| December 2011: budget for 2012 | Current cuts €2.1 bn; capital cuts €0.8bn, tax increases €1bn | €3.2 bn |

*Source*: Hardiman (2013, figure 6).

of which would come from European funds. In return for this funding, Ireland agreed a very detailed programme of reform targets and deadlines to restructure the banking sector, implement further fiscal adjustment, and introduce various social and other policy reforms. The agreement stipulated that, to return to sustainable growth, a €15 billion budgetary adjustment was required over four years, and that one-third of this would come from taxes and two-thirds from spending cuts (Hick, 2014). Social protection would contribute €2.8 billion of these spending cuts, representing a 13 per cent reduction from the 2010 spending level. In the event, while the agreement was adhered to closely—and the budgetary adjustment exceeded the level set—expenditure cuts in social protection did not achieve the desired level, mainly because of rising demand (see Table 7.2).

The crisis in Ireland also entailed a crisis of and for social policy, centred upon capacity to cope with increased demand and changing economic conditions and the consensus around the kind of social policy system that was 'fit for purpose' in the post-crisis world. Attention turned to the lack of structural reform during the Celtic Tiger period. As mentioned, spending on social protection rose sharply in real terms during the boom (albeit from relatively low levels) and the period saw generous increases in benefits. Coming out of the Celtic Tiger period, however, the weaknesses of the Irish system were thrown into sharp relief.

For one thing, there were still significant deficits in and underdevelopment of social services, resulting in coverage gaps and services that were too tightly targeted, too expensive, or of poor quality (not just for those on low incomes but also people on modest earnings) (NESC, 2009, p. 81). One could reference as examples here the high cost and low availability of childcare; difficulties in accessing public wards in hospitals; poor value for money in health spending; tight rationing in the supply of social housing; and limited reach of public transport networks (NESC, 2009, p. 81). In addition, a significant subgroup of people had continued on long-term unemployment benefits and other state support through the period of full employment, interpreted as a social welfare system that tolerated and encouraged welfare dependence. The NESC (2013) has suggested that the expectations of, and aspirations for, recipients of long-term social welfare programmes were low. Moreover, while Ireland had ALMPs in place, these were as much to serve a variety of other functions—such as local development, meeting gaps in service provision, and keeping people occupied—as they were about placing people in sustainable employment. In truth, the system had little orientation to activation as it is now understood, especially in terms of incentivizing entry to the labour market. Furthermore, very high levels of poverty continued throughout the Celtic Tiger period (see Tables 7.3 and 7.4).

All of this suggests the persistence of a sizeable subsection of the population for whom economic growth yielded little by way of short- or long-term prospects.

## 7.3 Financial Hardship through the Crisis

Figure 7.1 shows that the crisis hit Ireland hard, spreading financial hardship quite widely. Ireland had a lower proportion of its population suffering financial hardship than the average for the 30 European countries before the crisis, according to our composite measure. However, its hardship level increased rapidly during the crisis, from just over 16 per cent in 2008 to about 26 per cent in 2012–13, before coming down a little. Thus, hardship increased more drastically in Ireland than in Europe as a whole and it was rather sticky, in that it came down only modestly despite relatively good recovery of economic growth towards the end of the period. It was only in 2014 and 2015 that a significant improvement occurred. Even so, Ireland still had a significantly higher level of hardship in 2015 than before the crisis hit.

The information for particular sectors of the population shows a progressively worsening situation over time also, especially for low-income groups as a whole, the unemployed, households with children under 18 years, immigrants, and those with primary education only. The change for disability pensioners was more modest. Lone parents were at the second-highest hardship level before the crisis and they also suffered a significant increase of financial hardship during the crisis years.

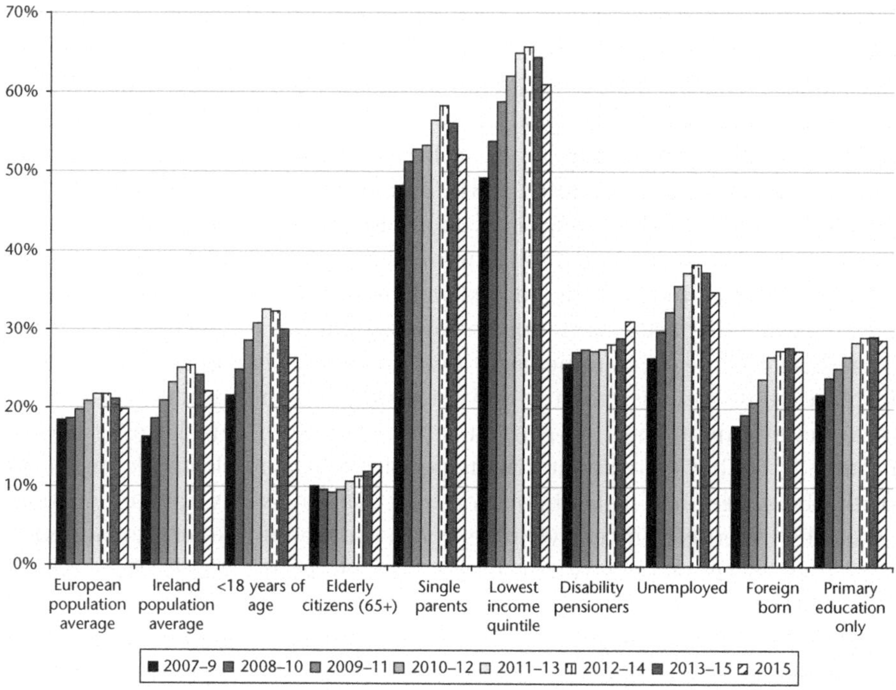


**Figure 7.1.** Financial hardship profiles through the crisis in Ireland, 2007–15

*Note*: This shows Ireland compared to the European average and disaggregated by main socio-economic groups. It is a composite measure based on income poverty, difficulties in making ends meet, and material deprivation (see the Appendix for explanation of the methodology) and shows proportion suffering financial hardship over three-year moving averages and in 2015.

The circumstances of lone parents worsened especially after 2010, when the impact of the benefits cuts started to bite (to be discussed further below). At the other extreme the relatively cushioned situation of those aged over 65 years is also starkly in evidence, with their hardship levels far below the population average and limited worsening in the latter part of the period. This will be explained in section 7.4 as closely connected to the strategy to protect old-age pensioners from the worst effects of the crisis.

How did the government respond to the crisis and what impact did the policies have?

## 7.4 The Overarching Strategy Pursued to Alleviate the Effects of the Crisis

The response of the Fianna Fáil government was immediate and clear-cut in terms of approach—an austerity orientation was needed and would be applied. From late 2008 onwards, a series of contractionary budgets was put in place. A similar cuts-in-public-spending-oriented policy was followed by the succeeding Fine Gael/Labour coalition government that replaced Fianna Fáil in 2011 (see Table 7.1). The mantra that 'there is no alternative' became a fixture in the Irish government's justifications for retrenchment and consolidation measures (Hardiman & MacCarthaigh, 2016, p. 2).

Between 2008 and 2010, fiscal adjustments of almost 9 per cent of GDP were implemented, making the Irish among the earliest adopters of an austerity approach in response to the financial crisis (Dukelow & Considine, 2014, p. 58). Public sector pay was cut, income taxes and VAT rates were raised, a universal tax on households was introduced, more workers were brought into the tax net by virtue of lower tax allowances, non-welfare current spending was cut, and capital spending slashed. The crisis was also taken as an opportunity to reform the public sector. While public sector redundancies were not a major strategy, salaries were cut substantially and a new public sector pension levy was introduced. In the private sector, wage reduction did not follow the same pattern, but employment did fall.

In regard to welfare there were two major strategies: to cut back or freeze the value of benefits; to reframe support for those of working age much more firmly around activation.

According to Dukelow and Considine (2014), in keeping with the framing of the crisis as a crisis of public expenditure, 'generosity' gained currency as a critique of Irish social protection. Political debate about the generosity of the welfare system emerged as a justification for its retrenchment, especially in the early stages of the crisis. Recipients of almost all categories of welfare benefits suffered direct cuts to their entitlements during 2009, while cuts or freezing of the payment rates continued for most benefits up to 2015. Among the most significant changes were the following: a cut of €12 to the weekly basic social welfare payment; a cut of €20 a month per child in the universal child benefit; cuts to rent supplement (paid to help tenants renting privately); the introduction of a new lower payment rate for young unemployed benefit recipients (first for those between the ages of 18 and 21 and subsequently for those aged between 22 and 24). In addition to the cuts in child-related benefits, the government also made numerous cuts to top-up benefits for welfare recipients and their families (such 'top-ups' for additional expenditure necessitated by circumstances—usually given on a discretionary basis—were a significant feature of the Irish income support system, with its roots in social assistance).

While social welfare pensions were largely protected from cuts, the retirement age was increased over time from 66 to 68 years. It was only from 2015 on that the cuts began to be reversed, starting with the universal child benefit which was increased in January 2016 by €5 per month per child, reversing the trend of the previous five years and representing the first increase since 2008. The other welfare payments—with the exception of the state pension—remained frozen at the 2011 rates and were slower to change. Not until March 2017 did benefit recipients over 25 years of age have their payments increased (by €5 a week).

As well as cutting back or freezing benefits, a much stronger orientation to activation was the second major systemic response to the social policy crisis. In fact, activation was the main type of institutional reform in Irish social policy—other than that, the reforms have been mainly incremental, leaving the welfare system less generous but essentially unreformed. While state-led job placement and training services predated the crisis, policy after 2008/9 saw both a concerted activation strategy and significant service reorganization and renewal. The new activation strategy—Pathways to Work (Department of Social Protection, 2011) first launched in 2011 and updated regularly since—focused on five key action points: more regular and ongoing engagement with non-employed people; greater targeting of activation; incentivizing the take-up of job and training opportunities; incentivizing employers to recruit the unemployed; reforming institutions to deliver better and more activating services. To realize these aims, a new integrated activation service—known as Intreo—was set up in 2012 within the Department of Social Protection to integrate three types of services for unemployed people—income support, job placement, and job matching—and oversee the design and supervision of ALMPs. These three services had been previously provided by separate agencies. In addition, a new national training agency (SOLAS) was established in 2013 and 16 regional education and training boards were created by merging local authority vocational education committees and the national training authority's local training centres.

These changes have seen a much more intensified programme of activation-oriented engagement, concentrating especially on the unemployed and other 'at risk' groups (mainly other categories of social welfare recipients and especially lone parents of older children). Ireland spends 0.26 per cent of GDP on these types of active labour market or direct employment programme, compared to the Organisation for Economic Co-operation and Development (OECD) European average of 0.1 per cent (OECD, 2014a). The low-grade-, status-quo-type activation measures, serving functions around keeping the unemployed occupied and implementing community-level service provision and local area development, came to be challenged by a much more focused (hard-core) activation policy, which makes much more extensive use of profiling systems, targeted provision, and behavioural controls. From 2011 to 2015 legal reforms put in place new penalties for unemployed job seekers, lone parents, and inactive young people (Murphy, 2016). These included sanctions such as benefit cuts in the event of non-compliance with a training or job offer and temporary disqualification. Profound change is also indicated by the contracting of the activation service for the long-term unemployed to two private sector companies from 2014, on a new pay-by-results activation programme.

The remainder of the chapter considers the impact and consequences of the policy approach followed.

## 7.5 Impact and Outcomes

The impact will be analysed in terms of four dimensions: the sectoral distribution of the budget cuts, poverty and deprivation, inequality, and employment and unemployment.

In terms of the sectoral impact, budget allocations by sector reveal a policy approach that especially targeted the welfare state. Health, education, and social welfare were all profoundly affected. In health, public spending declined by 18 per cent from 2009 to 2014, reductions that were largely driven by cuts in staff numbers and pay (Goldrick-Kelly, 2015b). Moreover, public capital spending declined by 36 per cent between 2008 and 2014. Education spending was also slashed, with nominal spending falling by €1 billion between 2008 and 2014 and real expenditure by 13 per cent between 2010 and 2014 (Goldrick-Kelly, 2015a).

In terms of social welfare expenditure, the period of the crisis presided over an overall decline of expenditure of around €1 billion between 2010 and 2015 (see Table 7.2), a fall in social expenditure as a proportion of the GNP of over 5 percentage points, and a strong increase in benefit and beneficiary numbers up to 2013 and only gradually decreasing numbers thereafter. Roughly a million

**Table 7.2.** Welfare expenditure and beneficiaries, 2005–15

| | Total social welfare expenditure | Social welfare expenditure as % of GNP | No. of social welfare recipients | No. of beneficiaries | No. of beneficiaries as % of total population |
|---|---|---|---|---|---|
| 2005 | €12.2 bn | 8.4% | 976,613 | 1,469,106 | 35.5% |
| 2006 | €13.6 bn | 8.5% | 1,003,517 | 1,508,824 | 35.5% |
| 2007 | €15.5 bn | 9.2% | 1,060,327 | 1,577,479 | 36.0% |
| 2008 | €17.8 bn | 11.1% | 1,208,883 | 1,799,875 | 40.1% |
| 2009 | €20.5 bn | 14.7% | 1,379,206 | 2,076,256 | 45.8% |
| 2010 | €20.9 bn | 15.1% | 1,430,833 | 2,179,428 | 47.8% |
| 2011 | €21 bn | 15.1% | 1,467,129 | 2,248,284 | 49.0% |
| 2012 | €20.8 bn | 14.7% | 1,468,481 | 2,267,499 | 49.5% |
| 2013 | €20.3 bn | 13.8% | 1,467,918 | 2,273,003 | 49.5% |
| 2014 | €19.8 bn | 12.5% | 1,440,876 | 2,219,662 | 48.2% |
| 2015 | €19.97 bn | 9.9% | 1,377,558 | 2,110,988 | 45.5% |

*Source*: Department of Social Protection (2017, table 2.2).

and a half people were in personal receipt of a weekly social welfare payment in each of the five years, with the number of beneficiaries exceeding 2 million. Up nearly 50 per cent on pre-crisis levels, in the height of the crisis almost half of the population were receiving support through the benefit system.

It is well known that the Irish social security system performs well in reducing market income poverty through transfers. In 2015 social transfers reduced the poverty rate from 46.3 per cent to 16.9 per cent (Central Statistics Office, 2017). In fact, Ireland is among the best-performing EU and OECD member states at reducing poverty from pre-transfer levels. This is because of low market income, high inequality in market income, and strong targeting in the benefit system. Success in reducing pre-transfer poverty notwithstanding, Ireland is a high poverty country.

Along with high poverty rates, two other facts are clear from Table 7.3. First, poverty was mostly stable over the early years of the crisis but started to increase significantly from then on and has remained high (at around 17 per cent). Secondly, deprivation is very high in Ireland and is on a different course to poverty in that: (i) up to the last year or so it was increasing quite rapidly; and (ii) unlike poverty it was relatively low during the Celtic Tiger period but has skyrocketed since 2010. There is little evidence to explain the rise in deprivation, other than that it is associated with a long-term depletion of resources entailed by living on a low income over a period of time.

Table 7.4 summarizes the change over time in poverty and deprivation. When the poverty rates are anchored at 2010 values, poverty actually increased in Ireland over the course of the crisis, although the impact of social transfers on the poverty rate also improved. Overall though, while they might have stabilized it, the policies pursued did little or nothing to reduce the prevalence of poverty. With such stubbornly high poverty rates, Ireland has made little or no progress in meeting its targets under the Europe 2020 headline poverty target—to lift 200,000 people out of poverty. To take the example of child poverty, meeting the child poverty target requires 102,000 children to be lifted out of poverty by 2020 on 2015 rates (as against 70,000 when it was first set) (Government of Ireland, 2017).

**Table 7.3.** Poverty and deprivation rates, 2008–15

| | 2008 | 2009 | 2010 | 2011 | 2012 | 2013 | 2014 | 2015 |
|---|---|---|---|---|---|---|---|---|
| Poverty rate (based on 60% of median income poverty line) | 14.4 | 14.1 | 14.7 | 16 | 17.3 | 16.5 | 17.2 | 16.9 |
| Deprivation rate (measured on the basis of enforced lack of two or more standard items) | 13.7 | 17.1 | 22.6 | 24.5 | 26.9 | 30.5 | 29 | 25.5 |

*Source*: Central Statistics Office (2017, table 5).

**Table 7.4.** Change over time in a range of poverty-relevant measures

| | Average 2005–8 | Average 2009–15 | Difference |
|---|---|---|---|
| Poverty rate (based on 60% of median income poverty line) | 16.6% | 16% | −0.6 |
| Deprivation rate (measured on the basis of enforced lack of two or more standard items) | 13.6% | 25.2% | +11.6 |
| Impact of social transfers on the poverty rate | 49.5% | 57.4% | +7.9 |
| Poverty rate anchored in 2010 values | 15.4% | 16.9% | +1.5 |

*Source*: Department of Social Protection (2017), Social Inclusion Monitor (2015, table 3.3).

Turning to inequality and redistribution, the income losses occasioned by the policies pursued during the crisis were not evenly spread. Modelling the impact of the annual budgets from 2009 to 2016, Callan and colleagues (2015) report that the highest losses were experienced by those in the top decile, who are estimated as having lost 14.3 per cent of their income due to the specific policy changes. But these households did not bear the burden of adjustment alone. The bottom decile is estimated as having the next highest income loss, suffering policy-induced losses of 12.8 per cent over the period. The lowest losses (7.5 per cent) were for the third income decile (which in Ireland includes a higher than average representation of pensioner households). Losses for other deciles were in a relatively narrow range, between 8.3 and 10.2 per cent. In terms of the effect across households, single unemployed people without children experienced by far the largest losses (more than 22 per cent); this reflects the cuts to Jobseeker's Allowance for the young unemployed in particular. Most family types saw losses of between 8 and 11 per cent. The factors contributing to the losses vary by income level. At the lowest income levels, the authors identify as causal the reductions in welfare payment rates, along with property tax and water charges. At the highest income levels, they point to increases in income-related taxes (income tax and the Universal Social Charge) and cuts in public sector pay as playing a pivotal role. The lowest losses, of between 5 and 6 per cent, were experienced by retired people, both singles and couples, reflecting the relative privileging of pension payments throughout the period of the crisis.

One can see these processes reflected in relatively static but high levels of inequality. The eight years represented in Table 7.5 show little or no change in overall inequality (although the benefit system is also highly effective in reducing gross income inequality—in fact in this regard Ireland was the best-performing EU member state in 2015, reducing income inequality by over twice the EU average and over four times more than in other deep-crisis countries, such as Italy, Greece, and Cyprus (cf. Department of Social Protection, 2017, p. 34)).

**Table 7.5.** Gini coefficient and income quintile ratio, 2008–15

| | 2008 | 2009 | 2010 | 2011 | 2012 | 2013 | 2014 | 2015 |
|---|---|---|---|---|---|---|---|---|
| Gini | 30.6 | 29.3 | 31.4 | 31.1 | 31.8 | 32 | 32 | 30.8 |
| Income quintile ratio | 4.5 | 4.3 | 4.8 | 4.9 | 5.1 | 5 | 5.1 | 4.7 |

*Source*: Central Statistics Office (2017, table A).

Looking at the period between 2004 and 2015 and pointing to the broad stability of the Gini coefficient over the period, Callan and colleagues (2017) consider that the automatic stabilization impact of Ireland's tax-transfer system at the start of the recession played a strong role in limiting the increase in inequality over the period. When they looked at the distribution of income by deciles between 2008, 2013, and 2015, they found that there was a sizable fall in the income share of the bottom decile between 2008 and 2013 (3.6 per cent as against 3.1 per cent at the latter date). Between 2013 and 2015, the income share of the bottom decile had recovered to 3.3 per cent (see also Figure 2.6 in Chapter 2). Savage and colleagues (2017) undertook further forensic analysis of the fall in incomes in the lowest decile. They report, first, that the sharpest falls in average income for this group occurred during 2009 to 2010 and 2010 to 2011 and, secondly, that the fall is attributable to sharp falls in income for those previously in deciles 2, 3, and above, which brought these individuals into the bottom decile (rather than a fall in income for those already in the bottom decile).

Table 7.6 provides some evidence on how these effects came about. It confirms that Ireland's taxation system made two main changes during the crisis. First, taxes were increased for all from 2008, unlike the preceding eight-year period where there were significant tax decreases across the board. Secondly, the increases were not generally progressive, with couples on higher incomes especially privileged.

**Table 7.6.** Effective taxation rates for selected household types, 2000, 2008, 2016

| | 2000 | 2008 | 2016 |
|---|---|---|---|
| Single earner | | | |
| Gross income €25,000 | 24% | 8.3% | 13.5% |
| Gross income €60,000 | 37.7% | 27.5% | 31.6% |
| Couple: 1 earner | | | |
| Gross income €40,000 | 20.2% | 9.4% | 12.9% |
| Gross income €60,000 | 29% | 19.8% | 24.1% |
| Couple: 2 earners | | | |
| Gross income €40,000 | 17.5% | 3.6% | 8.3% |
| Gross income €100,000 | 35.9% | 23.8% | 28% |

*Source*: Social Justice Ireland (2016a, table 5).

The fourth dimension to be considered relates to employment and unemployment. There are a number of elements here, all indicating inequality and continuing entrenched disadvantage.

Ireland's labour market was transformed by the crisis; the employment machine stopped working, and dramatically so. Over the nine years from 2007 to 2015 the labour force decreased by some 4 per cent, participation rates dropped, full-time employment fell by 13 per cent, representing almost 234,000 jobs, while part-time employment increased by 15.6 per cent (Social Justice Ireland, 2016c). Unemployment peaked at 15.1 per cent in 2012 and as of July 2017 stood at 6.7. per cent. The numbers during the crisis may have been even more dire, however. Murphy (2016, p. 434) underlines the need to treat these figures with caution since they do not include over 85,000 people on active labour market programmes, at least 100,000 underemployed workers, and the 70,000 who emigrated annually between 2011 and 2014. As well as large-scale unemployment, one other notable feature has been the high prevalence of long-term unemployment (defined as being out of work for 12 months or more). Since 2010 around a half of those claiming unemployment benefits are long-term unemployed. Ireland's jobs gap—the number of jobs that the Irish economy needs to create in order to return to peak performance levels while accounting for changes in the population and the labour force—stood at around 166,200 in March 2016 (Social Justice Ireland, 2016b).

The evidence indicates a concentration of labour market disadvantage and exclusion. A particular contributor to and consequence of this is Ireland's high rate of jobless households—one of the highest in the EU. As Table 7.7 shows this was high at the beginning of the crisis and remains high on the latest evidence, although on a downward trend. This suggests a strong concentration of disadvantage and reveals that some people in Ireland are adrift of developments in the economy.

Secondly, the effect of the crisis on unemployment was both dramatic and dramatically uneven. Comparing two cohorts of workers between 2001 and 2011, O'Riain (2014, pp. 257–8) shows that, while there was almost no difference in the employment rate of workers with third-level education at the two dates, there was a 15–20 per cent gap for those with low levels of education. The policy responses in the face of this situation have been mainly

**Table 7.7.** Percentage of persons in jobless households, 2009–15

| | 2009 | 2010 | 2011 | 2012 | 2013 | 2014 | 2015 |
|---|---|---|---|---|---|---|---|
| % of persons aged 0–17 | 16% | 19.4% | 20.1% | 20.1% | 18% | 16.2% | 14.9% |
| % of persons aged 18–59 | 12.3% | 14.3% | 15.2% | 15.9% | 14.9% | 13.7% | 12.4% |
| % of all persons aged 0–59 | 13.4% | 15.9% | 16.7% | 17.2% | 15.8% | 14.5% | 13.2% |

*Source*: Central Statistics Office (2015).

focused on activation, job creation, and also some measures to ease the income transition from benefits to employment. The response could be described as small in the face of the challenges.

## 7.6 Overview and Conclusion

How was the Irish welfare state changed by the crisis? There is no doubt that there has been retrenchment, with significant cuts and freezing of benefits as well as large reductions in social expenditure (which affected social services also). There were also changes to the focus and orientation of the Irish welfare state. The most notable and consequential of these was in the forceful turn to activation. The function of job placement became—and remains—a much more integral part of the Irish welfare state than heretofore and there is considerably less tolerance in the system for long-term benefit recipiency seen to be attributable to lack of engagement with employment. It must also be said that the international organizations took the opportunity of the financial bailout to push Ireland towards activation and other reforms. This, of course, has had an effect on the extent to which people can rely on the welfare state and also the conditions under which they receive public support. Overall though, the Irish welfare state proved resilient in a period which saw the overshadowing if not demise of social partnership.

In conclusion, I tend to agree with Hay and Smith (2013, p. 403) who—in a comparison of the crisis in Ireland and the UK—suggest that the crisis has been paradigm reinforcing rather than paradigm changing. The Irish welfare state played a key role in the adjustment and reform process—strategic use was made of the social protection elements of the welfare state, if not to maintain income levels among the most disadvantaged then at least to protect or cushion them from the worst effects of the crisis and the policies pursued. In this the welfare state did not oversee any major measures to adequately redistribute the costs of the crisis. There is little evidence of a change towards a redistributive logic as in Iceland. Hence, those who were economically vulnerable before the crisis remained so after it, although widespread housing indebtedness has generalized financial vulnerability in Ireland.

To a large extent, responding to the crisis saw business as usual in Ireland with no real restructuring. The significant welfare state exception was in regard to activation. Benefits to the unemployed were more tightly tied to measures to incentivize employment by tapering the withdrawal of benefits and supplementary payments. There was some movement also towards other elements of a social investment approach. The main activity in this direction over the years considered was the introduction of a free universal early childhood education and care year on a half-time basis for 3–4 year olds in 2015 (extended to a full year in 2016). This, while important for children and families, is a relatively minor change in the nature of the state and state/society/economy relations, however. As a percentage of wages, net childcare costs in Ireland are among the highest in the EU (European Commission, 2017a) and the availability and cost of high-quality, full-time childcare present barriers to female labour market participation and hinder efforts to reduce child poverty, which has fallen slightly but remains higher than the EU average (at 19.3 per cent in 2016) (Central Statistics Office, 2017).

Overall, the crisis leaves Ireland's service infrastructure underdeveloped and arguably weaker now than before the crisis (with housing and health services especially underdeveloped), while it leaves the welfare state in its highly targeted income maintenance mode rather than as an instrument that transforms economy and society.

# 8

# Iceland's Strategy of Redistribution

*Stefán Ólafsson*

## 8.1 Introduction: The Political Economy Context

Iceland was one of the first countries to fall in the Great Recession. The stock market began to slide in the autumn of 2007 and the currency (Icelandic krona) followed from the beginning of 2008. Then in late September to the beginning of October of 2008, the three main banks of the country collapsed, along with some other financial institutions. In total over 90 per cent of the banking system became bankrupt. All of this was the result of an exceptionally large bubble economy, which developed from 1998 and with increasing speed from 2003. When the bubble burst a severe financial crisis and a deep economic recession followed.

Iceland is thus an interesting case for studying the advent of the financial crisis as well as the ensuing economic recession and the policy reactions to it. Given the enormity of the crisis one might have expected that the consequences for levels of living would have been extensive and long lasting.

In 2018, a decade after the collapse, it appears that Iceland has done relatively well in dealing with and ameliorating many of the crisis consequences. It has been hailed by the International Monetary Fund (IMF, 2012), as well as by some well-known political economists—such as Paul Krugman, Joseph Stiglitz, and Mark Blyth—for its policy reactions and success in resurrecting the economy (see also Jónsson & Sigurgeirsson, 2016).

For some, Iceland is a case representing an alternative to the outright austerity policies that prevailed in Europe in recent years. That characterization may, however, call for some qualifications, as we show in this chapter. For some critics within Iceland the government was seen as having failed to reinvigorate the economy, by not sufficiently increasing growth-inducing investment, by failing to alleviate excessive debt burdens, and by increasing taxation on businesses and society. Those criticisms also need some qualifications. Iceland's growth rates from 2011 to date have, for example, been significantly higher than in most European economies and unemployment has, since 2014, come down to one of the very lowest levels in Europe—by end of 2017 it was in the region of 2–3 per cent.

Due to the shock of the collapse of October 2008, continuous and intense protests arose in the streets of Reykjavík, eventually leading to the downfall of the reigning government, as well as the removal of the governors of the Central Bank and the Financial Surveillance Authority (Bernburg, 2016).

In this chapter we analyse Iceland's pre-crisis position and policy reactions to the crisis and their success. We start by characterizing the advent of the crisis and the severity of the depression that followed. Then we look further at financial hardship developments and the strategies of dealing with the crisis. Lastly, we reflect on the outcomes and implications.

## 8.2 Characteristics and Severity of the Crisis

The crisis was multidimensional, featuring not just a banking collapse, but also a stock market collapse, a currency collapse, an economic crisis, and a political crisis of lost trust in institutions and politicians (Aliber & Zoega, 2011; Bergmann, 2014; Ingimundarson, Urfalino, & Erlingsdóttir, 2016). The economic contraction was swift and deeper than seen at any previous time from the founding of the Icelandic republic in 1944. IMF researchers estimated that the Irish and Icelandic financial crises were amongst the ten most costly financial crises in recent history, when assessed by direct fiscal cost, increased debt, and lost output taken together (Laeven & Valencia, 2010, 2013).

In many countries the Great Recession was the result of a housing bubble that became unsustainable and burst. This was not the main reason for the Icelandic crash. Business speculation played the biggest role, while a housing bubble from 2004 had but a minor role in the whole affair. An unsustainable accumulation of external debt was what eventually led to the financial collapse of 2008 (Ólafsson, 2011, 2016a). It increased more than tenfold from 1997 to 2008, as can be seen in column 4 of Table 8.1.[1] In their survey of international debt developments Reinhardt and Rogoff (2010) note that they have never before seen as rapid an accumulation of debt as in Iceland and Ireland leading up to 2008. Corporations and private investors took on most of the new debt, while the increase of household debt was more modest (see column 11 of Table 8.1).

[1] In addition to the escalating external debt there was also considerable accumulation of internal debt, not least to the Icelandic Occupational Pension Funds (OPFs).

**Table 8.1.** Political economy and welfare developments, 1990–2016

| | Real GDP per capita growth (%) | Real disp. income per capita (%) | CA balance (% GDP) | External tot. debt (% GDP) | Public revenue (% GDP) | Public exp. (% GDP) | Budget balance (% GDP) | Gen.gov. debt (% of GDP) | Unemployment (%) | Public welfare transfers (% GDP) | Household debt (% disposable earnings) |
|---|---|---|---|---|---|---|---|---|---|---|---|
| 1990 | 0.4 | −4.6 | – | 54 | 38 | 41 | −3 | 36.2 | | 7.7 | – |
| 1991 | −1.5 | 2.5 | – | 54 | 40 | 43 | −3 | 38.4 | 2.5 | 8 | – |
| 1992 | −4.5 | −3.3 | – | 64 | 41 | 44 | −3 | 46.2 | 4.3 | 8.6 | – |
| 1993 | 0.3 | −6.8 | – | 70 | 39 | 43 | −5 | 53.1 | 5.3 | 9 | – |
| 1994 | 2.7 | 0 | – | 64 | 39 | 43 | −5 | 55.7 | 5.3 | 8.6 | – |
| 1995 | −0.4 | 2.6 | – | 62 | 40 | 43 | −3 | 58.9 | 4.9 | 9 | – |
| 1996 | 4.2 | 4 | – | 62 | 41 | 42 | −2 | 56.3 | 3.7 | 8.6 | – |
| 1997 | 3.6 | 4.6 | −2.36 | 64 | 40 | 40 | 0 | 51.7 | 3.9 | 8.2 | – |
| 1998 | 5.9 | 6.6 | −7.25 | 70 | 40 | 41 | −1 | 43.7 | 2.7 | 7.6* | – |
| 1999 | 2.6 | 4.7 | −7.17 | 81 | 42 | 42 | 1 | 39.1 | 2 | 7.5 | – |
| 2000 | 3.1 | 7.5 | −10.32 | 103 | 43 | 41 | 1 | 37.6 | 2.3 | 7.5 | 87.5 |
| 2001 | 2.5 | 1.7 | −4.32 | 118 | 41 | 42 | −1 | 42.7 | 2.3 | 7.7 | 89.4 |
| 2002 | −0.3 | 3.2 | 1.14 | 106 | 40 | 43 | −3 | 39.4 | 3.3 | 8.4 | 90.2 |
| 2003 | 1.8 | 2.3 | −4.94 | 131 | 42 | 45 | −3 | 38.3 | 3.3 | 9.5 | 89.1 |
| 2004 | 6.8 | 5.2 | −9.83 | 168 | 43 | 43 | 0 | 33 | 3.1 | 9.2 | 91.2 |
| 2005 | 5.2 | 6.4 | −15.89 | 272 | 46 | 42 | 5 | 24.6 | 2.6 | 8.9 | 102.7 |
| 2006 | 2.1 | 5.6 | −23.29 | 422 | 47 | 41 | 6 | 29.2 | 2.9 | 8.1 | 110.6 |
| 2007 | 6.9 | 10.4 | −13.97 | 501 | 46 | 41 | 5 | 27.3 | 2.3 | 8.2 | 113.3 |
| 2008 | −0.9 | 0.1 | −16.64 | 760 | 42 | 55 | −13 | 67.1 | 3 | 8.5 | 120.7 |
| 2009 | −6.5 | −14.4 | 7.99 | 133 | 39 | 48 | −10 | 82.3 | 7.2 | 10.6 | 123.7 |
| 2010 | −3.2 | −13.4 | 6.78 | 123 | 39 | 49 | −10 | 87.8 | 7.6 | 10.6 | 121.1 |
| 2011 | 1.6 | 3.5 | 3.04 | 126 | 40 | 46 | −6 | 94.7 | 7.1 | 11.1 | 110 |
| 2012 | 0.8 | 0.6 | 2.91 | 107 | 41 | 45 | −4 | 92.1 | 6 | 10.6 | 106.6 |
| 2013 | 3.3 | −0.8 | 7.39 | 91 | 42 | 44 | −2 | 84.4 | 5.4 | 10.1 | 101 |
| 2014 | 1 | 5.3 | 5.24 | 80 | 45 | 45 | 0 | 81.9 | 5 | 10.1 | 94.3 |
| 2015 | 3.2 | 7.4 | 5.76 | 68 | 42 | 43 | −1 | 67.7 | 4 | 9.4 | 82.7 |
| 2016 | 5.9 | 6.9 | 6.74 | 62 | 58 | 45 | 13 | 52.8 | 3 | 9.1 | 76.6 |

*Note*: Public welfare transfers, in column 10, exclude what comes from the mandatory OPFs, which is the majority of old-age pensions and a sizable part of disability pensions. When public and mandatory private social expenditures are taken together Iceland approaches the expenditure level of Norway, as % of GDP.

*Source*: Central Bank of Iceland, Statistics Iceland, OECD, Eurostat.

The bubble economy period had relatively high economic growth rates (even though not historically extravagant; cf. Ólafsson, 2008). Real disposable household income increased significantly after 1995, but in the shadow of a greatly increasing inequality of incomes. Top incomes increased by far the most (Ólafsson & Kristjánsson, 2017). The overall contraction of gross domestic product (GDP) that came with the collapse of 2008 was in the region of 10–11 per cent, bottoming out in 2010 (see column 1 of Table 8.1). Growth resumed from 2011 and has been quite forceful in the last few years.

Paul Krugman, a Nobel laureate in economics, has remarked in his *New York Times* column that Iceland did not need a stimulus programme since its currency was devalued. The currency was devalued altogether by close to 50 per cent from the beginning of 2008 to 2010, leading to a very large cut in real disposable incomes (see column 2 of Table 8.1) due to the inflation spike that followed the devaluation. The average cut was in the region of 28 per cent, but that was more pronounced amongst the higher income groups than the lower ones, as we show later in the chapter (Figure 8.6).[2] This reduction of real purchasing power along with significantly increased debt burden for households (column 11 of Table 8.1) is what primarily affected the level of living of households, along with increased unemployment and generally reduced volumes of work. Household debt had increased significantly after 2004, for both mortgage debt and other consumer debt. All such debts are indexed to prices in Iceland and thus, when inflation took off with the decline of the value of the krona, the burden of servicing these debts increased significantly (Ólafsson & Vignisdóttir, 2012).

Iceland has for decades enjoyed exceptionally low levels of unemployment. When the crisis hit it went from about 3 per cent to a peak of 7.6 per cent in 2010, a big increase but still a relatively low level by European standards in 2010; in fact, below the EU average. It came down significantly as growth resumed from 2011 onwards, and since 2015 unemployment has regained its historically low level of 3 per cent or less. Some emigration of Icelanders (mainly to Norway) and return migration of recent immigrants from Poland and the Baltic states reduced the pressure on the unemployment register in Iceland. The strategy of dealing with the crisis, however, also managed to contain the increase of unemployment, as we show in section 8.5.

The devaluation of the currency strengthened the position of the main export industries (fishing, tourism, and the energy-intensive industry) and facilitated the return to a positive current account balance (cf. column 3 of Table 8.1). This, along with various government strategies, helped to produce

[2] The average reduction of real household disposable income of 28% includes the effect of increased debt burden, i.e. increased interest cost. If we exclude that and focus solely on incomes, the average decline was in the region of 20% (see section 8.6).

a swift turnaround to growth and a stronger base for financial resurrection (Jónsson & Sigurgeirsson, 2016). With currency controls (implemented towards the end of 2008) and the establishment of new banks, built on the ruins of the fallen ones, the process of restructuring debts of firms and households could proceed, with the aim of shifting the economy and households towards a healthier base.

The reduced purchasing power, increased debt burden, and increased unemployment, which emanated from these measures to help the economy, were also the prime drivers of increased burdens for households. The strategy of redistribution pursued by the left-of-centre government of 2009 to 2013, however, aimed explicitly to soften the burden on the lowest income groups. Nevertheless, increased financial hardship was inevitable, given the extent of the financial collapse and the ensuing recession. We show this in section 8.3.

## 8.3 Financial Hardship through the Crisis

Iceland, like the other Nordic nations, is characterized by a financial hardship level significantly below the European average (see Figure 8.1). This, of course, reflects a traditionally low level of poverty in an advanced welfare state, with considerable capacities for redistribution. While Sweden, Norway, and Finland reduced or maintained their financial hardship level from the beginning of the crisis to 2015, the story was different in Iceland, as is to be expected, given the country's very deep crisis experience.

During the deepest crisis years, 2009 and 2010, the financial hardship level increased significantly in Iceland, peaking in 2010. From then on it has continually come down again. That said, the level of 2015 is still somewhat higher than it had been in 2007–8. We know that further improvements were made in 2016 and 2017 so the pre-crisis best position has most likely been regained at the time of writing. The levels of GDP and unemployment certainly have, while the real disposable income has again approached the high level of 2007–8.

As in many other countries, the pre-crisis financial hardship was most extensive amongst low-income individuals in general, closely followed by single parents (who are mainly women). Both experienced greatly increased financial hardship levels during the crisis. Next come the unemployed and disability pensioners, who also experienced increased hardship levels, particularly the latter group. Amongst immigrants the increase in hardship level was particularly swift from 2008 onwards and peaked in 2010–11. The pre-crisis level amongst immigrants was one of the lowest, reflecting the fact that most immigrants were fully employed and in many cases made up for low wages by

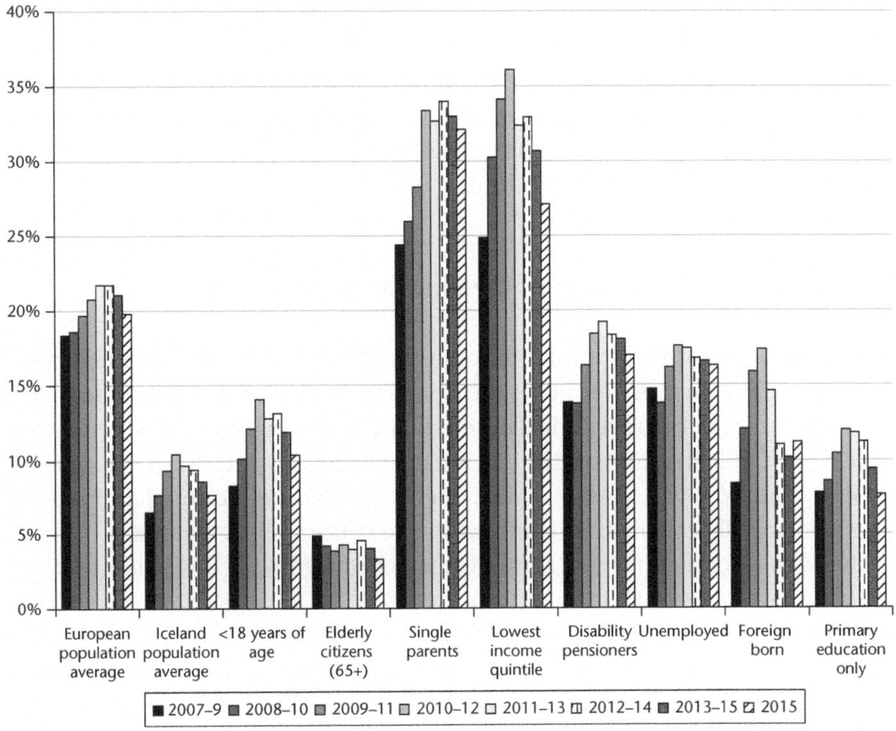


**Figure 8.1.** Financial hardship profiles through the crisis in Iceland, 2007–15

*Note*: This shows Iceland compared to the European average and disaggregated by main socio-economic groups. It is a composite measure based on income poverty, difficulties in making ends meet, and material deprivation (see the Appendix for explanation of the methodology), and shows proportion suffering financial hardship over three-year moving averages and in 2015.

*Source*: EU-SILC, author calculation.

working extra hours, a pattern for which there is a tradition amongst manual and middle-class workers in Iceland (Ólafsson, 1990; Stefánsson, 2012).

Households with children also saw a decisive increase in financial hardship after 2008, indicating that young families with children were particularly hard hit by the crisis. They entered the crisis with higher debt levels than typical for the same group in earlier decades and that made them vulnerable during the crisis (Ólafsson & Vignisdóttir, 2012; Stefánsson, Arnardóttir, & Karlsson, 2018). As in many other European countries the elderly were relatively modestly affected by the crisis and lowered their hardship level significantly from the beginning to end of our period. Their pre-crisis level was indeed far below the population average for Iceland.

On the whole, it appears that financial hardship of individuals increased less in Iceland than might have been expected, given the spectacular banking collapse and the severity of the crisis. This is confirmed by comparative statistics: Iceland had the fifth-largest overall contraction of GDP (from pre-crisis peak to post-crisis trough) but it comes below tenth place when European nations are ranked by maximum increase of financial hardship (from pre-crisis level to the maximum reached), as shown in Chapter 2 (Figure 2.12). That indicates significant success in softening the crisis consequences for the more vulnerable households in Iceland.

## 8.4 The General Strategy of Dealing with the Crisis

Iceland was in a difficult situation after the crisis hit. Public finances were devastated. The majority of the financial system was in total ruins and required emergency measures to keep the daily economy functional and allow new banks to be rebuilt, from the ruins of the old as it turned out. The Central Bank also had to be refinanced with excessive sums. On top of that the economy and the tax base were rapidly contracting, leading to large cuts in public revenues.

The Social Democratic government (the Social Democratic Alliance and the left–Greens coalition) that came to power early in 2009 pledged to approach the crisis management in the spirit of Nordic welfare policies. This referred to the goal of sheltering households, in particular those on the lower incomes, against the worst consequences of the crisis (Ólafsson, 2016b; Ólafsson & Kristjánsson, 2012). This was easier said than done, considering the condition of the public finances and unclear prospects about future debt levels for the government and the economy as a whole. It took in fact up to two years for the overall debt situation of the economy and future obligations of the state to become clear. Hence the first steps of the new government were undertaken in a situation of great uncertainty.

Iceland was thus neither in a position to save the banks with a massive injection of capital, nor to provide an exceptionally large fiscal stimulus (Jónsson & Sigurgeirsson, 2016). General government gross debt went from some 25–7 per cent of GDP before the crisis up to about 95 per cent, when it peaked in 2011. Iceland indeed increased its governmental expenditures greatly at the beginning of the crisis, at the same time as government revenues came down, as can be seen in Table 8.1.

Hence the budget deficit became massive, starting at 13.5 per cent at the end of 2008 and then gradually coming down to balance in 2014. On the surface this seems like a forceful Keynesian-style fiscal stimulus response. And indeed we see that nearly all the European countries responded similarly at the beginning of the crisis, albeit to differing degrees (see Chapter 4). The countries hardest hit by the financial crisis generally accumulated the greatest government deficit during the crisis (with only a few exceptions). Increased debt then stimulated the austerity emphasis.

With a massive deficit and a collapsed financial system Iceland had to seek assistance from the IMF. They came in soon after the collapse of the banks and worked out a plan with the government to deal with the deficit and the resurrection of the financial system.[3] This plan was accepted in November 2008 and involved defined steps to erase the deficit, to be monitored every three months. Unlike in some of the Southern European programme countries the IMF did not enforce excessive austerity policy in Iceland. The choice of means to eradicate the deficit was up to the government to determine. They could achieve it by cutting expenditures, raising taxes, or both. In fact they did both, in close to equal proportions.

During the summer of 2009 the labour market partners agreed to delay all pay rises until 2010 and drew up a 'Stability Pact' ('Stöðugleikasáttmálinn'), with the government as a third partner. According to this, the role of tax rises or other revenue increases in combatting the deficit should not be more than 45 per cent over the period from 2009 to 2011—as against 55 per cent from expenditure cuts. The role of taxes became larger, according to later claims by the labour market partners.

The pact also defined some characteristics of budgets for 2010 and 2011 and stipulated that the government would provide debt relief measures to aid households and facilitate job creation through large investment projects in industry and infrastructure, for example by negotiating with the OPFs for financing (the OPFs are governed by the labour market partners). Various other goals were stipulated in the pact, some of them quite unrealistic though, since they were beyond the powers of the partners to deliver (such as issues relating to monetary policy, which, of course, were in the care of the Central Bank, such as determining interest rates and influencing the development of the currency).

By August 2011 Iceland graduated from the IMF programme and at a major international conference held by IMF, the Central Bank, and the Icelandic government in Reykjavik in October the same year, the programme and its implementation were hailed as a major success. The upswing had already started at that time, but it still took until 2014 to balance the budget.

The left government lost its majority quite drastically in the elections of 2013. In came the two parties that had prevailed during most of the bubble economy period, (the right-of-centre Independence Party and the centrist Progressive Party). Despite the success of dealing with the crisis and the economic resurrection, the left government had exhausted its energy and

[3] Since Iceland is not a member of the European Union the European Central Bank (ECB) and the European Commission did not have a role in resurrecting the country—there was no 'Troika'! This fact may have influenced the differential policy emphasis in Iceland as against Ireland and Southern Europe to some extent.

goodwill amongst many voters in the battle with the deep-crisis conditions. The left government declared before the elections that they would not support households with their debt problems anymore and instead wanted to concentrate on stability and strengthen the foundations of the economy and governmental finances in the coming term. This sounded like a bad deal to voters, not least when the opposition offered a 20 per cent cut of the principal of all household mortgage debts. That was an offer the voters could not reject: hence the large swing from left to the centre-right (mainly to the centrist Progressive Party) in the election of 2013.

The new government, which lasted until autumn of 2016, will be mainly remembered for three issues. The first was its debt revision programme (more on that in section 8.5.2). The second was the very successful programme for lifting the currency controls in conjunction with a contract with the main claimants to the fallen banks for a major haircut of their claims. This was done in the interest of avoiding a major collapse of the Icelandic krona when the extensive foreign capital that had been locked in the country since November 2008 flowed out again. Due to the currency controls the Icelandic government had a strong bargaining position against foreign claimants, as their assets were stranded in the country. This plan was successfully finalized in 2016 and improved the finances of government by some 15–16 per cent of GDP (see column 5 of Table 8.1). Thereby the government reclaimed most of the cost it had shouldered with the collapse (Jónsson & Sigurgeirsson, 2016).

The third part of the legacy of the new government is what brought it down a whole year before the end of term, namely the fact that both the prime minister and the minister of finance featured in the Panama Papers as significant owners of assets in foreign tax havens, particularly the former. This was more than the voters were prepared to swallow; hence the fall of the government and early elections in October 2016 (see further on other responses to the crisis in various chapters of Ingimundarson et al., 2016).

So while there was clearly a limit to the application of Keynesian stimulus measures as well as for increasing social protection, the Social Democratic government of 2009–13 could target expenditures more towards those with lower incomes and those in more vulnerable positions. It could also shift expenditures from one area to another, such as from services and administration to transfers. It could redistribute the tax burden and equalize other burdens with various measures. This brings us to the strategy of redistribution.

## 8.5 The Strategy of Redistribution

The overall welfare strategy was shaped by the stated goal of the Social Democratic government of 2009 to 2013 to shelter the more vulnerable households. Since resources were indeed limited, the approach had to involve some shifting of resources from one area to another and also a more efficient use of available resources for the most vulnerable groups, even with cuts for the better off. In effect, this involved both a redistribution of available resources and an increased targeting on the worst off. The strategy of redistribution had four major aspects, which we address under the titles of welfare effort, debt relief, activation and job creation, and shifting of the tax burden (from lower to higher income groups).

### 8.5.1 *Welfare effort*

First we look at the shifting of expenditures from one area to another. Welfare transfer expenditures were increased but expenditures on welfare services (mainly health and education) and administration were cut. The increased expenditures on transfers to households were not simply due to the increased unemployment level, as can be seen from Figure 8.2. When expenditures on unemployment are excluded from the data for total transfers they still show a higher real value level during the crisis years. And the welfare transfers were also increasingly directed at the lower income groups. At the same time what previously went to higher income groups was cut. The net effect was a higher level of overall welfare expenditures than ever before in the history of the Icelandic republic, both in real value Icelandic krona and as a per cent of GDP.

So it was a mixed development, with a considerable increase of social protection transfers to households while expenditures on health-care services and education were markedly cut during the crisis. The main factors that contributed to increased expenditures were unemployment benefits (due to increased numbers, extension of rights period, and a modest rise of the benefit level), activation measures, housing cost subsidies, and minimum pension guarantees. The cuts in health care were generally across that sector, except that disability pensioners enjoyed some increase of their minimum pension and services. Hospitals, health-care centres, and subsidies on medication costs and services were all cut. In education the cuts affected all levels, from primary to tertiary education.

As Figure 8.2 shows, the real expenditures on health care and education began to increase again in 2012 (health care) and 2013 (education). Health care got an extra boost in 2016, bringing it to the pre-crisis level (more has been added in 2017 and in the budget for 2018), while education was still, in 2016, below the pre-crisis level. Expenditures on housing support (mainly debt relief) were more than doubled from 2007 to 2011, with an increase of 112 per cent. Since then they have contracted again.

As figures on the aggregate categories of public expenditures are not particularly sensitive to the targeting of expenditures, we provide in Figure 8.3 an

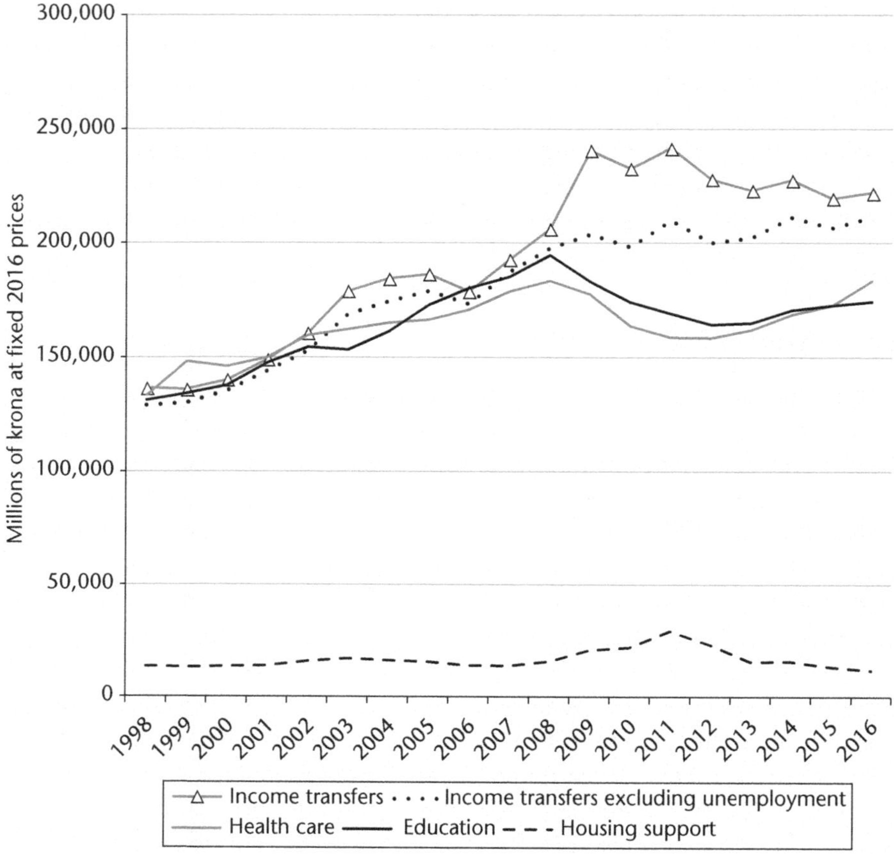


**Figure 8.2.** Development of real public welfare expenditures, by main categories, 1998–2016

*Note*: Shown at fixed 2016 prices.

*Source*: Statistics Iceland.

indication of how payments and benefits primarily aimed at lower income groups increased (in comparison to the average wage index), from the height of the boom to the bottom of the bust.

The minimum pension guarantee for a single old-age pensioner and for single disability pensioners were raised the most, at about the same as the increase in the price index for the period from 2007 to 2010 (about 41 per cent).[4] That means that the pensioners with the very lowest earnings maintained their purchasing power and were in fact kept above the poverty line through the deep crisis years. Social assistance (the ultimate safety net), the

[4] In fact the minimum pension guarantee for old-age and disability pensioners was raised by 20% on the first of January 2009.

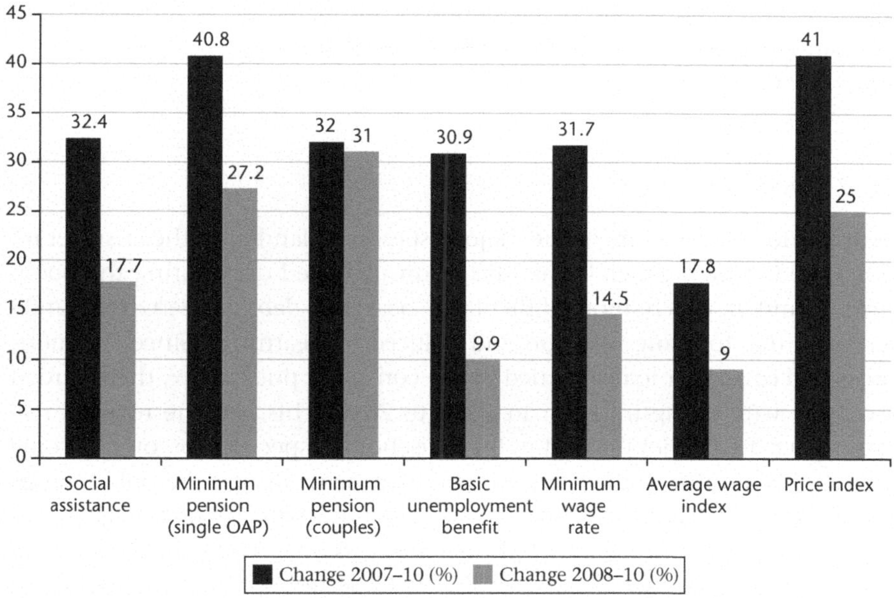


**Figure 8.3.** Development of benefits and wages directed at the lower income groups, 2007–10

*Note*: Includes a comparison to the change of average wage index (in %).

*Source*: Social Security Administration and Statistics Iceland.

basic unemployment benefit, the pension minimum for each member of a pensioner couple, and the minimum wage were all increased in this period by about 32 per cent, while the average wage index (reflecting general wage earners overall) rose by just under 18 per cent. The pattern is similar when looking at the 2008–10 period, but not as marked. Hence the benefits aimed at the lowest earning groups got an extra boost during the crisis.

When compared to the price index we also see that due to inflation (which was caused by the devaluation of the currency) the real purchasing power declined for these groups other than the single lowest earning pensioners.

Another change of importance is the alteration in the duration period for the unemployment benefit. That was first lengthened from two to three years and then later to four years. That was of major importance for long-term unemployed people, the numbers of whom grew at unprecedented speed during the crisis.

Towards the end of its term, the government increased child benefit by some 30 per cent (on 1 January 2013), a move which can be criticized for coming too late. It would have been a valuable addition to the strategy of redistribution earlier in the crisis, since the beneficiaries of the child benefits are often the same people who were amongst the hardest hit by the debt crisis, that is, young families who had bought flats at inflated prices at the height of the bubble, from 2004 to 2008 (Ólafsson & Vignisdóttir, 2012; Stefánsson et al., 2018).

### 8.5.2 *Debt relief*

Debt burden became one of the major issues in Iceland after the crisis set in. Households which generally had taken on increased debt during the boom years found it much more difficult to bear the debt burden from 2009 onwards, due to rising inflation and reduced real earnings. Since the mortgages and consumer loans are tied to the consumer price index, their burden increased with rising inflation in 2008 to 2010. This and the reduced real earnings created major difficulties for households, especially for lower income households and those that had bought apartments during the bubble years (2003–7) at elevated prices, typically young families with children (Ólafsson & Vignisdóttir, 2012; also Ólafsson, Kristjánsson, & Stefánsson, 2012).

The government had pledged to shelter households and therefore had to provide some measures of debt relief. They started early, by making it possible to reschedule repayments or get a temporary freeze on repayments. Soon after, the government introduced more direct measures for cutting housing loan principals of households in the greatest difficulties. Two main measures were featured. The first was a general cut of housing debt for those with debt more than 110 per cent of the value of their flat or house. The principal could be cut down to 110 per cent, capped by the value of a modest family house. The second was for those in gravest difficulties and with very low earnings, involving a special cut down to 70 per cent of the value. Relatively few households got access to the latter measure, but the 110 per cent measure helped a considerable number of households (Ólafsson & Vignisdóttir, 2012).

The household debt level increased rapidly in Iceland during the bubble years, from about 90 per cent of GDP in 2003 to about 124 per cent in 2009. From then on it came down, ending at 76.6 per cent in 2016, a more extensive reduction than in any other OECD country, except Ireland, where it was similar. Denmark had the highest household debt level from 2006 onwards and it came only modestly down from 2009.[5]

The IMF surveyed the debt relief programmes of some Western countries in its staff report on Iceland for 2012 (IMF, 2012). They found that the debt relief measures taken by the Icelandic government were more extensive than other measures taken during the crisis. The only programme they found to

[5] See Central Bank of Iceland, Financial Stability Report 2017, https://www.sedlabanki.is.

be of comparable relative size to the Icelandic one was Franklin D. Roosevelt's debt relief programme from the Great Depression in the USA. No comparable measures were taken in the USA or the UK in the 2008 crisis, nor in Finland or Sweden when they were severely hit by financial crises in the early 1990s.

The other part of the debt relief programmes was the increased subsidy for the housing interest cost of mortgages. Figure 8.4 shows how those were drastically increased during the crisis, after having been eroded gradually from 1995 to 2007. The share of the housing loan interest cost paid by government went from about 13 per cent in 2007 on average to about 35 per cent in 2011. This support was, however, well grounded in the redistribution strategy, giving more support to lower income households than to the median and higher income ones. Thus the households with the lowest income (the lowest decile of income groups) got close to 45 per cent of their housing interest cost paid by government in 2011, while the median household got about a third and the top income group (highest decile) got about 10 per cent or less (Ólafsson, Kristjánsson, & Stefánsson, 2012).

The debt relief measures of the left government (2009–13) were generally hailed as good, including by the IMF, but Icelandic households wanted more support. As remarked, the opposition offered voters a further cut of household mortgage debt principals by 20 per cent across the board, in the run-up to the

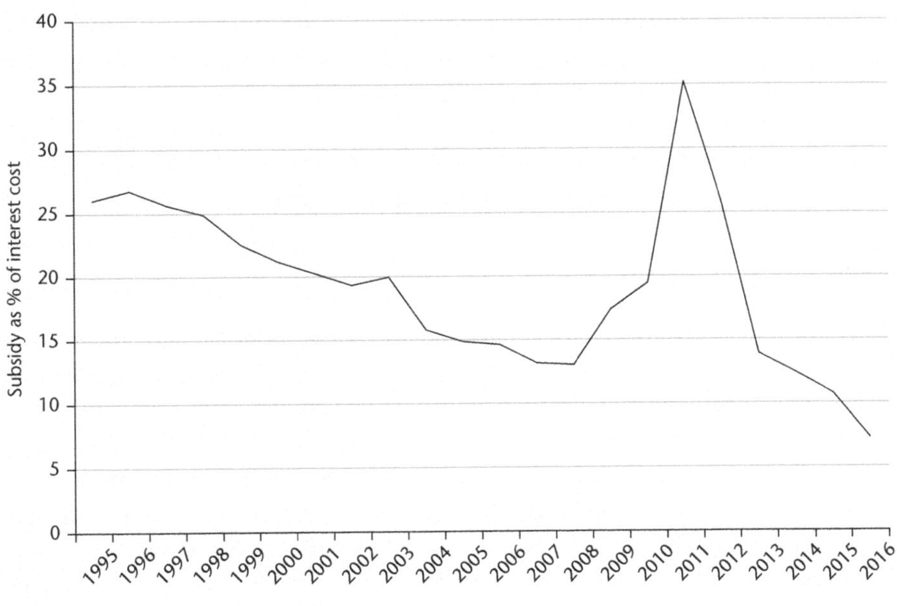


**Figure 8.4.** Average public subsidy of mortgage interest as % of average interest cost in Iceland, 1993–2016
*Source*: Statistics Iceland.

election of 2013. This was indeed a tempting offer, as many middle-income households were still hard-pressed by debt burdens. Hence the two main opposition parties were swept to power. They soon started to work out their new debt relief plan, in order to honour their main election promise.

By the end of 2013 the government introduced its programme in more detail. Half of the promised debt cut would come directly from government, financed by a new tax on financial institutions, including the estates of the fallen banks. The other half would come from the debtors' own voluntary pension savings accounts (Prime Minister's Office, 2013). A ceiling on total support for individual households was set, with the aim of limiting the regressive feature of the programme. The use of private pension savings for down payments of mortgage debt would be tax free, unlike when such savings are taken out as a pension supplement.

The implementation of this programme seems to have attained its goal of reducing household debts by about 20 per cent on average, but since the received support from the previous (left) government was subtracted from the right to the later debt relief programme the regressive character of the latter debt relief programme was considerable, mainly benefiting the middle- and even upper middle-income groups (Ministry of Finance & Economy, 2016).

At the same time, the new government greatly reduced the interest cost subsidy, as can be seen in Figure 8.4. That support, which was heavily targeted at households with lower incomes and less equity in their accommodation, has been at a historically low level since 2013, even though housing prices have increased to a historically high level in the last few years. Thus this part of the redistribution strategy was scaled back after 2012.

To sum up: the debt relief programmes of the two governments that reigned from 2009 to 2016 have provided considerable debt relief to households in general, probably more extensive than seen elsewhere.

### 8.5.3 *Activation and job creation*

Despite a significant loss of jobs there was still some room for activation from early on in the crisis, as a sizable part of the population emigrated after the onset of the crisis. Immigrants returned to their countries of origin to some extent (about a fifth of those that had come to Iceland between 2004 and 2008 returned to their country of origin) and Icelandic natives moved in considerable numbers to Norway, where the employment situation continued to be good. Altogether about 1.5 per cent of Icelandic natives went to Norway (Ólafsson, 2014). This created some job opportunities for those on the unemployment register.

The government also took various initiatives to maintain employment and create jobs. Amongst these were investments in various maintenance and infrastructure projects. An example was the full construction of the extravagant Harpa music hall in Reykjavik (which had been started before the crisis, but was only a skeleton when the banks fell). For such projects the government could use borrowed funds from the OPFs. The funds also set up an investment corporation to channel their investments into Icelandic firms, including by refinancing and taking ownership shares. The pension funds could not invest abroad due to the currency restrictions in force from late 2008 to 2016 and this made a big difference for restructuring and expanding the Icelandic economy when such a stimulus was badly needed. In a sense this was a special form of 'privatized Keynesianism', since the OPFs were not a part of the public sector, but owned by members of the funds (all working people) and managed by the labour market partners (see Crouch (2009) for a different version of 'privatized Keynesianism').

The government also provided tax incentives to owners of accommodation if they engaged in maintenance and restructuring projects on their own houses (including on second-home country cabins). This was meant to stimulate work for skilled and unskilled manual workers and proved to be a great success.

It is quite clear from official data that the activation measures were drastically increased. Prior to the crisis Iceland had for decades enjoyed very high employment participation rates and low unemployment. Hence the need for active labour market policies (ALMPs) was not greatly felt and such measures remained modest. Programmes promoting educational participation were offered to the unemployed from 2009 onwards, including long-term study in secondary schools and special educational tracks. These increased in scope up to 2011 when they peaked in terms of numbers of participants. There were also various efforts to facilitate employment, with the use of a wage subsidy from the Unemployment Insurance Fund; these peaked in 2012.

The Directorate of Labour, with its public employment offices, successfully aimed to involve all those on the unemployment register—some of which took part in many lines of activation measures.[6] In-work or rehabilitation measures were also stepped up from 2009.

An evaluation survey of those registered as unemployed from 2009 to November 2013 indicated that about 75 per cent of those that had taken part in ALMPs were back in employment or education by December 2013 (Maskína, 2014). It seems clear that the activation measures and related labour market efforts were quite successful in Iceland and greatly helped to alleviate the negative consequences of the crisis. Since unemployment generally hits the lower income groups hardest this support for re-employment benefitted those groups disproportionally.

[6] The participation was over 100% in 2010–12 since some of the unemployed took part in more than one type of activity (Ólafsson, 2016b).

But the largest impact for creating new jobs at this trying time was the great expansion of the tourist industry, which flourished after the early years of the crisis, particularly after 2010, following the large devaluation of the krona which made Iceland much more affordable as a tourist destination. That expansion has continued to the time of writing, making the tourist industry by now the largest earner of export revenues. So the political economy conditions were indeed very favourable, mainly due to the booming tourist trade.[7]

### 8.5.4 *Shifting the tax burden*

The last part of the redistribution strategy is taxation policy. As seen in Figure 8.5 the direct tax burden was greatly lowered on the top income groups from about 1995 to 2007, while the burden on middle and lower income groups was significantly increased. This was a consequence of the prevailing neoliberal policies and the great expansion of financial incomes during the bubble years—financial incomes were taxed more lightly than employment and pension incomes. Financial incomes primarily went to the top income groups and when they became a rapidly growing part of overall top incomes the tax burden of high income earners was significantly lowered.

The increased tax burden of the lower and middle-income groups was mainly due to the reduced value of the personal tax allowance (which was greatly lowered in value from 1995 to 2004, thus enlarging the taxable part of lower income earners' pay). Child benefits and interest rate subsidies were also greatly reduced, similarly increasing the tax burden of the lower income groups.[8]

The Social Democratic government of 2009 to 2013 reversed this policy and greatly increased the tax burden of the higher income groups, while actually reducing the tax burden of the lower and middle-income groups towards 2010. This was done by introducing higher tax brackets on higher incomes, by doubling the financial incomes tax rate (which primarily impacted on the top income groups), and by implementing a special wealth tax on large assets. Increased benefits and personal tax allowances lowered the burden on the lower and middle-income groups, even if only modestly.

As a result the real direct tax burden for the lowest earning 60 per cent of households was reduced while it was increased for the top 40 per cent, more

[7] While the tourist boom was fundamentally facilitated by the large devaluation, the government of 2009–13 made an effort to promote Iceland as a tourist destination, for example with a wide-ranging and influential campaign called 'Inspired by Iceland!' A prominent volcanic eruption in Eyjafjallajökull glacier in 2010 also made the news all over the world, which seems to have aroused interest in the country. Hence devaluation, luck, and active promotions all contributed to the rapid growth of tourism during the crisis years.

[8] These benefits are subtracted from the calculated tax. When reduced in value the effective tax burden increases, most decisively for the lowest income groups. For more details, see Ólafsson and Kristjánsson (2017).

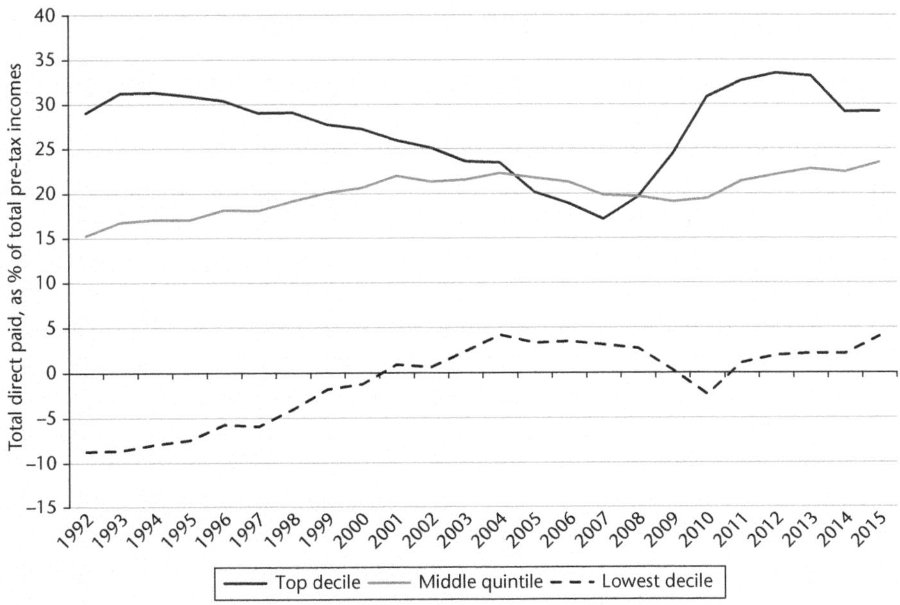


**Figure 8.5.** The shifting tax burden before and after the crisis hit

*Note*: Shows direct taxes paid, as a % of total pre-tax incomes. Analysed by main income groups: lowest and highest deciles and the middle quintile, 1992 to 2015.

*Source*: Ólafsson and Kristjánsson (2017).

greatly the higher up the income scale one went. The change was greatest for the top 1 per cent of income earners, a shift from 13 per cent direct tax burden up to 33.3 per cent. This change in the distribution of the direct tax burden was a major reversal of the trend that had prevailed for the 12 years prior to the crisis, as Figure 8.5 clearly shows.

With growing incomes after 2011, the tax-reducing effect of the benefits that particularly favoured the lower and middle-income groups were eroded somewhat again. Then the new government of 2013 abolished the special wealth tax, with effect from 2014 onwards. That reduced the overall tax burden of the top income group. On the whole the policy on direct taxation played a significant role in the overall strategy of redistribution.

## 8.6 Impact and Outcomes: How the Burdens were Shared

### 8.6.1 *Equalization*

The logical consequence of the strategy of redistribution is that income distribution should have become more equal during the crisis years. The welfare expenditures, the debt relief measures, the activation and job creation measures as well as the shifting of the tax burden all had an equalization effect. In that sense the strategy of redistribution is a strategy of equalization.

As we showed with OECD data in Chapter 2, Iceland appears to have been in a class of its own as regards equalization of the income distribution during the height of the crisis. According to Eurostat data, the Gini index for household equivalized disposable earnings declined by 18.9 per cent between 2008 and 2011, while it came down by 9.9 per cent in the runner-up country (Lithuania), which was also a deep-crisis country. The next two in line were, however, only modestly affected by the crisis, namely the Netherlands and Norway, with about 6 per cent reduction of the Gini coefficient. The UK and Portugal also reduced inequality. In contrast, inequality increased in a number of deep-crisis countries during the crisis years, such as Spain, Estonia, Cyprus, and Greece.

Prior to the crisis, income inequality had been increasing fast in Iceland, in fact all the way from 1995 to a peak in 2007, just before the bubble burst. The Gini index of inequality for disposable earnings, with all taxable incomes counted, went from 0.21 to 0.43 in 2007, an unprecedented speed of change in OECD countries.[9] Then it came down again to about 0.25 in 2010–12—also an unprecedented reversal of trend.[10] A part of the reversal towards greater equality was due to a decline of financial earnings during the crisis, but a sizable effect was due to the changed governmental strategy of tax and benefits policies.

The strategy of redistribution thus ensured that the average cut in real earnings for the household sector was softened by tax and benefit policies, so that the cut in living standards for the lower income groups was significantly less than the average, while the highest income group lost much more than the average. This can be seen in Figure 8.6.

The real disposable earnings of the lowest two deciles (the lowest earning 20 per cent of households) lost about 9 per cent while the median households lost 14 per cent and the top decile lost 38 per cent of their earnings level of 2008.

While the overall setback for economic living standards was large by any standards, it was a fall from a great height. The level of living was generally quite high before the crisis hit, not least due to the overrated Icelandic krona during the boom years (making imports more affordable). The real wage index started to come up again in the latter part of 2010 and more decisively from 2011. From 2014 the increase of real disposable income has been quite forceful (cf. Table 8.1).

[9] This is based on Icelandic tax data, counting all taxable income, including capital gains. The only incomes missing are those evading tax, including by use of foreign tax havens. See Ólafsson and Kristjánsson (2013, 2017).

[10] If we instead look at the OECD and Eurostat Gini coefficients for equivalized disposable earnings, *excluding capital gains*, the story is the same, but at a lower inequality level, as the inclusion of capital gains primarily adds to the top incomes (Ólafsson & Kristjánsson, 2013, 2017).

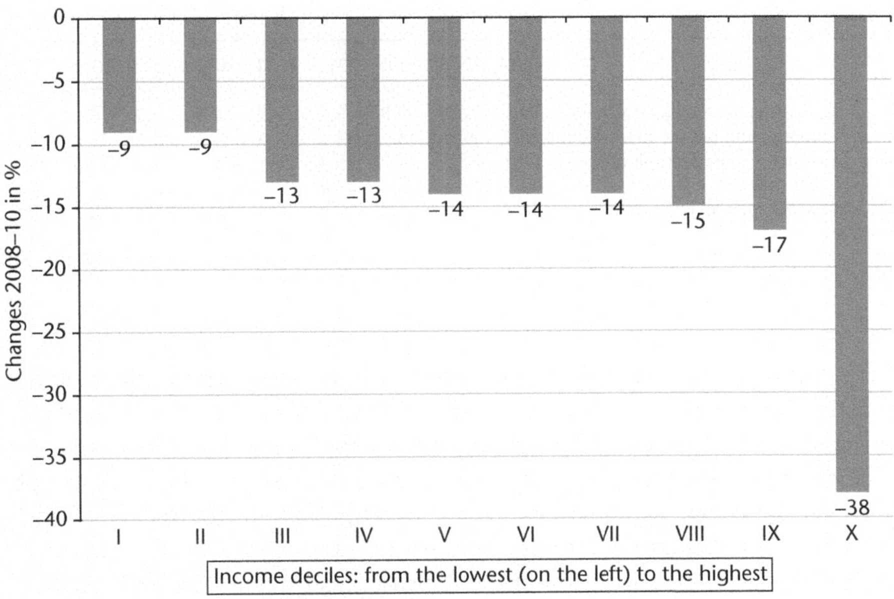


**Figure 8.6.** Change in real disposable earnings by income deciles

*Note*: Ranges from pre-crisis level of 2008 to the bottom at 2010. The income concept is all taxable incomes after tax and benefits.

*Source*: Icelandic tax data, Ólafsson & Kristjánsson (2012).

## 8.6.2 *Poverty reduction effort*

Lastly we assess the poverty reduction effort further, with classical Eurostat data on relative poverty rates (based on the 60 per cent median cut-off point), both yearly nominal rates and using the fixed real value poverty line of 2005 throughout (anchored). The anchored poverty rate takes more account of changes in income levels and shows an outcome that is more in line with the proportion of respondents that say they have great difficulty in making ends meet (see Table 8.2).

The relative poverty rates, after all transfers (including pensions; cf. row 1 in Table 8.2) show a decrease during the crisis years, after having remained more or less at around 10 per cent from 2003 to 2008. This reflects the fact, which we have already shown, that the disposable incomes of the lowest income groups contracted less than those of the median and higher incomes. By comparing that to the pre-transfer rate we get an estimate of the poverty reduction effort of the welfare system. There we see that pre-transfer poverty increased significantly during the crisis (from 27 per cent to 34–5 per cent), while the decline of the post-transfer rate indicates a greater efficiency in reducing poverty after the crisis (as shown in rows 3 and 4 of the table).

**Table 8.2.** Poverty reduction effort and difficulties making ends meet, 2007–15

| | 2007 | 2008 | 2009 | 2010 | 2011 | 2012 | 2013 | 2014 | 2015 |
|---|---|---|---|---|---|---|---|---|---|
| Relative poverty rate after all transfers | 10.1 | 10.2 | 9.8 | 9.2 | 7.9 | 9.3 | 7.9 | 9.6 | 8.8 |
| Relative poverty rate before all transfers | 26.9 | 27.4 | 33 | 34.6 | 34.4 | 34.4 | 32.5 | 32.4 | 30 |
| Poverty reduction (percentage points) | 16.8 | 17.2 | 23.2 | 25.4 | 26.5 | 25.1 | 24.6 | 22.8 | 21.2 |
| Poverty reduction (in %) | 62.5 | 62.8 | 70.3 | 73.4 | 77 | 73 | 75.7 | 70.4 | 70.7 |
| Great difficulty making ends meet | 5.2 | 5 | 7.8 | 12.8 | 12.3 | 10.6 | 11.7 | 8.9 | 8.6 |
| Relative poverty rate anchored in 2005 | 6.1 | 7 | 9.7 | 11.6 | 13.2 | 12.5 | 8 | 8.0 | 5.1 |

*Source*: Eurostat.

The net poverty reduction went from around 17 up to 26.5 percentage points in 2011 (a proportional reduction of about 63 per cent to 77 per cent), and this has come down to about 21 percentage points (or 71 per cent) since then.

Relative poverty rates, based on the yearly nominal poverty rate, do not, however, reflect the experience of the general public during the crisis years. Most people felt increasing financial hardship (as our measures in Figure 8.1 indeed show). Hence we show more realistic measures in the lower part of Table 8.2. Those saying they only make ends meet with great difficulty went from about 5 per cent up to nearly 13 per cent in 2010, before coming down to just under 9 per cent in 2015—still higher than before the crisis started. A similar pattern emerges from the anchored poverty rate, which gives a more realistic impression of the changing income poverty rates during the crisis than the nominal relative rates.

This outcome is in harmony with relatively good results in averting unemployment and protecting the lowest income groups, and it hence supports our impact analysis of the strategy of redistribution.

## 8.7 Conclusions

Despite suffering a major financial collapse and economic recession, Iceland appears to have done relatively well in its recovery phase. The crisis bottomed out by mid-year 2010 and from then on growth has been significantly above the EU average. The record in combatting unemployment is even better. All the other countries that went deep into the financial crisis (Ireland, Spain, Portugal, Greece, the Baltic States) suffered considerably higher unemployment rates. Even Sweden and Finland experienced higher unemployment rates than Iceland, despite their more modest contraction of GDP. The Icelandic unemployment rate also came down faster after 2010 and has, since 2014, been amongst the very lowest in Europe.

In this chapter we analysed Iceland's strategy of dealing with the crisis consequences in the context of policy debates about Keynesian-style stimulus and austerity measures (Blyth, 2013; Krugman, 2012; Skidelsky, 2010). We then mapped the characteristics of the Icelandic approach and found that there were elements of both stimulus and austerity policies. Governmental finances were particularly under strain at the start of the crisis, but the welfare system was still strategically used to soften the worst consequences of the crisis for levels of living.

The main characteristic of the Icelandic crisis management strategy is what we call the strategy of redistribution. This is exemplified by the fact that welfare expenditures were both increased and cut (depending on types), but the primary emphasis was on redistributing them so that they would benefit the lower income groups to the greatest extent, while benefits were cut for higher income groups.

These strategies succeeded in softening the relative cuts in living standards of the lower income groups while cutting earnings in the higher income groups. The latter also lost significant financial earnings that had increased greatly during the boom years prior to the crisis. Activation measures and job creation programmes were greatly stepped up and proved very successful in combatting unemployment.

Given the low generosity of child benefits in the pre-crisis situation in Iceland we suggest that the government might have done better by increasing the benefit more well before the end of their period (which was 2013), as young families with children were particularly hard hit with an increased debt burden early in the crisis period. The cuts in welfare services (health and education) worked well at the beginning but gradually became of greater concern as quality standards reduced. This concern has been very prominent in the very last years and even up to the time of writing.

The redistribution strategy was a good addition to Keynesian-style stimulus measures, as the lower income groups give better impetus to private consumption by spending most of what they have—unlike higher income groups. This strategy thus facilitated a higher level of demand than otherwise would have prevailed. That, along with the devaluation of the currency, is likely to have helped in keeping the unemployment rate low and facilitating renewed growth.

Iceland's strategy was not just a more equitable way of dealing with deep crisis by sheltering the more vulnerable in society to a greater extent than in most other deep-crisis countries. It was also a good economic crisis management strategy.

# 9

# Finland

## From the Deep Crisis of the 1990s to the Great Recession

*Olli Kangas*

### 9.1 Background: The Two Crises

The 1980s was the heyday of the Finnish welfare state. The booming economy allowed the government to improve the main transfer schemes and expand social services. The liberalization of the banking sector and the financial markets in the 1980s created a credit bubble. International lending fuelled the economy: the level of investments increased rapidly and easy access to housing loans caused housing prices to explode. Towards the end of the 1980s, prices had more than doubled in five years (Korhonen, 2011, pp. 11–14). The end of the boom was abrupt and dramatic. Due to economic problems in major Western countries, Finland's exports to the West ran into severe difficulties. The collapse of the Soviet Union suddenly nullified exports to the East, which had amounted to 15–20 per cent of the total export volume. A tight fiscal policy, combined with a strong currency policy, led to increased interest rates and ruined the competitiveness of Finnish export-oriented enterprises.

These developments resulted in a situation called the 'Great Depression', which lasted from 1990 to 1994. To improve the international competitiveness of the Finnish industry the government carried out a devaluation of the Finnish markka by about 40 per cent. Simultaneously, the Finnish information and communication technology (ICT) sector experienced explosive growth from then on, not least due to the success of Nokia. Nokia's share of the total value of production and hours worked in Finland were 6 per cent and 7 per cent respectively around 1995, but by year 2000 they were 18 per cent and 21 per cent (Pohjola, 2014). Consequently, the latter part of the 1990s was characterized by strong economic recovery. The flip side of this strong economic tide was that it did not lift all boats equally: unemployment stayed at a high level and income inequalities expanded rapidly (see Blomgren et al., 2014).

When the first signs of the international crisis in 2008 became visible, the Finnish minister of finance, later prime minister and commissioner in the European Union, Mr Jyrki Katainen, believed that the crisis would not concern Finland. The Finnish economy and state finances were in a good shape. However, the optimism was very much premature (see Figure 9.1). Finland is a small and open national economy that is exposed to international economic cycles and cannot avoid turbulence in the world market. No wonder that the 2008 crisis hit the country badly. Since then, gross domestic product (GDP) growth has been very weak, unemployment has increased, and domestic demand is being held back by rising unemployment, low-income growth, and weak consumer confidence. For nine years, the national budget has been running a deficit. The municipal finances have been in deficit for even longer. Consequently, the public debt has exceeded the critical 60 per cent threshold required by the Euro's Stability and Growth Pact. In these circumstances, Juha Sipilä's centre-to-right government (nominated 29 May 2015) launched austerity measures aimed at balancing the budget, seeking cuts in various places, and planning structural reforms to meet future sustainability challenges for the welfare state.

The aim of this chapter is to describe the causes and consequences of these two crises in the Finnish economy: the deep depression in the early 1990s and the post-2008 recession. There are many similarities and some differences in the causes, the characteristics, and the depth of the crises, as well as in the measures prescribed for the economy to recover. The structure of this chapter is as follows. First, we survey the anatomy of the crises. Section 9.3 deals with crisis management strategies. Section 9.4 analyses changes in the social policy system and taxation, while section 9.5 concentrates on the social and economic consequences of the two crises in Finland. Section 9.6 summarizes our key findings and provides some thoughts on the future of Finland's economic situation.

## 9.2 The Anatomy of the Two Crises

Economic and social policy developments in the 1980s and 1990s were strikingly different. While the GDP growth in 1989 was close to 5.4 per cent, it dropped to −6.3 per cent two years later. Unemployment skyrocketed from 3 per cent in 1990 to 17 per cent in 1994. Although major income transfer schemes were cut, social spending expanded from 23 per cent in 1990 to 30 per cent in 1995. The state budget ran a deficit for seven consecutive years and the public debt increased from 14 per cent of the GDP in 1989 to 56 per cent in 1994 (see Figure 9.1).

The second half of the 1990s witnessed a strong recovery and a booming economy. The average annual GDP growth was 5 per cent, which was primarily a result of the growth of the information and communication sector, with Nokia as a flagship. The devaluation of the Finnish markka by 40 per cent facilitated the rapid recovery of the export sector. As early as 1992, the volume of exports increased by 10 per cent. This recovery led to a fundamental shift in the composition of the labour market as well, as it led to serious imbalances in the supply and demand of labour (Vartiainen, 2011). Unemployment did not decrease in lockstep with the growth of the economy, and the labour market simultaneously faced a high level of long-term unemployment due to the vanishing of traditional industries and a lack of skilled labour in the new high-tech sector.

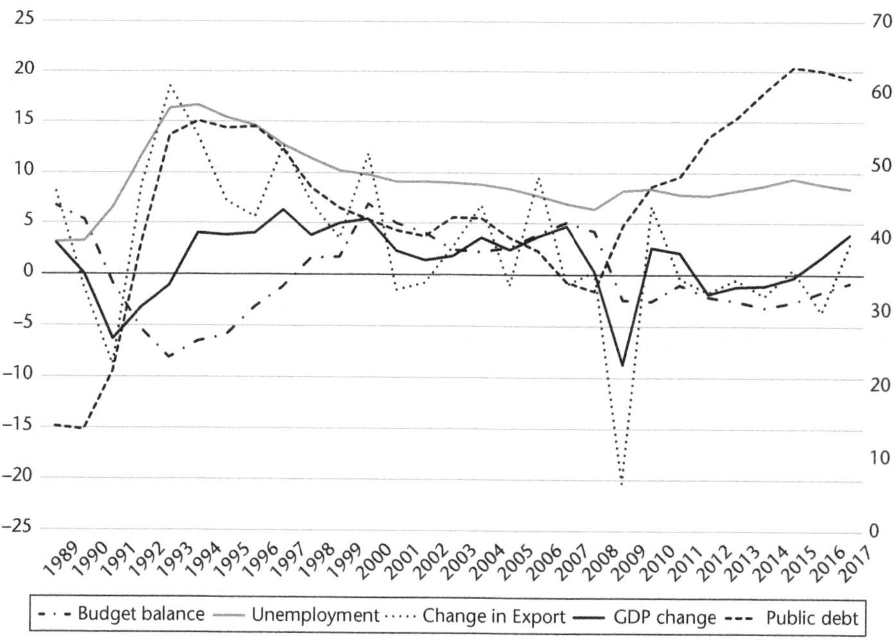


**Figure 9.1.** Economic indicators of the deep crisis of the 1990s and the post-2008 recession

*Note*: Balance of the national budget (% of GDP), change of the real GDP (%), change of the export volume (%), and unemployment rate (%) on the left-hand axis; public debt (% of GDP) on the right-hand axis.

*Source*: Kiander (2001); Statistics Finland (2005, p. 251; 2017, p. 93); http://findikaattori.fi/en/44; Statistics Finland, General government debt and deficit, Statistics Finland, Imports and exports, http://findikaattori.fi/en/table/80; Statistics Finland, Unemployment rate, http://findikaattori.fi/en/34.

The international financial crisis, the Great Recession, which originated from the problems in the US banking sector, gradually made landfall in Europe. Contrary to the optimistic scenario painted by the Finnish government in 2008, the crisis also hit Finland. In 2009, the GDP declined by 8 per cent, but grew by more than 2 per cent again in 2011. However, the hope that the depression might be over was premature. During the early 2010s, the growth rate was very weak. Exports remained subdued. The global demand for capital goods in the Western market weakened and exports to Russia collapsed as a result of the Western embargo against Russia due to the annexation of the Crimean Peninsula. Simultaneously, domestic demand was being held back by rising unemployment, low-income growth, people's weak confidence in the economy, and their inclination to save and pay back housing loans rather than to make new purchases. The unemployment rate increased—albeit much more modestly than in the early 1990s. Nevertheless, social spending rose from 25 per cent of GDP in 2005 to 31 per cent in 2015. Needless to say, while the social protection system provides financial security and help for the unemployed and other crisis-stricken sectors of the population, the flip side of the coin is deterioration in the sustainability of the welfare state. Finland has a long-standing public sector deficit, and in 2017 the public debt exceeded the EU warning level of 60 per cent of GDP.

There are many similarities between the 1990s and the post-2008 crisis. In both cases there was an economic recession in important Western markets, while exports to the East simultaneously decreased. In the 1990s, the reason for this was the collapse of the Soviet economy, and after 2008 the problems were again caused by the collapse of exports to Russia. The Western embargo on Russia in particular caused problems for the food-processing industry, for which Russia was a substantial market. The post-2008 crisis was reinforced by the decline in the ICT sector in the wake of the Nokia collapse. The Nokia case is indicative of the Finnish industrial structure as a whole: a few big companies dominate the market and if they run into problems the whole national economy is imperilled.

In addition to macroeconomic problems, in the two to three decades from 2018 the rapid ageing of the population will bring about demands to increase income transfers and social services targeted at the greying population. The sustainability deficit is a device to evaluate the severity of these demands. It estimates the ability of a welfare state to maintain its current social policy programmes, spending levels, tax, and other policies in the decades to come. On the basis of these estimates, it is possible to forecast what the needs are for long-term tax increases or benefit cuts in order to maintain government solvency (providing that no policy changes are made). The size of the required adjustment is usually indicated as a percentage of the GDP. Despite all the uncertainties linked to such long-term prognoses, they give a hint about the magnitude of the reforms required to reconcile projected revenues with expenditures. Finland's sustainability deficit is in the range of 3 per cent to 9 per cent, depending on who is making the calculations.[1] The concept of the sustainability deficit has been an effective weapon in the post-2008 political discourse in Finland. It has been used successfully to justify austerity measures and to cut down on public spending (Kangas, Palme, & Kainu, 2017).

## 9.3 Policy Responses Then and Now

### 9.3.1 *Muddling through the depression of the 1990s*

The crisis in the 1990s changed Finland's industrial structure. While the stagnation in international trade with the West halted exports from the paper, metal, and electronic sectors, the collapse of trade with the Soviet Union hit the textile industry, which virtually disappeared in the turmoil of the depression. The German Central Bank raised its interest rates, which raised the costs of the currency loans that had been taken out in the wake of the liberalization of the financial markets in the 1980s. Borrowed money turned out to be too expensive and even healthy enterprises ran into difficulties. Bankruptcy proceedings increased from the 'normal' level of 2,500 a year (in the 1980s) to over 7,000 in 1992 (Statistics Finland, 2013, p. 575). Exports suddenly stopped, domestic consumption shrank, the economy contracted massively, and unemployment skyrocketed.

The centre-to-right government of Centre Party leader Esko Aho (1991–5) tried to bring about an 'internal devaluation', that is, wage cuts to increase the external competitiveness of the economy. However, neither the strong metal- and wood-processing unions nor the employers, who regarded the measures as insufficient, accepted a proposed agreement. Gradually, pressures from the global actors became too strong and the currency (markka) had to be devalued by 40 per cent against the German mark and the US dollar. The record high unemployment had the effect of harnessing inflation, which had previously been associated with the economic growth brought about by devaluations. The devaluation rapidly improved the profitability of the export sector, but the economic tide did not raise all boats equally. Income inequalities grew rapidly due to these imbalances, cuts in social benefits, and the differing taxation of work income and capital income, that is, the lower taxation of the latter. Thus, at the same time, there was an increase in factor income inequality and a decrease in the redistributive effects of the transfer and tax systems (Tuomala, 2017).

[1] The sustainability deficit varies from the low figures of Germany (1.4%), France (1.9%), and Sweden (2.4%) to a deficit of almost 10% in Belgium.

The two consecutive 'rainbow' coalitions led by the Social Democrat Paavo Lipponen (1995–2003, consisting of the Social Democratic Party (SDP), the Conservative Party, the Left Wing League, the Swedish People's Party (SPP), and the Greens) tried to combat the expanding public deficit and debt by cutting almost all social benefits. Most income transfer schemes were cut and access to benefits was made more restrictive. Some minimum daily allowances and the universal flat-rate portion of the national pension were abolished, and the national pension was changed to be fully tested against employment-related pensions. Furthermore, the period for calculating the earnings-related pension was extended from the last four years in employment to the last ten. The general idea was not to change the basic structure of the Finnish welfare state, but to make it leaner. The unintended consequence of this was that the welfare state also became meaner towards the lower income groups, as will be seen in Figure 9.3 in section 9.4.1.

### 9.3.2 *The post-2008 recession*

As the US banking crisis gradually expanded to Europe, country after country started running into problems. During the 2007 electoral campaign, the Conservatives wanted to create a new image of themselves as the biggest workers' party. First of all, they wanted to get votes from the expanding lower white-collar and non-manual workers. They created a fictive 'Sari the Nurse', a person who deserved a pay raise of at least €500 a month. The nurses' conservative-led trade union, the Union of Health and Social Care Professionals (Tehy), took this proposed alliance seriously and in the wage negotiations—which were carried out decentrally at the union level this time, rather than in the form of the traditional centralized bargaining—Tehy set a very high baseline for wage increases. In response, the strong male-dominated unions then demanded much better deals as well. The employers were happy to oblige in order to show that decentralized union-based bargains were better than centralized top-level labour market agreements. In these circumstances, where Eurozone membership meant that Finland was unable to manipulate its currency using devaluations to solve its problem of international competitiveness—as it had done before—the 2007–8 wage increases appeared to be too expensive. Once again, they would erode Finland's competitiveness, as had happened in the early 1990s.

The cabinet of Centre Party leader Matti Vanhanen (2007–10), consisting of the Centre Party, the Conservatives, the Greens, and the SPP, adopted austerity policies to try to keep public finances sustainable, and aimed for balanced central government finances and restrictions in public spending. Population ageing was one starting point for planning economic and social policies. While the Lipponen SDP-led governments of the early 1990s had also cut basic social security benefits, the emphasis in Vanhanen's Centre-led government was to fortify basic social security. Thus the old social policy divide between the SDP's emphasis on worker insurance and the Centre's inclination towards 'basic security' was reinforced (see Kangas, 2006; Kangas, Niemelä, & Varjonen, 2014).

The Vanhanen government set up a special committee to evaluate the structure and adequacy of basic social security. The goals of the committee were ambitious, including a gradual movement towards a basic income system. The results were more modest. Most of the reforms were paralysed by joint opposition from representatives of the employer federation and the trade unions. In their joint contract—which came as a surprise to the rest of the committee—the social partners agreed upon on a 'Social Policy Incomes Policy Pact'. This pact included abolishing the employers' contributions to the national pension scheme, which was a direct subsidy by employers. The magnitude of this subsidy was about 1 billion euros; this sum was to be paid, instead, directly from the state budget—which at the time was about €50 billion. The 'pact' precluded the possibility of implementing any of the other major reforms the committee had planned. However, the government decided to introduce a guaranteed pension, payable after the pension income test, to low-income pensioners. This new pension became effective just a month before the parliamentary elections in 2011. It increased the level of minimum pension by about 15 per cent, making it the biggest single improvement in the national pension system.

In return, the prime minister proposed raising the retirement age from 63 to 65 in the employment-related pension scheme, which had been reformed in 2005. His idea was immediately strongly opposed by the Central Organisation of Finnish Trade Unions. The prime minister had to withdraw his proposal, which indicates the powerful position of social partners in Finnish social policymaking, especially in matters of pension policy. The Finnish employment-related pension system is run by private pension insurance companies that are jointly administered by social partners. Therefore, the social partners have an institutional veto on matters of pension politics. If, in the Scandinavian countries, politics have been used against markets (Esping-Andersen, 1985), then in Finland labour markets have been often used against politics (see Kangas, 2007).

### 9.3.3 *Austerity in the 2010s*

The cabinet negotiations after the 2011 elections were difficult. Finally, the Conservative Party leader, Jyrki Katainen, managed to build an 'unholy' coalition cabinet, in which the Conservatives, the SDP, the Greens, the Left Alliance, the SPP, and the Christian Democrats (CD) participated. The European financial crisis greatly influenced the work of this cabinet. Furthermore, the wide political spectrum of the various parties featured conflicting policy goals, which eroded the Katainen cabinet's ability to act effectively. For example, whereas the Conservatives and the SDP were willing to curb the home-care allowance (a cash-for-care system for parents of children younger than 3) in order to enhance female employment, the CD forcefully opposed this idea. The SDP did not accept raising the pension age, but agreed that a special committee working under the social partners could be nominated to prepare a new pension reform. When the cabinet decided to lower the corporate tax rate from 24.5 to 20 per cent, the Left Alliance strongly disagreed. As a result, and due to broader disagreements on the austerity policies, the Alliance left the cabinet. Katainen eventually stepped down as the party leader and instead became an EU commissioner. The new leader of the Conservative Party, Alexander Stubb, was appointed prime minister in June 2014. However, his prime ministership lasted only a year and after the 2015 elections the Centre Party Leader, Juha Sipilä, formed a coalition cabinet with the True Finns and the Conservatives (29 May 2015).

The Sipilä government prescribed tough austerity measures to secure the sustainability of public finances. In order to stop debt financing, the government committed to making the necessary savings and structural reforms, prioritizing social and health-care reform (SOTE) and finalizing pension reform. The government aimed to carry out cuts totalling €6 billion by 2021. In addition to direct cuts, amounting to €4 billion, the government decided on an extra €1.5 billion in cuts and tax increases, in case the 'social contract' (as explained later in this chapter) was not accepted by social partners. In the care services, reallocations were made to enhance informal care and to limit the universal right to full-time childcare. Rhetorically, these measures were presented to the public by emphasizing the creation of a public–private partnership (PPP), opening up public services for private competition and, at the individual level, giving people more opportunities to make their own decisions. Furthermore, user fees were increased in municipal health-care and day-care services.

Interestingly enough, the priorities of Sipilä's centre-to-right cabinet regarding childcare differed from the two previous 'rainbow coalitions'. The previous cabinets planned to limit the home-care allowance period, in order to increase the labour market supply of mothers. However, they did not have enough political power (or courage) to carry out this reform. The Sipilä government—following the centrist policy line and the True Finns' rhetoric about traditional families—is, as of 2018, moving forward with significant cuts in the public day-care system and emphasizing the greater responsibility of parents.

Soon after his nomination, Prime Minister Sipilä called the social partners to negotiate a broad agreement on wages, working hours, and terms of employment. The prime minister planned that by means of this 'social contract' the annual work volume would be increased by 100 hours per employee without any extra compensation. The alternative was a wage cut by at least 5 per cent. The purpose of this agreement was to improve the international competitiveness of the Finnish economy. Thus, it repeated Esko Aho's idea of internal devaluation from the early phases of the deep depression of the 1990s. Whereas the Employer Federation welcomed the initiative, the trade unions were largely sceptical, saying that the burden would fall too heavily on the employees. The 'social contract' pact never materialized as such. But after long and difficult negotiations, the Competitiveness Agreement was reached, which included lengthening the annual working time by 24 hours, increasing employees' social security contributions by 2.1 percentage points, and correspondingly reducing employers' social security contributions. In return, the government promised employees tax reductions totalling €0.5 billion. It appears these tax reductions, which are supposed to fuel the economy, have coincided with an economic boost and hence are pro-cyclically accelerating economic growth.

In income transfers, the biggest cuts are, as of 2018, taking place via direct cuts and the freezing of indexes. All basic social benefits except social assistance are subject to freezing. In the long run, the measures will yield substantial savings in public spending, but it is questionable to what extent social assistance will compensate for the inadequate level of other basic social benefits. This will mean a gradual shift from universalism towards a more conditional and targeted social policy model.

It is not only central government that is cutting benefits but local governments—that is, municipalities, which currently provide the lion's share of social services—are applying austerity measures when trying to solve their economic problems. Too often, solutions have been based on practical short-term cameralistic bookkeepers' considerations, geared towards balancing the budget, and neglect long-term social investment perspectives. Municipalities concentrate on those measures they are legally obligated to adopt. Consequently, they emphasize spending on 'heavy' services—that is, child protection measures such as foster homes and child custody services—instead of 'light' investment-like services, such as home help and support for families. For example, while in the late 1990s some 60,000 families got home help, as of 2018 this is only 10,000 families, and, correspondingly, costs for 'heavy' measures have tripled. Some municipalities have made successful efforts to reverse this vicious cycle and, by investing more in home help and family services, have been able to considerably cut expenditures on more costly child protection measures. These innovative municipalities show that it is possible to cut costs without jeopardizing social investment objectives and vice versa (Kangas & Kalliomaa-Puha, 2016).

There are also some large structural changes taking place in Finnish social policy. The pension reform, which was planned by an expert group (Eläkekysymysten asiantuntijatyöryhmän raportti, 2013) and approved by the social partners, became effective in 2017. It combats the costs of the rising number of pensioners and the increasing life expectancy. The reform introduced a 'double link': the pension age will be linked to increasing life expectancy, and there will be a lifetime coefficient. The lower pension age will be 65 and the higher one 70. The pension accrual rate is 1.5 per cent for each year in employment (previously 1.5 per cent for those younger than 53 years of age, 1.9 per cent in the age bracket 53–62, and 4.5 per cent in the age group of 63–7 years), which may deteriorate the adequacy of pensions for those with shorter careers.

SOTE, which three previous cabinets have tried to implement without success, is supposed to improve the delivery and access to health care and social services. The implementation of this reform is seen to be vital for combining social welfare, health care, and long-term care into one system. The reform would be the biggest in the history of social welfare and health care in Finland. Social and health-care services that are currently being provided by the municipalities will be concentrated in 18 counties. After the reform, the public administration in Finland will be organized at three levels: the state, county, and municipal levels. The counties will be responsible for arranging all public social welfare and health-care services and decisions will be made by elected county councils.

In the planned SOTE model (as it stands now) the money-follows-the-patient principle will be applied: state funding to counties will be a fixed sum according to 'needs-based capitation'. A wide set of freedom-to-choose options will be introduced and the clients will be able to choose between public or private providers (Brommels et al., 2016).

There are many questions surrounding the SOTE reform, and the Constitutional Committee of the Parliament has, on a number of occasions, returned the proposed bill to the government for further elaborations and improvements. Social policy and health-care experts are critical of the heavy reliance on private providers and the unclear administrative structure. According to the critics, there is a danger that there will be a private monopoly of multinational corporations, which will eliminate national and small-scale actors. There are also fears that the administrative model may be expensive and will lead to an increase in spending rather than saving money (Hiilamo, 2017).

The Sipilä government has made numerous political compromises in constructing the bill and a political logrolling process has ensued. The Centre Party will get 18 counties (which no other party wants to have) and in exchange the Conservatives will get their extended freedom of choice model (which no other party wants). Thanks to this logrolling, both the Conservatives and the Centre Party have secured their key demands.

In order to reduce unemployment and create stronger incentives for the unemployed to accept job offers, the Sipilä government has been introducing three measures: transferring old long-term unemployment benefit receivers to the pension system, cutting benefits, and increasing conditionality.

In 2016 in Finland, there were about 35,000 unemployed people over 60 years of age. About 15 per cent of these had been unemployed for more than five years. For an older unemployed person, it is practically impossible to find a job (HE 226/2016, 4-5). This was the reasoning behind the government's decision to implement a special measure, pension assistance, which allows all unemployed people who reached the age of 60 before the first of September 2016 and who have received basic unemployment benefits for longer than five years to qualify for special pension assistance until they qualify for the regular old-age pension or turn 65. The special law will be effective until 2021, when the last benefits will be paid out.

In 2016, the government also decided to limit the access to unemployment benefits.[2] The unpaid waiting period was extended from 5 to 7 days, and the duration of income-related benefits was shortened from 500 days (2 years) to 400 days (1.5 years) for those who had worked longer than 3 years before becoming unemployed and to 300 days (1.2 years) for those whose employment record is shorter than 3 years. Unemployed people over 58 years of age were not affected by these changes: their benefits period remained at 500 days.

The government also increased the conditionality of benefits and imposed harsher consequences should an unemployed person not fulfil certain conditions of actively searching for a job. According to this 'activation model', which entered into effect at the beginning of 2018, the unemployed must document at least 18 hours paid work every 3 months, a monthly income of €241 from self-employment, or 5 days of participation in labour market measures organized by employment offices. If the claimants fail to document such activities, their benefits are cut by 4.65 per cent for the next three months.

## 9.4 Changes in Benefits and Taxation

The heyday of the Finnish welfare state was just before the deep depression of the 1990s. Major social transfer schemes were reformed during the 1980s, with social services expanded and health care made free of charge. Finland reached the level of her Nordic neighbours with regard to social benefits. During the early years of the 1990s, benefits were cut by approximately 10 percentage points. The most dramatic decrease has taken place in the relative value of the

[2] HE 113/2016 vp, Hallituksen esitys eduskunnalle laiksi työttömyysturvalain muuttamisesta [Finnish Government's Bill on changes in the Unemployment Security Act].

basic pension, which has dropped the most (Figure 9.2). The introduction of the guaranteed pension has improved the compensation level, though not enough to reach the levels of the early 1980s.

One way to assess the development of minimum income protection schemes is to inspect them in relation to the 60 per cent poverty line, as is done in Table 9.1. The problem in Finland is that all the basic social security benefits have lost their value in relation to the 60 per cent poverty threshold. During the 2000s, only basic pensions (mostly due to the introduction of the guaranteed

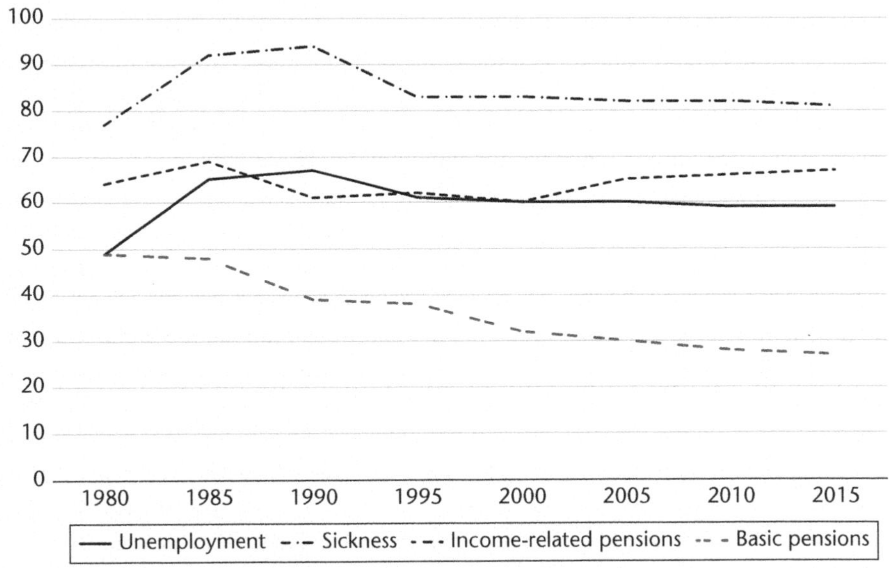


**Figure 9.2.** Compensation levels of sickness, unemployment insurance schemes, and earnings-related and basic pensions in relation (%) to the average wage, 1980–2015
*Source*: Kangas and Niemelä (2017).

**Table 9.1.** Relation (%) of minimum social benefits to the 60% poverty line in Finland, 1995–2015

| Year | Basic unemployment benefit | Basic pension | Housing allowance | Minimum sickness benefit | Social assistance | Study allowance | Child allowance |
|---|---|---|---|---|---|---|---|
| 1995 | 58 | 69 | 77 | 48 | 55 | 69 | 45 |
| 2000 | 50 | 61 | 48 | 30 | 48 | 55 | 37 |
| 2005 | 45 | 55 | 42 | 35 | 41 | 47 | 31 |
| 2008 | 41 | 53 | 36 | 30 | 38 | 44 | 29 |
| 2010 | 42 | 53 | 37 | 42 | 38 | 46 | 28 |
| 2015 | 48 | 62 | 27 | 42 | 40 | 41 | 25 |

*Source*: Honkanen (2017).

pension in 2011) and the minimum daily sickness allowance have maintained their relative position vis-à-vis the poverty threshold, compared to 1995. Due to these developments, many of the Finnish basic social security benefits fall below the agreed European standards. Nevertheless, there have been some improvements during the crisis in the levels of basic unemployment and basic pension benefits, as well as in minimum sickness benefits and social assistance.

In the present economic situation of 2018, it is, however, hard to imagine that there will be substantial increases in the level of benefits. As mentioned, in order to combat budget deficits, the Sipilä government has suggested cuts in benefits and freezing the indexes, except in the case of social assistance. An interesting question is what will happen to the distribution of labour between social assistance (not frozen) and other basic social security benefits (frozen). The most probable scenario is that social assistance will compensate for the inadequate level of other basic benefits. Gradually, this trend will change the whole character of the Finnish welfare system: there will be a slow shift towards a more selective or targeted welfare state.

However, there may be other scenarios as well. The Finnish basic security benefits are scattered and many clients receive a number of benefits aimed at guaranteeing a basic livelihood. The benefits system has a number of overlapping schemes. For example, the Social Insurance Institution (Kela) pays a housing allowance to 52 per cent of the recipients of basic unemployment benefits and the labour market subsidy.[3] In addition, about 20 per cent of the recipients of the basic unemployment benefits and 32 per cent of the recipients of the labour market subsidy are also receiving social assistance. Since 2017, Kela has begun to pay out social assistance, so it will now be possible to streamline the scattered basic benefit system and make it more coherent.

In fact, one important aspect of reforming and streamlining the basic social security system is to get rid of the worst monetary disincentive problems, which are currently leading to effective marginal tax rates of 80 per cent to 100 per cent (see Kangas & Pulkka, 2016). Furthermore, there are some bureaucratic hindrances that are making unemployed people cautious of accepting short-term work offers. There are fears of losing the right to unemployment benefits after the termination of the new job and fears of long waiting periods while the unemployment bureaucracy makes the decision whether the claimant has the right to benefits.

In addition to economic disincentives and bureaucratic traps, there is a 'housing trap'. There are currently over 40,000 vacant jobs, while at the same time the unemployment rate is around 8 per cent. The problem is that while vacancies are in the southern and western parts of the country,

[3] Kelasto, Beneficiaries of Kela's benefits and paid benefits, http://www.kela.fi/web/en.

unemployment is primarily a problem in northern and eastern Finland. The specific hindrance for geographical labour mobility is the huge variation in housing prices. In the capital area, where most job vacancies can be found, housing prices are high. Consequently, the unemployed residing in other parts of the country are not willing to move. One important public sector investment objective could be the construction of houses in developing areas in order to secure reasonable housing prices.

### 9.4.1 *Distributive effects of transfer and tax policies*

When analysing the distributive effects of the welfare state, there are two important elements: social transfers and taxation. In 1970, the redistributive effect of income transfers was 15 per cent—that is, due to transfers, 15 per cent of the poor were lifted above the poverty line—and the redistributive effect of direct taxes was 10 per cent. In the deep depression of the 1990s, the corresponding numbers were 35 per cent and 20 per cent. Not surprisingly, the redistributive effects of transfers and taxes increased during the 1990 depression (43 per cent and 19 per cent in 1996) and went down again during the period of economic growth (32 per cent and 12 per cent in 2008). The post-2008 recession again increased the redistributive effects of transfers (35 per cent in 2015), as well as of taxes (14 per cent) (Tuomala, 2017). All of this indicates that the Finnish welfare state cushioned the most detrimental effects of the economic downturns.

In the late 1990s, the pendulum swung towards a more unequal income distribution when taxes on capital and on higher income groups were lowered and the level of income transfers was cut. Consequently, the distributive profile of the Finnish welfare state changed dramatically. Whereas during the construction period of the Finnish welfare state (1966 to 1990) the income of the lowest decile increased by 5.2 per cent and that of the highest decile by 2.3 per cent, the corresponding numbers for the post-1990s period are reversed: 0.8 per cent for the lowest and 2.5 per cent for the highest decile (see Figure 9.3).

Figure 9.3 also gives micro-simulation estimates of the effects of the austerity and other policy measures the Sipilä government has carried out. Whereas the biggest losers are the low-income groups, and especially the lowest income decile, the 8th and 9th deciles are the biggest winners, providing the government does not change its policies.

Changes in the level and volume of transfers, and changes in the structure of taxation, are directly mirrored in income differences. In 1990, the Gini coefficient for disposable income was 0.21, which was among the lowest in the Western hemisphere. However, it rapidly increased to 0.27 in 1994. Since then, the coefficient has hovered around 0.27. Thus, after the mid-1990s, Finland moved towards the group of Central European countries in regard

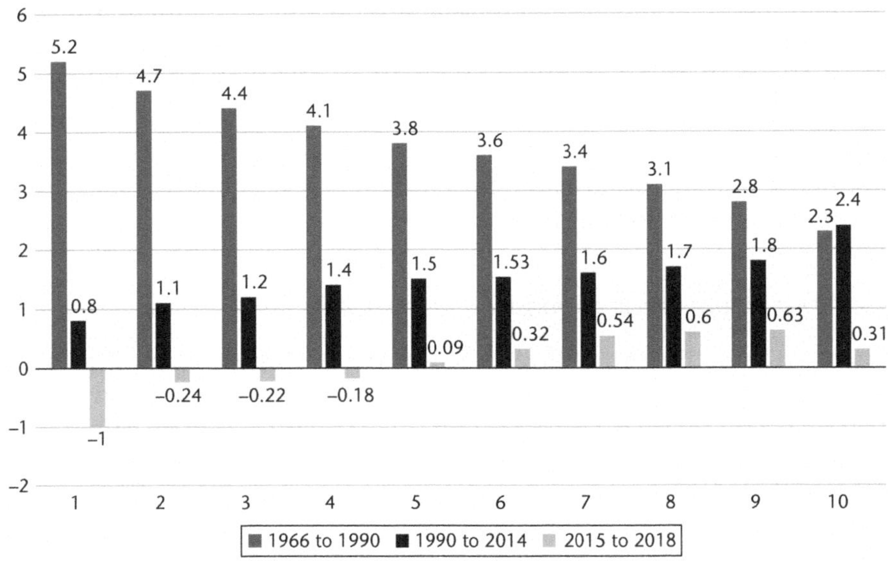


**Figure 9.3.** Increases in the real income (%) of different income deciles in Finland due to taxes and transfers

*Note*: Figures are given during the welfare state's construction (1966–90) and austerity periods (1990–2014 and 2015–18).

*Source*: Tuomala (2017); Parliament's Information Service (2017).

to income inequality. Since 2010, the Gini coefficient has been quite stable. The problem is that it is not especially sensitive to changes in the tails of income distribution. There are signs that the depth of social exclusion among the poorest groups has increased, but the conventional statistics do not reflect these problems on the margins. When and where the welfare state fails, the responsibility of the well-being of those worst off falls to the third sector, for example, by providing charity food aid, an activity that has expanded and established itself in Finnish society (Ohisalo, 2017).

## 9.5 Economic and Social Consequences of the Recessions

Although the post-2008 recession seems to be much more long-lived than the deep depression of the 1990s, the impact in terms of unemployment and employment rates has been much more modest in the current decade. What is worrying is that the unemployment rate remains high, at 8.6 per cent in 2017. During the post-2008 recession, long-term unemployment rose from 100,000 persons in 2008 to 220,000 in 2015. When the economy finally began to improve in 2017, long-term unemployment came down to 180,000 persons.[4]

Despite the increase in unemployment, in some age groups—in the older groups, in particular—employment rates have been increasing considerably and without interruptions. As can be seen in Figures 9.4a and 9.4b, whereas the age group of 55–64 year olds has managed the post-2008 crisis period well, youngsters seem to have been hit the worst. Since 2015 the situation has been improving gradually.

Needless to say, growing and prolonged unemployment creates severe economic problems for the unemployed. Whereas the risk of poverty (60 per cent poverty threshold) rapidly increased during the economic boom of the late 1990s, the post-2008 crisis has not increased poverty rates among the unemployed as dramatically. However, the risk of poverty is now higher, almost 40 per cent, among the unemployed. Students and other youth groups also have a high poverty risk, whereas poverty among employees is negligible. The old adage that employment is the best medicine against poverty seems to be true—and in Finland it is especially true for paid labour.

If we compare the financial hardship in Finland with that in many other countries, the overall picture is favourable (Figure 9.5). Whereas the average proportion of the European population suffering from financial hardship is around 20 per cent, it is well below 10 per cent in Finland, and for many population groups hardship rates are declining or remained at similar levels through the crisis. There was, though, commonly an increase of hardship after 2010, which has, however, reversed towards the end of the period. Thus, one can conclude that the country has managed to muddle through the post-2008 recession, thanks to the welfare state. This being said, however, the hardship rates among individuals in the lowest income quintile, single parents, and immigrants are still alarmingly high (there is an overlap between these groups).

An additional problem is that employment rates among single parents are still low and many of them rely on social benefits. The way to improve their situation is to encourage their labour market participation. The same goes for the unemployed, the foreign born, and those with low educational attainments. The picture of the adequacy of the Finnish pension scheme very much depends on the measure used. According to the 60 per cent at-risk-of-poverty line, the Finnish scheme does not fare well in comparison to many other EU countries. The poverty rate of elderly women in particular tends to be high. As Table 9.2 indicates, during the post-2008 recession, the at-risk-of-poverty rates for pensioners has declined. The same can be seen in Figure 9.5.

[4] See Statistics Finland, http://findikaattori.fi/en/34.

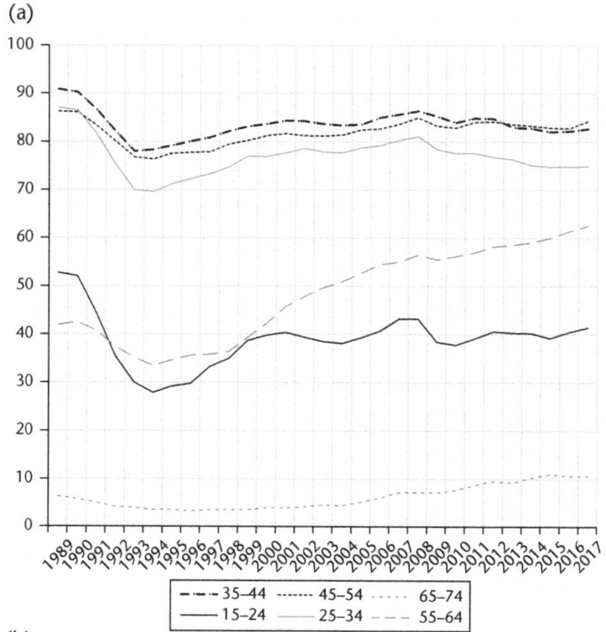


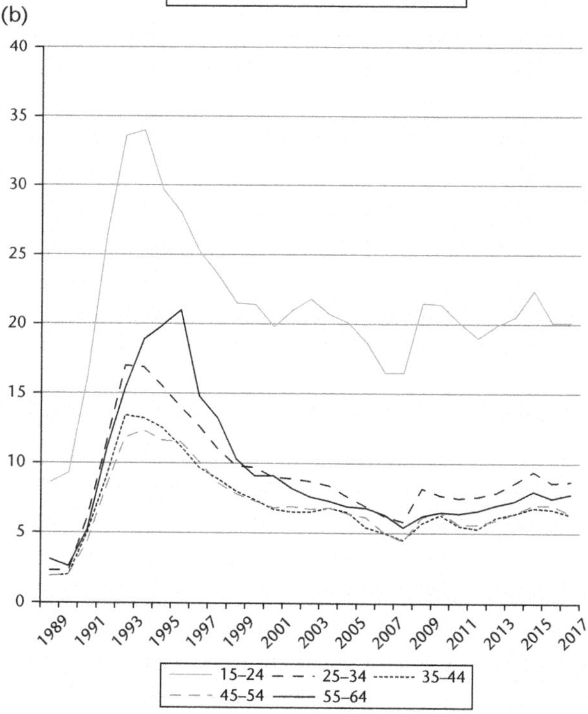


**Figure 9.4a.** Age-related employment in Finland, 1991–2016
**Figure 9.4b.** Age-related unemployment in Finland, 1991–2016

*Source*: Statistics Finland, Employment and unemployment in 2016, https://www.stat.fi/til/tyti/2016/13/tyti_2016_13_2017-04-12_kat_002_en.html.

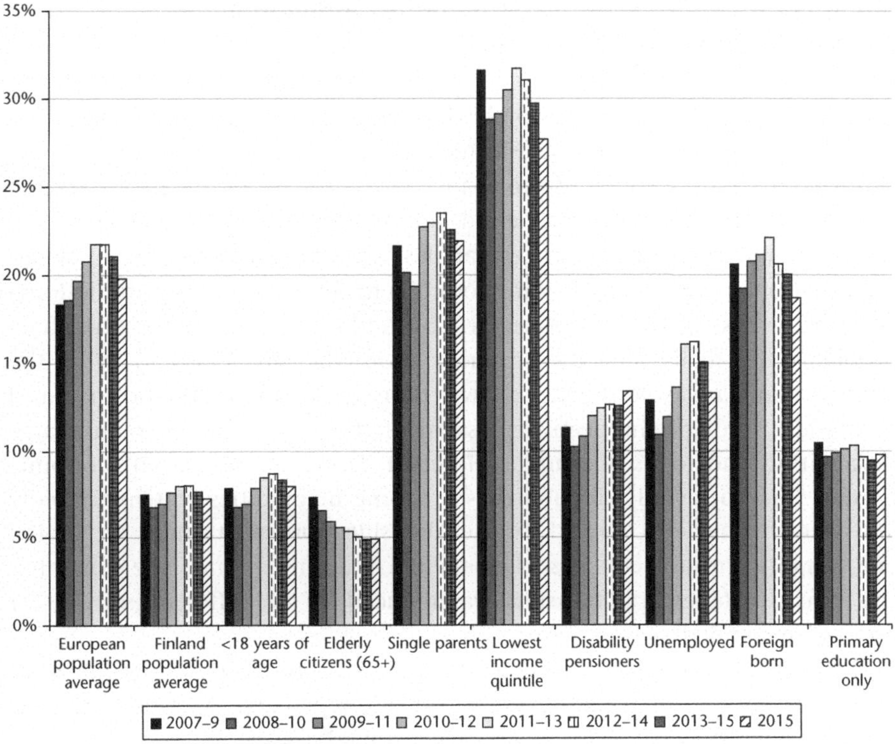


**Figure 9.5.** Financial hardship profiles through the crisis in Finland, 2007–15

*Note*: This shows Finland compared to the European average and disaggregated by main socio-economic groups. It is a composite measure based on income poverty, difficulties in making ends meet, and material deprivation (see the Appendix for explanation of the methodology), and shows proportion suffering financial hardship over three-year moving averages and in 2015.

**Table 9.2.** Risk of poverty (60% poverty threshold) in Finland among different socio-economic groups, 1995–2015

| Socio-economic group | 1995 | 2000 | 2007 | 2010 | 2013 | 2015 |
|---|---|---|---|---|---|---|
| Self-employed | 15 | 16.1 | 14.2 | 15.2 | 13.4 | 14.4 |
| Employees | 1.2 | 1.6 | 2.5 | 2.5 | 2.4 | 1.4 |
| Students | 19.1 | 21.6 | 27.8 | 27.7 | 28.4 | 29.7 |
| Pensioners | 10.1 | 14.7 | 22.3 | 19.3 | 16.4 | 13 |
| Unemployed | 17.4 | 31.8 | 42.9 | 42.3 | 45.7 | 38.1 |
| Others | 5 | 9.8 | 13.9 | 14.1 | 12.7 | 11.4 |

*Source*: Statistics Finland, Sosioekonominen asema ja pienituloisuus [Socio-economic status and low income], https://www.stat.fi/til/tjt/2015/01/tjt_2015_01_2017-03-03_kat_004_fi.html.

## 9.6 Increasing Competition, Increasing Individual Choices, Increasing Differences?

Among the Finnish socio-economic developmental peculiarities have been the late but rapid structural transformations of the economy and the strong changes throughout different economic cycles. The economic history of the country displays strong growth periods followed by years of deep crisis. When the economy was booming, wages, salaries, and prices rose rapidly, accelerating inflation and gradually leading to problems in terms of the international competitiveness of the export sector. The traditional remedy to solve these problems was to devalue the currency. From the late 1950s to 1992, the Finnish markka was devalued no fewer than seven times. Finland managed to muddle through the deep depression of the 1990s thanks to this large devaluation and to its booming ICT sector. However, this rapid economic growth was not evenly distributed so income inequalities widened rapidly and were further exacerbated by the diversification of tax rates on capital and work income and cuts in social benefits. As a consequence, the redistributive effect of taxes and transfers was reduced as the differences in factor incomes expanded.

The overture of the post-2008 recession came in the form of the collapse of American banks, which had severe worldwide repercussions. Due to the EU embargo against Russia, Finnish exports eastwards ceased.

Both in the deep depression of the 1990s and the Great Recession of 2008 and onwards, the economic and fiscal policy followed the 'traditional Finnish way', that is, the fiscal policy was more pro-cyclical than countercyclical (Pekkarinen & Vartiainen, 1993). During recessions, governments imposed heavier taxes and cut public spending to save money, while in economic growth periods they gave tax reliefs and increased public spending. This pro-cyclical policymaking bolstered the economic cycles by deepening recessions and accelerating growth. In both crises, excessive wage increases further undermined the price competitiveness of the Finnish export industry. However, when Finland adopted the euro in 2000, recovery through devaluation was removed from the policy options. Slowly, perhaps too slowly, the country is learning this lesson and perhaps therefore the post-2008 recession has lasted longer than the deep depression of the 1990s.

During both periods of economic crisis, the government has adopted austerity policies. These have included some structural changes, but mainly they have consisted of index freezing and smaller cuts to social transfers, hikes in user fees, and increases in an individual's responsibilities, both in terms of finances and of taking care of social services themselves, with increased user fees. According to the governments in power, regardless of their political colour, austerity was argued to be the 'only alternative'.

The social investment paradigm has been an overarching theme in Finnish policymaking, from the prenatal phase to that of university level. However, the cuts the austerity package introduced in the educational system may jeopardize the good results that have been achieved and reflected in good Programme for International Student Assessment (PISA) outcomes. These cuts endanger the social investment objectives, and in the long run, may have detrimental consequences. The Sipilä government's 'neo-familial' emphasis on long-term care and the planned cuts in child day-care services may further deepen the Finnish deviance from the 'Nordic' social investment perspective, with its strong emphasis on using public services to facilitate the reconciliation of childcare and employment.

Since 2008, different governments have tried to reduce public expenditure, make service production more effective, and increase consumer choices and private initiatives. This marketization has occurred most rapidly in elderly care. The expansion of private alternatives has eaten up public services. Furthermore, the formerly strong third sector of non-profit providers has also been replaced by for-profit actors. This is partially due to the (too) strict adoption of EU regulations: previously, Finland's Slot Machine Association (RAY) had been permitted to subsidize the third sector, but according to the prevailing interpretation, the EU does not accept such a 'market distortion', and consequently the third sector is losing ground to bigger market-oriented enterprises (Anttonen & Karsio, 2016; Karsio & Anttonen, 2013). In fact, the largest social service actors in Finland and Sweden are private for-profit multinational corporations (Meagher & Szhebely, 2013, p. 250). As a rule, these corporations are based in various tax havens. When the SOTE reform opens up social and health care for private providers, the most likely scenario is that the big companies will win the competition and a handful of private actors will divide the market among themselves.

Given the gloomy economic prospect, the municipalities—which have the main responsibility for the delivery of social services—will seek solutions to ease the growing financial burden of the local sector. Different forms of PPPs will offer promising possibilities for this. At the local level, decision makers tend to be pragmatic rather than ideological and eager to find practical solutions to balance the municipal budget. If users are compelled to pay higher and higher user fees for public services, the natural follow-up question will be why they should stay on public waiting lists, why not pay for private services that are available here and now. The question is not any more whether the role of private providers will expand the delivery of social services, but how, on what terms, and with what kind of actors will the service markets function.

The deep depression of the 1990s, and more so the post-2008 recession, showed that the universal welfare state was able to cushion most of the economic shocks and guarantee security when most needed. Despite unemployment and increases in differences in factor incomes, differences in disposable incomes or poverty did not change greatly and poverty and social exclusion have in fact been in decline since 2008. However, the prolonged recession may have long-standing consequences and growing 'pockets' of poverty and social exclusion may only become visible in the coming decades. This underlines the question of the adequacy and tightness of basic income transfer schemes and access to social and health services. In particular, the adequacy of pensions, the level and access to basic unemployment benefits, minimum sickness allowances, and social assistance are of utmost importance.

## Acknowledgements

This chapter has received support from the Strategic Research Programme, Academy of Finland (grant #293120).

# 10

# UK

## Changing Politics of Crisis Management

*Fran Bennett*

### 10.1 Political Economy Context in the Lead-Up to the Crisis

An examination of the initial position of the UK when the crisis and associated recession hit in 2007–8 reveals some strengths and some weaknesses. The UK economy had enjoyed average annual gross domestic product (GDP) growth from 1992 to 2007 of 2.8 per cent and unemployment was at a low of 5 per cent in 2007. But the economy was quite vulnerable, given the recent boom in housing and its dependence on the finance sector (OECD, 2009, p. 22). Labour was in government at that time and onwards up to 2010.

The UK was one of the first European countries to be affected by the crisis. In 2007, one bank received two financial bailouts; in 2008, a major mortgage lender was nationalized; and the financial sector was supported further later in 2008, with a £500 billion bailout (Chung & Thewissen, 2011, p. 362). The creeping credit crunch thus put increasing pressure on the UK financial system from 2007 and mortgage lenders became choosier about loan risks.

The causes of the UK crisis are still contested, with some blaming high public expenditure. Labour governments had increased public spending since 1997, in part to improve the quality of services and eradicate child poverty. But the international nature of the crisis contradicts the idea of this as the main cause. Any increase in public expenditure in later years was in part a response to the crisis itself. By 2010, government borrowing was over 10 per cent of national income (Johnson, 2016).

The alternative view is that the crisis was primarily caused by financial deregulation, or failure of regulation to match developments, and that in 2010 policymakers were convinced by the theory that fiscal contraction can be expansionary (Wren-Lewis, 2015)—though many argue that the economy was unbalanced, in the build-up of private debt (Elliott, 2015b) and in its dependence on the financial sector.

According to Emmerson and Tetlow (2015), the hole in the UK's public finances after the crisis hit did not simply arise from optimistic fiscal forecasts. It was also caused by the changing composition of the economy (to being less tax rich) and a substantial downward revision to trend output relative to expectations. Adam, Browne, and Elming (2015) argue that countries experiencing the largest deterioration in their underlying public finances relied most on financial sector revenues and taxation of property and other assets, as was the case in the UK.

The UK has been identified as a liberal welfare regime (Esping-Andersen, 1990) and a liberal market economy (LME) (Hall & Soskice, 2001). Its benefit system, when 'stress tested' by crisis, cannot protect income in unemployment adequately unless there are other earners in the household (Figari, Salvatori, & Sutherland, 2010). On the whole, the capacities of the UK social protection system to shelter the population from adverse crisis effects on levels of living are thus likely to be constrained and quite heavily dependent on the prevailing political orientation of the government of the day.

In order to examine the role of the welfare state in tackling the crisis in the UK, it is thus crucial initially to describe the wider context. There were three periods of post-crisis government: Labour, until May 2010; the Conservative/Liberal Democrat coalition, until May 2015; and the Conservative government since (with Theresa May taking over as prime minister from David Cameron in July 2016). Scotland, Wales, and Northern Ireland have also developed their own strategies since 1998, with varying power over different policies (Simpson, 2017), and there has been some devolution to local government. This complicates somewhat the idea of giving a straightforward analysis of the post-crisis role of the welfare state.

## 10.2 Governments' Crisis Strategies

The UK was amongst the first countries to implement a post-crisis stimulus package. The November 2008 Budget included tax cuts, investment in housing, education, and transport infrastructure, and higher social spending, with an estimated cost of 1.6 per cent of GDP over 2008 and 2009 (OECD, 2009, p. 53). A temporary top rate of tax of 50 per cent on the highest incomes was introduced in 2010. Changes also meant that individuals could keep some savings if banks collapsed, and significant 'quantitative easing' was arranged by the Bank of England (in total, £375 bn; cf. Johnson, 2016). Lupton and colleagues (2016) argue that Labour continued to spend as before but, as a percentage of GDP, spending shot up because GDP fell. The government also continued to index benefits at least to inflation, 'supporting the most vulnerable families through the downturn' (2009 Budget).[1] Real reductions did not therefore happen until some time after the coalition took office. The 50 per cent tax rate also continued until 2013. Analysis of the coalition's policies depends crucially on whether Labour's pre-election Budget 2010 policies are seen as part of the coalition's record (Lupton et al., 2016); if so, they appear more progressive.

The May 2010 election saw a change of direction—described by Elliott (2015a) as (together with the Eurozone crisis) snuffing out what resembled a 'promising recovery'. The coalition government wanted to reach structural current budget balance by 2015, though poorer than expected economic growth prevented this (Crawford & Johnson, 2015). Emmerson and Tetlow (2015) argue that UK governments have planned and (so far, only partially) implemented significant fiscal tightening to cut borrowing in order to achieve a surplus. The Bank of England gained more control of the financial sector under the Financial Services Act 2012. Alongside this, a key emphasis was retrenchment of social programmes and austerity rather than stimulus. But though the coalition government said that its most urgent task was to tackle the country's record debts, it also claimed that fairness was at the heart of its decisions so that those most in need were most protected (Lupton et al., 2016).

The major plank of the strategy was cuts in public expenditure, in particular social security. Lupton and colleagues (2016) describe this as 'selective austerity'. The June 2010 emergency Budget introduced 'cut-backs of exceptional scale, speed, composition and distributional impact' (Taylor-Gooby, 2012, p. 63), with 13 per cent of public spending being cut. The plan was to reduce the deficit from 8.4 to 0.4 per cent of GDP in four years, with service cuts accounting for 36 per cent, tax increases 30 per cent, and benefit cuts 18 per cent. The Budget also extended private sector provision in public services (Lupton et al., 2015, p. 19). But some planned cuts did not take effect until later, because of time lags. The coalition initially continued to protect benefits and tax credits from inflation (albeit using a different, lower, index). It was hard to cut social security spending because of additional demand from an ageing population, rising rents, and so on. And in some areas the Liberal Democrats either had a restraining influence on policy or pushed for specific measures (Bochel & Powell, 2016). But between 2009–10 and 2014–15, public spending fell from nearly 46 per cent to just over 40 per cent of national income (cf. Crawford & Johnson, 2015).

[1] As Jenkins and colleagues (2013) explain, the UK normally uses formulae that uprate most benefits automatically each year by the increase in prices. One of the most significant changes by the coalition government was to break with this.

'Fiscal consolidation' was initially planned as to be composed of some 80 per cent reduction in spending versus some 20 per cent tax increases. However, under the Conservatives from 2015 fiscal consolidation was made up of 86 per cent public spending cuts versus 14 per cent tax rises (Emmerson & Tetlow, 2015) and then 89 per cent versus 11 per cent for its austerity programme plans through to 2020 (de Henau & Reed, 2016a). The summer 2015 Budget, including plans to cut social security spending by £12 bn annually by 2020, would bring UK public spending levels down to those of the USA by 2018–19 (subsequently 2020) (Taylor-Gooby, 2015).

The coalition government attempted to kick-start the market with a scheme in 2012 for lending to small firms and individuals. But by 2013, the IMF and OECD argued that excessive spending constraint was slowing recovery. There was a temporary rise in public spending of some £47 bn in 2013–14, largely in support for bank lending and home purchase, and an infrastructure programme—but with plans to continue cuts after the 2015 election (Taylor-Gooby, 2015).

Some policies did protect those on low incomes, or boost services for them. For example, the 'pupil premium' was introduced—an additional amount given to schools for each child from a low-income or disadvantaged family (spring 2011)—while free school meals were introduced for all 5–7 year olds (autumn 2014). Both these policies were attributed to the Liberal Democrats' influence.

Some spending areas were also protected, including health and schools (as well as pensions) (Bozio et al., 2015), meaning that these now make up a larger share of total expenditure (Emmerson & Tetlow, 2015). Spending on the state pension was 4 per cent of GDP, but since the recession has risen to 5 per cent. Taylor-Gooby (2015) argues that spending on 'old social risks', which enjoyed popular support, was protected, with provision for 'new social risks' involving less popular groups being significantly reduced. Protection did not necessarily ensure sufficient funding to keep pace with social and demographic changes. But protected areas did better than unprotected ones. Furthermore, funding for local authorities was reduced significantly between 2009–10 and 2014–15—disproportionately for those in poorer areas (Innes & Tetlow, 2015; see also Crawford & Johnson, 2015).

Spending cuts meant departments having to make administrative savings, including staffing cuts. Hermann (2015) reports 420,000 jobs shed by 2012, with a goal of cutting the public sector workforce by 10 per cent by 2015. The government also aimed for ambitious restructuring of state services (extending 'new public management' principles and encouraging private providers in health care, for example) (see Taylor-Gooby, 2015, pp. 606–7). Sales of public assets have also helped to meet debt targets.

The other clear element of later strategies was saving on benefits/tax credits to avoid (larger) cuts in other departments, with social security seemingly seen as a burden (Bennett, 2015) rather than as positive protection and an automatic stabilizer. In Budget 2014, the coalition set a cap for 'annually managed expenditure' on benefits (excluding only pensions and cyclical benefits). This cap has been breached already in practice, however (Crawford & Johnson, 2015; Rhodes, 2016). Recent governments have also increased discretion and decreased rights, in particular in social security, and have reduced access to ways of challenging decisions about these rights (e.g. through increases in employment tribunal fees and cuts in legal aid).

The Conservatives' Chancellor declared that 'we are all in this together' in resolving the crisis, but this was challenged by many because of the disproportionate impact on those on low incomes. Those at the very top of the distribution did contribute a higher share of their income through tax changes, but below this, average losses were higher for lower deciles, hit hardest by austerity (Blyth, 2013). The Women's Budget Group (2014) also argued that governments were not tackling the real deficits—of care services, affordable housing, and high-quality work—which all had a particular impact on women.

## 10.3 Policies on Social Security

Post-crisis social security changes have targeted families with children, in particular larger families. Early cuts affected young children in particular. The 'benefit cap', limiting benefits for workless households, is not adjusted for number of children, and in April 2016 was reduced again, affecting many more families. Some means-tested benefit child additions are withdrawn for third or subsequent children born from April 2017 (with limited exceptions).

The UK's minimum income scheme has also been undermined by a range of cuts, including the 'bedroom tax' ('underoccupancy charge' or 'abolition of the spare room subsidy') in social housing, local limits to the amount of private rents covered by benefit, restricted housing benefit for single under-35s, real cuts, the failure to uprate child tax credits, and the localization (and reduction) of council tax support. It is difficult to see the effects of all these changes, especially measuring poverty 'before housing costs'. But they are very real. The poverty gap (how far incomes fall below the poverty threshold on average) increased for families with children both before and after housing costs between 2007–8 and 2013–14. Local authorities are given 'discretionary housing payments' by government to ease the impact of certain cuts, although this gives only partial compensation. Northern Ireland and Scotland have also developed various mitigations, including compensation for those excluded from disability benefits by tighter eligibility rules (Simpson, 2017). But it is clear that the social security element of the welfare state in the UK has been severely weakened by successive post-crisis measures, in particular for those of working age and their dependants.

One major structural reform is the introduction of 'universal' credit (UC) (HM Government, 2018) for those of working age and below, replacing six means-tested benefits/tax credits for those in and out of work. ('Universal' here means comprehensive, not non-means tested.) Its aims are to simplify benefits and provide clearer incentives (aided by support and conditionality) to enter work and progress. The devolved administrations have decided to vary how UC is paid.

UC has also been designed to be in line with a key goal of recent governments, to reduce so-called 'welfare dependency'. It has been delayed, however, and the Cameron government's desire to make further benefit cuts led to planned UC reductions. A revolt by Conservative MPs and others led to tax credit cuts being reversed, but the proposed UC cuts are proceeding under the new prime minister, Theresa May, though the rate of withdrawal of benefit due to additional income will now be slightly lower. De Henau and Reed (2016a) note that, taking tax/benefit changes from 2015–20 announced in 2015 as a whole, the outcome is clearly more regressive than previously, if temporary transitional protection is excluded. These and other cuts led to the then Secretary of State for Work and Pensions complaining, when resigning in spring 2016, of Treasury pressure to 'salami slice' benefits.

Another key structural reform is the (higher, flat-rate) single-tier state pension payable from April 2016, ending earnings-related state pensions more quickly than previously planned. This is not an integral part of post-crisis policies—except that it does tilt the UK system further towards private provision for anyone wanting more than a basic pension.

## 10.4 Policies on Taxation

In late 2008, Labour increased tax allowances and reduced VAT from 17.5 to 15 per cent as a response to the crisis (restoring the 17.5 per cent rate in early 2010). It introduced a taper on the personal allowance once taxable income reached £100,000 per year. It also introduced a top tax rate of 50 per cent from 2010; the coalition reduced this to 45 per cent from 2013. Capital gains tax was increased for higher rate taxpayers by the coalition government in its emergency Budget in June 2010, but was reduced again in 2016—even further for basic rate taxpayers (Seely, 2016). The June 2010 Budget also raised VAT from 17.5 to 20 per cent from early 2011, though the prime minister then pledged not to raise it again. The effects of a VAT increase on living standards are, of course, not visible in the disposable household income measures often used to track changes in poverty, but they generally fall disproportionately on lower income groups.

Another tax increase—presented as a social security cut—was the high-income child benefit charge from January 2013, for households with someone earning £50,000 or more annually. This increases income tax until child benefit is reduced to zero unless the claim is dropped.

Recent governments have been opposed to increases in taxation for individuals and corporations. A Liberal Democrat manifesto pledge in 2010, for real increases in the personal tax allowance, was adopted by the coalition and then Conservative governments. These increases are very significant, taking the tax allowance to £11,000/year in 2016–17 for most (withdrawn for those with income of £100,000/year or more, as noted), and will continue. This represents a huge spending commitment and a 1.5 per cent average increase in living standards (Lupton et al., 2016). Income tax is largely individual in the UK, but the coalition introduced a transferable marriage tax allowance (also applicable to registered civil partners) allowing a partner not using up their allowance to transfer one tenth of it to the other if neither pays higher rate tax.

Lupton and colleagues (2016) calculate that, compared to price linking of relevant benefits and tax credits in line with inflation, revenue from benefit/tax credit cuts by the coalition from 2010 to 2014–15 was spent on direct tax cuts, rather than contributing to deficit reduction as claimed. These resources were in effect redistributed to others (de Agostini, Hills, & Sutherland, 2014), but those suffering benefit cuts were generally on much lower incomes than those receiving most from direct tax cuts. Furthermore, though the annual/lifetime allowances on pension tax reliefs were cut significantly in 2011 and 2014, affecting the highest paid saving the most, fiscal welfare is still regressive and yet seldom considered for cuts.

## 10.5 Employment and Labour Market Policies

The focus on activation, including increasing and extending conditionality, if anything intensified post-crisis. Labour introduced an employer subsidy for recruiting someone unemployed for over six months and invested £3 billion in active labour market policies in 2009 (Chung & Thewissen, 2011, p. 362). The coalition government in 2010 brought together programmes for different workless groups in the Work Programme. This leaves (largely private) providers to develop services and be rewarded for getting people into sustainable employment, especially those with greater barriers. At the time of writing, there are plans for restructuring this, in particular because it is criticized for being insufficient for sick/disabled people.

Governments since 2010 have put increasing emphasis on apprenticeships, latterly proposing a levy on large companies (at the same time as corporation tax continues to decrease). But there is concern about many apprenticeships being filled by older workers, rather than younger starters, as well as about the quality of these schemes and their often gendered nature.

The Conservatives introduced the 'National Living Wage' in April 2016—a higher minimum wage for those aged 25 or over, aiming to reach 60 per cent of the median wage by 2020—saying that this helped towards their goal of a 'high wage, low tax, low welfare' economy.

Whilst the new UC may facilitate the transition to work, there is concern that it may act as a subsidy to low hours. In-work support and conditionality are intended to counter this, so that people move on from such 'mini-jobs'. But many claimants appear reluctant to accept the possibility of sanctions, given that they have already shown willingness to work (Wright et al., 2016). Knowledge about employers' roles and how to overcome structural barriers to more intensive work is needed for this to succeed (House of Commons Work and Pensions Committee, 2016).

UC includes a 'claimant commitment', with up to three years' loss of benefit for breaches, which was introduced into Jobseeker's Allowance in advance of full UC rollout. Most claimants are expected to spend 35 hours per week looking for work. UC also extends conditionality to many partners of claimants in or out of work (with modified conditionality for those with caring responsibilities for children).

## 10.6 Housing and Household Debt Policies

Labour introduced a mortgage rescue scheme to help low-income households, allowing those eligible to sell a part share of their home and reduce payments, or sell their home but stay there, paying affordable rent. This was claimed by fewer than anticipated. The home-owner mortgage support scheme allowed lenders to reduce mortgage payments by deferring some interest payments for borrowers who had lost their jobs or experienced a large fall in income (OECD, 2009, p. 42).

The recession was associated with a collapse in house building, which by 2012–13 reached rock bottom, with the fewest completions since 1949. Housing supply recovered slightly in 2014–15, and in 2015–16 improved further, largely due to the 'Affordable Homes Programme', with a target of 80,000 by March 2015. However, 'affordable' does not always mean social housing; and housing associations were allowed to charge up to 80 per cent of private rents on some properties.

House prices increased, particularly in London and the south-east, affecting young people especially (Halifax, 2015)—though properties were more affordable in 2014 than in 2007 (except for in London) (Wilcox, Perry, & Williams, 2015). The coalition government introduced a Help to Buy scheme in 2013 for first-timers (subsequently modified) and, more recently, a lifetime savings scheme to be used for house purchase or pension. Housing association tenants got the right to buy their homes in 2016, but Scotland and Wales are abolishing this scheme altogether. In 2014 stamp duty was revised in England and Wales, with more tax on higher value homes; Scotland introduced a more progressive structure. The planning system is being speeded up and other measures are intended to stimulate house building.

Housing benefit cuts and other restrictions mean that many social housing tenants have suffered severely and the future of social housing is uncertain; a four-year rent cut announced in 2015 may make investment even harder. Private rents have increased, with housing benefit cuts for four out of five private tenants due to local limits and altered uprating policies. Many people must now pay part of their rent out of other benefit income; though this cut is less visible than many others, it can have a serious impact on low-income household budgets.

Local authorities have been allowed to fulfil their homelessness duties by offering homeless people a private property. In the 2016 Budget, in the face of rising homelessness and rough sleeping, the Conservative government announced that it would spend £115 m to tackle these problems.

## 10.7 Economic and Employment Position

Emmerson and Tetlow (2015) argue that permanent damage has been caused to public finances and the economy is not expected to regain the growth trajectory predicted pre-crisis. Elliott (2015a) judges that Britain coped with this recession better than other countries did, but 'this has been the slowest recovery in living memory'. In deindustrialized and deprived areas, the recession may just have compounded long-standing decline and disadvantage. The UK economy has 'dragged itself from the depths of recession' but 'is still fragile', according to Johnson (2016); he noted that despite positive employment news the national debt, at over £1.5 trillion, was over 80 per cent of national income and not yet falling. The UK has a large current account deficit and public spending cuts are substantial. Furthermore, 'we don't quite know why it is taking so long for the economy to return to normal'. Whilst objective measures of national well-being improved from 2012–14, subjective measures worsened (Office for National Statistics, 2016).

Johnson highlights additional uncertainty because of the 'leave' vote in the EU referendum in mid-2016. The media is predicting that a recession is very likely. In the Autumn Statement in November 2016 the Chancellor confirmed that Theresa May's government would drop the plan to bring the public finances into balance by 2020. However, the National Institute for Economic and Social Research warned that low-income households are likely to shoulder a disproportionate share of the costs of 'Brexit'.

Adam and colleagues (2015) argue that 2010–15 saw a remarkable rise in employment. Robust average income growth in 2014–15 resulted in particular from a strong labour market recovery (Hood, Joyce, & Cribb, 2016). The Labour Force Survey shows the employment rate for 16–64 year olds rising to 73.2 per cent in 2014–15, the highest since 1971, driven by the private sector; 2 million more are in work than in 2007 (Johnson, 2016).

Workless households have decreased in number, with children in such households falling by 450,000 since 2010 (House of Commons Hansard, 2016). Although recent employment growth was in full-time jobs in particular, there was growing disquiet even before the crisis about insecurity, with increasing 'zero hours contracts' and underemployment, and concern about unpaid internships. Citizens Advice, the largest UK network of advice bodies, said in mid-2016 that 4.5 million people in England and Wales were in some form of insecure work (MacInnes, 2016). Employees' average real gross earnings grew slightly in 2014–15 (Hood et al., 2016). But average weekly earnings remain below pre-recession levels (Bell, 2016)—an unprecedented decade without earnings growth. This is largely because productivity has barely risen—again unprecedented (Johnson, 2016). Indeed, the Institute for Fiscal Studies says that real wages are unlikely to reach pre-crisis levels until 2020–21 at the earliest, the longest such period in 70 years. In 2014, the Office for National Statistics reported that output per hour worked was 18 percentage points below the other G7 group members' average. And 'rebalancing' from public to private sector tends to disadvantage women—a majority of public sector workers (Bennett, 2015).

In addition, ministers expressed concern about jobs disproportionately going to immigrants rather than to British citizens, with the new higher National Living Wage seen as a potential 'pull' factor. The scope for immigration may now be curtailed because of the EU referendum vote. Others argue for more restrictions on exploitative conditions, to avoid undercutting by unscrupulous employers using immigrant labour for this purpose.

## 10.8 Incomes, Inequality, Housing, and Housing Debt

How were the burdens of the crisis shared in the UK? The next few sections, 10.8 to 10.11, examine this crucial question.

Whilst Labour, and initially the coalition government, protected people to an extent from the economic 'cold climate', after 2013 the pace of change intensified and they were much more exposed (Lupton et al., 2016). The latest (2014–15) data on income distribution with a focus on low incomes (Department for Work and Pensions, 2016) show that for the first time, average (median) disposable incomes have increased to levels above those before the 2008–9 recession.

Following increases in disposable incomes across the distribution, income inequality is unchanged from 2013–14 (0.34 using the Gini coefficient) (Department for Work and Pensions, 2016), as it has been since 2011–12 (with a slight decrease before that). It is lower than before the recession—as large earnings falls between 2009–10 and 2011–12 tended to hit higher income households most—and at its lowest since 1990 (Hood et al., 2016). But the very top has continued to accelerate away. Intergenerational inequality has also grown to a significant level, with pensioners owning most of the nation's wealth and having average incomes higher than those of non-pensioners (Johnson, 2016). Wealth inequality is not included here (see Lupton et al., 2016), but Standard & Poor's (2016) argues that quantitative easing and low interest rates helped the wealthiest 10 per cent raise their share of net financial assets from 56 to 65 per cent from 2008–14. This also favoured those in London and the south-east.

Coalition government tax/benefit changes reduced household incomes by an average of £1,127/year (Browne & Elming, 2015), with low-income working-age households and the very richest losing most (Adam et al., 2015). Analysis of the 2010–15 tax/benefit policies showed children and those in their 30s and early 40s hit hardest, with those in their 20s and early 60s benefiting from tax changes; pensioners benefited from the 'triple lock', but older pensioners were negatively affected by other benefit cuts (Institute of Social and Economic Research, 2016).[2]

Beatty and Fothergill (2016) find older industrial areas, poorer seaside towns, and certain London boroughs losing most from benefit cuts after 2015, though other areas will also be hit hard.[3] Theresa May, as incoming prime minister in July 2016, noted the 'gaping chasm' between London and the rest of the country.[4]

Elliott (2015a) argues that ultra-low interest rates and mortgage lenders' forbearance meant no repeat of the record home repossessions of the early 1990s. Mortgagors gained from low interest rates, whilst savers lost. It is hard to get a complete picture, however. Mortgagors' gains are invisible in 'before housing costs' income measures.

[2] The 'triple lock' was introduced in 2010 by the Conservative–Liberal Democrat coalition government. It was a guarantee to increase the state pension every year by the highest of inflation, average earnings, or a minimum of 2.5%.

[3] This analysis excludes changes in other policies.

[4] She also drew attention to energy bills having 'rocketed' recently.

## 10.9 Poverty and Material Deprivation

Recent official data (Department for Work and Pensions, 2016) show the percentage in relative poverty before and after housing costs in 2014–15 as relatively stable compared with 2013–14, at 16 per cent and 21 per cent respectively. Examining anchored ('absolute') low income, using 2010–11 incomes uprated with inflation, 20 per cent were in poverty after housing costs. Hood and colleagues (2016), however, note that this is only slightly below the level a decade earlier—a long period of little income growth for low-income households. The proportion of pensioners in absolute poverty after housing costs decreased by 2 percentage points to 13 per cent—probably largely due to the 'triple lock', with most other benefits uprated only by inflation (or less) (Department for Work and Pensions, 2016). However, the recent change in the inflation measure may have resulted in reduced numbers recorded as being in absolute poverty.

Disentangling the distributional impact of recent governments' 'fiscal consolidation' strategies is complex, however. One reason is the simultaneous or sequential changes to different policies (de Henau & Reed, 2016a). For example, benefit cuts took place alongside increases to the National Minimum Wage (especially on the introduction of the National Living Wage) and direct tax reductions, but these did not always affect the same people—those affected by some policies are not necessarily compensated by others. Policy intent is also different from reality, as EUROMOD (2016) shows: despite the policy to keep benefit increases below inflation, benefits kept pace with prices in practice due to very low inflation in 2014 and 2015.

In addition, since the July 2015 Budget the government no longer produces a distributional analysis of Budget and Financial Statement policy changes. The Treasury argues that this is misleading because it presents spending funded by additional borrowing as an unequivocal gain to households (and vice versa), and that this is not helpful, because without sound public finances there is no economic security for working people, and unsustainable deficits result in the poorest suffering most (Stewart, 2015). Instead, the share of net spending and tax for different income groups is given (de Henau & Reed, 2016a). The government has also refused to undertake cumulative impact assessments, arguing that this is too complex and requires too many assumptions. This view has been challenged, however, and alternative impact assessments have been carried out, covering overall distributional outcomes or impact differentiated by equality groups.

A third problem is that many analyses include only changes to tax and benefits (e.g. Browne & Elming, 2015); however, Crawford and Johnson (2015) argue that changes in the labour market were more important determinants of living standards overall under the coalition than these. In addition to changes to gross incomes, it is often argued that the value of services should be taken into account in calculating overall changes to living standards; the government argued that the increased hours in free early education for 3 and 4 year olds in 'working families' should be included, for example. Some investigations (e.g. simulation modelling by Landman Economics) have included the impact of changes in funding for services. This is more difficult, however, given the differential use of services by households, the fact that services often cater to greater need, and local-level funding allocation (Taylor-Gooby, 2015, p. 605). But Lupton and colleagues (2016) find that benefits in kind for the bottom fifth were lower in 2013–14 than in 2007–8 as a proportion of overall income, whereas they were unchanged for the top fifth.

Beatty and Fothergill (2016), examining the prospective losses from benefit changes from 2015 onwards, show the four-year benefit freeze affecting the most households, followed by cuts to UC and tax credits. The most significant losses result from disability benefits changes, the lowered benefit cap, and the planned loss of housing benefit for 18–21 year olds from 2017 (later abandoned). De Henau and Reed (2016a) include tax changes as well and estimate that the cumulative impact for 2010–20 means the bottom decile of households losing up to a quarter of their disposable income on average in 2020, with the next decile losing one-fifth, compared with a loss of one twentieth of income for the top 30 per cent; these calculations exclude any policy changes made in the 2016 Budget.

One group that has lost out disproportionately in the UK is families with children, especially large families and those with young children (Innocenti: UNICEF Office of Research, 2014, p. 2). Whilst the basic state pension was protected by the 'triple lock', and other pensioner benefits were largely maintained, benefits for families with children have suffered many reductions, as described. Bozio and colleagues' (2015) comparison of six European countries in the 'Great Recession' finds that whilst in France and Italy households with children lost less from tax/benefit reforms than pensioner households, the opposite applies for Ireland and the UK.

De Henau and Reed (2016b) note that, as UC makes up much of the announced benefit spending cut, families with children would lose out in particular (though this excluded the impact of reducing the taper from 65 per cent to 63 per cent). Looking at the cumulative impact from 2010–20, they find female lone parents most affected overall. Beatty and Fothergill (2016) calculated that 83 per cent of the benefit cuts after 2015 would fall on families with children, totalling £10.7 billion annually. The Institute for Fiscal Studies projects an increase in 'absolute' poverty amongst children from 15.1 per cent in 2015–16 to 18.3 per cent in 2020–21, driven entirely by a sharp rise in poverty among families with three or more children resulting from planned tax/benefit cuts. Relative child poverty is also projected to rise significantly, from some 17.8 per cent in 2015–16 to 25.7 per cent in 2020–21, undoing most of the falls since 1997–8 (Browne & Hood, 2016).

Several benefit changes result in a restriction of the areas in which those on lower incomes can afford to live. Furthermore, more children living in homes in the private rented sector means more mobility and less security for them. In social housing, three-quarters of those affected by the 'bedroom tax' have had to cut back on food, with many landlords concerned about the well-being of their tenants (Cambridge Centre for Housing and Planning Research & IPSOS MORI, 2015). The number of tenants evicted by bailiffs reached a record high in 2015 in England and Wales. The collapse in house building led to an increase in homelessness, which moderated in 2014 but increased again in 2015. Rough sleeper counts (especially in London) have risen yearly since 2010.

## 10.10 Financial Hardships through the Crisis

There were real falls in wages immediately after the crisis hit (Elliott, 2015b), but transfer payments were protected at first, including following the 2010 change of government (Lupton et al., 2016). Unemployment was also much lower than anticipated, peaking at just over 8 per cent. This meant that initially the pain of the crisis was shared more broadly (Elliott, 2015a), as can be seen in Figure 10.1. But this was before later government strategies had an impact.

Median (net) income fell by 4 per cent between 2009–10 and 2011–12; it then grew by 5 per cent (weakly in 2012–14, but with robust growth of 3 per cent in 2014–15), and it is now 1 per cent above its 2009–10 peak (Hood et al., 2016). Taylor-Gooby (2015) argues that the distinctive features are the depth of the 2008–9 recession, and a slow recovery only becoming established after 2012.

The UK had a significantly lower financial hardship level than the European average before the crisis hit, but the increase during the crisis was steeper in the UK (see Figure 10.1). It peaked in 2012–14 and it was only in the last two years that it started to come down again. The 2015 level is still higher than the pre-crisis level.

The most striking feature of Figure 10.1 is the increase in financial hardship from 2012 overall and, in addition, for many subgroups, except the elderly. In particular, there are significant changes for the worse for those households containing someone on disability (incapacity) benefits and for lone parents. This is not surprising, given the policy emphasis of the coalition government and the lagged effects of the legislation passed from 2010 onwards described in several sections above, which imposed the bulk of the burden of 'fiscal consolidation' on those reliant on social security benefits in or out of work.

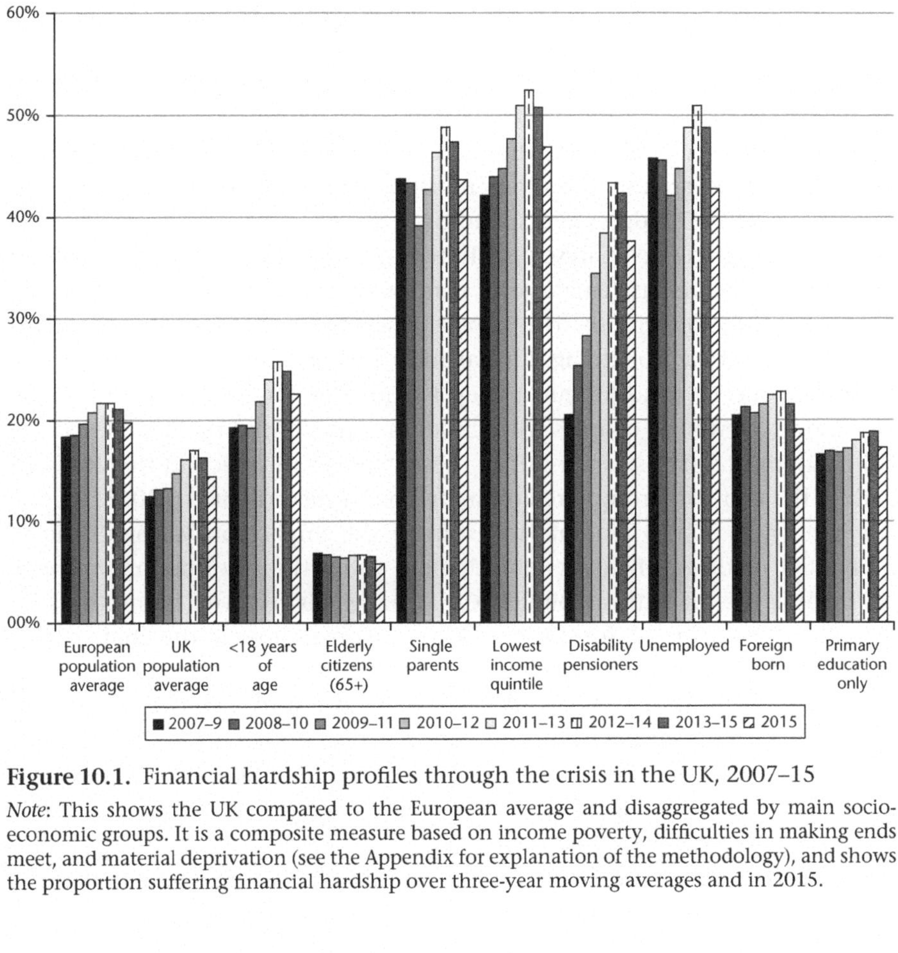


**Figure 10.1.** Financial hardship profiles through the crisis in the UK, 2007–15

*Note*: This shows the UK compared to the European average and disaggregated by main socio-economic groups. It is a composite measure based on income poverty, difficulties in making ends meet, and material deprivation (see the Appendix for explanation of the methodology), and shows the proportion suffering financial hardship over three-year moving averages and in 2015.

## 10.11 Gendered Effects of the Crisis and of Post-Crisis Measures

As Bennett (2015) notes, initial analyses of the crisis described a 'man-cession', in which men's jobs (largely private sector) were lost first, female breadwinners were increasing, and the gender pay gap declined somewhat. However, once the effects of post-crisis policies were included, this picture changed (McKay et al., 2013). Indeed, the Fawcett Society described a 'triple jeopardy' for women, as they were more likely to be hit by cuts in benefit income, services, and public sector jobs. The Fawcett Society filed for judicial review in 2010 after the 'emergency Budget', arguing that the government had not carried out its gender equality duty fully. A limited gender impact assessment of the 2010 spending review was then produced. But since then (Conley, 2012), the coalition government back-pedalled on this kind of exercise, with

Prime Minister Cameron, in late 2012, describing equality impact assessments as an unnecessary 'tick box' exercise.

Most distributional data are traditionally presented at the family/household level, with limited information about within-household distribution of income and well-being (Bennett, 2013). However, in the UK a vigorous strand of research by the Women's Budget Group and others focuses on gender analysis of Budgets and spending.

First, it is possible to analyse distributional impact by gender of household head (e.g. male versus female lone parents or single pensioners) (Browne, 2011). A study on cumulative impact assessment (Reed & Portes, 2014) included the impact of changes in taxation and benefits, and also in service provision due to funding cuts. They found that lone parents and single pensioners, as well as couples with children, experienced the largest average fall in living standards as a result of these changes in policy in the 2010–15 period; the first two groups are dominated by women (Bennett, 2015).

Secondly, it is also possible to estimate the impact on women's/men's individual incomes of tax/benefit changes using the information we have on income receipt within couples. Child benefit is received by mothers by default; child tax credit, for those on lower incomes, goes to the 'main carer', usually the mother. Family benefit cuts therefore hit women's incomes disproportionately. Some changes affect women's access to their own independent income; for example, limiting contributory employment and support allowance (for those who cannot work through illness/disability) to one year for those in the work-related activity group may leave many women (and also men) with no income of their own.

Reed and Portes (2014) found that, as a result of direct tax/benefit changes planned and/or implemented from 2010–15, women's average losses would be twice men's as a percentage of individual income. The latest House of Commons Library figures at the time of writing (including 2016 Budget measures) show that, cumulatively, 86 per cent of savings in 2010–20 come from women's pockets—an increase from 81 per cent after the November 2015 spending review (cited in Women's Budget Group (2016); see de Henau & Reed (2016a)—with various assumptions about the counterfactual and baseline used in such exercises). Given that mothers in low-income families with children tend to manage the household budget, qualitative research also reveals the costs to women when money is tight (Lister, 2006).

Underlying many gender analyses (e.g. Perrons et al., 2015) is a concern that whilst resources for physical infrastructure are seen as investment—and were meant to be boosted as part of the rebalancing of the economy away from the City and London towards other industries and areas—those for social infrastructure (such as caring services) are seen as consumption (Himmelweit, 2016). This argument is now being taken up by various other voices, from the consultancy firm KPMG to community-based groups. In addition, gender analysis highlights that repeated freezes of duty on fuel and beer are more likely to benefit men.

## 10.12 Conclusions

Before the recent referendum on the UK's EU membership, Austin (2015) argued, on the basis of European Social Survey data, that in the crisis there was widespread 'hunkering down' into security-related goals such as safety and certainty, especially among socio-economically vulnerable groups and young people. The referendum also revealed a range of fault-lines in the UK, including rurality versus urbanism, liberalism versus social conservatism, and differences between generations. One major driver of voting divisions was 'the shape of our long lasting and deeply entrenched national geographical inequality' established in the 1980s—which, Bell (2016) argues, requires a focus on building more housing, providing decent non-university routes into careers, and supporting local areas to progress economically.

There is some evidence of public attitudes changing now (Curtice, Phillips, & Clery, 2016), with a majority opposing further social security cuts and more supporting higher benefits for those in poverty. Almost as many (45 per cent) now want increases in spending and taxation as support the current balance (47 per cent)—back to pre-crash levels. However, whilst there is more support for higher spending on benefits for some, there is continuing lack of sympathy for the jobless. Polling after the EU referendum in 2016, analysing the four most important reasons for voting 'leave', was also interpreted by some as highlighting the backlash of a protest vote against austerity, precarity, and economic stagnation, and in favour of more public investment.

Whatever its meaning, however, there has clearly been a loss of trust by many, especially the more disadvantaged, in UK politicians and institutions to deliver security, well-being, and a better life. Despite the new prime minister's declaration in her first speech of her government's commitment to the 'just about managing', and the announcement by the (then) new Secretary of State for Work and Pensions that there would be no further social security cuts, the pressures both on time and resources of the post-Brexit situation suggest that (leaving aside some minor measures in the devolved nations) there will be little or no positive development in welfare state provision in the near future in the UK.

# 11

# Denmark

## The Welfare State as a Victim of Neoliberal Economic Failure?

*Jørgen Goul Andersen*

Denmark entered the Great Recession with a strong economy, but also a housing and credit bubble beginning to burst. The bubble, nourished by credit liberalization in 2003, contributed to constraining private consumption (and housing investments) for a long period as home equity evaporated. Unaware of these constraints, the government switched abruptly in May 2010 to zero growth in public consumption and to social and tax policies that were intended to promote labour supply but also entailed less economic security. This approach was largely maintained or radicalized under the Social Democratic government 2011–15 and basically left exports as the only possible driver of growth for an extended period. It took ten years for private consumption per capita to catch up with 2007, while the number of public employees declined by 5 per cent from 2010 to 2016.

Taken together, the reforms have contributed to an erosion of social citizenship, accompanied by more aggressive rhetoric (and administrative practices) questioning the deservingness of people in a vulnerable position outside or at the margins of the labour market. The weakest groups are increasingly being excluded from the protection of the welfare state. If long-term stagnation or decline in welfare services continues, it may crowd in private welfare and generate 'voluntary exit' from the welfare state among the upper middle classes. But in a context of prosperity, retrenchment is also likely to meet stronger resistance.

## 11.1 Economic and Political Context before the Crisis

In Denmark the Great Recession came as a break in 15 years of solid economic growth. After two decades of mass unemployment in the wake of the oil crises (1975–95), unemployment had declined steadily and by 2007–8 the country was back to full employment—and even a shortage of labour power. At the beginning of the crisis Denmark had a budget surplus of 5 per cent of gross domestic product (GDP) in 2007 and net state debt had been eliminated. From 1990, three decades of permanent current account deficits had turned into a more or less permanent surplus and a substantial foreign debt was gradually replaced by a positive net international investment position (NIIP) reaching more than 50 per cent of GDP by 2017.

Further, the long-term welfare challenge of ageing had largely been solved (Goul Andersen, 2011). The state was relieved of pension costs via a multipillar pension system (with the highest pension savings in the Organisation for Economic Co-operation and Development (OECD)—above 200 per cent of GDP by 2016). Further, in a broad political compromise, the 2006 welfare reform indexed retirement age to life expectancy at 60 years of age. By and large, the welfare state was considered to be sustainable long term without higher taxes or welfare retrenchments. Finding the labour power for future welfare services was a bigger concern than their financing. Taken together, the period from 1992 to 2007 could be described as a second 'golden age' of the welfare state, with a cumulative growth in public consumption of 37 per cent (30 per cent if calculated on a per capita basis). From 1990 most cash benefits were indexed to wage increases in the private sector. Nonetheless, because of lower unemployment and debt repayment, total public expenditures as per cent of GDP declined by 11 percentage points from the peak in 1993 to 2007 (Goul Andersen, 2012).[1]

In this context, there was little room for attacks on the welfare state. The Social Democratic coalition government lost the 2001 election because of voters' dissatisfaction with immigration policy (Goul Andersen, 2003). The incoming Liberal Prime Minister Anders Fogh Rasmussen was previously a figurehead of neoliberalism, but he had realized that this was incompatible with winning an electoral majority. Accordingly, until 2010 the Liberal–Conservative government (supported by the Danish People's Party) continued a pro-welfare policy, albeit with stricter conditionality and sanctions for the unemployed, with a promise not to raise any taxes and with more use of vouchers in welfare services. However, the government imposed severe cuts in

[1] Calculated from http://www.statistikbanken.dk. The 1993 figures are corrected upwards by 1.6 of GDP as the 1994 tax reform made more cash transfers taxable and raised the amounts accordingly.

benefits for various target groups where non-Western immigrants constituted a majority, including much lower social assistance ('start help') for people arriving from non-EU countries and granted permission to stay after 1 July 2002 (Goul Andersen, 2007).

With full employment, a large budget surplus, and positive current accounts, the Danish economy did not appear vulnerable in 2007. Nonetheless, Denmark ended up in a long recession. It took seven years to recover GDP to 2007 levels in real terms and ten years to recover GDP per capita.[2] It will be argued that the lengthy recovery was attributable to policy failures prior to the crisis (credit liberalization), to an inadequate diagnosis of the crisis, and to economically counterproductive side effects of social policy changes—most of which had been prepared before the crisis, but became politically possible because of it.

Eventually, the prolonged crisis served to legitimize the path-breaking welfare reform proposals of the government. By 2018, this mobilization seems to have run out of steam, but policies have changed or are close to changing in a way that could promote a double exit from the welfare state: on the one hand, the formation and exclusion of an 'undeserving' underclass and, on the other, a crowding in of private solutions for the upper middle classes if public welfare is considered inadequate.

## 11.2 Nature and the Severity of the Crisis

When Denmark was hit by the international recession, a self-inflicted national crisis was already under way as a housing and credit bubble was about to burst. Denmark entered the recession with negative quarterly growth rates from the beginning of 2008. With different emphasis, the Economic Council (De Økonomiske Råd, 2009), the Central Bank (Dam et al., 2011), and researchers (e.g. Birch Sørensen, 2010; Goul Andersen, 2011, 2013; Sørensen, 2010) have all pointed at three national sources of the crisis: (i) a housing and credit bubble that accelerated because of credit liberalization in 2003; (ii) the stoppage of the property value tax which further nourished the bubble; and (iii) a too lenient fiscal policy in 2006–7.[3] However, Danish governments (and opposition parties) did not focus particularly on these sources of the crisis.

[2] Because of revenues from net foreign assets, national income figures look better than GDP figures. By 2016, GDP was 4% above 2007, but GNI (gross national income) was 9% above 2007. Disposable net national income, which is the most relevant figure for assessing the wealth of Danish society, increased by 10.4%, reaching the 2007 level by 2012 (calculations based on http://www.statistikbanken.dk, tables NAN1 and NAN2).

[3] Fiscal policy was considered too lenient in spite of a budget surplus of 5% of GDP, partly because Denmark had the strongest automatic budget reaction in the OECD.

Ironically, attention was never drawn to the similarities with the 'Nordic banking crisis' of Finland, Norway, and Sweden in the early 1990s—a crisis that was mainly self-inflicted by excessive increases in real property prices and in loans, driven by credit liberalization (Tranøy, 2000).[4] The lesson was that credit liberalization is dangerous—and that crises caused by asset value bubbles tend to be long (in Finland it took seven years to catch up—and in Japan it took decades to fully recover from the 1990 slump). In Denmark, liberalization before the 2008 crisis culminated in the introduction of mortgage loans without repayment by October 2003 (reluctantly supported by the Social Democrats). This set fire to an already overheated housing market. From the 4th quarter of 2003 to 2006, housing prices increased on average by over 60 per cent. Taken as a whole, average prices for single family houses and apartments quadrupled from 1993 to the culmination in 2006–7 (for details, see Goul Andersen, 2011) and mortgage loans increased from 40 per cent of GDP in 1993 to 80 per cent in 2009.

Failure to diagnose the crisis adequately and to draw on earlier Nordic experiences delayed recognition of the crisis and eventually spurred a rather counterproductive austerity strategy from May 2010 onwards. The initial decline of GDP by 0.5 per cent in 2008 and by further 4.9 per cent in 2009 was roughly similar to that of Sweden, but recovery in Denmark was slower because of lower public and private consumption and investments (Goul Andersen, 2013, pp. 102–12).

The banking crisis was the first shock of the Great Recession. From 2004 to 2008, Danish banks had developed a large savings deficit, drawing on easy access to cheap money on the international market. Accordingly, the banks—in particular the largest bank having invested heavily in Ireland—were in a dire situation when credit markets froze after the bankruptcy of Lehman Brothers in September 2008. They were kept afloat with support from pension funds in the most critical days (*Berlingske Business*, 11 December 2012; *Berlingske Tidende*, 15 December 2012) before the government could provide a total guarantee of all deposits (amounting to some 250 per cent of GDP).

By comparative standards, the banking crisis was handled quite well. Through six bank packages bankruptcies were prevented, or at least controlled,[5] and the state did not lose money on bailouts. The banking sector itself contributed 35 billion DKK to a so-called Private Contingency Association taking care of banks in trouble and the state demanded very high

[4] As regards the housing bubble and banks in trouble, the Great Recession also resembles the Danish situation after 1987, which left the banks in a dire situation (Berg & Bech, 2009, p. 32). However, the Danish banking crisis of the early 1990s was not severe enough to become part of the collective memory.

[5] Nearly 20 banks went bankrupt, and the number of banks declined from 146 in 2007 to 76 in 2015. But consequences were alleviated.

**Table 11.1.** Welfare reforms in Denmark related to the Great Recession

| | Reform | Main elements |
|---|---|---|
| June 2006 | Welfare reform | 1) Indexing age brackets in the retirement system to life expectancy at 60 (1979–95): 14.5 years of life expectancy after pension age<br>2) First increase (by two years) in 2019–22 for early retirement allowance and in 2024–7 for pension age |
| 1 March 2009 | Tax reform | 1) Reduced marginal tax rates<br>2) Higher EITC<br>3) Broader tax base/tax value of deductions lower |
| May 2010 (package; agreement 19 May, adopted by law June 2011) | Reform of unemployment insurance | 1) Duration of unemployment benefits cut from four to two years<br>2) Requalification increased from 26 to 52 weeks of ordinary employment |
| | Freezing the growth in public consumption | Public consumption growth put at a hold as from autumn 2010.<br>Cumulative maximum to child benefits (benefits only for the first three children or less) |
| May 2011 (political compromise, adopted by law December 2011) | Retirement reform | 1) Age for early retirement allowance raised from 60 to 62 years (2014–17) and pension age from 65 to 67 years (2019–22), five years earlier than agreed in 2006<br>2) Age for early retirement allowance raised to 64 years and duration cut to three years (2018–23)<br>3) Higher deduction for pension assets—de facto abandoning the scheme over time<br>4) People entitled to exit the voluntary early retirement scheme and claim their contributions back (tax free)<br>5) New senior disability benefit scheme without works testing |
| December 2011 | Abandoning 'poverty benefits' | 1) Replacing start assistance with ordinary social assistance<br>2) Cumulative ceiling to support for social assistance recipients abandoned<br>3) Requirement of 450 hours of unsubsidized work for social assistance recipients abandoned |
| 2012 | Tax reform | 1) Lower marginal tax rates<br>2) Higher EITC<br>3) Means testing of child benefits (by parents' income)<br>4) First explicit co-financing by social benefit cuts: indexation of social transfer payments reduced by *c.*5% (implemented 2016–23) |
| June 2012 (adopted by law December 2012) | Flex job reform | Changing the subsidy for employers into a subsidy for employees, and reducing the ceiling markedly |
| | Reform of disability pension | Disability pension as last resort after one to five years of testing ability to work<br>Average decline about 50% in disability pension grants 2013–17 |
| 2013 (adopted by law 28 June 2013) | Social assistance reform | 1) Claimants under 30 years lose right to social assistance. Instead they obtain education assistance (at the same level as students' benefits) and are required to take an education course or be available for efforts aimed at preparing them for education<br>2) People above 30 years and younger people with a completed education are subject to three months of intense job search; afterwards they are required to work in return for social assistance |

| | | |
|---|---|---|
| | | 3) More sanctions for people who undertake insufficient job searches<br>4) Cohabiting unmarried couples obliged to provide for each other, not Social Assistance on an individual basis (abandoned in 2015 budget compromise) |
| 2013 (adopted by law 11 June 2014) | Sickness benefit reform | 1) More early follow-up<br>2) Entitlement reduced from 52 to 22 weeks, but with opportunities for extension (7 possible conditions) occasionally beyond 52 weeks. If no conditions are fulfilled, people are transferred to work test sessions with social assistance-level benefit |

interest rates for the capital provided in the second package. Hence, the state altogether earned a net surplus of 18 billion DKK (1 per cent of GDP) from loans and guarantees.[6]

The government did not jump the gun to impose restrictions on the financial sector (and when it acted it was too late and something of an overreaction), but it was not sufficiently aware of the ensuing credit squeeze for small- and medium-sized firms and others. This contributed to low investment. There was an increase in public investments from a low point in 2006 to a peak in 2012, but few initiatives to support housing investments apart from support for housing renovation. The number of housing starts continued to decline and between 2009 and 2013 reached the lowest level since 1945.[7]

Housing prices declined markedly. From the peak in 2006 till the lowest point in the 1st quarter of 2009, the average price for an apartment declined by 30 per cent.[8] For single family houses the decline from 2nd quarter of 2007 to 1st quarter of 2012 amounted to 20 per cent. However, because of extremely low interest rates, foreclosures remained far below the level of the early 1990s (see footnote 7, table TVANG1). Still, the home equity of home-owners was almost halved from the peak to the trough (47 per cent, cf. Realkredit Danmark in *Berlingske Business*, 2 August 2013).

Danish households were (and remain) extremely indebted, but this must be viewed against their enormous pension savings. However, pension savings do not provide a buffer in case of liquidity problems and home equity had evaporated or was uncertain. Hence people had a strong incentive to increase savings and reduce private consumption. And so they did: the level of private consumption in 2007 and 2008 was not surpassed until 2015. As regards private consumption per capita, the 2007 figure was not reached until 2017.

[6] According to the Ministry of Business and Growth (Erhvervs-og Vækstministeriet), Status Report, 1 April 2016. The government was slow to realize the danger, but afterwards acted quickly with professional support from Rothschild & Co.

[7] Cf. Denmarks Statistik, Statistikbanken, http://www.statistikbanken.dk/statbank5a/default.asp?w=1440.

[8] By 2016, however, apartment prices had recovered to above the 2006 level.

This reflected a significant increase in savings propensity, leaving exports as the only significant driver of growth. As investments also remained low, Denmark's balance of payment surplus increased from 1.4 per cent of GDP in 2007 to 8.9 per cent by 2014.

As population growth/decline is quite different among European countries we should analyse consumption per capita rather than with absolute figures. To take an example, Luxembourg experienced the highest increase in private consumption (18 per cent) among EU countries in OECD 2008–16 but also a population increase of 19.1 per cent, leaving Luxembourg with falling private consumption per capita. By 2016, private consumption per capita in Denmark was 1.3 per cent lower than in 2008. Higher rates of decline were only found in Greece, Spain, Italy, the Netherlands, Ireland, and Portugal (see Figure 11.1). Corresponding figures for Norway, Sweden, and Germany reveal a growth of 9 per cent—much the same as the USA, Canada, and Australia—and even crisis-ridden Finland had an increase of 3.9 per cent.

Still, unemployment in Denmark did not explode. Gross unemployment (national figures) increased from 2.6 per cent in 2008 to 6.1 per cent in 2010

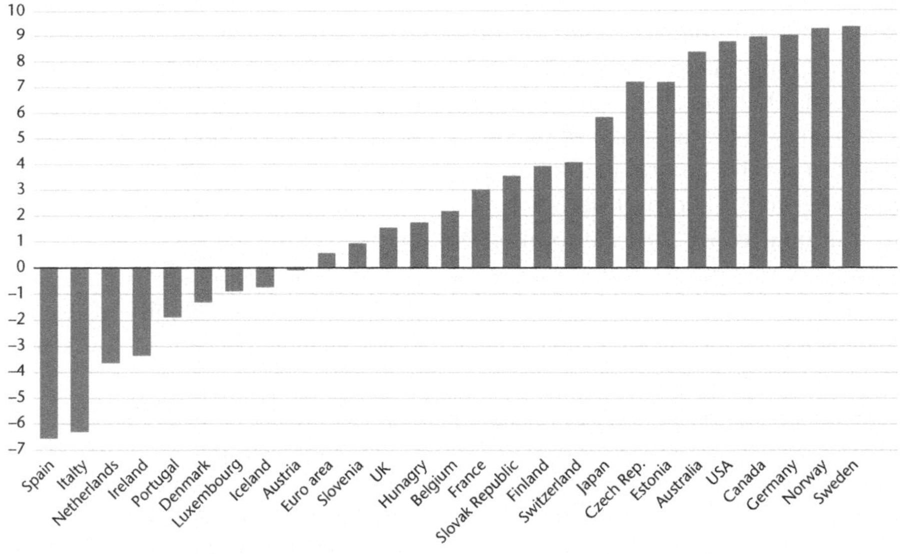


**Figure 11.1.** Cumulative increase in private consumption per capita, 2008–16 (%)

*Note*: * Four extreme countries omitted: Turkey (+34.3%), Poland (+22%), Latvia (+15.1%), Greece (−23,6%). Cumulative growth for household final consumption expenditure 2008–16 is divided by the growth rate of the population.

*Sources*: Calculated from OECD, National accounts at a glance (http://stats.oecd.org). Population data for Europe are from Eurostat (1 January 2008 and 2016). For Australia the date is 30 June (Statistical Yearbook plus demographic statistical releases from Australian Bureau of Statistics). For Canada reference date is 1 July (Statistical Yearbook plus quarterly demographic estimates). For the USA it's 30 June (population clock plus intercensal estimates 2000–10 from US Census Bureau). For Japan data refer to October (Japan Statistical Yearbook 2018).

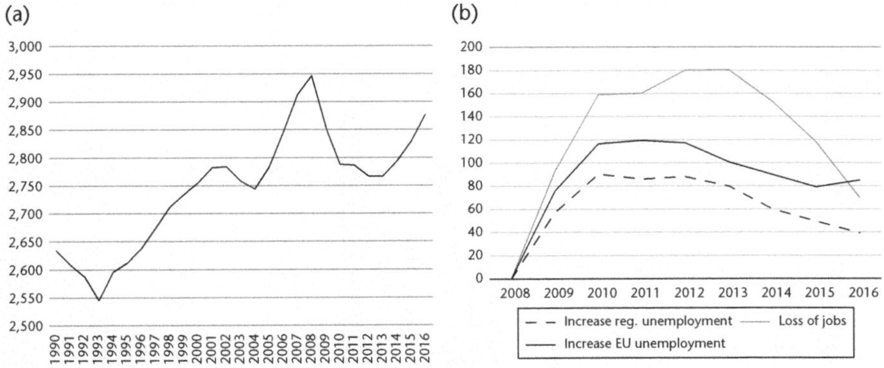


**Figure 11.2a.** Full-time employed in Denmark, 1990–2016

**Figure 11.2b.** Loss of jobs and increase in unemployment after 2008, according to national and EU measures

*Note*: Registered unemployment only includes those who receive unemployment benefits or social assistance. EU figures include all active jobseekers, also e.g. students looking for a part-time job.

*Source*: Denmarks Statistik, Statisticsbanken, http://www.statistikbanken.dk. Tables NAN1, AUL01, AKU300 compared.

(4.2 per cent in 2016). The immediate increase in unemployment was much lower than the decline in employment (see Figures 11.2a and 11.2b). In the first place, the working-age population declined; secondly, many students and pupils gave up trying to find a part-time job; this group used to have exceptionally high employment rates in Denmark, but served as a 'reserve army' during the crises. A total of 180,100 jobs were lost from 2008 to 2012 but unemployment only increased by 88,100 persons according to official figures and by 117,250 according to the EU definition, including those who were not eligible for unemployment benefits/social assistance (or had become ineligible).

## 11.3 Financial Hardship Experiences through the Crisis

Even though the Danes cut private consumption, the causes should not be conflated with the situation in Southern Europe. For most people it reflected voluntary consolidation rather than economic hardship. In spite of zero interest rates, savings of wage earners and pensioners in cash accounts in banks reached unprecedented levels—39 per cent of GDP from 2010 onwards—and consumers' reluctance to spend surprised economic forecasters.[9]

[9] Net savings (savings minus loans) in banks doubled from about 10% of GDP in 2007–8 to about 20% in 2016–17, as calculated on the basis of data from the Danish Central Bank and Realkredit Danmark.

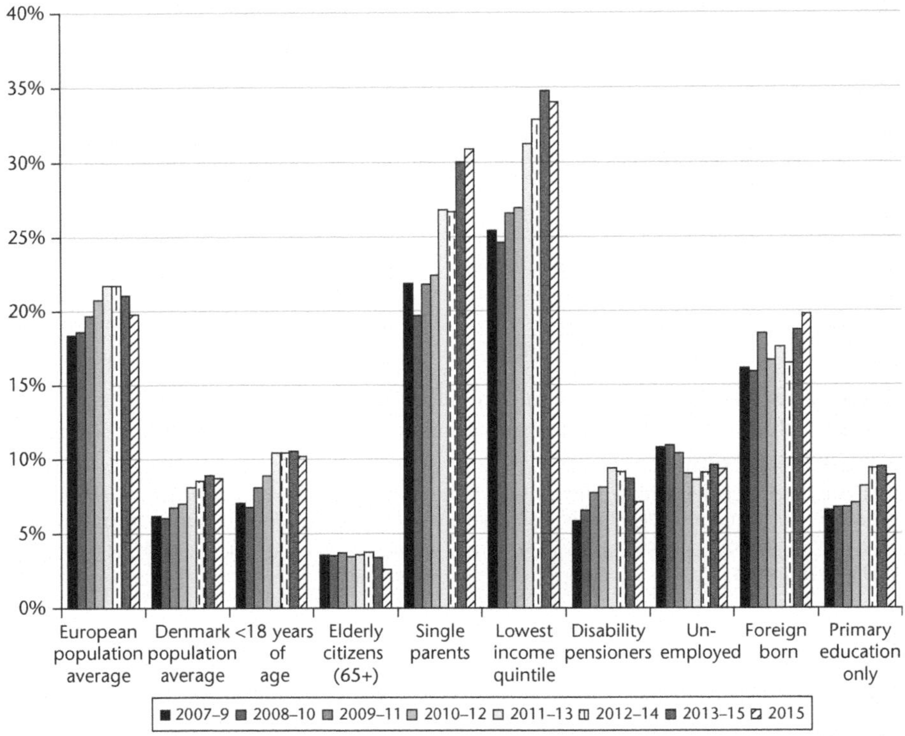


**Figure 11.3.** Financial hardship profiles through the crisis in Denmark, 2007–15

*Note*: This shows Denmark compared to the European average and disaggregated by main socio-economic groups. It is a composite measure based on income poverty, difficulties in making ends meet, and material deprivation (see the Appendix for explanation of the methodology), and shows proportion suffering financial hardship over three-year moving averages and in 2015.

Looking at financial hardship profiles for Denmark (Figure 11.3), Denmark had a very low level before the crisis (about a third of the European average) but there was a decisive increase from 2011 onwards. While there was improvement in 2013–15, Denmark still remained at a significantly higher level in 2015 than in the pre-crisis situation.

The highest financial hardship levels experienced are, by far, by the low-income individuals (lowest quintile) and single parents. Both of these groups suffered greatly increased hardship during the latter part of the crisis years and improved only slightly by 2015. Immigrants are third in line as regards financial hardship level, but their increase of hardship was more modest than in the two former groups. Households with children under 18 and disability pensioners experienced a significantly increased hardship level around the middle of the period, as did those with the lowest educational level. The elderly and the unemployed are the only groups to systematically experience lowered financial hardship levels during the crisis years.

Danish data on income distribution largely confirm these patterns, with one exception. National data reveal increasing reliance on social assistance rather than unemployment benefits among the unemployed. Subjective insecurity among social assistance recipients is very high; it is lower, but increasing, among people receiving unemployment benefits (Andersen, Hede, & Goul Andersen, 2015, 2017).

After the crisis, public data reveal increasing inequality for both gross and disposable incomes (Goul Andersen, 2018; Ploug, 2017). Furthermore, regardless of definition, the proportion of poor had doubled from the beginning of the century until 2016—and there is more increase under way. One of the first actions of the new Liberal government in 2015 was to abandon the official poverty measure. Surveys reveal that people have become more insecure about their welfare protection in the future. Insecurity has declined since 2015, but remains far above the level at beginning of the crisis (Andersen et al., 2017). This seems strongly related to policy changes during the crisis.

## 11.4 Government Crisis Strategies

As indicated, the government's approach to the crisis changed radically by 2010. At the first stage (2008–9) the priority was to keep the wheels turning. Public consumption grew at high speed. Next, the government enabled people to withdraw their money with a tax rebate from a mandatory pensions savings scheme.[10] Coincidentally, the government's unfinanced tax relief in 2007 became effective in 2009 and was formally counted as an effort to stimulate aggregate demand.[11]

The pension withdrawal actually echoed an initiative that was implemented in the wake of the oil crisis of 1973–4. But the 'recovery package' in May 2010 marked a transition to a second stage. The government was convinced that recovery was under way and decided to halt and reverse the economic stimulus (in retrospect, this was premature). This led to immediate cuts in public consumption; in five out of six subsequent quarters the quarterly growth rate

[10] This 'private Keynesianism' should stimulate demand without putting strain on the state budget (which would even be relieved by incoming taxes). Unfortunately, the savings were partly invested in shares, and the decision coincided with the stock market hitting the bottom (12 months earlier or 18 months later, stock prices were twice as high). Hence, the government misled people into sell their financial assets at the worst possible moment, and in the end withdrawals were so large that the scheme had to be terminated.

[11] Financing was to be provided by a labour market reform, and by 2008 a Labour Market Commission was appointed to come up with proposals, but its proposals were considered economically and politically unfeasible in 2008 and 2009.

was negative.[12] Public consumption per capita remained at the same level in 2016 as in 2010. From that time on, much political rhetoric was borrowed from the crisis of the 1980s—even though the context was almost the opposite. In the 1980s Denmark suffered from too high a level of private consumption, permanent budget deficits and current account deficits, and escalating state and foreign debt.

From May 2010 Danish governments used the burning platform of the crisis to adopt long-term structural reforms that had been prepared before the crisis, all aiming at increasing labour supply. This holds also for the Social Democratic coalition government which held office between 2011 and 2015. The pivotal party, the Radical Liberals, made their participation conditional on the economic strategy of the outgoing government being preserved in the new government programme—the main difference being a stimulus to public investments in 2012–13.[13] This led to severe losses in opinion polls and the third coalition partner, Socialist People's Party (SF), leaving the government in 2014.

To quote the Social Democratic prime minister at the World Economic Forum Davos Summit in 2013, the government was caught by 'reform frenzy', and according to the minister of finance did not conduct crisis policy but long-term structural policy. However, a side effect of these reforms (presented in detail in section 11.5) was a marked deterioration of social protection for some groups. Besides, in the short run, these policies were ineffective and perhaps even counterproductive in promoting domestic economic growth.

After the 2015 election, the new Liberal government used economic stagnation as justification for an ambitious plan with path-breaking tax cuts and welfare retrenchment in order to restore dynamism in the Danish economy. Ironically, before negotiations took off, a thorough revision of the Danish national accounts in November 2016 ruined the discourse as GDP was elevated by 2 per cent. This removed the apparent stagnation in productivity and GDP: since 2013, Denmark had performed at least as well as other countries. By 2017, the government (now a minority coalition including the Conservatives and the ultra-liberal 'Liberal Alliance') recycled the proposals. However, it missed the burning platform and a political accommodation between the Social Democrats and the Danish People's Party strengthened the latter's hand at blocking tax cuts and retrenchment.

[12] See http://statistikbanken.dk (table NKN1). In addition, elements of the 2009 tax reform were postponed, in particular the implementation of higher brackets for the so-called 'top tax' of 15 percentage points.

[13] A new regulation in 2008 had imposed penalties on municipalities for exceeding their budgets; this worked a little too well as municipalities reacted by under-consuming, thereby weakening the fiscal stimulus.

## 11.5 Welfare and Tax Reforms

Whereas retrenchment in public consumption was an austerity measure, the other reforms from 2010 onwards should be seen in the light of the structural reforms of the previous decade that were aimed at increasing labour supply. However, the purpose was less self-evident and the negative social side effects were larger when the reforms were introduced during a recession (see Table 11.1 for a detailed overview of welfare reform in Denmark related to the crisis).

### 11.5.1 *Reform of unemployment benefits in 2010*

This holds in particular for the reform of the unemployment benefit system in May 2010. Duration was reduced from 4 to 2 years and the requalification requirement was raised from 26 to 52 weeks of employment. The Social Democrats and the SF criticized the reform in the 2011 election campaign, but accepted it as the price for government power. Unemployment protection had been cut before but not during a recession. According to government estimates (and the Labour Market Commission 2008–9), dropout from unemployment benefits to social assistance (or no support at all) would be small. It turned out it was 10–20 times higher than expected (Goul Andersen, 2017).

This forced the government to postpone implementation by one year. As the problem continued, various temporary benefits on a social assistance level were invented to prevent people from losing rights to benefits altogether (e.g. because of a spouse's income). After the 2015 election the Social Democrats, the Liberals (now in office), and the Danish People's Party were keen to close the issue by a compromise that offered somewhat better opportunities for requalification through temporary and part-time jobs. This closed the case politically and in the media. A full assessment of the impact is currently lacking.

### 11.5.2 *Retirement reform of 2011*

The 2011 retirement reform was also inherited from the Liberal–Conservative government. It is linked to the 2006 welfare reform which indexed future age brackets in the retirement system to life expectancy at 60,[14] with 1979–95 as reference point (19.5 years). As a first step, the lowest age for voluntary early retirement (*efterløn*) would increase from 60 to 62 years in 2019–22 and the pension age to 67 for the same cohort in 2024–7. Subsequently, retirement age

[14] As the Social Democrats participated in the 2006 reform, the 2011 reform could not be formally adopted until after the 2015 election (following Danish parliamentary norms). Accordingly, the Social Democrats had to vote for the 2011 reform.

would be adjusted every five years. The 2006 reform was presented as an alternative to abolishing the early retirement scheme,[15] but the latter was effectively phased out with the 2011 reform. First, the age brackets of 62–7 were phased in five years earlier than announced in 2006. Next, early retirement was cut to three years from 2018. Finally, deductions for private pension assets were increased, regardless of whether pensions were paid out. Hence, as labour market pensions mature income replacement becomes negligible.[16]

By 2012–16, life expectancy at 60 had increased by 3.6 years and all the signs are that this trend will continue. Accordingly, from the birth cohort of 1953 to the birth cohort of 1971, the earliest time of (voluntary) retirement increases from 60 to 70 years. The 2011 reform introduced a 'senior disability pension' as compensation for worn-out workers, with a shorter administrative road without working tests but based on the same eligibility criteria.

### 11.5.3 *Disability pension and flex job reform in 2012*

The criteria for disability pension have been tightened on several occasions since the 1980s when pensions were sometimes granted on the basis of 'social' criteria; municipalities had perverse incentives as pensions were financed by the state—unlike social assistance. The next 20 years witnessed a series of reforms to change incentive structures and tighten eligibility criteria. Most importantly, a reform in 2003 installed the principle of ability to work (*arbejdsevne pricippet*) instead of *lost* ability to work (*tab af erhvervsevne*). Focus was shifted towards the remaining resources of the individual who could be employed in an 'inclusive' labour market. As an alternative for people with reduced work capacity, so-called flexible jobs had been introduced in the 'active social policy' reform of 1998 in order to make labour markets more inclusive; typically recipients work fewer hours. The scheme initially subsidized employers and enabled them to employ flexijob workers on ordinary conditions, in principle with the same income as ordinary employees. While the scheme contributed to a reduction of disability pension grants,[17] it was expensive and there was suspicion of abuse. Changes had been under way for years but the crisis became a vehicle for reform.

[15] Conditions are membership of an unemployment insurance fund and paid contributions to early retirement allowance. In 1998 the allowance was reduced by 9% for those who retire before 62. Besides, there were deductions for all pension savings for this group. From the age of 62, deductions only applied to pensions actually paid out. Hence, by postponing payment of pensions, people could typically obtain maximum allowance from the age of 62.

[16] Actually, the number of people receiving the early retirement allowance decreased by more than 30% from 2007 to 2013, before the reform was implemented on 1 January 2014. Consequently, the decline in the number of recipients before the reform was practically as strong as after the reform when the 60–1 year olds gradually lost eligibility.

[17] This is visible when we look at age groups. Because of changing age composition (fewer young people, more middle aged and older), the improvement is less visible from aggregates.

In June 2012, the government, along with the Liberals, Conservatives, and others, agreed on a reform of disability pension and flexible jobs (formally adopted December 2012). Subsidies for flexible jobs became a subsidy for the employee, albeit with a low ceiling. This made the scheme attractive only to people with low incomes. Disability pension claimants became subject to work test sessions (*ressourceforløb*) where the job centre could assess their work capacity. The new scheme improves opportunities for those who have some work capacity and want to find a job within their capabilities. However, this is a stressful experience for those with little capacity and few job opportunities. Benefit claimants experience a deteriorating economic situation as they typically end up on a social assistance-level benefit. From 2012 to 2016 the number of disability pensions granted on average declined by a half.

The efforts to activate and integrate people with a reduced work capacity seem to have positive employment effects. But it comes at the cost of reduced social security. Until the 2000s elderly unemployed were protected by long benefit duration and special rules preventing dropout from the unemployment benefit system. After the reforms of 2010 to 2012, worn-out workers may drop out from unemployment insurance and receive social assistance-level benefits while being work tested. Not surprisingly, surveys have found increasing insecurity about being able to continue working and a much strengthened association between self-declared health and political trust from 2011 to 2013 (Goul Andersen, 2016).

Opportunities for voluntary early retirement are also closing and the retirement age is being raised. Early retirement was used especially by unskilled workers and women (Friis, 2012a, 2012b). As the social gradient in health and life expectancy is strong and increasing (Brønnum-Hansen & Baadsgaard, 2008, 2012), the one-size-fits-all approach embodied in the new rules de facto constitutes a breach of universalism (which in this case requires that people should be treated differently in order to be treated equally from an outcome perspective).

### 11.5.4 *Sickness benefit reform*

The sickness benefit reform in 2013 (formally adopted 2014 and implemented in 2014–15) pulls in the same direction. Earlier follow-up and stronger and more coordinated efforts reduce the risk of labour market marginalization. Further, although sickness benefit entitlement was reduced from 52 to 22 weeks, there are some opportunities for prolongation, even beyond 52 weeks. However, those who do not fulfil one of seven conditions of extension are transferred to a work test session with a social assistance-level benefit resembling the one for disability benefit claimants. It does not take into account a spouse's income but most people have a supplementary disability insurance scheme as part of their labour market pension which is fully deducted. In other words, some people find themselves in a much more critical economic situation than they had ever anticipated, depending on somewhat arbitrary circumstances like the ability of a doctor to predict exactly whether and when return to the labour market is possible. Finally, complaints about being subject to control and suspicion are widespread.

### 11.5.5 *Social assistance reform*

The year 2013 also witnessed a social assistance reform aimed primarily at extending existing requirements for 18–24 year olds to 25–9 year olds. A main element was that people deemed able to participate in education were required to do so. Accordingly, benefits were, as a point of departure, reduced to the equivalent of the state education grant (which is usually generous in Denmark, it must be noted). Those assessed as currently unfit for education generally receive individualized support to become fit and move on to a job or education.

Unemployed people above 30 years of age and people below 30 with a completed education were subjected to a requirement to work in return for social assistance after three months—having a benefit job (*nyttejob*) in municipal activity. This was aimed at those ready for a job in order to motivate them, positively or negatively, to find work themselves. More generally, incentives to enrol in education were strengthened and control and sanctions were intensified. The reform took a step away from emphasis on social rights towards paternalistic help and control.

A final element was a requirement that cohabiting, but unmarried, couples should be subject to the same requirement as those who were married. However, this was never fully implemented and was abandoned in 2016.

### 11.5.6 *Removal and reintroduction of 'poverty benefits'*

The Social Democratic government deviated from its predecessor on one occasion. Soon after its instalment in 2011 it repealed the former government's so-called 'poverty benefits'. These included: (i) start assistance, the heavily reduced social assistance for people immigrating from non-EU/European Economic Community (EEC) countries after 2002; (ii) a cumulative ceiling of support for social assistance claimants (*kontanthjælpsloftet*); and (iii) a rule demanding that married social assistance recipients should have 450 hours of non-subsidized work as a precondition for remaining eligible for social assistance.

After the 2015 election, however, all of these arrangements, de facto targeted mostly at people with immigrant backgrounds, were reintroduced. Start assistance was called introductory support and this time did not apply only to newcomers. The cumulative ceiling for public support to social assistance recipients was reintroduced with exceptions for certain groups of disabled people. Two hundred and twenty-five hours of unsubsidized employment within the previous 12 months was made a condition for entitlement to social assistance. Benefits would be reduced for unmarried people failing to comply. For married people social assistance/introductory support would normally lapse, but only for one of the spouses.

### 11.5.7 *Tax reforms*

Like the other reforms, tax reforms were aimed at increasing labour supply. Tax reforms in 2009 and 2012 (the sixth and seventh big tax reforms since 1985) reduced marginal taxes at all levels, partly via an earned income tax credit (EITC) for people in employment and partly via higher tax brackets or lower tax rates for the highest incomes. Financing was mainly obtained by broadening the tax base—reducing (the tax value of) deductions. In 2012 cuts in social benefits were, for the first time, explicitly included to co-finance income tax cuts. The distributional impact of each individual reform was modest, but, cumulatively, the tax reforms made a considerable contribution to higher inequality (Goul Andersen, 2018). For people earning 167 per cent of an average worker (AW), Denmark was second only to Hungary in reducing tax on wages as a per cent of gross wage expenditures from 2000 to 2016.

As all reforms took the same direction, marginal taxes on labour in Denmark eventually reached a low level. For high incomes (167 per cent AW), marginal tax rates remained 3 per cent above the average of EU–OECD members. However, for average incomes and low incomes (67 per cent AW) marginal tax rates on labour were almost 10 percentage points below the EU–OECD average (Goul Andersen, 2018; OECD, 2017b) and for an AW they were even below the USA in 2016.

### 11.5.8 *Limits to public consumption*

As mentioned, public consumption grew quite fast until 2010. With the 2010 'recovery package' the growth stopped overnight. This course was basically maintained when the Social Democrats were in office between 2011 and 2015. For the first time in a generation, the number of public employees declined: by the third quarter of 2017, the number of (full-time) public employees had declined by 4.7 per cent as compared to the second quarter of 2010. Aggregate public consumption grew slightly between 2009 and 2016 but public consumption per capita remained almost constant. Because of demographic change (population growth and rapid ageing), the current standard estimate for a neutral or status quo development of public consumption is an annual growth rate of 1.1 per cent in aggregate public consumption. Since 2015, the maximum claim among the major parties was 0.8 per cent (made by the Danish People's Party).

## 11.6 Conclusion

In Denmark the crisis did not only come as a tsunami from abroad. It was also self-inflicted by the bursting of a housing and credit bubble nourished by credit liberalization, in particular the introduction of interest-only loans in 2003. However, the diagnosis and awareness that crises caused by asset value bubbles often tend to be prolonged barely entered government interpretations of the crisis. Rather, governments followed practices from the 1980s in addressing government deficits and competitiveness as the main challenges. Furthermore, even more significantly, they used the crisis as a vehicle for implementing structural reforms that were planned before the crisis and aimed at increasing labour supply. Alongside ageing, general crisis awareness, and the lower home equity of homeowners, the reforms may have contributed to the significant drop in private consumption which served to prolong the crisis.

As Denmark enjoyed full employment and large public surpluses before the crisis, it may come as a surprise that financial hardship increased during the crisis. It appears that this was, to a large extent, a side effect of reforms carried out during the crisis: social protection became less adequate for people at the margins of the labour market and subjective measurements indicate many were increasingly concerned about avoiding unemployment and being physically unable to keep working (Andersen et al., 2015, 2017).

This marks a huge change. Up to about 2000 Denmark used to have a very generous social protection system aimed at securing full citizenship for everybody regardless of employment and health status. Denmark probably held a world record in avoiding social marginalization (Goul Andersen, Albrekt Larsen, & Jensen, 2003). Although rules were tightened in the 1990s, this happened in tandem with the improved employment situation. There was no increase in dropout from unemployment benefits to social assistance. From 2002 conditions were gradually tightened for immigrants and poverty increased. But structural policy reforms aimed at increasing labour supply were radicalized by the crisis, and all created losers. The main exception was the repeal of start assistance, work requirement, and maximum support for social assistance clients, which was undertaken between 2011 and 2015, but these were reinstalled with a vengeance in 2015–16 and it seems likely that substantial increases in poverty rates are under way.

Welfare for the poor has become increasingly weak, a development accompanied by a negative political rhetoric. Even though reforms to some extent succeed in bringing people back to work, a corollary is the formation of an underclass of 'undeserving poor'—initially mostly an ethnic underclass, but increasingly extended to include people of Danish origin. In this sense one could say that some of the most vulnerable people are kicked out of the welfare system.

Obversely there may be a voluntary exit from public to private welfare among the upper middle classes as a reaction to the reduction in public consumption and the declining number of public employees. It remains to be seen if the government is able to keep a very low growth rate in public consumption that is insufficient to maintain the status quo. In January 2018, the Liberal coalition government and the Danish People's Party failed to reach an agreement on lower taxes in exchange for tighter rules for immigrants. The public consumption prospects embodied in the 2018 budgets are well above the government's initial targets and it seems that the government failed to exploit the momentum in 2016. With solid economic growth since 2013–14 (according to heavily revised GDP figures), voters' crisis consciousness has evaporated. This could pave the way for more welfare-friendly policies, perhaps including some damage repair for the most 'deserving' among those threatened by poverty or radical income decline.

# 12

# Norway

## Averting Crisis through Coordination and Keynesian Welfare Policies

*Jon Erik Dølvik and Johannes Oldervoll*

As Norway entered the 1990s in deep crisis, prominent observers argued that the Norwegian model during the 1980s had undergone transformative change (Fagerberg, Mjöset, & Skarstein,1990; Moene & Wallerstein, 1993). Dismantling central elements of the model, the Conservatives deregulated credit and housing markets and put an end to the state capitalist features of the Norwegian economy. Far from ushering in a period of Social Democratic resurgence, however, Labour's return to power in 1986 signalled, according to Fagerberg and colleagues (1990), the definite demise of the social democratic model of capitalism when full employment was abandoned as the principal policy goal. Exchange rate stabilization had taken precedence, and between 1986 and 1993 unemployment trebled.

In this chapter, we make three principal arguments. First, we argue that the 1980–90s crises eventually inspired a Social Democratic resurgence. Unlike Sweden and many Continental European countries, Norway avoided segmentalist labour market reforms. In fact, further restrictions were introduced on temporary employment contracts, against employer protests, while vast investments were made in education and skill formation. Moreover, renewed commitment to solidaristic wage bargaining was accompanied by successive efforts to shore up coordination across sectors and policy domains. Reinforced in the aftermath of the financial crisis, the social partners appear more committed to the front-runner model of wage coordination today (2018) than a few decades ago. Further, amidst a series of deregulatory reforms in product markets, Norway exited the 1990s with a welfare state that was significantly more Scandinavian than when entering it. Together with further revisions in the macroeconomic policy mix, these adjustments made Norway better equipped to handle the next large crisis hitting in 2008.

Secondly, we show how Norway benefited from the lessons of the 1980s crisis and placed faith in its traditional institutional structures—the coordinated labour market and inclusive welfare state—to cushion the social impact of the 2008–9 financial meltdown and the recession following the 2014 oil-price plunge.

Thirdly, showing that coordination and solidarity are not necessarily linked (Thelen, 2013), we argue that while the Norwegian political economy—in spite of international market integration—has retained its capacity for policy coordination, it has been less able to maintain egalitarian outcomes. Faced with rising immigration and low-wage competition after the 2004 EU/European Economic Area (EEA) enlargements, Norway has been unable to prevent rising wage and wealth gaps (Förster, Llena-Nozal, & Nafilyan, 2014; OECD, 2011a).

## 12.1 The Political Economy Context

In contrast to liberal market economies (LMEs), Norway belongs to the Northern European group of coordinated market economies (CMEs), which are distinguished by institutionalized coordination between key producer groups, political stakeholders, and social actors in the varieties of capitalism (VoC) literature (Hall & Soskice, 2001). In empirical comparisons, the Nordic countries have stood out—also among CMEs—for low inequality and high efficiency (Sapir, 2005), commonly associated with encompassing wage coordination, active stabilization policies, and social-investment-oriented welfare and training systems (Dølvik, Andersen, & Vartiainen, 2017).

In the 1980s, flawed deregulation of credit markets and failed policy coordination sent Norway into severe crisis, prompting significant economic policy changes. In our view, the lessons from this critical juncture—followed by further revisions around the turn of the century—were essential for Norway's ability to ride out the Great Recession, thereby also averting the grave social consequences seen elsewhere. Measured by welfare state indicators Norway was long a laggard in the Nordic family, along with Iceland. Yet, since the 1980s Norway surpassed its bigger neighbours in gross domestic product (GDP) per capita, not least due to its flourishing petroleum sector. That notwithstanding, the Norwegian exchange rate and economy fluctuated in line with oil prices, and caused difficulties for export manufacturing and sectoral tension in wage and policy coordination. Combined with its special outsider/insider relationship with the EU, these traits imply that Norway has been viewed as an outlier—virtually irrelevant—in comparisons of European political economies. However, despite the surge in prosperity, repeated slumps—most lately when the oil price fell over 70 per cent in 2014—have reminded the actors of Norway's vulnerability to international political-economic swings and the quandaries they pose for domestic coordination.

In light of this, there are, in our view, useful lessons to be drawn from Norway's privileged management of crises. First, based on the Norwegian responses to the deep crises it underwent in the late 1980s, 2008–9, and again in 2014–15, relying on strengthened wage coordination, automatic welfare state stabilizers, and expansionary fiscal policy, we argue that this demand-side-oriented policy approach has proven successful over time and more important than structural labour market reforms and supply-side policies in promoting growth and employment. Secondly, the Norwegian model has—affluence notwithstanding—proven to be poorly equipped to ensure the egalitarian distribution of wealth and the benefits and burdens of increased labour mobility from Eastern Europe (Dølvik, Eldring, & Visser, 2014). Although wage inequalities are still low in comparative terms, they have increased faster in Norway than elsewhere in Europe (Förster et al., 2014; OECD, 2011a).

In what follows, section 12.2 reviews the 1980–90s crisis and section 12.3 the responses to it. Section 12.4 describes how the financial crisis affected Norway and section 12.5 the social consequences of it, while section 12.6 reviews the responses to the past decades' turbulence. Section 12.7 draws the chapter to a close with a concluding discussion.

## 12.2 The Self-Inflicted 1980s Crisis and the Responses to it

According to liberal observers, the deep crisis into which Norway—and soon after, Finland and Sweden—fell in the 1980s was evidence that the Nordic model was incompatible with globalization. But these crises had little to do with labour market rigidities or bloated welfare states. They arose from policy blunders in the process of credit market deregulation and the huge asset bubbles to which they gave rise (Dølvik et al., 2017). The increased petroleum wealth magnified the impact, but also enabled politicians to shield the welfare state and eventually apply forceful expansionary policies. The crisis led to a revision of the Norwegian economic policy regime, but, contrary to expectations, this critical juncture inspired a revitalization of the traditional labour market regime and renewal of the welfare state.

The traditional Norwegian model was built on tight fiscal policies—usually with budget surpluses—while monetary policies (with political interest rate setting, strict banking regulation, and numerous state banks) was used for Keynesian stabilization purposes. Centralized wage coordination aimed to secure manufacturing competitiveness and productive reallocation of labour and capital. Welfare state expansion was thus conditioned by the growth in revenues.

With the breakdown of the Bretton Woods system and the first oil shock in the 1970s, this economic policy model came under pressure. Anticipating rising petroleum incomes, countercyclical fiscal policies were applied to bridge the international slump. As this fuelled soaring pay increases, inflation, and current account deficits, the Labour cabinet eventually turned to austerity and enacted a wage freeze in 1978–9 (Kleppe, 2003). The second oil shock in 1979 helped balance the current account, but to experts in the Ministry of Finance and elsewhere it seemed clear that the old regime with low, politically determined interest rates was unable to contain the pressures building with the rising oil wealth (Lie & Vennesland, 2010). When a Conservative government took office in 1981, it soon announced that it would deregulate the housing and credit markets.

Swiftly dismantling restrictions on banks' lending, the government nonetheless continued to keep interest rates low while offering tax relief and maintaining tax deductions on interest payments. Unable to curb public spending, wage growth, and tax deductions, the result was an unprecedented consumption boom until the bubble eventually burst. Similar policy failures were committed under Social Democratic leadership in Sweden and Finland in the 1980s, with similar results (see Chapters 13 and 9, respectively).

### 12.2.1 *Pro-cyclical policies: From bubble to bust*

Amid accelerating inflation and current account deficits that triggered speculative attacks on the currency, an employer lockout in 1986 prompted large-scale industrial conflict and sharp labour cost increases. This, along with a collapse in petroleum prices and government attempts to curb spending, led to the ousting of the Conservative Willoch coalition. The incoming Labour cabinet devalued the krona by 12 per cent and declared that Norway would shift to a fixed exchange rate. Interest rates were raised accordingly, along with introduction of harsh austerity measures and restrictions on bank lending. Exploiting its ties with the social partners, the government imposed a wage law in 1988 whereby a modest settlement between the main employer and labour confederations (NHO and LO) was generalized and all further wage negotiations were banned (Stokke, 1998). The government sweetened the pill by contributing to the establishment of a collectively agreed early retirement scheme (AFP). When the wage law was repealed in 1990, the social partners sought to prevent local wage drift by establishing criteria for company-level wage formation.

Meanwhile, rising interest rates and fiscal austerity brought the economy to a halt. Consumer spending and building investment plunged, house prices dropped by 40 per cent, and unemployment surged (Lie & Vennesland, 2010). As ever more firms and households could not service their debts, the bursting bubble unleashed a veritable financial meltdown in 1991–2 and major banks were permitted to fail. Contrary to several EU states during the 2008 crisis, however, the state refused to bail out shareholders and large investors (Lie & Vennesland, 2010, p. 459). It also enacted legislation enabling it to nullify the stock value of bankrupt banks. By effectively nationalizing the three largest banks, the state could restructure and consolidate the financial sector, allowing it to eventually sell its shares profitably. Underpinned by the enactment of stricter funding rules and supervision, a long-term consequence was that Norway met the 2008 meltdown with a fairly sound financial sector (Mjøset & Cappelen 2011, pp. 215, 247).

### 12.2.2 *Returning to Keynes and refurbishing the model*

Alongside the shift to a hard currency regime—in 1990 the krona was pegged to European Currency Unit (ECU)—and state-imposed wage restraint, the crisis inspired a slate of further adjustments to economic policy. While fiscal policies shifted towards an expansionary stance as the recession deepened, completion of the financial deregulation was followed by liberalization of international capital flows in 1990 and the energy and telecom sectors in 1992. Also in 1992, a major tax reform introduced gross taxation of personal income and a unified lower tax rate for capital incomes, and lowered marginal tax rates on labour to spur employment. The reform broadened the tax base and abolished a host of tax deductibles that had rewarded perverse company behaviour. However, the tax deductions on interest payments that had fuelled the former bubble were retained, albeit at a modestly reduced level. At the height of the European currency crisis in 1992, the ECU peg was abandoned in favour of exchange rate stabilization against Norway's main trading partners.

From 1988, unemployment rose to levels unseen in the post-war period—in 1993 passing 9 per cent, including those on activation schemes. Against this backdrop, the government appointed an employment commission made up of representatives of the social partners, political parties, experts, and civil servants. Its report 'A National Strategy for Full Employment in the 1990s' (NOU, 1992:26) recommended a comprehensive approach coined the Solidarity Alternative, combining countercyclical fiscal policy and monetary policy attuned to the stable exchange rate regime with income policies aimed at securing competitiveness and low inflation. Regarding employers' call for more flexibility, the report collated theoretical and empirical insights into the workings of imperfect labour markets and drew heavily on Rehn–Meidnerian insights (LO, 1953). In contrast to Sweden and other countries, which undertook segmentalist reforms (or partial deregulation; see OECD (1994)), the report emphasized the beneficial constraints emanating from stringent job security rules. Hence, in 1994, Norway tightened the rules on temporary employment. Further, the commission highlighted the efficiency-enhancing aspects of wage compression and advocated more active labour market policies, with emphasis on investment in skills and work-oriented welfare policies.

In many respects, the Solidarity Alternative merely codified policy responses that had evolved incrementally during the crisis. The novelty was that it coupled the various policy areas and instruments (together) in a coherent strategy that clarified the responsibilities of different political and social actors—emphasizing the social partners' crucial role and the need for policy coordination to achieve complementarities and multiplier effects. In this way, the Solidarity Alternative represented the first attempt to configure a revised Norwegian model in the context of open global markets without jeopardizing its ability to reconcile equality and efficiency (Dølvik et al., 1997).

### 12.2.3 *Renewing and expanding the welfare state*

Facilitated by steady rising oil revenues, the 1980–90s crisis became a harbinger of the renewal and expansion of the welfare state (Fløtten, Hippe, & Christensen, 2007). The AFP adopted in 1988 to secure dignified exits for elderly workers was transformed into a supplementary labour market pension, eventually leading to introduction of a universal, flexible retirement age (from 62). At the other end of the life cycle, expanding further and higher education, and an overhaul of the vocational and educational training regime (VET), upgraded the skill structure (Tønder & Nyen, 2014).

From 1990 to 2007 the share of the working-age population with tertiary education rose from 16 to 34 per cent. During the crisis, educational reforms were supplemented by significant investments in active labour market policies, with participation peaking at approximately 3 per cent of the workforce. Further, the fiscal expansion from 1989 spurred job growth in public welfare services. Expenditure on health and social protection rose during the 1990s by roughly 70 per cent in real terms, while employment in the sector rose by 32 per cent in full-time equivalents (Fløtten et al., 2007, pp. 78–80). Parental leave was increased from 12 weeks in 1980 to 44 weeks in 1993 with a capped 100 per cent wage compensation rate, whereas childcare coverage rose from 20 to 80 per cent between 1980 and 2006 (Fløtten et al., 2007, p. 83). To further enhance female labour supply, a government White Paper advocated stronger follow-up of the activation approach (St.melding 35, 1994–5). Rather than cuts, this was mostly pursued through conditionality requirements, whereas unemployment benefit duration was increased from one to two years in 1997. In sum, Norway emerged from the crisis with a welfare state that was significantly more Scandinavian than when entering it.

## 12.3 Lessons from the 1980–90s Crises: Recalibration and Continuation in the New Century

The Norwegian economy recovered strongly from 1993. Rising manufacturing production and employment even spurred some reindustrialization. There was no magic bullet behind this turnaround, which relied on mainstream economic policy to adjust to the international regime of low inflation and free capital movements. The same pertained to the renewed emphasis on supply-side policies and liberalization of product markets. Underpinned by adjustments to the EU/EEA single market, this left more room for market competition and spurred industrial restructuring and productivity growth. The demand impetus from surging offshore investments clearly helped, but the point here is that these supply-side policies worked when underpinned by expanding demand.

The distinguishing feature of the Norwegian crisis response in the 1980s and 1990s was that market liberalization was linked with a strengthening of the social model's key tenets. First, reinvigoration of the collectivist regime of wage and employment regulation provided the social partners with key roles in tripartite concertation; secondly, the expansion of the welfare state was coupled with renewed emphasis on work and investment in human and social capital.

The oil revenues enabled Norway—in contrast to Finland and Sweden—to overcome the crisis by using welfare state expansion as a demand booster. Notable here is the seeming absence of negative effects on productivity, inflation, and the labour market. This suggests that Keynesian demand strategies can work even in an environment of free trade and capital mobility if they are complemented by proper wage policies, skill formation, and activation on the supply side.

A striking difference between Norway's way out of its financial crisis in the 1980–90 period and the Eurozone's recipe after the recent crisis, was the ability to adjust the exchange rate. In contrast to the recent crises of Denmark and Finland—both tied to the euro, albeit by different means—the swift recoveries in Norway, Finland, and Sweden in the 1990s were propelled by substantial devaluations (see Chapters 9 and 13). This sparked swift export-driven recoveries, which enabled fiscal consolidation in a context of solid growth. A similar example is the Icelandic recovery after the Great Recession of 2008 (see Chapter 8). By contrast, under the Economic and Monetary Union (EMU) regime, Finland had to undertake a pro-cyclical shift to austerity in the recent slump, a policy even Denmark—pegged to the euro—felt compelled to follow, reinforcing and prolonging the downturn (see Chapter 11). Sweden and Norway, however, benefited from currency depreciation and autonomous interest rate policies attuned to domestic needs. Without monetary policy instruments—the exchange rate and interest rate instruments, recently supplemented by quantitative easing—countries tied to the EMU are bound to counter negative economic shocks with internal devaluations, that is, cuts in wage costs or public expenditure which reduce labour demand and increase unemployment. To counter the latter, the EU crisis recipe commends 'structural reform' of labour markets and welfare arrangements. Norway also undertook welfare reforms in the 1990s to enhance labour supply, but, supported by rising labour demand, such reforms were more likely to succeed and less consequential for the bargaining power and protection of workers.

In sum, the incremental revision of the Norwegian economic policy was accompanied by reinvigoration of the social model and tripartite policy concertation. As similar adjustment patterns were seen in the other Nordic countries, international observers begun talking of a new, hybrid Nordic model combining elements from CMEs and LMEs (Campbell & Pedersen, 2007; Pontusson, 2011). According to some observers, such 'unholy marriages' were doomed to be short-lived, as the neoliberal market forces were expected to dismantle the social institutions on which the Nordic models rested (Baccaro & Howell, 2011; Bieler, 2012).

### 12.3.1 *Soaring employment: New tensions in wage setting*

Today, it is widely acknowledged that wage and policy coordination under the Solidarity Alternative helped the Norwegian economy return to a growth path consonant with high employment and low unemployment. Faced with rapidly rising unemployment around 1990, coordinated wage setters placed a high premium on aggregate employment and provided policymakers with room to pursue fiscal stimulus without risking inflation (see Gjedrem, 2002 and Figures 12.1a and b).

By 1998, unemployment had fallen to 3.2 per cent and employment rates had climbed to unprecedented heights. As the labour market became increasingly tight, the collective wage formation system appeared—as in Sweden under the late 1980s boom—decreasingly able to deliver the prescribed wage restraint. When the 1998 bargaining round resulted in wage increases that far exceeded those of Norway's trading partners, along with a series of public sector strikes and defections from the 'rules of the game' on the part of service sector trade unions, the viability of the bargaining system was called into question. Hence, a commission was appointed to supervise the 1999 midterm revisions, and two tripartite commissions were appointed to propose

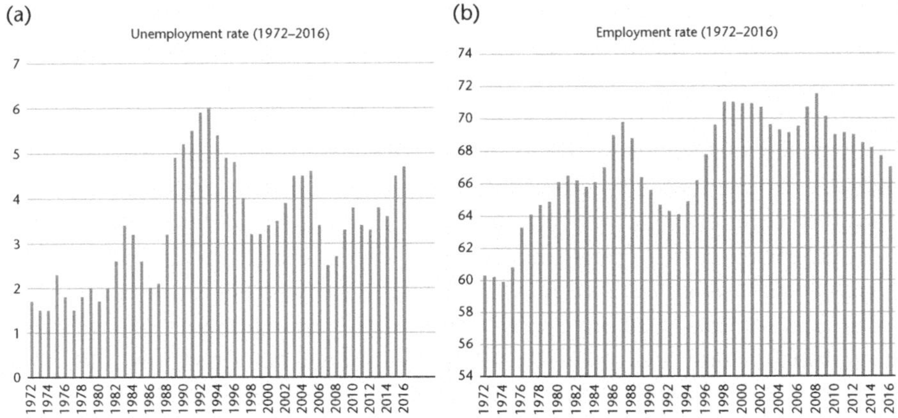


**Figure 12.1.** Unemployment and employment rates (ages 15–74), 1972–2016
*Source*: Statistics Norway, Labour Force Survey.

adjustments to the collective bargaining system and ways to strengthen the social partners' coordination capacity.

Given the tensions between export manufacturing and the public sector, the commissions concentrated on rendering the front-runner model more palatable to public sector trade unions. Importantly, embraced by the social partners, the estimated wage norm set by the trendsetting industries was broadened to include wage increases both among blue- and white-collar workers in export manufacturing. These exercises helped solidify the central premise of the wage coordination system, namely that wage increases in the export industries should set the norm for wage developments elsewhere.

## 12.3.2 *Restoring monetary policy discretion*

Following the 1986 devaluation, Norwegian monetary policy transitioned from a non-credible to a more credible exchange rate regime.[1] Largely successful, the new regime also implied that monetary policy could not—as currently in Denmark—be used for stabilization purposes. When the aforementioned wage settlement of 1998 sparked something of a political crisis, this was in no small part because the Central Bank found it impossible to defend the krona amid the financial turmoil after the Asian crisis (Steigum & Thøgersen, 2015, p. 14). When a doubling of the interest rate proved insufficient, the Central Bank in effect abandoned exchange rate stabilization as its principal policy goal (Gjedrem, 2010). The regime shift was not formalized until 2001, when

[1] Between 1976 and 1986, the Norwegian krone was devalued seven times. As a result, the currency proved largely indefensible towards the end of the period.

the Labour cabinet announced that Norway would officially introduce a flexible inflation target of 2.5 per cent.

Although instructed to set its key policy rate in light of activity and employment levels, the Central Bank initially took a non-accommodating stance. In 2002, the new monetary regime was brought into conflict with the collective wage-setting system when pay increases well in excess of those among Norway's trading partners were agreed. Fearing inflation, the Central Bank punished wage setters by raising its key policy rate. Elsewhere, the information and communication technology (ICT) crisis and 9/11 were met with more lax monetary policy, and the krona appreciated sharply (Eika, 2008). The Bank's hawkish approach would prove costly, as the currency appreciation and wage increases severely impaired competitiveness (16 per cent) and over 30,000 manufacturing jobs were lost between 2000 and 2003 (according to Strukturstatistikk from Statistics Norway 2004). A new commission was thus appointed to consider the compatibility between the front-runner model and inflation targeting. In its report, the commission argued that the front-runner model was both necessary and durable, provided that wage setters and the Central Bank could learn to get along (NOU, 2013:13). Experience in the years that have passed testify to the wisdom of this approach.

When the turmoil was overcome, Norway's international fortunes took a turn for the better. Oil prices trebled from 1999, leaving the state—through its recently established Petroleum Fund—with unanticipated windfall in revenues. This sparked a heated debate on fiscal policy guidelines—or lack thereof—in the context of highly volatile petroleum revenues (Lie & Vennesland, 2010). It was widely held that fiscal policy of the 1970s and the 1980s—when budgets were balanced (pro-cyclically) directly through petroleum revenues—had exacerbated the 1980s malaise. As price volatility could well prove destabilizing once more, the Labour government in 2001 introduced rules for the use of oil revenues. Supported by all but the populist Progress Party, the fiscal rule implied that budget deficits over time should not exceed the expected real rate of return on the Petroleum Fund (4 per cent).[2] Over time, the fiscal rule would allow the fund to grow and enable governments to gradually phase in petroleum revenues, while shielding the economy and the budget process from oil-price volatility. Importantly, the fiscal target provided scope for countercyclical fiscal policy. In times of contraction, deficits could exceed the target; in times of expansion, deficits should return to the stipulated bounds.

[2] The Petroleum Fund had been established in 1996, tasked with investing petroleum revenues abroad.

## 12.4 Riding out the Financial Crisis and the Oil-Price Plunge in 2014

Quickly recovering from the slump following the ICT crisis and the 2002 monetary policy failure, Norway experienced its strongest, most durable economic boom in decades. By 2007, employment had reached an all-time high while registered unemployment fell towards 2 per cent. In 2008, however, activity ground to a halt and annual growth fell from over 6 per cent to 2.2 per cent. Soon after the Lehman Brothers collapse, the red–green government presented a modestly expansionary budget, primarily aimed at buffering a mild contraction prior to the financial crisis. The budget made no reference to the imminent meltdown, but it was soon evident that the Norwegian financial system needed to implement extraordinary measures to survive. As credit lines for the Norwegian banks dried up, the parliament passed a slate of bills to provide liquidity to the financial system.

The principal fiscal response came in January 2009, when the government presented a large fiscal stimulus package. As the Petroleum Fund had accrued large revenues, the government faced the crisis in a solid fiscal position and with a mandate to counteract downturns with sizable budget deficits. Combining spending increases and selective tax cuts, the stimulus package had a distinctly Keynesian tenor.[3] As the crisis deepened over the next months, further spending increases were adopted in May 2009. In total, the red–green government increased oil revenue spending by roughly 50 billion krona from 2008 to 2009, amounting to a fiscal stimulus of 2.7 per cent of mainland GDP (NOU, 2013:13).

Monetary policy, too, played an important part in the Norwegian crisis response. Unlike the 1980–90s slump, monetary policy could now—as in Sweden—be used to stimulate economic activity. From October 2008 to June 2009, the Central Bank cut its key policy rate by 4.5 percentage points. Owing to high household indebtedness and floating mortgage rates, this had a fairly immediate effect on household consumption (Steigum & Thøgersen, 2015, p. 25).

Contributing to softening the blow, the LO–NHO bargaining round conducted at peak level generated a modest settlement, containing also a derogation clause allowing the central increment to be forfeited or postponed through local agreement.

[3] Although the lion's share of the stimulus package sought to bolster economic and labour demand directly, 20% was devoted to temporary tax cuts targeted at struggling businesses to prevent needless job losses. As compensated businesses were required to pay additional taxes upon recovery, the measure did not harm the long-term fiscal position.

By spring 2009, most of the extraordinary financial measures had been discontinued and by October the minister of finance and the Central Bank's governor declared that Norway had largely steered clear of the financial crisis. The main reasons, according to observers, centred upon a virtuous combination of sound institutional arrangements, a competent and resolute macroeconomic response, and *luck* (Gjedrem, 2010). The director of the Financial Authority highlighted that Norwegian authorities and central financial players had learned important lessons from the 1980s banking crisis and recession—entering the 2008 financial crisis with more stringent banking standards than most other countries (NOU, 2011:1). The Central Bank's governor also pointed to the institutional resettlement at the new century's turn. The new fiscal rule, coupled with vast revenues during the boom phase of 2004–7, provided substantial fiscal leeway, while the abandonment of exchange rate stabilization enabled the Central Bank to focus on economic stabilization (Gjedrem, 2010).

The importance of the latter points was further highlighted when Norway, in 2014–16, fell into a new and deeper recession owing to plunging oil prices and an associated halt in offshore investments. Largely applying a similar recipe, the newly elected Conservative government responded with expansionary fiscal policy, including sizable tax reliefs and record-high spending of oil revenues (NOU, 2016:15). As the Central Bank kept interest rates low and the exchange rate fell by 20–30 per cent, while the social partners contributed with zero-wage growth—in effect, real wage decline—competitiveness improved, domestic demand was maintained, and by 2017 the economy had recovered, with unemployment in October 2017 standing at 4 per cent.

## 12.5 Financial Hardship through the Crisis Years

As shown in Figure 12.2, the share of the Norwegian population experiencing financial hardship is very low in comparison with other European countries—only about a quarter of the European average. The crises in 2008–9 and in 2014–15 had very little impact on the overall picture. Some subgroups did, however, experience an increase of hardship, such as the unemployed and those with the lowest educational level. The prevalence of hardship is highest amongst individuals in the lowest income quintile and amongst single parents. Both had an increase at first and then a return towards their pre-crisis position. Immigrants had the third-highest level of financial hardship before the crisis, but they improved their position during the crisis years. The unemployed had, by 2015, approached their pre-crisis level again. Even in these groups, however, the shares experiencing financial hardship are markedly lower than the European average.

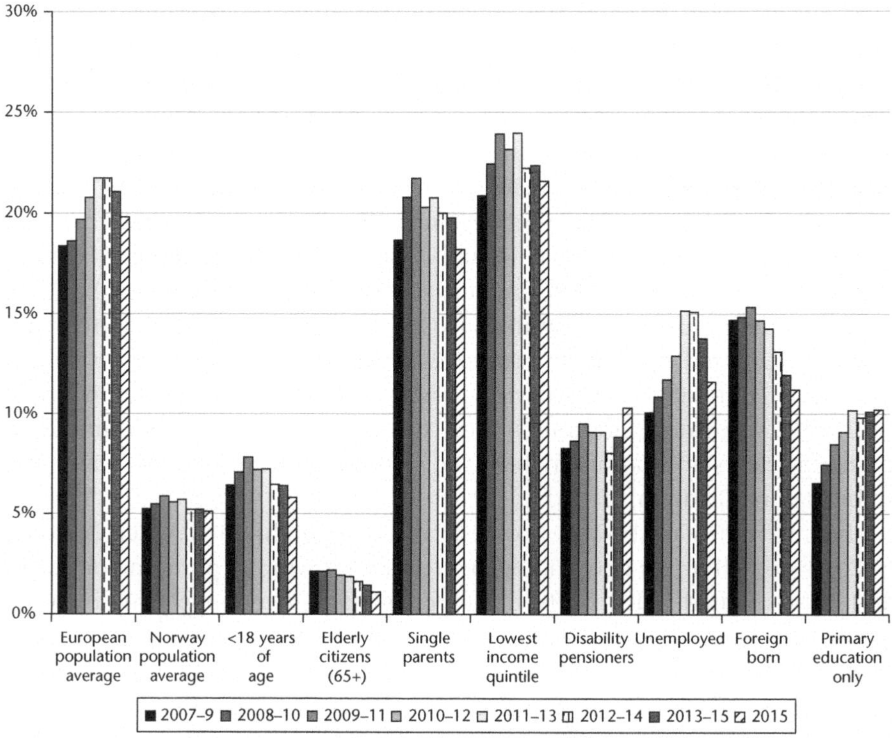


**Figure 12.2.** Financial hardship profiles throughout the crisis in Norway, 2007–15

*Note*: This shows Norway compared to the European average and disaggregated by main socio-economic groups. It is a composite measure based on income poverty, difficulties in making ends meet, and material deprivation (see the Appendix for explanation of the methodology), and shows proportion suffering financial hardship over three-year moving averages and in 2015.

Households with children under 18 experienced a small increase of hardship early on, topping in 2011, and then dropped to a lower level again. They ended the period close to the very low pre-crisis level. Disability pensioners had a mixed and modest development of hardship during the crisis years, albeit at a low level for that group in the wider European context.

As the majority of those in risk of poverty in Norway are people outside the labour market, the low shares falling into the hardship category bear witness, first, to the robust system of income transfers marking the Norwegian welfare state and, secondly, to the effectiveness of the interplay between Keynesian crisis management and solidaristic wage setting in curbing unemployment and in-work poverty. The elderly, who only had a financial hardship level of around 2–3 per cent even saw this reduced in the latter part of the crisis.

A worrying tendency, however, is that the rate of employment since 2007 has shown a mild downward tendency, leading in 2018 to the appointment of a new employment commission assigned to assess, in view of comparative experience, how welfare, training, and labour market arrangements can improve inclusion and job and income opportunities, especially for groups at risk of marginalization (NOU, 2017:2; St.melding 29, 2016–17).

## 12.6 Responses to Recent Turmoil: Coordination Restored, Solidarity Lost?

As seen, lessons learned over the course of the preceding decades, along with large petroleum revenues, have helped Norway ride out the international upheavals more or less unscathed. In the years following the financial crisis dip, the Norwegian economy continued along its merry path, largely decoupled from developments elsewhere in Europe, not least owing to rapidly rising oil prices, beneficial terms of trade, and soaring investments on the offshore shelf. Indeed, between 2008 and 2015, the real wage of a median wage earner rose by 17.2 per cent.

The flipside of the boom, however, was that the competitiveness of Norwegian manufacturing deteriorated sharply (NOU, 2013:13). This incited renewed debate on the functioning of the wage-setting system. As per usual practice, a commission with representatives from all the main employer and labour confederations was appointed to consider the fit between multi-tier bargaining and macroeconomic policy in a petroleum-driven economy. In its report, the commission concluded that changes in the composition of the front-runner industries—entailing an increased share of petroleum-related production—had weakened the cost competitiveness of traditional manufacturing but also ensured that a large share of wage earners had benefited from beneficial terms of trade (NOU, 2013:13). As a result, the capital/labour ratio of value added had remained relatively stable since the 1970s.

The commission also sought to address the recurring dissatisfaction with the front-runner model on the part of public sector trade unions. In 2012, a large strike erupted in the public sector where the trade unions questioned the credibility of projected wage increases in exposed industries. In response, the commission proposed measures to strengthen adherence to the wage norm, amongst others, that NHO—in agreement with LO—should publish a credible estimate of wage growth in the trendsetting industries. Including pay rises among the individually negotiating white-collar employees, this entailed a strong commitment on the part of the NHO to curb white-collar pay drift. Apart from these incremental adaptations, the codification of former practice renewed and consolidated the social partners' commitment to the front-runner model.

The employer associations' capacity to deliver on that commitment has thus far not been really tested, due to the subsequent recession unleashed by the 2014 oil-price plunge. Grinding the petroleum-related industries to a halt—losing 50,000 jobs in ensuing years—the downturn was met with very modest settlements, in 2016 even resulting in falling real wages. The public sector unions have largely conformed with the norm. Hence, the central stakeholders in the Norwegian wage-setting system acted according to script, while the Conservative government and the Central Bank secured ample stimuli to bridge the slump.

### 12.6.1 *Coordinated stabilization from the top: Widening gaps from below?*

While confirming the Norwegian model's capacity for flexible adjustment to economic shocks (Katzenstein, 1985), the turbulent period after the turn of century has nevertheless called its ability to secure egalitarian outputs into question. Despite increased immigration of groups with low employment rates from countries outside the EU/EEA, Norway has, due to its generous welfare transfers, only seen modest growth in household income inequality (NOU, 2017:2). More striking, however, is the stark increase in wage inequality in the lower half of the income distribution.

Norway entered the new millennium with a wage structure that was comparable to those of Finland and Sweden. In the intervening years, Norway appears to have departed from the Nordic trajectory (see Figure 12.3). By 2016,

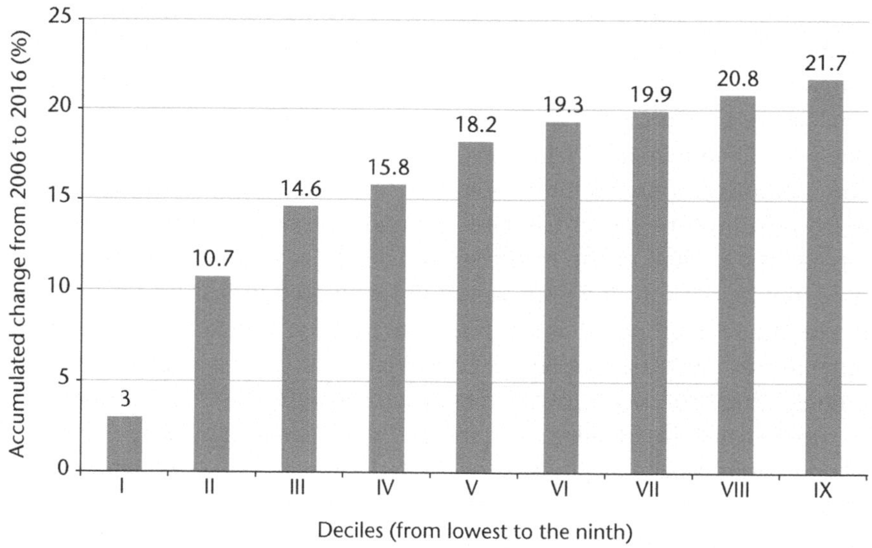


**Figure 12.3.** Real wage increases by earnings deciles, accumulated 2006–16 (%)
*Note*: Shows wage increases per decile for full-time equivalents, adjusted for inflation.
*Source*: Statistics Norway, TBU 2017.

dispersion in the lower half of the wage distribution was closer to that of Britain than Sweden (Jordfald & Nymoen, 2016).

Despite rising challenges in regulating work in transnational labour markets, Norway and its Nordic neighbours have—unlike most European governments—not introduced a statutory minimum wage. Leaving wage setting to the social partners, the Norwegian system of wage bargaining has never been underpinned by rates of organization and collective agreement coverage comparable to its Nordic neighbours (Alsos & Eldring, 2014). Still, Norway has historically been characterized by a compressed wage structure (NOU, 2016:15), reflecting the fact that even unorganized firms have tended to follow the wages set by collective agreements in order to attract and retain labour in tight labour markets. This changed profoundly when Norway, from 2004, experienced a massive influx of migrant and posted workers, predominantly from Poland and the Baltic countries (Dølvik et al., 2014). This opened new scope for competition on pay and conditions, especially in instances of cross-border subcontracting where, according to EU rules (PWD 71/1996), the posted workers are subject to home country rules except for a nucleus of minimum labour standards including minimum pay regulated by statute or extended collective agreements. To counter the spread of low-wage competition, some unions hesitantly begun to invoke the dormant 1994 law on extension of minimum terms in collective agreements—today covering nine industries—underpinned by a range of statutory control and enforcement measures. In spite of these measures, which in several home market sectors gained support from employers, it has proved difficult to halt the contagious abuse of migrant labour, especially when migrants are employed by international subcontractors or staffing agencies.

In our view, these developments can hardly be attributed to an insider orientation on the part of Norwegian trade unions. Although union density among low-skilled service workers is low, a number of unions in low-wage service industries have merged or amalgamated with stronger manufacturing unions that have invested considerable organizational resources in lifting their respective low-wage groups.[4] In the last few years alone, manufacturing-based trade unions have even gone on strike in support of improved relative wages for low-wage workers. Nonetheless, with increased layers of unorganized firms, often with highly internationalized workforces—steadily fuelled by extra EU/EEA jobseekers arriving through the 'humanitarian' gates—such efforts have proven insufficient to curb the tendency towards a more dualized job market in parts of the private sector.

[4] For instance, hotel and restaurant workers are now organized alongside manufacturing and construction workers in the United Federation of Trade Unions.

Hence, while the Norwegian model has proven efficient in handling the globalization challenges stemming from increased trade and foreign direct investment (FDI), it has proven much less efficient in dealing with low-wage competition and disorganization stemming from the internationalized labour market. A rising concern is hence that the twin effect of declining employment rates and emergence of a low-wage job market will spur growing welfare state dependence and call the viability of the generous Norwegian income transfers into question when the effects of the ageing population make themselves felt in the decades to come (NOU, 2017:2).

## 12.7 Discussion and Conclusions

In this chapter we have argued that the renewed Norwegian model of coordinated wage setting, welfare, and economic policies has stood the test over 30 years with huge swings. While the oscillating oil price has fuelled volatility, offshore investments and revenues have boosted growth and enabled Norway to pursue countercyclical Keynesian policies and welfare state expansion to bridge the slumps. Through learning from earlier crises, the means of coordination have become better attuned while specific policy instruments have been subject to incremental recalibration. As the fiscal rule for use of oil revenues was introduced in 2001 along with the change in monetary policy towards inflation targeting and a floating exchange rate, the independent monetary policy could be used for stabilizing purposes in response to the Great Recession and after the oil-price plunge in 2014. The wage formation system, too, has been subject to cautious adaptation, so that the upper wage norm defined by the trendsetting trade has been strengthened, for instance, by including white-collar employees in calculations of wage drift. Thus, in contrast to the management of crises in the 1980s, the refurbished Norwegian model has, after the turn of the century, proved to be quite successful in counteracting and cushioning negative demand shocks in the swinging Norwegian oil economy.

Therefore, the first main conclusion from our analysis is that—in spite of liberalization of product markets and propelling globalization of trade and FDI—the Norwegian capacity to and repertoire for managing economic crisis by means of coordinated economic, wage, and welfare policies has improved and become more sophisticated over the past 25 years (see e.g. NOU, 2016:15). Rather than a definite demise of the social democratic model of capitalism (Fagerberg et al., 1990), this has implied a revival of traditional features of the Norwegian social model within an economic context that has indisputably become more market liberal. In view of the broader European controversies in the wake of the Euro crisis over the merits of demand-side versus supply-side policies, the Norwegian case clearly indicates that demand-stimulating policies still work—even in small, open economies—insofar as they are underpinned by effective wage coordination, autonomous monetary policy, and sound public finances.

Our second conclusion is that the Norwegian model has been much less successful in coping with the labour supply shock and ensuing structural shift in the labour market following the extension of the EU/EEA single market from 2004. With modest coverage of collective agreements and low organizational density in many private industries, the Norwegian labour regime has not been able to stem the growth of low-wage competition, social dumping, and downward inequality in affected sectors. The consequences has been increased wage dispersion at the lower end and growing segmentation of the job market (Bratsberg, Dölvik, Nergaard, & Raaum, 2015; Jordfald & Nymoen, 2016). A related effect has been increased dependency, especially among migrant workers and the growing immigrant population, on welfare benefits, and deteriorating employment rates among young people in particular (Friberg, 2016; NOU, 2017:2). These tendencies have spurred debates about why Norway, in such a prolonged period of economic affluence, has not managed to halt the rise in income inequalities and bring down the rate of welfare dependency among disadvantaged groups (St.melding 29, 2016–17). As well as failing to curb the inequality-enhancing dynamics of contemporary capitalism, a related cause of concern is the past decade's surge in Norwegian housing prices and household debt—which currently is among the highest in Europe.

Although Norway has been successful in protecting its citizens against financial hardship during the recent crises, a looming question is how resilient the Norwegian model will prove if the leeway for fiscal expansion and welfare state spending diminishes. While the institutions of the Nordic countries were renowned for their ability to reconcile growth and distribution—efficiency and equality—in the era of industrial mass production and relative closure, they appear less well equipped to maintain that capacity in a context of unfettered free movement, digitalization of production, and financialization of investment. With the prospect of diminishing oil revenues and a rising elderly population, Norwegian policymakers and wage setters are thus well advised to prepare for harder policy choices in the decades to come. If they continue to learn from experience, however, the Norwegian actors will probably be better positioned to tackle these choices than their counterparts in most other comparable European countries.

# 13

# Sweden

## In Times of Two Crises

*Joakim Palme*

### 13.1 Introduction

The Great Recession evokes a number of questions in relation to the Swedish welfare state and invites historical as well as comparative perspectives. A natural starting point is to ask how the encounter with the Great Recession compares with other crises that the country has experienced. Comparisons with other countries can also help us to assess the consequences of the Great Recession, not only for human conditions but also for policymaking. This can provide new insights about the capacity of the welfare state to protect the population against economic policy failures and/or external shocks. We can also ask if these processes are changing the political economy of the 'Swedish Welfare State Model' as we know it. Ultimately, this is about lessons learnt for future policymaking in Sweden and, possibly, in other country contexts.

Historically the most important reforms of the Swedish welfare state have taken place in times of crisis, which would suggest that every crisis opens up an opportunity for transformational change. The Great Depression triggered state interventions in many countries in ways that did not seem possible before the 1930s. In Sweden, this holds true for economic policies in general and employment-related policies in particular (Furåker, 1986). In the interwar period, many European countries experienced falling birth rates and the threat of population decline. In Sweden this was framed as the 'Crisis of the Population Question' (Myrdal & Myrdal, 1934) and became the starting point for new social reforms aimed at supporting families with children, as a strategy to simultaneously respond to poor social conditions and falling birth rates.

Even if the oil crises of the 1970s meant declining growth rates and put public finances under pressure, unemployment did not increase much and the Swedish welfare state saw little change (Hort, 2014). The economic crisis of the 1990s was a tougher challenge, not only for the welfare state but also for most elements of the post-war Swedish model (Palme et al., 2003). The management of the crisis in the financial sector in the 1990s could also be seen as a rehearsal for the kinds of pressures triggered by the Great Recession. It meant that different levels of government and various public authorities actually had a game plan (Lundgren, 2009). In a Swedish perspective, it is therefore impossible to analyse and discuss the Great Recession and its consequences without referring to what happened during the 1990s. The chapter approaches this by making systematic comparisons between Great Recession and the 1990s crisis in order to identify similarities and differences, as well as historical legacies.

The chapter is organized in the following way. First, the characteristics of the crises are described and analysed in section 13.2 to capture their depth and severity. Section 13.3 offers an account of financial hardships upon the advent of the crisis, including comparisons to the 1990s crisis and to the crisis experiences of other countries. Thereafter, section 13.4 describes and analyses political responses to the crisis in terms of policy. Section 13.5 offers a discussion of how burdens were shared, including considerations of both structural changes and policy decisions. Section 13.6 discusses the relevance of social policy in how Swedish society has fared during times of crisis and the role of the Swedish Welfare State Model in this context.

## 13.2 Two Crises

### 13.2.1 *Sweden's first dip*

In retrospect, the Swedish crisis of the 1990s not only seems home-grown but also the result of unlucky timing of a number of reforms and events, where international trends served to magnify the consequences of domestic mistakes. A disturbing fact is that decisions were taken that could have been avoided if the lessons from similar reform strategies previously pursued by other countries had been learnt. What eventually triggered the crisis was the bursting of a real estate bubble that had started to build up following the deregulation of financial markets during the 1980s. The bubble had been growing for some time but burst only when policy reforms taken to put a break on the drivers of the bubble started to come into effect. The 'mistakes' reveal many similarities with what has been recorded for Finland (see Chapter 9).

Here the 1991 tax reform, labelled the 'tax reform of the century', is of crucial importance (Perbo, 1999). It followed the pattern established in many other countries, including a broadening of the tax base, a lowering of marginal taxes, and a separation of taxes on capital and labour. It is clear that the reform had important repercussions for the financial sector. The intended effect was the changed incentive structure: it became much more expensive to borrow and more profitable to save. The unintended impact was a drastic—and, as it turned out, destructive—drop in domestic consumption in 1991 (10 per cent of GDP) as reformed incentive structures actually changed behaviours.[1] At the same time the inflationary wage negotiation system had been subject to a kind of overhaul, with a nationwide wage deal that meant a virtual wage freeze in 1991 and modest increases the following year. This, of course, had an immediate impact on wage inflation, which then spilled over to lower price inflation. In combination with the tax reform and the increasing cost of borrowing money, the real estate and housing sector bubbles burst. The driving factor was the borrowing rate, which had exceeded 100 per cent during the high inflation years because investors and individual consumers were under the impression that inflation would continue. It did not.

The economic downturns in the early 1990s in the UK and the USA, Sweden's most important export markets at the time, coincided with the domestic demand fall. The financial sector was first to be hit and many companies went bankrupt, including some major banks. The only two banks that survived without direct state support lost about 80 per cent of their value on the stock market (Lundgren, 2009). The consequences were massive for growth, employment, and public finances.

From 1991 to 1993, GDP growth rates were negative for three years in a row, which had not been experienced even during the Great Depression of the 1930s. In GDP per capita terms the total fall was also deeper in the 1990s. The negative growth rates were, to an important extent, driven by a dramatic fall in employment. In an active labour force of 4.5 million, employment fell by 500,000. Open unemployment went from below 2 per cent to above 8 per cent. On top of that, the proportion of the labour force that was engaged in active labour market policies (ALMPs) was virtually tripled to reach 6 per cent. The fall in employment and growth eroded the tax base. The costs of unemployment were massively increasing public expenditure. The result was that the deficit in the public finances 'skyrocketed' and in 1994 eventually reached 13 per cent of GDP (Palme et al., 2003).

In addition, Sweden experienced the most dramatic waves of refugee immigration since World War II. The wars in the Balkans and the African Horn were major sources of these flows of people and the costs for the public sector were high and immediate. The positive effects, stemming from the labour market integration of these mainly young persons, took time to emerge. Here it is

[1] Note that income levels had remained the same.

important to see the employment crisis in sequence. First, the economic crisis hit the manufacturing sector. This increased unemployment, particularly among men. When the municipality sector, which in Sweden is highly dependent on the ability to tax the residents, was hit by the crisis the municipalities were more or less forced (by central state regulations) to cut back on spending, which meant that the crisis spread to the public sector by lowering employment, mainly in social services. This resulted in the unemployment rate of women reaching that of men. The employment crisis was sticky: employment in 1998 was still lower than in 1993. In 1999, however, employment figures saw a strong recovery, not least for the immigrant part of the population (Palme et al., 2003).

The financial sector had been the first to recover and was already in profit again by 1994. Eventually economic growth picked up, partly because the international business cycle became more favourable, partly as a consequence of policy changes to which we will return in section 13.4. Public finances improved faster than expected, and faster than employment. Despite this, Sweden left the 20th century with an economic deficit. As we will develop further in section 13.6, there was also a 'social deficit' which, even if it was identified (SOS, 2006), was not fully recognized. By the turn of the millennium the Swedish economy was booming, fuelled by an expanding information and communication technology (ICT) sector. Yet the first years of the 21st century did not really serve as a honeymoon for this vibrant 'new economy'. Part of the booming ICT bubble burst. Economic downturns in different parts of the world contributed to high volatility, not least on the stock market. Unemployment increased again, especially among youth. This continued to contribute to an unfinished recovery from the 1990s, which in a way paved the way for a policy supply-side shift that will be described in section 13.4.4.

### 13.2.2 *Sweden's second dip*

The Great Recession of 2008 and onwards differed in a number of important ways from the crisis of the 1990s. It was caused by different, external, factors and it was quicker. However, although the Great Recession drop was faster it was not much deeper than in the 1990s. Recovery was also quick in most respects, which contrasts with the first dip (SCB, 2018). As we will expand on in section 13.4, policy responses to the Great Recession were similar to those of the 1990s with regard to the financial sector but different with regard to social policies. The implosion of the global financial markets during the autumn of 2008 had immediate repercussions for the Swedish economy. This is not surprising given the deep integration of the Swedish economy in global financial and product markets. The effects were particularly strong for financial institutions and for the manufacturing sector.

The financial sector was challenged by the global credit crunch, which shook the entire sector. While the Swedish banking sector did not have to struggle with bad loans to the same extent as in the 1990s, a complicating factor was the exposure of some of the Swedish commercial banks in the Baltic countries. This was, in reality, the biggest source for concern for the Swedish regulatory authorities with regard to the financial markets. With the state guarantees in place, all banks eventually survived the Great Recession. There was perhaps only one commercial bank—with low exposure in the Baltics—which would have survived without such guarantees. In contrast to the 1990s and to the developments in many other European countries, not to speak of the USA, the Great Recession did not trigger a crisis for the housing sector in Sweden.

In 2009, the fall in manufacturing was broad and deep—a result of the drastic fall in international demand. It triggered fast reactions from companies, first in issuing advance notices and then in actually laying-off a large number of workers, though a substantial number of layoffs were subsequently withdrawn. Unemployment showed strong regional correlation with the relative importance of the manufacturing sector. GDP started to fall in 2008 and fell by more than 5 per cent in 2009; altogether more than 6 per cent over these two years. Recovery was fast, however, and GDP growth was not only positive again in 2010 but on par with the negative rate of 2009—it has since continued to be positive with the exception of a small dip in 2012. Compared to the rest of Europe the fall in GDP was not remarkable and the recovery not outstanding. The fall was definitely smaller than in the worst affected countries but fairly close to the median. The recovery was better than average but not as fast as in, for example, the Baltic States (see Chapter 2).

In contrast to the 1990s, the Great Recession remained a crisis for the manufacturing sector and did not spread to the public sector. An explanatory factor here was the fact that the public finances in the municipality sector were much stronger than they had been in the 1990s. The (central) state finances were in general in remarkably good shape and the deficit never reached above 1 per cent of GDP. Domestic demand remained strong. Low interest rates and a reasonably stable housing sector, as well as a large inflow of refugees during the years before the crisis, also contributed to reducing the impact of the Great Recession. While implying large short-term costs, the population increased, and so too did public expenditure to low-income groups. The recovery was helped by the fact that Sweden had a floating currency, which meant that the competitiveness of the export sector was strengthened by the automatically depreciated Swedish krona. This stands in contrast to the Finnish situation inside the Eurozone and Denmark where the krona is pegged to the euro, and, of course, to the initial situation in Sweden during the autumn of 1992.

## 13.3 Financial Hardships during Two Crises

### 13.3.1 *A prolonged employment crisis*

The financial hardship tales of our two crises of the 1990s and the Great Recession are, in more than one respect, very different: it is clear that the first crisis generated significantly more hardship for individuals and households than the latter.

Following Palme and colleagues (2003), we can look back at the 1990s crisis in various ways: the late but fast recovery more or less across the board meant that by the end of the 1990s, some aspects of living standards were actually better than at the beginning. Some were on par with what had been recorded before the crisis, whereas others failed to recover, such as unemployment, economic buffers, and mental health (anxiety). This overall pattern is true for financial as well as other hardships. To illustrate the point: real hourly wage rates improved over the decade and this was the case also for low-paid workers. Since employment levels had not fully recovered, this resulted in the fact that average disposable incomes remained on roughly the same level in 1999 as in 1991.

Such a perspective on the 1990s crisis fails to capture how deep the economic downturn was for the economy at large and for individual households. For example, in the midst of the crisis a family with two children had on average lost about 30,000 SEK (€3,000) per year in disposable income and it was only by the end of the decade that disposable income levels had, on average, recovered fully. Here it should be noted that the economic margins of households to cover unexpected expenditures had not recovered by the end of the 1990s, suggesting that the prolonged employment crisis had taken its toll on the economic reserves of many households.

Poverty rates developed in—what at first would appear to be—unexpected ways. The relative rates actually went down during the worst years of crisis. This could, however, be explained by the fact that 90 per cent of the population experienced an absolute decline in income, but as safety nets were not reduced in general people on low incomes were less affected by the crisis. When growth started and income levels for those in employment and those with capital income increased, the relative poverty rates actually started to grow (since low-income groups lagged behind), but still absolute poverty declined (see Chapter 8, Table 8.2, for a similar pattern).

### 13.3.2 *An instant shock*

The hardship indicators for the period that we associate with the Great Recession are surprisingly clear and consistent. The pattern described in Chapter 2 and Figure 13.1 correlates very strongly with what has been reported in national surveys and reports (Bengtsson, Edin, & Holmlund, 2014; Björklund & Jäntti, 2011; Cronert & Palme, 2017). It may be possible to summarize the trends as follows: most indicators do not change significantly during the Great Recession, the trend is for declining financial hardships, and, while some indicators actually change for the worse, they do so without being primarily affected by either the crises as such or by crisis-related policy changes.

Figure 13.1 helps us to see how financial hardships in Sweden have developed from 2007 to 2015, and makes comparisons with European averages as well as of different population groups possible. The average level of hardship in Sweden is not only much lower (around 5 per cent) than the European average (around 20 per cent) but also declining. It can be noted that by 2015 no single population group of those displayed in Figure 13.1 experience a higher hardship level than the European average. Compared to European average, what is different with the Swedish development over time is that hardship declined for all groups from 2007 to 2009, that is, during the worst

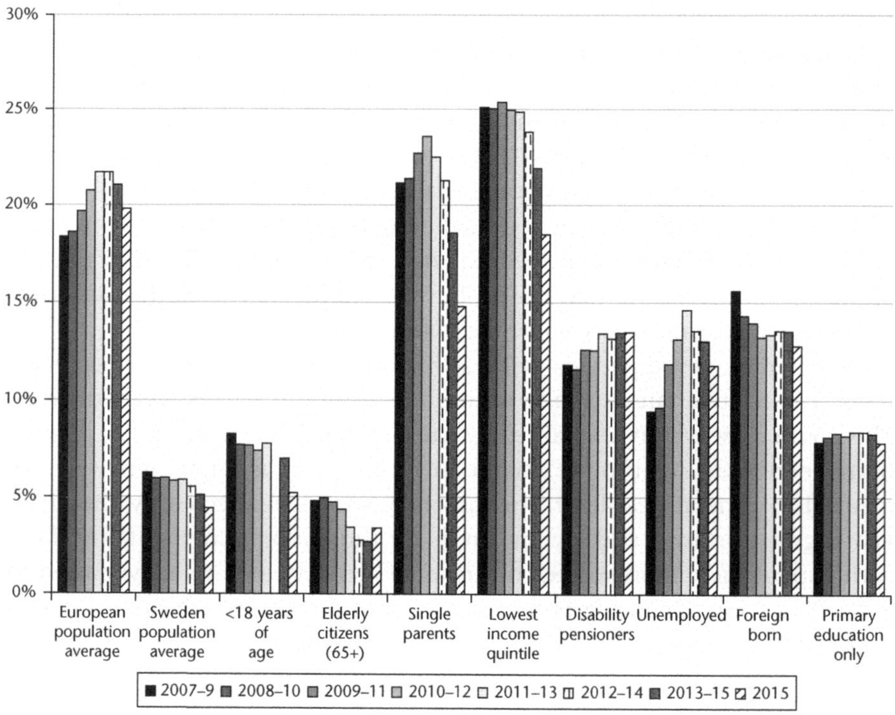


**Figure 13.1.** Financial hardship profiles through the crisis in Sweden, 2007–15

*Note*: This shows Sweden compared to the European average and disaggregated by main socio-economic groups. It is a composite measure based on income poverty, difficulties in making ends meet, and material deprivation (see the Appendix for explanation of the methodology), and shows proportion suffering financial hardship over three-year moving averages and in 2015.

years of economic crisis. Then there was a common increase to 2011, and thereafter a universal decline.

Children and the elderly share low levels of hardship with small fluctuations and a declining trend to below 5 per cent in 2015. Single parents and those in the lowest income quintile show similar levels and development trends. Both groups start above 20 per cent and peak around 2011, approaching 25 per cent, but they decline substantially to 2015, not least single parents. Disability pensioners, the unemployed, and immigrants end up with similar hardship levels but changes over time differ. Disability pensioners show modest changes and no declining trend. The unemployed group displays a peak around the middle of the period and then come down again. Foreign-born persons start above 15 per cent in 2007 and, after ups and downs, end around 12–13 per cent. Low educated people in Sweden have higher than average hardship rates but below 10 per cent. They experienced only small changes and a somewhat declining trend.

Compared to the 1990s crisis, the development of hardships for different population groups during the Great Recession display less problems for all groups during the crisis as well as in the aftermath. The positive contrast to the 1990s is particularly sharp for the foreign born, as well as for single parents.

However, the Swedish Great Recession case warrants a disaggregated analysis of different hardship indicators. As shown in Chapter 2, unemployment in Sweden increased at the onset of the crisis but less than in most other European countries and from modest levels. In contrast to not only the worst affected European countries, but also the Swedish experience in the 1990s, the unemployment rates had already started to come down in 2010. Indicators that are expressions of some kind of absolute financial status report the crisis had little effect. Material deprivation was not increasing and the indicator of economic strain was also unaffected. This stands in contrast to the Southern European countries where the crisis has been both deep and long-standing. It is also different from the Baltic countries were the crisis was deep but recovery reasonably fast.

The important exception from this positive picture of the Swedish Great Recession crisis concerns relative poverty rates, which, in contrast to the 1990s experience, increased significantly during not only the recession but also subsequent years. Moreover, the increase was particularly significant for a number of groups that many would label 'vulnerable'. What turns out to be a common factor here is that poverty increased among those groups that lack income from employment. As we will discuss in section 13.4.4, this is a result of tax policy changes. It should be underlined that these policy changes predated the crisis and hence were not occasioned by it.

The figures in Chapter 2 indicate that increasing relative poverty was a consequence of changes in different areas of income distribution: specifically, income decreased at the bottom and increased at the top. Any discussion of the Swedish Welfare State Model hence has to incorporate reflections about the broader social and economic conditions of the population, especially when it comes to equality. This raises the question of how the welfare state matters for equality in general and for the effects of the crisis in particular. This is important as economic inequalities have continued to increase although the patterns are somewhat different when we compare the two crises. In the 1990s, not only relative poverty but also overall inequality went down in the midst of the crisis, but inequalities went up during recovery as the rich were galloping ahead. An exclusive focus on the years of the economic crisis is, however, problematic. This is illustrated by the development of income from capital, which was the primary driver behind the increasing inequalities after 1994. During the actual crisis years, income from capital actually declined and this is true for both the 1990s and Great Recession. Values at the Stockholm Stock Exchange came down massively in the early 1990s and by almost 60 per cent in connection to the Great Recession.

The other trend of importance is that groups without employment income were losing out. While wage inequalities increased in the 1990s due to elevating wage premiums for managers, they have remained remarkably stable in the 21st century. There were only modest changes in the redistributive effects of the tax/transfer system in the 1990s but during the Great Recession redistributive effects of the system actually declined.

## 13.4 Sweden's Policy Responses

### 13.4.1 *Legacies of past crises*

It can be argued that the 1930s was a formative period for the Swedish Welfare State Model, relating to two parallel but very different crises: the Great Depression and the 'Crisis of the Population Question'. Whereas the implemented policies were relatively modest, the agenda that was formulated for Keynesianism as well as for modern family support was very important for later policy developments (see Chapter 3). In common with other kinds of crises, World War II created a 'moment' for the reform and expansion of systems of social protection. Eventually post-war development turned into the heyday of welfare state expansion. In Sweden this included universal pensions and equally universal child benefits. The next phase in the universalization process came to encompass universal health-care reform as well as earnings-related social insurance for sickness and old age.

Keynesianism continued to be the main frame for economic policymaking and in Sweden it was complemented by Schumpeterian elements. An ALMP was introduced to facilitate structural transformation by investing in skills and subsidizing mobility. Capitalism's destructive forces would thus be complemented by socially constructive policies that supported new and more wealth-producing structures (Kangas & Palme, 2005). Sweden also entered a new phase in the construction of its modern social model when implementing the gender equality policy agenda from the 1930s with universal social services for the elderly and children, as well as other reforms that incentivized female labour force participation.

The structural changes and reforms that the Swedish economy went through during the second part of the 1970s following the oil crises implied strong challenges not only for the Swedish welfare state but also for the economic paradigm. Keynesian deficit spending generated public deficits and the Schumpeterian approach was temporarily abandoned as the centre-right government tried to beat structural transformation with huge subsidies to industrial firms. For the Social Democrats, the 1980s became a kind of defence battle for Swedish Welfare State Model, in ideational terms but also in 'realpolitik'. The neoliberal critique of the 'big' Swedish welfare state suggested that the country's economic problems not only became the crisis of the welfare state but that the welfare state was causing the economic problems. At the same time, part of the defence battle paved the way for the crisis of the early 1990s. In retrospect, the timing of deregulatory and other reforms appear particularly problematic. In early 1990, the Social Democratic government resigned, only to be reinstalled soon after. But the political crisis paved the way for a change of government the following year when a centre-right four-party coalition government took over the cabinet.

### 13.4.2 *Centre-right government 1991–4*

Swedish centre-right parties have not been lucky with the timing of their electoral successes. After being out of power for 44 years they formed their first post-war government in 1976 in the middle of a crisis period. In 1991 it was even worse and they did not really have a macroeconomic strategy that was appropriate to deal with the emerging crisis. The election platform had been based on big tax cuts but when the Liberal Party leader(s) saw the social policy consequences of that they backed away from it and the government actually increased spending on services for disabled and introduced a home care allowance as a new spending item. However, as the economic crisis deepened and public finances deteriorated, the government responded by cutting social benefits more or less across the board.

Yet the fixed exchange rate became a bigger problem than could be handled by the government. International speculation drew Sweden into a series of massive interest rate increases in order to defend the Swedish currency from speculation. These increases were part of several 'package deals' between the government and opposition. It turned out that a 500 per cent interest rate was not enough to safeguard the currency and eventually the government took the wise decision to let it float, thereby following a number of other countries such as the United Kingdom. While this would eventually help the Swedish economy to recover by lowering interest rates and improving competitiveness, acute problems within public finances had to be dealt with more promptly. The package deals between the government and opposition made policy priorities more diffuse on both sides.

In the midst of the crisis, a major reform of the pension system was undertaken in 1994. The reform as such was not a response to the crisis but an outcome of, first, a long review process and, secondly, the Liberal minister for social security finding a window of opportunity to initiate a big reform. Many commentators have argued that this reform was made possible by the crisis and the sense of urgency that surrounded it. Yet the reform actually meant increased contributions and increased short- and medium-term spending (Palme, 2003). It is surprising that the public finances crisis did not render such changes impossible, especially in a context where the retired population was more or less sheltered from the effects of the crisis, not least regarding economic indicators (but also with regard to mental health indicators) (Palme et al., 2003).

In 1992, the social services were also subject to reform. This was part of an ideational agenda shared by the coalition parties rather than about crisis management. The implications for the political economy of the Swedish Welfare State Model are obvious. The reform allowed for-profit companies to provide publicly funded services in any policy area. The way the reform did this was subject to variation between policy areas. Since then, a series of reforms have moved the entire sector towards a consumer choice model (Palme, 2017a).

### 13.4.3 *Social Democratic government 1994–2006*

After the election in 1994, the Social Democratic Party formed a minority government that had to handle a difficult situation for public finances. Their strategy was to rely on the Left Party to push through a large number of tax increases. When they followed up in a second phase by cutting virtually all cash transfers, the support of the Left Party evaporated. Instead the Social Democrats turned to the Centre Party and were successful in establishing a collaboration that lasted up to the next election in 1998.

In order to understand the 1990s crisis it is important to recognize how prolonged the employment crisis was (Palme et al., 2003). While public finances improved quicker than expected, employment rates did not and unemployment remained stuck at high levels. Looking back, the Ministry of

Finance, in their review of the 1990s, concluded that both monetary and fiscal policies had been too tough. This had held back domestic demand and contributed to the fact that it was not until 1999 that a clear improvement in employment was registered. The tough policies were not out of free choice but a result of the fact that the foreign creditors, and key actors at the Bank of Sweden, did not believe the government was able to achieve control over public finances and hence kept interest rates high, which gave little or no leeway for the government to act differently. While the basic social policy structures had been kept intact, benefit levels had been trimmed down. Social services had been politically prioritized but nevertheless were diluted, albeit in different ways. For children the universality acted to increase day-care and education but per capita resources fell. For the elderly and disabled resources were concentrated on the most vulnerable. In 1998, social policy reform changed direction and the levels of cash benefits started to increase again.

Two policy reforms that had taken place during the 1990s were aimed at dealing with some of the underlying problems of the macroeconomic policy regime (Hassler, 2010). One was the reform of the Bank of Sweden that gave it independence from the Ministry of Finance and contributed to establishing a wage negotiating system that sustained a non-inflationary wage development in contrast to the past pattern. The other was a new budget process with nominal cost limits, which has proved very effective in terms of bringing public expenditures under control. At the same time it includes mechanisms that allow for democratic influence on spending priorities.

Nevertheless, it can be argued that a policy deficit also emerged as a result of the crisis (in addition to the social and economic deficits). This is most obvious in social insurance and other cash benefit programmes where the expansionary changes made towards the end of the 1990s did not bring the benefit level to pre-crisis levels. The different kinds of changes that were made in social services also cast some doubt on the adequacy of the services. This also applied to the health services—the source of elevated public discontent after the crisis. It deserves to be noted that expenditures on ALMP were massively increased and a special programme was set up to enable unemployed persons to take a secondary school examinations. In addition to the expansion of expenditures on tertiary education that the centre-right government had initiated in the early 1990s this contributed to a human capital orientation of the policy response to that crisis (Palme et al., 2003).

### 13.4.4 *Responses to the Great Recession*

In order to understand observed patterns of financial hardships during the crisis of 2008 and subsequently, it is warranted to describe policy changes that took place before the Great Recession. These changes can be understood partly as a supply-side approach inspired by the seemingly jobless growth during the first years of the 21st century, partly as anchored in ideational differences between the Social Democrats, in government until the autumn of 2006, and the centre-right coalition, which governed from 2006 to autumn 2014. In 2007 two types of changes took place, which then, successively, were implemented over the following years (Cronert & Palme, 2017). The most important was the stepwise introduction of a Swedish version of an earned income tax credit (*jobbskatteavdraget*). This lowered taxes for all those with earnings above a certain minimum level compared to those without employment earnings. This system eventually generated tax expenditures amounting to over three times the spend on ALMP. Social insurance also saw a move towards more basic security in the social insurance systems, by trimming down benefit levels. There was, moreover, a distinct increase of differential premiums for unemployment insurance funds.[2] Lower benefit levels meant lower earnings for those who became sick or lost their jobs. Differentiation of unemployment insurance premiums reduced coverage from 87 per cent of employees in 2006 to 74 per cent in 2008, as many opted out from the core unemployment insurance programme (Kjellberg, 2018). Most of those who opted out were, however, covered by the basic unemployment benefit.

When it comes to the actual management of the response to the Great Recession, two features are striking. The first is how closely and effectively the protocol from the 1990s was followed in dealing with the financial institutions. Without swift state intervention, the effects could have been disastrous, but the Swedish politicians and those placed in central positions of influence were very well rehearsed (Lundgren, 2009). The main perceived task was to maintain the liquidity in the financial system and restore the capital base, but also, by other means, to restore confidence in the system. This included guarantees to the banks but also increased guarantees for depositors. This part of crisis management did not generate any important political conflicts but much interest from international observers who studied policy actions carefully.

The other feature is the strong reliance on automatic stabilizers as a macroeconomic strategy. When we discuss the consequences of the Great Recession crisis, it should therefore be repeated that the direct effect of the crisis on policy change has been negligible. There were some targeted efforts towards the elderly (tax cuts and housing supplements) and families with children (via housing supplements) but by and large any measures taken were very modest (cf. Starke, Kaasch, & Van Horen, 2013). It deserves to be emphasized that the centre-right government pursued a clear rhetoric about public spending: that automatic

[2] In Sweden, the Ghent model of unemployment insurance prevails.

stabilizers were enough. However, the anticipation of the upcoming election campaign in 2010 appears to have changed their minds, and an additional 17 billion SEK was directed to the municipality sector. The explicit motivation was to secure the finances and service levels of the municipality sector. The fact that this package emerged during an election year and after having been deemed unnecessary by the minister of finance suggests that there were electoral motives behind it. Interestingly enough, the inflow of refugees that had preceded the crisis was increasing the burden on the public sector but the population increase contributed to sustain the level of demand in the economy.

The supply-side shift eventually took over in macroeconomic policy-making. This change was inspired by the perception of Swedish economic development during the subsequent years as being an illustration of the concept of 'jobless growth', where economic output is increasing by technological change such as automation without engaging more workers in the production. This view persisted until the autumn of 2006. The impression was that labour supply reforms were not only desirable but also necessary in order to exit this scenario. As will be described in section 13.4.4 it also formed the basis of the political challenge of the 'New' Moderates to the Social Democrats and a reformulation of the Swedish Welfare State Model. As regards the tax/transfer system, the main avenue was to continue with additional steps of earned income tax credits. This strategy was strongly and exclusively supply-side oriented (Cronert & Palme, 2017). However, it is also clear that it was increasing demand, because taxes were decreased not only for rich people but also for low- and middle-income persons.

The unwillingness of the government to increase subsidies to Swedish industrial firms in economic difficulties, illustrated by the case of Saab Automobiles, indicates a strong historical legacy of Schumpeterianism. This has generated surprisingly little political controversy but it should be seen in the perspective of failed industrial subsidies in the mid-1970s and the successful socially constructive responses to the destructive forces of competitive capitalism since. It may however have come as a surprise, not least for those who traditionally have perceived the Swedish welfare state as overburdened, when the Swedish government was criticized both by domestic observers such as the Swedish Fiscal Policy Council (2011) and the International Monetary Fund (IMF), as being too restrictive in their fiscal policies, because of the destructive consequence for the economy, both inside and outside the country.

## 13.5 The Consequences of the Crises and the Sharing of Burdens

For the 1990s, we highlighted some differences between the centre-right and the Social Democratic governments but also observed that these were somewhat blurred by the fact that the government and opposition in late 1992 agreed on a number of package deals. This makes the analysis of the politics of burden sharing complicated. Since the Social Democrats' government (1994+) eventually had the strongest influence on crisis-related policy changes, we focus on the Social Democratic cabinet, even if also their period in government included deals with different opposition parties (Palme et al., 2003).

The Social Democrats made two explicit strategic priorities when they entered government after the 1994 election. First, in order to balance the burdens of the crisis-induced policy changes, they aimed at using tax increases as much as benefit cuts to restore the balance of public finances. Secondly, in order to avoid irreversible imprints of crisis measures, they aimed at cutting transfers rather than services. In macroeconomic terms they also wanted to avoid what they saw as a mistake in Finland, where the crisis started earlier and the retrenchment was immediate with very destructive effects on the economy, eventually leading to two-digit unemployment figures (cf. Chapter 9). This led to a gradual implementation of austerity measures in Sweden. In terms of burden sharing the success of this strategy was at best incomplete: in the end, benefit cuts exceeded tax increases and municipalities cut back on social services despite the continuity of central state support, and even if the Swedish crisis was not as drastic as that in Finland it continued longer than necessary.

While differences in class and gender earnings persisted during the crisis, these, by and large, did not increase. For that part of the population of working age, it can be observed that they, on average, were affected both by falling earnings and benefit levels. For the retired population, pensions were not fully indexed but they did not experience the same losses in terms of earnings. Three other groups instead stand out as the most vulnerable: youth, immigrants, and single mothers. A common factor is that all groups were adversely affected by the employment crisis. In addition, youths and immigrants are often newcomers to the labour market and have no savings to insure themselves against unemployment or sickness. Even if there was a shift in emphasis towards more targeted benefits, the direct public support of single mothers was not diminished. The losses single mothers made were in terms of earnings. What is clear for these groups is that they were not only suffering more in financial terms but also in health, as well as other levels of living conditions. An important lesson from the crisis is that macroeconomic factors have clear effects on the human conditions of people in general, and particularly on vulnerable groups in society.

Due to the fact that the same centre-right government was in power throughout the entire Great Recession period, it is reasonably straightforward to analyse the politics of burden sharing during this time. The government's expansionary measures were modest and targeted when it came to social protection (social transfers). Furthermore, the government gave priority to social services, albeit for slightly different reasons as compared with their predecessors. This should not conceal the fact that the tax and transfer system had been subject to a number of changes immediately before the crisis hit. The consequence of these changes was that the relative position of those outside employment deteriorated. This was primarily caused by the stepwise introduction and expansion of an earned income tax credit (*jobbskatteavdrag*) but also by cutbacks in some transfer programmes that also had some absolute effects on income levels (Fritzell et al., 2016). The result was that those who were or became unemployed during the crisis lagged behind the rest of the population in economic standards. What emerges here is a clearer division of welfare between the employed and unemployed.

The role of the now much larger share of the population that is foreign born is another social division, although it has obvious overlaps with the division between employed and non-employed. Due to their lack of firm attachment to the labour market, modest earnings, and heavy reliance on social benefits, we can be sure that the large inflow of refugee migrants during the years that preceded Great Recession added to the problems of relative poverty. We also know that these groups tend to be underreported in surveys. This is particularly the case with the presumably increasing number of 'undocumented migrants'. Nevertheless, according to the data that we have, the immigrant group on the margins was less affected than the 'unemployed' group by financial hardship (see Chapter 2 and Figure 13.1).

This speaks to the question of how the social protection system worked in terms of cushioning the impact of the crisis. When we look at the crisis of the 1990s, it is clear that the system worked well to protect those who were employed at the onset of the crisis and that the social safety nets were tight enough to prevent relative poverty to increase for the rest. The 1990s crisis highlighted three groups—youth, immigrants, and single mothers, the first two of which are somewhat newcomers to the labour market and less well protected. Social insurance works but requires that you have an income to insure in the first place. Since safety nets have lagged behind in Sweden as well as in other parts of Europe (Kuivalainen & Nelson, 2011), this implies that the cushioning effect has become less effective in terms of preventing poverty. The policy tools appear to be in place but their capacity has been eroded by policy drift and/or austerity measures (Cronert & Palme, 2017; Palme, 2017b).

## 13.6 Beyond the Double Dip: Adequate Policies for Hard Times?

There is evidence to suggest that the two crises examined in this chapter have left their imprint on the level of living conditions in Sweden. While there are a lot of indicators that captured the broad-ranging effects of the 1990s, the data show much more restricted effects of the Great Recession on population hardship both when it comes to who was affected and how much. Most of the effects in the 1990s appear to have been temporary but the prolonged employment crisis meant that, even at the end of the decade, there had been a build-up of social deficit in addition to the deficit in public finances. In turn, this points to the emergence of policy deficits.

The effects of the 1990s crisis were partially mediated by the retrenchment effects that the crisis had on social protection systems across the board. During the recovery from that crisis, a number of benefit programmes were made more generous—although not to pre-crisis levels—which can be described as another form of crisis imprint. We can see this as an institutional deficit in relation to the ideal type of universalism that is often associated with the Swedish Welfare State Model (cf. Beland et al., 2014; Blomqvist & Palme, 2016). In contrast, there were no retrenchment effects of the Great Recession on social protection systems as such, but policy changes made before the crisis actually increased the identified universalism deficit. Despite this, the very modest effects of the Great Recession on financial hardships in the Swedish population show that the capacity of the welfare state to protect the population at the onset of an external shock has been remarkably good.

Another thing to highlight is the Swedish management of the crisis in the financial sector. The policy lessons had been well learnt and the same kind of strategy was repeated. The implications of crisis management here were similar for other advanced industrial nations and, indeed, during the onset of the Great Recession many countries showed strong interest in the Swedish policy response in the 1990s (Lundgren, 2009). It might have been helpful here to state that it was centre-right governments which pursued a rescue strategy that included the temporary socialization of private banks.

For the 1990s, it seems fair to conclude that the direct effects of the macroeconomic crisis per se on employment, earnings, and health, were more severe than the effects of retrenchments, particularly for vulnerable groups such as single mothers (Palme et al., 2003). This illustrates that bad macroeconomic policies are also bad social policies (and vice versa). It also indicates that it is important to be concerned about potential negative effects of social policy on macroeconomic development. On the other hand, the positive economic impacts of well-designed social policies have been 'rediscovered' during the Great Recession—recognition of unemployment insurance as an automatic stabilizer is the clearest example. The conclusion from the Swedish crisis experience is hence that economic and social policies need to be combined; this echoes the recommendation from the first broad study of the welfare state in crisis (OECD, 1981).

Any discussion of the Swedish Welfare State Model ponders the issue of a Swedish exceptionalism. How does the Swedish welfare state compare with other European countries after the crises? The brief answer is: it is certainly less exceptional than assumed. This is an answer that deserves to be qualified, however. If Sweden's welfare state really was exceptional, this had less to do with the individual programmes as compared with the comprehensiveness of the entire system of benefits in cash and kind. While social expenditure increased massively during the 1990s crisis, overall social expenditures came down not only as a result of recovery after the crisis but also due to the political priorities of the centre-right coalition government before the onset of the Great Recession. In a European perspective, Sweden had become more mainstream even if expenditure levels as such may have hidden very important country differences in social entitlement structures (cf. Kangas & Palme, 2007). An important point here is that many European welfare states have become more like Sweden's. The activation turn is one important area where there has been a clear expansionary reform trend. Another is the modernization of family policy in Europe: not only by reforming parental leave benefits but also expanding childcare provisions; this also makes Sweden less exceptional.

The Swedish welfare state has changed in important ways since the early 1990s. Most of the reforms have not been caused by the crisis in any direct way. They stand out as political priorities of different governments. In light of the massive refugee migration that took place in 2015, the Swedish welfare state appears to be at another crossroads today. It is not that the immediate effects have been devastating for the welfare state as such. It is rather that there are problems of social integration and potentially far-reaching policy proposals. One proposal is to increase earnings inequalities to make an expansion of a new service economy for low productive immigrant workers possible. While this could help to raise employment levels it also opens up a goal conflict for those who see both equal wages and high employment as important cornerstones of the Swedish Welfare State Model. The position of women is particularly interesting in this perspective. The dual-earner model has been a successful strategy for combatting child poverty by increasing the family income with a second person's earnings. Employment levels among foreign-born women are, however, substantially lower than for the Swedish born. If their employment levels could be increased then social integration as well as family income would be improved, and this would presumably ensure households were better insured for future times of crisis.

A decade after the onset of the Great Recession, in 2018, Sweden may be in an advantageous position when it comes to both employment levels and public finances but there is room for improvement when it comes to both the coverage and adequacy of social protection. This would have the immediate effect of halting increasing inequalities but would also ensure the population weathered the storms of the next crisis.

# Part III

# Outcomes and Lessons

# 14

# How Institutional Environments and Policies Impacted Hardship

*Stefán Ólafsson, Agnar Freyr Helgason, and Kolbeinn Stefánsson*

This chapter seeks to establish a more comprehensive understanding of what shaped the varying welfare consequences of the Great Recession in Europe. We take our lead from the explanatory diagram outlined in Chapter 1 (see Figure 1.1). We do not claim to be testing a comprehensive causal model but rather exploring patterns of associations between welfare outcomes, on the one hand, and institutional environments and policy responses, on the other, based on theoretical mechanisms suggested by prior chapters in the book. Hence we aim to paint a wide comparative picture at this stage, with relatively broad strokes, by relating financial hardship developments to the depth and persistence of the crisis, to welfare regime characteristics, and to the policy reactions of governments. We also assess relationships between financial hardship and other relevant aspects, such as the pre-crisis affluence level of nations, governmental debt position, bargaining coverage in the labour market, and currency regimes.

The international financial crisis was primarily the result of a failure of the financial markets. Even though the state also shares a part of the blame, by insufficiently regulating and restraining the market's tendency towards excesses, it became the primary role of the state to deal with the economic and social consequences, as in previous financial crises (Bermeo & Pontusson, 2012; Epstein & Wolfson, 2013; Gourevitch, 1986; Krugman, 2012). While there has been some progress in economic crisis management techniques since the days of the Great Depression of the 1930s, it seems that the same general contrasting perspectives prevail: in the realm of the economy it is interventionist Keynesian demand management versus laissez-faire (self-correction of the market), or stimulus versus austerity (Alesina & Ardagna,

2010, 2013; Blyth, 2013; Guajardo, Leigh, & Pescatori, 2014; Krugman, 2012; Romer & Romer, 2014; Skidelsky, 2010). In the social realm it is a question of more or less social protection (Korpi & Palme, 2003; Levy, 2010; Pierson, 1994, 2001; Starke et al., 2013; van Kersbergen, Vis, & Hemerijck 2014; see also Chapter 3). Modern additions mainly involve some detail variations and technical modifications of the basic underlying approaches.

The social protection system of the welfare state aims to shelter people in general against the vagaries of the market society, by securing means of subsistence for those left behind or hampered by temporary or permanent inactivity in the labour market during normal times. As such, the welfare state is also a straightforward crisis management instrument, that automatically or discretely reacts to the consequences of crises, such as increased unemployment, lowered incomes, increased debt burdens, and the like (Castles, 1989, 2010; Starke et al., 2013; Taylor-Gooby, Leruth, & Chung, 2017; van Kersbergen & Vis, 2014). Thus the welfare state is society's main automatic stabilizer. It reacts quickly, quietly, and effectively to welfare shortfalls during crises. But to what extent is it capable of fully countering increasingly adverse crisis conditions varies by welfare regime, the resources available for social protection, and the effectiveness of organizational/institutional designs? It also depends on government policies and financial capabilities during the crisis period itself.

The modern welfare state is the biggest institutional innovation in European societies since the interwar years (Castles et al., 2010). It should have been of major importance for better sheltering contemporary populations against the negative welfare consequences of the Great Recession, as compared to the Great Depression of the 1930s. The welfare states of the 1930s were generally much less advanced in structure and had less capabilities for sustaining the unemployed, the sick, the elderly, and families with children, by means, for example, of income transfers and services. The Keynesian lessons from the 1930s helped modern governments save banks and avert deeper economic recessions in 2007 to 2009, while modern welfare states softened the negative welfare impact of the recession well beyond what was possible during the 1930s. But such impacts still varied between countries and we want to account for such differences.[1]

In the following sections, we discuss relevant institutional and policy variables one at a time, and evaluate their association with our chosen measure of

[1] It is not our aim here to dive deeply into a search for explanations of government responses to the crisis, only to study how such responses related to changing financial hardships. See, for example, van Kersbergen et al. (2014), Starke et al. (2013), Streeck and Schäfer (2013), and Bermeo and Pontusson (2012) for interesting explanations of differing governmental actions or policies.

welfare outcome: financial hardship. In the concluding section, we assess to what extent welfare outcomes were purely driven by the depth of the crisis and whether welfare states and policy responses played any independent role in ameliorating the effects of the crisis on national populations. Our findings suggests that depth alone cannot fully account for welfare outcomes and that both the welfare state and particular policy responses played a key role in mediating how the crisis was felt by individuals and households around Europe.

## 14.1 How the Depth of the Crisis Related to Welfare Outcomes

It has emerged quite clearly in previous chapters that the depth of the crisis and its perseverance had a major impact on populations' welfare outcomes. We start by probing further into that issue here. Figure 14.1 shows the average severity of financial hardship experienced by countries differently exposed to the crisis. Based on the contraction of gross domestic product (GDP) experienced by countries from 2007 to their post-crisis trough, we group countries into three categories: those which did not experience or experienced only a

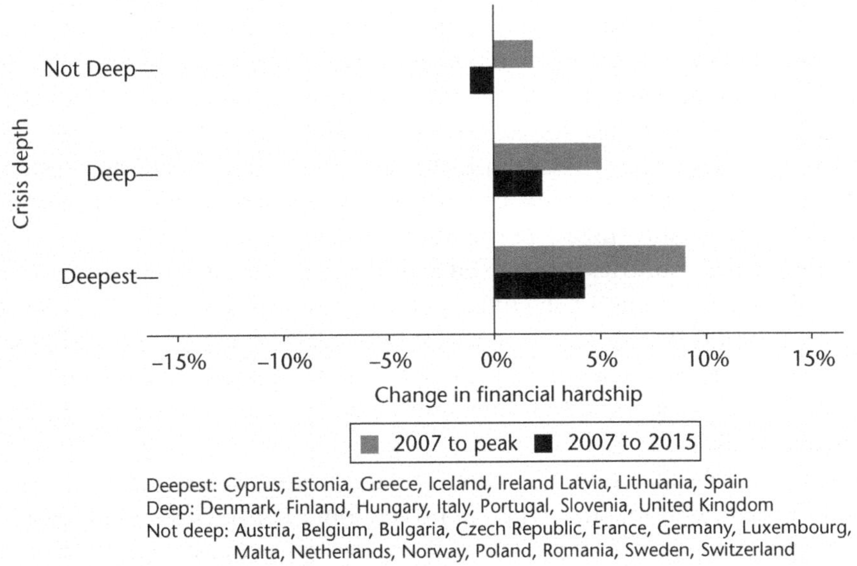


**Figure 14.1.** Association between crisis depth (maximum contraction of GDP) and changing financial hardship in 29 European countries

*Source*: OECD and European Union Statistics on Income and Living Conditions (EU-SILC), authors' calculation.

limited contraction in GDP; those which experienced a modestly large drop in GDP; and those which experienced a substantial fall in GDP over the crisis years.

We measure the impact on financial hardship in two ways: first, from 2007 to the highest level reached during the crisis years (the peak) and then from 2007 to 2015, taking account of the progress after the peak was reached. Thus the former measure shows the maximum impact on financial hardship (grey columns) and the latter (the black columns) is an indication of the persistence of the crisis impact on hardship outcomes. As can be seen from Figure 14.1, the depth of the crisis is strongly associated with the severity of financial hardship experienced by national populations.

Looking first at the development towards the peak level of financial hardship, a strong direct relationship emerges, with significantly more increases in financial hardship as the depth of the crisis increases. In the countries that experienced the deepest crisis in terms of GDP contraction the increase of financial hardship from 2007 to peak was about three times larger than in the countries least affected by economic contraction.

When looking at the whole period from 2007 to 2015 (black columns) the relationship is the same, but at a significantly lower level, incorporating the improvements in living standards in the years after the peak was reached. The countries that were unaffected or only modestly affected by economic contraction had, by 2015, actually reduced their financial hardship level below what had prevailed in 2007. The most prominent amongst these were the Eastern European countries that in general were on a convergence path in the pre-crisis years (Bulgaria, Czech Republic, Poland, Romania, and Slovakia, as well as the more heavily affected Baltic States of Estonia, Latvia, and Lithuania). They had a setback during the crisis but returned to their previous path of reducing financial hardship and poverty. The same applies for Sweden, Norway, Austria, and Finland on the more affluent end.

Amongst the countries most severely affected the financial hardship level was still, by 2015, some 4 percentage points on average above the 2007 level. The most prominent strugglers in that group, apart from a few Eastern European countries, were Greece, Cyprus, Spain, Italy, Ireland, and the UK. The Baltics, as well as Iceland, bottomed out early and were on a recovery path from about 2011–12.

On the whole the Great Recession impacted quite differentially on each European nation, from only a mild or no economic contraction (as in Poland) to a massive fall (as in Greece). The welfare consequences were largely shaped by the extent of the economic contraction, but as was shown in Chapter 2 the associated increase in unemployment and financial hardship deviated also to some extent. The welfare states in place in European countries no doubt made a great difference in softening the crisis consequences for populations and households. Nevertheless, the protective impact of the welfare state varied amongst European countries, as we show in section 14.2.

## 14.2 The Importance of the Welfare State

It almost goes without saying that the more advanced the welfare state of a country is, the more universal its coverage, and the more resourceful and generous its provisions of benefits and services, the better an insurance system for citizens—both in ordinary times and during crises—it should be (Barr, 2001; Starke et al., 2013). The welfare system has both a 'Robin Hood' function for reducing poverty and redistributing income and wealth generally, and a 'piggy bank' function providing insurance and consumption smoothing over the life course, as Nicholas Barr puts it.

As Gösta Esping-Andersen revealed in his *Three Worlds of Welfare Capitalism* in 1990, the amount of money spent by government on welfare is not necessarily a good indicator of people's welfare or level of living, since it may, for example, reflect a sizable unemployment problem—which, of course, is not a positive quality of life. Hence, his welfare regime approach measured the quality of welfare states by indicators of rights (such as coverage and generosity) and impacts for decommodification and reduction of stratification effects, instead of by welfare expenditure levels.

But a rising level of welfare expenditures associated with growing unemployment in hard times may indeed reflect positively on the quality of the welfare state itself as an insurance system and an automatic buffer against economic hardship. As such it contributes towards demand stability from a Keynesian perspective and softens crisis consequences for the publics, either automatically or discretely—or both. Thus the welfare state can at the same time have an economic and social stabilizing effect on the economy and society during a serious crisis. The welfare state is important for improving the competitiveness of the economy and the overall functionality of society in good times, but its importance increases greatly in hard times (Castles 2010; Dölvik & Martin, 2015; Hay & Wincott, 2012). Our interest here is more on the insurance and smoothing functions of European welfare states than on their implications for general living standards, even though these aspects are, of course, interrelated.

A highly advanced and efficient welfare state should in principle fully avert increased financial hardship in crisis periods, even if the economy contracts and unemployment significantly increases. Similarly, one could claim that efficient economic crisis management should be able to fully avert booms and busts—or at least greatly restrain the swings of the economic cycle.[2] But even if unemployment increased greatly due to ineffective or wrong economic management strategies an advanced welfare state should still avert increased financial hardships amongst the unemployed or at least sufficiently insure their level of living.

The Great Recession shows that most European welfare states did not fully manage to shelter the victims of the economic and financial crisis. Levels of living came down in most countries, as has been shown in previous chapters (see also OECD, 2014b). But some welfare states did better than others in averting increased financial hardship. For example, Finland and Sweden experienced significant economic contraction and increased unemployment but financial hardship actually came down (Sweden) or remained at level (Finland) in those countries during the crisis years.[3] On the other hand, the studies of Ireland, the UK, Spain, and Greece in this book show that these countries' welfare states did not rise fully to the task. This was also the case with other Southern European countries and the less advanced welfare states of Eastern Europe.

Figures 14.2 and 14.3 show the varying capacity of different welfare regimes (or different 'families of nations', using the terminology of Francis G. Castles (1993)) to avert crisis depth and increased financial hardship. Following that we assess the increased welfare effort expenditures by individual countries during the crisis years.

In Figure 14.2 we see a clear association between welfare regimes and financial hardship experiences, on the one hand from 2007 to peak, and on the other from 2007 to 2015. The Nordic and the Continental regime countries stand out as groups that experienced less increase of financial hardship than most.[4]

The Continental group of countries (excluding southern and eastern countries) generally did not go deep into crisis, either in terms of economic contraction or increased unemployment, and only experienced a modest increase of financial hardship, slightly more than the Scandinavian countries (i.e. Nordics minus Iceland). Looking at the whole period from 2007 to 2015 the Continentals ended the period slightly above their level of 2007, mainly

[2] In his 2012 book, *End this Depression Now*, economist Paul Krugman argues that the large stimulus provided by governments at the beginning of the Great Recession was frequently not large enough, hence the sluggish recovery and prolonged unemployment in both the USA and Europe. The return to austerity after 2010 then slowed the economic recovery and in fact reversed it into a second dip, particularly in Europe, further aggravating the welfare consequences.

[3] In Finland the associated cost was an increase of social spending from 25% of GDP in 2008 to 32% in 2016, and a rapidly increasing public deficit.

[4] If we exclude Iceland from the Nordic group the increase of hardship from 2007 to peak would be less, if any, for that group, and the reduction of hardship for the whole period from 2007 to 2015 would be larger, since Iceland was the exception in that group, going much deeper into crisis than the others and also experiencing a larger increase of financial hardship.

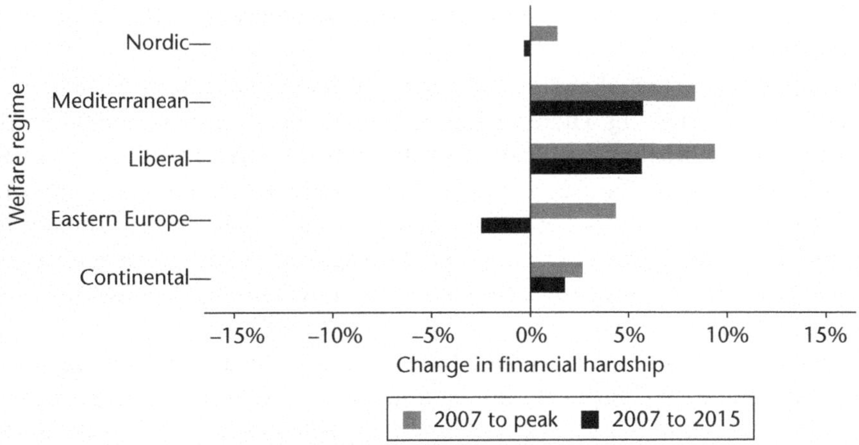


Nordic: Denmark, Finland, Iceland, Norway, Sweden
Mediterranean: Cyprus, Greece, Italy, Malta, Portugal, Spain
Liberal: Ireland, United Kingdom
Eastern Europe: Bulgaria, Czech Republic, Estonia, Hungary, Latvia, Lithuania, Poland, Romania, Slovenia
Continental: Austria, Belgium, Switzerland, France, Germany, Luxembourg, Netherlands

**Figure 14.2.** Financial hardship development during the crisis, by broad welfare regime characteristics in Europe
*Source*: OECD and EU-SILC, authors' calculation.

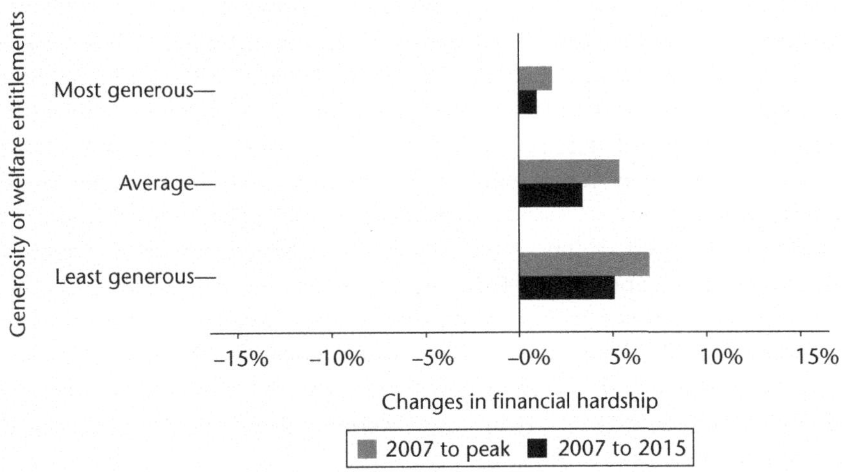


Least generous: Germany, Greece, Italy, Portugal, United Kingdom
Average: Austria, Denmark, Finland, Ireland, Spain
Most generous: Belgium, France, Netherlands, Norway, Sweden, Switzerland

**Figure 14.3.** Financial hardship development during the crisis, by welfare generosity in European countries, before the crisis hit
*Source*: Lyle Scruggs' Comparative Welfare Entitlements Dataset (CWED) and EU-SILC, authors' calculation.

due to some increases in the Netherlands and Luxembourg in the latter years of the crisis period.

Comparing the liberal regime countries (UK and Ireland) to the Mediterranean ones is interesting. There we have a similar degree of increased financial hardship, on both time variables, even though the crisis was deeper in the Mediterranean countries as a whole, particularly when compared to the UK. This may indicate lesser efficiency of the liberal welfare states in sheltering the more vulnerable parts of their population against welfare consequences of the crisis, at least in comparison to the Nordic and Continental ones (see also Chapters 7 and 10).[5]

The Eastern European countries have a pattern of a sizable increase of hardships from 2007 to peak, but, following a swift recovery (particularly amongst the Baltic States), they ended the crisis period at a significantly lower level of financial hardship that in 2007—which also reflects their underlying catch-up path from a lower affluence level.

In relation to the favourable outcome for the Western Continental countries one may ask if that is not more due to the fact that they were only modestly impacted by the financial crisis and economic contraction. The same argument might apply to Norway, Sweden, and Finland. This would cast doubt on the importance of their welfare states as insurance systems that would soften financial hardship consequences. Nevertheless, all these countries managed to avert increases of financial hardship despite a significant increase of unemployment. These doubts may, however, also be countered by reference to the varieties of capitalism (VoC) literature (cf. Hall & Soskice, 2001; also Hay & Wincott, 2012; Dölvik & Martin, 2015). The Western Continental countries with their more coordinated economies, and with a tradition of significant state interventionism, may indeed also have had institutional environments that prevented their financial markets from having too much freedom, as well as having significant consumption smoothing due to their more advanced welfare states. There is a strong support for such an argument on the importance of the legacy of Keynesian economic management and an advanced welfare state for generally averting economic crisis tendencies as well as negative welfare consequences in Chapter 12. Lessons learned from the Scandinavian crises of the early 1990s may have reinvigorated these tendencies in Norway and Sweden during the Great Recession (see also Chapter 13).

Looking beyond the welfare regime/families framework, by examining the association between welfare state generosity and financial hardship experiences,

[5] Both Ireland and the UK reduced pre-transfer poverty quite significantly, but the pre-transfer poverty levels were comparatively high, hence the generally higher levels of post-transfer poverty and financial hardship there than in the Nordic countries and in some of the Continental ones.

has further implications regarding the importance of contemporary welfare states for softening financial hardship consequences during the Great Recession (see Figure 14.3).

Here we see a considerable correlation between the generosity levels of European welfare states in 2007 and financial hardship experiences, on both time variables. There is not, however, a large difference between the countries in the groups with average and least generous levels, although the most generous welfare states had by far the least increase of financial hardship.

## 14.3 Increased Welfare Expenditures during the Crisis

Given the role of modern welfare states as automatic stabilizers and insurance systems for coping with level-of-living crises we would have expected the European states to have increased public social spending during the crisis period. That was indeed the case (OECD 2016b, 2016c; also Adema, Fron, & Ladaique, 2014). Figure 14.4 maps the changes in public social spending from 2007 to its peak and onwards to 2016.

Public social spending went up on average by some 3 percentage points from 2007 to 2009 for all Organisation for Economic Co-operation and Development (OECD) countries (Adema, Fron, & Ladaique, 2014, p. 20).

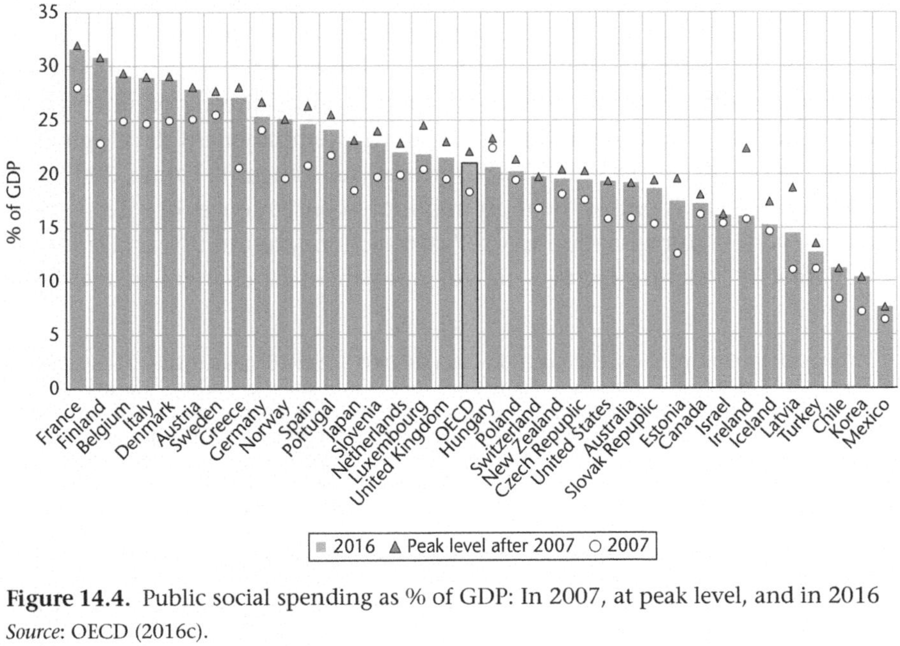


**Figure 14.4.** Public social spending as % of GDP: In 2007, at peak level, and in 2016
*Source*: OECD (2016c).

That year was also the peak year for many, but not all the countries.[6] As Figure 14.4 shows, all the European countries increased their public social spending ratio (to GDP) from 2007 to peak, but some more than others. The expenditure ratio had come down again by 2016 in most of the countries, except the few with the highest public expenditure level (France, Finland, Belgium, Italy, Denmark, Austria, Sweden, and Norway). This gives an impression of a general automatic response to increased unemployment levels and lowered incomes at the beginning of the crisis—and then when the recovery gathered speed the welfare effort receded. This is also generally in line with the 'stimulus at the beginning and then a swing to austerity' pattern identified by Helgason in Chapter 4.

On the whole the more advanced welfare regimes, the Western Continental ones and the Nordic ones, have the highest public welfare expenditures. Iceland, however, has unusually low public welfare expenditures for a Nordic country. The reason for that is an unusually large share of social expenditures that comes from mandatory occupational pension funds, run by labour market partners. Including those expenditures, which should be done, brings Iceland to a similar welfare expenditure level as Norway.[7]

But welfare expenditures measured as a ratio to the GDP can increase not simply due to increased real expenditures levels in response to growing need, but also because the GDP contracts during the crisis. Hence we need to look also at real value expenditure levels across countries. Total social protection expenditures do, however, mask various countervailing effects and merge expenditures on cash benefits and benefits in kind (services). When a country increases transfers but reduces service expenditures the explanatory role of the overall average becomes murky. Instead of building too much on overall welfare expenditures, we focus, in what follows, more directly on unemployment benefit expenditures and relate them to unemployment developments during the crisis years in individual countries (see Kangas & Palme, 2007).

Unemployment is one of the most important consequences of a deep crisis, having a very high correlation to GDP contraction (around 0.8, cf. Figure 2.4 in Chapter 2). Relating changes in unemployment to changes in real level

[6] The peak level of public social expenditures was 2009 for Sweden, Germany, Luxembourg, Hungary, Poland, the UK, Estonia, and Iceland (all countries either mildly affected or that bottomed out early and made a quick recovery, like the last two). Then came Ireland and Latvia (with a peak in 2010), Spain and Japan (2011), Greece and Mexico (2012), Belgium, Czech Republic, Denmark, the Netherlands, Portugal, Slovenia (2013), France, Italy, Israel (2014), and Austria, Chile, Slovakia (2015), while Australia, Finland, Korea, Norway, the United States, and Switzerland peaked in 2016 (see OECD, 2016c). We include non-European data here as this data comes from the OECD.

[7] In the Finnish case, similar expenditures for mandatory occupational pensions are included in public outlays, despite the fact that they are operated by private pension insurance companies. Thus, the seemingly heterogenous Nordic block is not so different in terms of overall welfare expenditure levels.

expenditures on unemployment benefits (in cash and kind) targets the response of the welfare state quite narrowly and clearly. That should give us an indication of how well the respective welfare state responded to growing need in this important area.

In Figures 14.5 and 14.6 we thus analyse the responsiveness of welfare states in Europe to increased unemployment by two periods: first from 2007 to 2010, covering the initial impact of the crisis, and then for 2007 to 2013, covering also the second dip of GDP development.

In the first dip the welfare states generally responded quite well to increased unemployment by increasing real expenditures on unemployment benefits. The correlation is 0.68. But when we extend the period to 2013 the correlation goes down to 0.33, reflecting the fact that many countries, including deep-crisis countries, had by then shifted policy towards austerity. Similarly, in some countries the right to unemployment benefits had been outrun, with loss of unemployment benefit. When that happens the unemployed can often go onto social assistance, which usually offers benefits at a lower level—or at

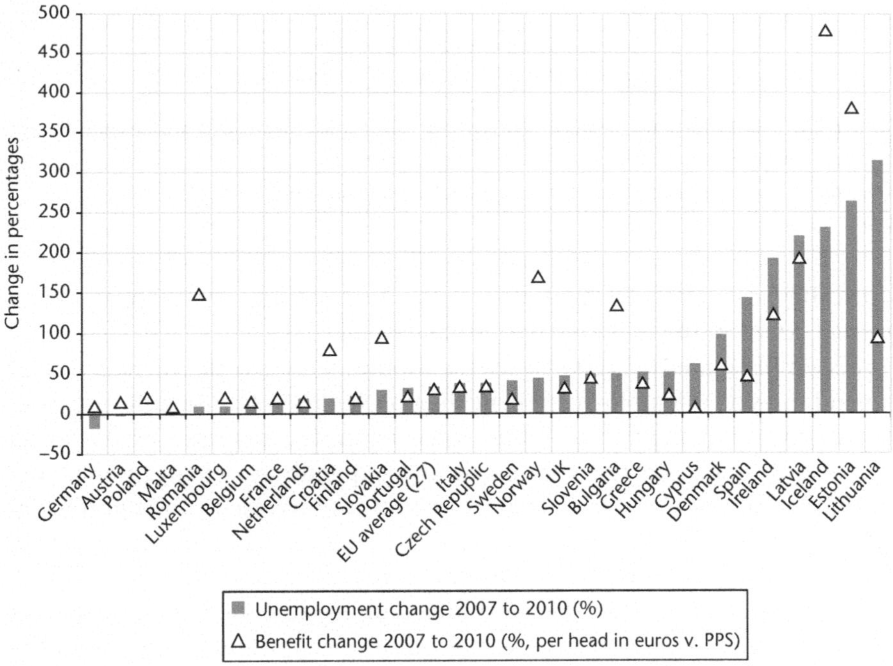


**Figure 14.5.** Relationship between growth of unemployment and real expenditures on unemployment benefits (in cash and in kind), 2007–10

*Note*: Ranked by increase in unemployment level. Pearson correlation r = 0.68. PPS = purchasing power standard.

*Source*: Eurostat.

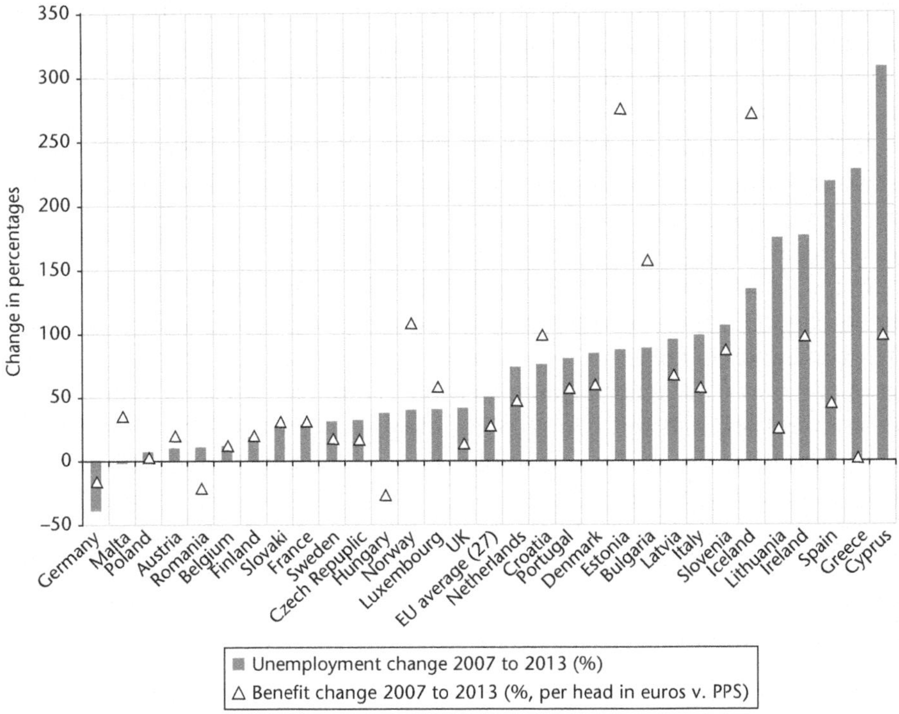


**Figure 14.6.** Relationship between growth of unemployment and real expenditures on unemployment benefits (in cash and kind), 2007–13

*Note*: Ranked by increase in unemployment level. Pearson correlation r = 0.33.

*Source*: Eurostat.

worst they lose nearly all support from the welfare state. That happened to a greater extent in the less advanced welfare states.

As seen in Figure 14.5 (2007 to 2010), around ten countries increased their expenditures on unemployment benefits proportionally less than the increases of the unemployment level, while seven countries increased expenditures significantly more. In the rest, needs and expenditures changed similarly. In Figure 14.6 (2007 to 2013) some 14 countries increased expenditures significantly less than the increased need (the changed unemployment level), while those who increased expenditures more remained around 7.

Of the deep-crisis countries, Estonia and Iceland were prominent for increasing unemployment benefit expenditures significantly more than the relative increase of unemployment for the 2007 to 2013 period, albeit both from a very low level. On the other hand, in Greece, Spain, Cyprus, Ireland, Lithuania, Italy, Slovenia, Latvia, Denmark, Portugal, the UK, and the Netherlands the expenditure response lagged behind the rising need for unemployment benefit support. Amongst the least affected, Norway increased unemployment benefit expenditures more than twice as much as the relative increase of unemployment. Amongst the less affluent nations, Bulgaria stands out with a large expenditure increase, albeit from a very low level. The increased discrepancies between the earlier and later period reflect how the shift to austerity policies after 2010 reduced the capacity of welfare states to shelter individuals and households from loss of living standards due to unemployment.

Two contrasting cases of responses to increased unemployment can be found in the country studies of Greece and Iceland, which are relevant in this context. In Greece the coverage of unemployment benefit insurance came significantly down between 2010 and 2014, from 36 per cent to 13 per cent of all jobless workers (see Chapter 5). In Iceland the benefit period was extended from 2.5 to 4 years during the crisis period and thus all unemployed were fully covered for up to four years. Activation efforts were offered to all registered unemployed individuals, with large increases in expenditures per individual. When the benefit right was fully used the jobless could go onto social assistance, which provided only a slightly lower level of assistance than the general unemployment benefit (see Chapter 8). While on unemployment benefit, many also enjoyed supplements from their municipality's social assistance scheme. Thus Greece could only offer a very limited insurance against unemployment, which rose to extreme heights. The ultimate minimum income safety net in Greece was also very weak or largely absent and thus could not shoulder the burden of uninsured unemployed individuals (see Chapter 5).

On the whole it is difficult to disaggregate the 'automatic' effects of the welfare state and government policy efforts, even though we do so in organizing our narrative. Focusing on the characteristics and generosity of the welfare state in place before the crisis hit primarily shows the importance of the welfare state structure. But changes during the crisis period, such as increased expenditure on unemployment benefits in the face of an increased unemployment problem, still have to be underwritten and accepted by the reigning government in its budget each year. The 'automatic response' is thus also shaped by government effort (policy and will) and tied to current decision-making on how to use limited resources and even increase government debt. In that sense the 'automatic response' of the welfare state is never fully automatic (cf. Kangas & Palme, 2007). This should be kept in mind.

Another important factor which emanates from welfare state structure is how transfers are distributed to the population, and to what extent they are directed towards the lower income groups or to the middle and higher groups. The more they go to the lower income groups the more income security they provide against increased financial hardship overall, since the lower income groups are most vulnerable to hardship. The differing ways welfare states secure living standards for different age groups is also an important aspect in this context (as shown in Birnbaum et al., 2017). A generational balance which is tilted towards the elderly and leaves the working-age population less covered may provide weaker security against increased hardship in deep crises.[8]

## 14.4 The Modest Role of Affluence Level

One may wonder if the affluence level of nations is not the most important determinant of how they fare in hard times. After all, the more affluent nations should have better capabilities and particularly more resources for tackling crisis problems. This does not, however, seem to be an important factor, as indicated by Figure 14.7.

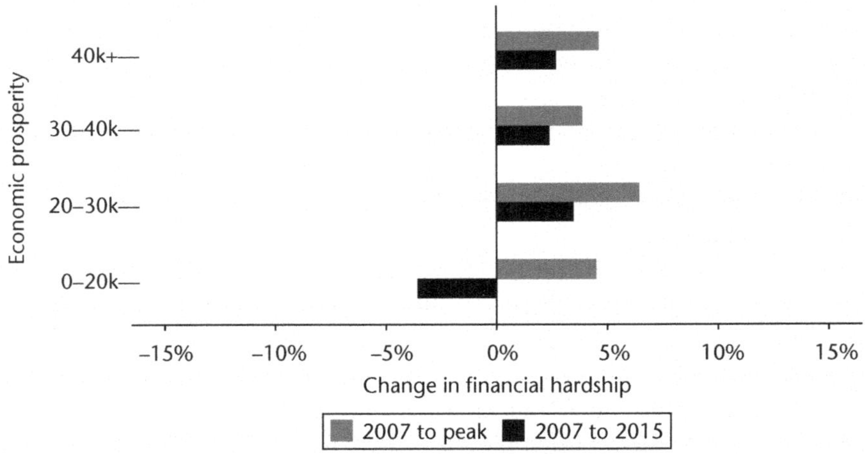


Economic prosperity measured as average real GDP PPP per capita ($), 2002–7
40k+: Iceland, Ireland, Luxembourg, Netherlands, Norway, Switzerland
30–40k: Austria, Belgium, Cyprus, Denmark, Finland, France, Germany, Italy, Spain, Sweden, UK
20–30k: Czech Republic, Greece, Malta, Portugal, Slovenia
0–20k: Bulgaria, Estonia, Hungary, Latvia, Lithuania, Poland, Romania

**Figure 14.7.** Relationship between pre-crisis affluence level and development of financial hardship

*Note*: PPP = purchasing power standard.

*Source*: OECD and EU-SILC, authors' calculation.

[8] See also data from OECD which indicates that the Mediterranean countries (Italy, Greece, Portugal, Spain) channelled transfers disproportionally towards middle- and higher income groups, in effect proportionally more towards the elderly than the unemployed (OECD, 2014b). Hence, the working-age individuals, including young families with children, who endure unemployment are more prone to experience increased financial hardship in these countries.

There is no direct association between affluence level of countries in the years leading up to the crisis and increase of financial hardship experienced by national populations during the crisis years. In each of the four affluence-level groups there are two or three countries that were particularly hard hit by the crisis. So affluence is no security at all against falling prey to financial crises.

The most interesting feature of the data in Figure 14.7 is the fact that when looking at the period from 2007 to 2015 it is in the least affluent countries that financial hardship ended at a significantly lower level than it had been on average in 2007. These are the Baltic States, Bulgaria, Hungary, Poland, and Romania. Again, this probably reflects their process of progress to lower levels of poverty and financial hardship that were in effect before the crisis hit. And the deep-crisis countries in that group also bottomed out early and recovered quickly, as previously shown.

It seems to apply in this context, as it does in the area of poverty in general, that politics, the strength of the welfare state, and redistribution seem to matter more for averting poverty than the affluence level of nations (Brady, 2009; Caminada & Goudswaard, 2010; Kenworthy, 2011; Smeeding, 2006). The more affluent nations do not automatically protect their vulnerable citizens better than other nations in hard times.

## 14.5 Relevance of Labour Market Regulation

Labour unions have played a large role in the build-up of the welfare state in Western countries, particularly amongst the Nordic nations (Christiansen et al., 2006). Labour market regulation through collective bargaining is also an important feature of the VoC perspective (Hall & Soskice, 2001), indicating a greater influence in coordinated capitalist countries (the Nordic and Continental ones) than in the more liberal Anglo-Saxon ones. The history of labour unions (and welfare states) was, on the other hand, very different in Eastern Europe, and their influence in contemporary society is significantly less notable there than in the Western countries. Eastern European countries have both a very low membership level and also a restricted coverage of collective bargaining. With the highest membership density in the Nordic countries and Belgium, the labour movements in these countries should have the greatest power to influence governments and employers.

In general we should expect that labour union influences through collective bargaining should be significantly associated to strength of welfare states, and hence possibly work in the same directions as welfare states in general, with respect to averting increased financial hardship of populations during deep crises (see Chapter 12 for a detailed treatment of the importance of labour market regulation and coordination).

Labour unions have generally been facing reduced membership (in relation to size of labour force) in Western countries over the last three to four decades, and hence their power and influence has potentially been reduced (OECD, 2016a, 2017a). Nevertheless, the regulatory influence of labour unions is more influential in Western Europe than might be expected from trends in union membership levels, since collectively bargained wages and conditions by unions and employers have significantly more coverage than membership density would indicate. In Figure 14.8 we examine the relationship between this institutional feature and experienced financial hardship during the crisis in Europe.

In general we have a similar relationship here as between welfare state generosity and financial hardship increase from 2007 to peak level. Where the bargaining coverage is larger, the financial hardship increased significantly less. The main deviation is when the period 2007 to 2015 is examined (the black columns). In the group with the lowest bargaining coverage the recovery towards lower financial hardship levels is the most decisive. That is, again, the main effect of the prominence of Eastern European countries in that group, who, despite a big setback at the beginning of the crisis, quickly returned to their convergence path of catching up with the more affluent European

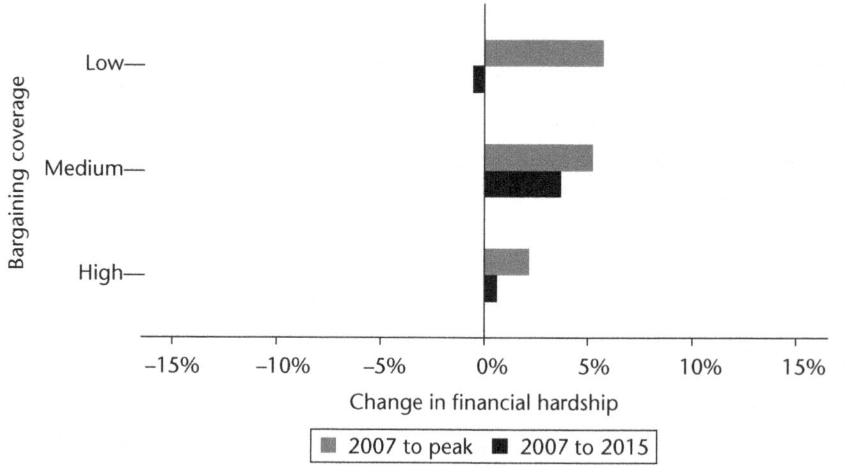


Low: Estonia, Hungary, Ireland, Latvia, Lithuania, Poland, Slovak Republic, Switzerland, United Kingdom
Medium: Czech Republic, Denmark, Germany, Greece, Italy, Luxembourg, Netherlands, Norway, Portugal, Spain
High: Austria, Belgium, Finland, France, Iceland, Slovenia, Sweden

**Figure 14.8.** Relationship between bargaining coverage in 2007 and development of financial hardship during the crisis

*Source*: OECD and EU-SILC, authors' calculation.

countries. Hence those effects amongst the Eastern countries are probably unrelated to welfare state or labour union influences.

## 14.6 The Role of Government Responses during the Crisis

The policies governments emphasized during the crisis is the second intermediary explanatory factor in our scheme, as shown in Chapter 1. Based on lessons of Keynesian demand management versus laissez-faire perspectives, or stimulus versus austerity options, government reactions should have made a major impact on the extent of economic contraction, for better or for worse (Alesina & Giavazzi, 2015; Krugman, 2012; Seidman, 2012; Stiglitz, 2016). The survey of government responses in Chapter 4 shows the general, by now well-known, pattern of initial stimulus response, followed by a growing emphasis on austerity. First we look at a conditioning factor that would affect the capacity of governments to react with a stimulus response, namely the overall debt level of governments prior to the onset of the crisis, that is, in 2007. The higher the debt level the less the scope for a strong stimulus response that might have averted increasing financial hardship.

There is quite a strong link between these, indicating that populations of countries with higher government debt level before the crisis hit were more prone to suffer financial hardship. This was, of course, mediated by the depth of the crisis. The rationale behind this would be that more indebted governments had less room to manoeuvre, either by providing economic stimulus (to avert increased unemployment) or by increasing expenditure on automatic stabilizers, such as unemployment and other benefits countering primary income losses. A more indebted government would either refrain from or simply not be able to finance the needed growth of expenditures for the welfare state to honour its pledge as an insurer of last resort for the households. Similarly, the pressure for a shift to austerity policies would be larger in those countries from the start and, given the size of welfare expenditures, they would be disproportionally affected by austerity cuts.

This is indeed supported by the data in Figure 14.9. The initial impact of increased financial hardship was largest in the countries with the most heavily indebted governments when the crisis hit, and there the recovery was also slowest (cf. the black columns). On the other hand, in countries where the debt level was lowest, recovery was more robust, even though the initial impact was also significant. So initial debt level was most likely a conditioning factor shaping what and how much governments could do to counter the negative welfare consequences of the crisis.

But let us now look more directly at the austerity policy option and its relationship with financial hardship developments, in Figure 14.10.

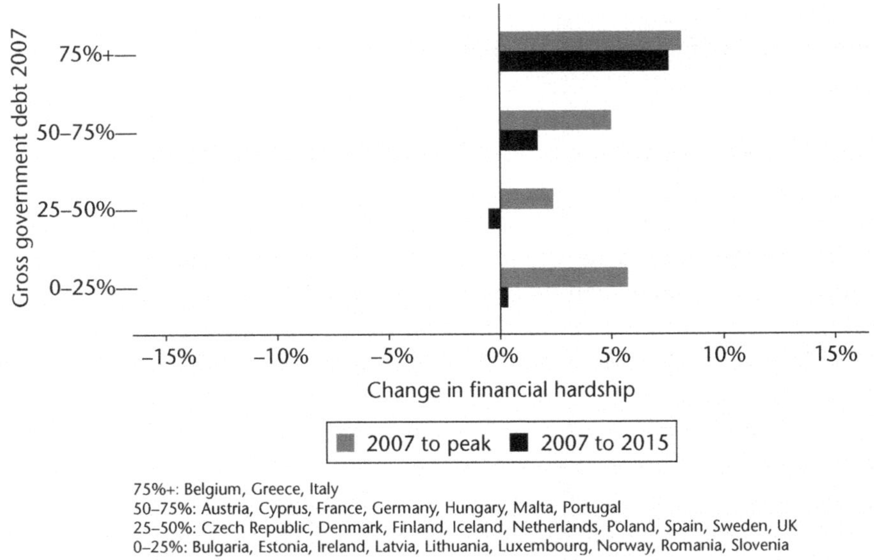


**Figure 14.9.** Relationship between debt levels of governments in 2007 (% of GDP) and experienced financial hardship of populations during the crisis years

*Source*: OECD and EU-SILC, authors' calculation.

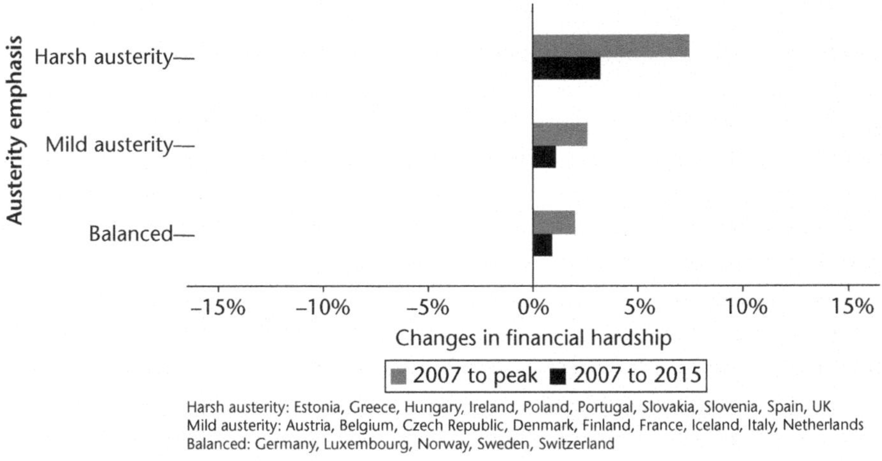


**Figure 14.10.** Relationship between austerity emphasis 2009–13 and experiences of financial hardship

*Note*: Austerity emphasis determined on the basis of changes to underlying government revenues and spending between 2009 and 2013.

*Source*: OECD and EU-SILC, authors' calculation (see also Chapter 3).

Here we have a strong link, with the countries that pursued austerity measures to a greater extent between 2009 and 2013 also having the populations that were most impacted by financial hardship, and vice versa. This is particularly strong when considering the impact from 2007 to the peak level of financial hardship (grey columns).

One may, of course, argue that we have here a selection effect, with more deep-crisis countries in the group applying 'harsh austerity' and fewer in the other groups. In that sense the depth of the crisis called for more reactions, as did a more difficult debt situation at the beginning of the crisis, thus increasing the likelihood of austerity measures being disproportionally applied in the deep-crisis countries. Nevertheless, one may also argue that austerity was the wrong measure, in the sense that it made things even worse than they already were (Blyth, 2013; Krugman, 2012; Stiglitz, 2016).[9]

This is the drama of interlinking negatives that made the consequences of financial hardship more likely in some of the deep-crisis countries—but as in the more nuanced approach of Iceland and some other countries there was another option available, that is, a more modest dose of austerity and a minimization of the hardship consequences for the most vulnerable. A related issue comes up when we consider the role of currency regime, which we examine in Figure 14.11.

Joseph E. Stiglitz argues in his book about the euro (2016) that, given the inadequate structural foundation for the common currency in Europe, this exposed the peripheral Euro countries to a greater risk of bubbles and overextended debt accumulation in the pre-crisis years—they were left with no other option than to apply forceful austerity policy after the crisis hit. With the euro there was no longer the classical option of devaluing the currency to mend the negative current account balance and to strengthen exports. The only option left was to adopt austerity and internal devaluation (lower wages and benefits, and even raising taxes), which unfortunately deepened the crisis further (hence the second dip in most Euro countries). This route caused greater and longer lasting financial hardship for populations (Blyth, 2013).[10] The euro thus did not provide any security against falling into a financial crisis, but

[9] An interesting recent study by Stefano Ronchi (2018) disaggregates social protection and social investment expenditures from 2000 to 2014, taking account of need levels in EU countries (expenditures per numbers of receivers in each benefit category). His overall finding is that both categories of expenditures were increasing in the years leading up to the crisis (some of this due to a catch-up effect amongst less advanced countries). But as the crisis hit the expenditure level on social protection came down significantly between 2009 and 2013, while social investment expenditures maintained their level much better. This would seem to indicate that austerity policies affected social protection more than social investment probably when social protection was most needed, at least in the deep-crisis countries.

[10] Again, an interesting example is given by comparing Eurozone Finland and Sweden with its own currency. Whereas the former suffered from a long-lasting crisis, the latter had more options at its disposal to adapt to and exit the crisis earlier.

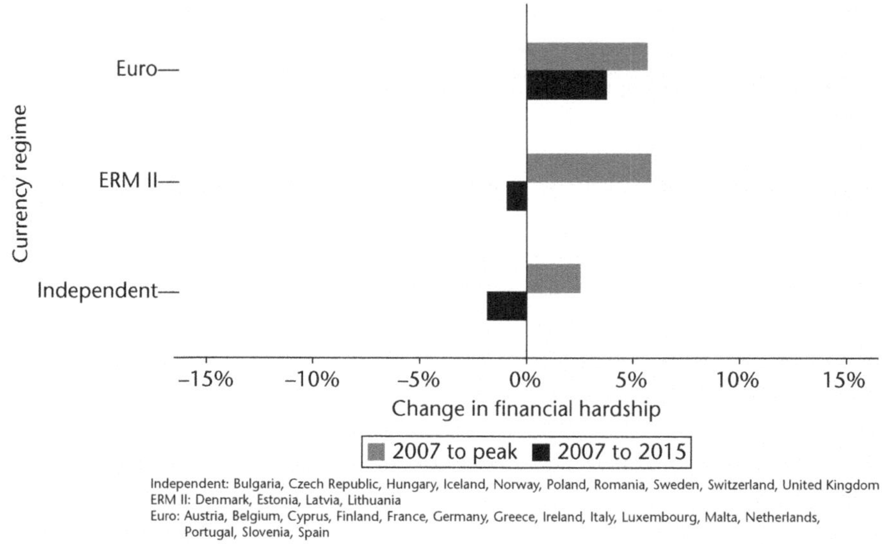


**Figure 14.11.** Relationship between currency regime and financial hardship developments
*Source*: OECD and EU-SILC, authors' calculation.

more likely increased that risk in less economically affluent nations. It also restricted the options available once the crisis hit.[11]

The ERM II (Exchange Rate Mechanism) group, that is, those with their currency pegged to the euro (the three Baltic States and Denmark) were more or less in the same boat. The Baltics succeeded in applying considerable internal devaluation and that helped them to recover quite rapidly, whereas Denmark remained sluggish for longer (see Chapter 11). Those countries that had their own independent currency were, in general, less severely hit with increased financial hardship in the early crisis years and recovered better on average.

Looking at this issue in a micro context we can compare Ireland with the euro and Iceland with its own independent currency. Ireland enforced a mixed policy response of internal devaluation and austerity (lowered wages and benefits) and it suffered a larger increase of unemployment, which also was more prolonged, than in Iceland. Iceland's strategy involved a milder dose of austerity with a more strategic redistribution and sheltering of the most vulnerable groups. It also lowered direct taxes on the lower half of income

[11] Furthermore, the richer Euro countries subsidized more crisis-stricken Euro countries, thus weakening their own possibilities for domestic stabilization. Non-Euro countries did not participate in the rescue operations despite the fact that the biggest creditors, for example to Greece, were Swiss and UK banks. Even the Swedish banks (outside the Eurozone) were much bigger creditors to crisis-stricken countries (particularly the Baltics) than the Finnish banks.

groups while increasing the tax burden on higher income groups, the wealthy, and on firms, in conjunction with various efforts at job creation and activation. Iceland's great devaluation strengthened export competitiveness, which was particularly effective for the rising tourist industry. While the devaluation reduced the disposable earnings of households considerably on average the strategy of equalization countered that to a significant extent amongst the lowest income groups. The overall effect was a much lower unemployment level at peak and a more successful recovery towards one of the lowest unemployment rates in Europe after 2014 (see Chapters 7 and 8).

Similarly, Finland with the euro is now experiencing more restraint on its options in the face of slowing economic growth in the latter years, with the concomitant pressure on unemployment, while Sweden with its own currency (which has been maintained at a relatively low level) is experiencing stronger growth (see Chapters 9 and 13).

## 14.7 Poverty Reduction and Redistribution

Probing further into government efforts during the crisis, we lastly look specifically at how governments reacted to underlying pressure on poverty levels during the crisis (that is, increased poverty rates before transfers) and at redistribution levels. This involves a narrower focus than in section 14.6, but perhaps a more realistic assessment of governmental responses that aimed to counter negative effects of the crisis on the populations, particularly for the more vulnerable groups.

Again, we emphasize the difficulty of disentangling the influences of the welfare state in place before the crisis hit and government actions after. Perhaps the issues in this section should be seen as involving an interrelationship between automatic stabilizing influences of welfare states and government efforts during the crisis.

What the data on changing poverty reduction efforts in Figure 14.12 show is the difference between poverty levels before and after public transfers and how this changed during the crisis. We look first at changes between 2007 and the peak level reached during the crisis and then at the changes between 2007 and 2016. The first measure gives an indication of the maximum effort to counter the tendency of the crisis to increase poverty. The latter one gives an indication of how the period ends. Those countries that recovered better could reduce or end their poverty reduction effort in later years. Those that recovered more slowly or entered the crisis later still had a high poverty reduction effect on the latter measure (change from 2007 to 2016; cf. the grey columns).

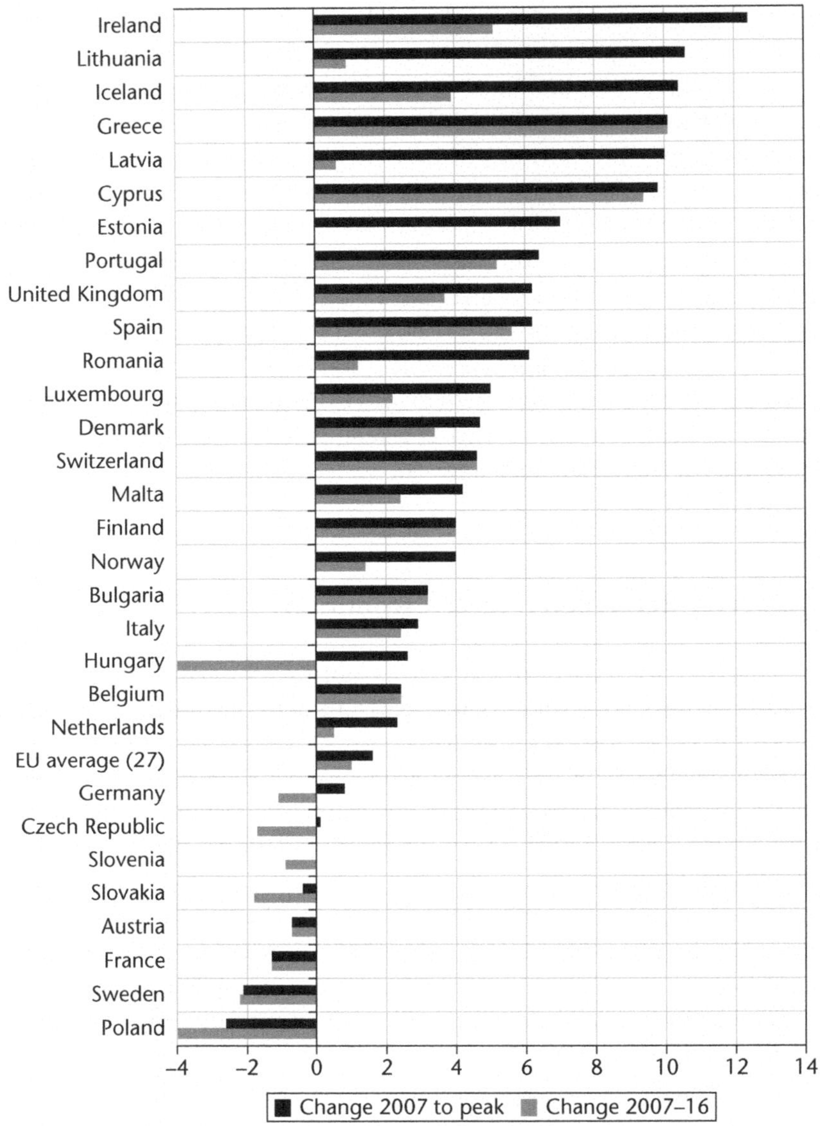


**Figure 14.12.** Changing poverty reduction during the crisis

*Note*: Measured as difference between poverty rates before and after transfers (pensions included in transfers). Maximum reduction of relative poverty from 2007 to peak, and development from 2007 to 2016.

*Source*: Eurostat.

What is interesting in Figure 14.12 is the fact that the greatest increases of poverty reduction were in the countries that were hardest hit by the crisis. While Greece should be at the top, if crisis depth was the determining factor, it comes in fourth place—still high for a less advanced welfare state. The Baltic States are all near the top, along with Ireland and Iceland. All of these five countries had scaled back their poverty reduction levels by 2016, most decisively the Baltic States (cf. the grey columns). On the other hand Greece and Cyprus, and also Spain and Portugal at a lower level, still exhibit a big difference between pre- and post-crisis poverty rates by the end of the period.

While capacity was different among countries (differing debt levels and differing capacities of welfare states to act as providers of last resort), it is still interesting that all those that were hardest hit made a significantly increased effort to counter poverty development during the crisis years. That is a positive message about governmental concerns, despite differing capacities to act and reap success. Of the Scandinavian countries, Denmark, Finland, and Norway increased their efforts while Sweden lowered its poverty reduction level during the crisis.

Lastly we examine changing redistribution efforts by European governments during the crisis years and compare these to the redistribution level in the pre-crisis year of 2007 (Figure 14.13). This is simply the reduction in market income inequality due to taxes and transfers in 2007 (grey columns) and changes in the redistribution levels, first from 2007 to 2010 and then from 2010 to 2014. This figure shows quite clearly the combined importance of both the welfare state structure (the redistribution level in 2007) and changed efforts during the crisis years.

Iceland and Latvia both had a low redistribution level before the crisis and they also increased redistribution the most in the early years of the crisis (2007 to 2010). In the case of Iceland the originally low redistribution level is due to a low level of inequality in market incomes, which is a result of the great influence of the Icelandic labour movement on wage compression. In Latvia it primarily reflects a low level of welfare state development. Ireland, however, had a very high level of redistribution in 2007 and yet had the third-largest increase at the beginning of the crisis. All these three countries were hit very hard by the crisis early on and increased redistribution to the greatest extent.

Other deep-crisis countries increased the redistribution more modestly, such as Greece, Spain, and Italy, while the UK and Portugal increased redistribution significantly. Hungary increased redistribution a little at the beginning of the crisis and then reduced it decisively between 2010 and 2014.

Amongst the less affected countries with advanced welfare states, Finland, Norway, Belgium, Luxembourg, and the Netherlands increased redistribution, while Denmark did not show any change and Sweden actually reduced its redistribution level.

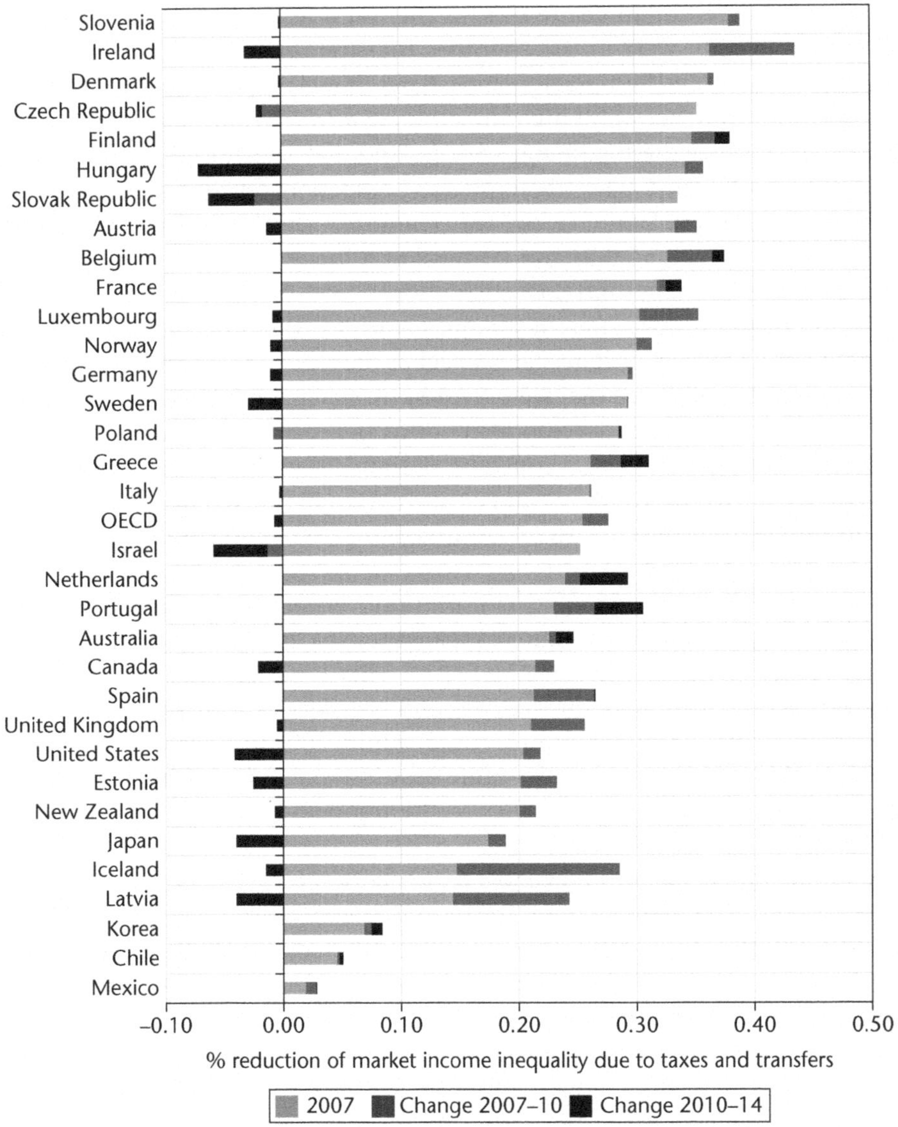


**Figure 14.13.** Changing redistribution during the crisis

*Note*: Percentage reduction in market income inequality due to taxes and transfers in 2007 and changes from 2007 to 2010 and 2010 to 2014. Countries are ranked by the redistribution level in the initial position of 2007.

*Source*: OECD (excluding non-European countries).

## 14.8 Controlling for Depth of Crisis

Given the difficulties in disentangling interrelationships between depth of crisis and governmental responses, and similarly between welfare state structures and governmental responses, we have refrained from setting up multivariate models with estimates of these relationships. Instead we draw conclusions mainly from the data-based narrative that we have presented in this chapter. Nevertheless, to go beyond the bivariate associations that we have typically shown, we lastly present some three-dimensional cross-tabulations of financial hardship developments by welfare state characteristics and austerity emphasis, controlling for depth of GDP contraction (Tables 14.1 and 14.2).

For countries that had 3 per cent economic contraction or more (Table 14.1, rows 2 and 3) the increase of financial hardship was decisively larger in those with less advanced welfare states. This relationship is more marked at the higher level (over 7 per cent) of economic contraction. In the 'more advanced'

**Table 14.1.** Financial hardship development from 2007 to peak by broad welfare regimes

| GDP contraction | Broad welfare regime | | Grand total |
|---|---|---|---|
| | More advanced | Less advanced | |
| Less than 3% | 2.1 | 1.2 | 1.7 |
| 3% to 7% | 2.5 | 8.3 | 5.4 |
| More than 7% | 1.6 | 8.6 | 7.2 |
| Grand total | 2.1 | 6.4 | 4.6 |

*Note*: Table controls for GDP contraction from 2007 to trough. The figures in the table are increases of financial hardship experienced by individuals, in percentage points.
*Source*: OECD and EU-SILC, authors' calculation.

**Table 14.2.** Financial hardship development from 2007 to peak by application of harsh austerity measures, 2009–13

| GDP contraction | Harsh austerity | | Grand total |
|---|---|---|---|
| | No | Yes | |
| Less than 3% | 2 | −6 | 1 |
| 3% to 7% | 2.5 | 7.7 | 4.7 |
| More than 7% | 3 | 10 | 7.4 |
| Grand total | 2.4 | 7.4 | 4.4 |

*Note*: Table controls for GDP contraction from 2007 to trough. The figures in the table are increases of financial hardship experienced by individuals, in percentage points.
*Source*: OECD and EU-SILC, authors' calculation.

group we have the Nordic and Western Continental welfare states, and in the 'less advanced' group the liberal, Southern European, and Eastern European welfare states. We have to work with broad categories since the number of countries on which the tabulation is based is too limited. The general indication is that the presence of a more advanced welfare state softened financial hardship consequences significantly, especially when taking into account the degree of economic contraction. Table 14.2 does the same for government emphasis on harsh austerity measures during the crisis.

Again, when we look at countries that experienced economic contraction of 3 per cent or more the application of harsh austerity measures is closely associated with a greater increase of financial hardship during the crisis. This is also more decisive at the higher level of economic contraction (over 7 per cent). So the larger the emphasis on austerity measures the greater the negative welfare consequences for populations, taking account of differing degrees of economic contraction.

## 14.9 Summary

The comparative analyses of this chapter have been undertaken within the general framework of our explanatory scheme outlined in Chapter 1. We have considered various statistical materials that reflect on the importance of the depth and persistence of the economic and financial crisis. The crisis is, of course, the fundamental source of the negative welfare consequences experienced by populations of European countries from 2008 onwards. We have also produced various data on the importance of the welfare state and governmental responses for softening, or aggravating, the welfare consequences of the crisis.

The general conclusion of the chapter is that the main elements of our explanatory scheme of Chapter 1 all had an important influence on welfare outcomes for populations of European countries during the crisis years. The welfare states functioned as an insurance or protection system, as providers of last resort, softening the negative consequences of the crisis; the policies of governments also had independent impacts on welfare outcomes, for better or worse. Governments' policies were often conditioned by pre-crisis levels of government debt or by the sheer depth of the crisis—or both, in the most severe cases. Those hard-hit countries that had adopted the euro and that had to seek assistance from the International Monetary Fund (IMF), the European Central Bank (ECB), and the European Commission (for example Greece, Ireland, Portugal, and Spain), also had to comply with stringent conditions which generally left them with barely any options except to implement harsh austerity measures. This impacted negatively on financial hardship amongst their respective populations. Those governments that could apply strategic social protection measures and other related policy instruments, such as job creation, activation, and tax cuts on lower income groups, could significantly soften negative welfare consequences. The underlying point is that aspects of the institutional environment interacted with government policies to affect welfare outcomes.

# 15

# Conclusions

*Stefán Ólafsson*

Crises are commonly conceived as 'hard times'. We generally expect them to be a setback to our continuous progress towards better levels of living. Indeed they are. The Great Recession is the largest crisis to hit the Western world since the Great Depression of the 1930s. But not all nations were affected equally by the Great Recession. Robust differences were found within countries, especially in the extent to which and how different population groups were affected.

It is these varieties of crisis experiences that we have surveyed and analysed in this book. While the depth of the initial crisis impact was of pivotal importance, we also show how welfare states made a difference for welfare outcomes, as did the policies and approaches adopted by governments and other conditions of the crisis situation. European countries were characterized by different levels of affluence, debt, employment, and welfare when the crisis hit. Institutional and political environments were also different. Some belonged to the Eurozone and others had independent currency regimes. That conditioned options in different ways, for instance. Thus capacities for coping with the crisis varied considerably and so did the actual usage of such capacities.

Now a decade later, in 2018, we can survey the Great Recession's broad effects on economies, finances, democracies, markets, and people's levels of living. Our focus has primarily been on individual and household welfare outcomes through the crisis years, both across European countries and amongst the main socio-economic groups, both from a pan-European comparative perspective and in more detail in nine country case studies.

In this last chapter we pull the threads together and discuss lessons learned along five dimensions: varieties of crisis experiences, how the burdens were shared, how the welfare state made a difference, how politics mattered, and lastly crises and the political economy of welfare futures.

## 15.1 Varieties of Crisis Experiences

The crisis started for most countries around 2008 and economic contraction generally peaked in 2009–10. Those countries that went into a second dip, most typically some of the Eurozone countries, had another economic contraction in 2012–13. Increased unemployment and financial hardship consequences followed the economic contractions and in some cases were quite protracted. Those countries that had a significant second dip generally faced more serious consequences in terms of population hardship. The depth of the crisis experiences varied and was generally in proportion to the size and characteristics of the bubble economy period leading up to 2008. Figure 15.1 provides a comprehensive overview of the depth and extent of crisis experiences of European nations and reveals the relationship between economic contraction and unemployment and financial hardship developments (see Chapter 2 for a more detailed analysis).

Greece is in a class of its own as the greatest victim of the Great Recession. Greece was very vulnerable with high government debt level before the crisis and a weak social protection system (see Chapter 5). The country experienced the biggest economic contraction, resulting in the largest increase of both unemployment and financial hardship. Most of the Mediterranean EU countries

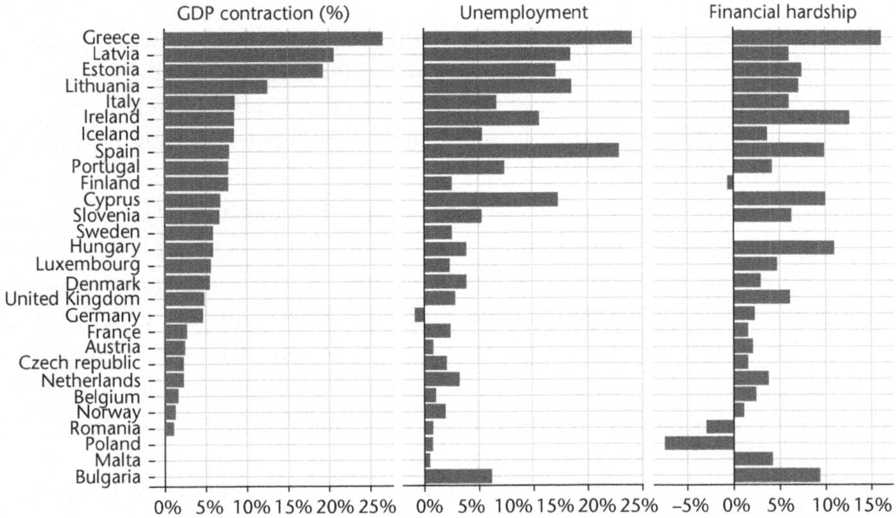


**Figure 15.1.** Maximum crisis impacts in European countries

*Note*: This shows economic contraction from 2007 to trough (%), change of unemployment and financial hardship from 2007 to peak during the crisis years (% points). Countries are ranked by extent of maximum contraction of gross domestic product (GDP).

*Source*: Eurostat, author calculation.

experienced a very deep and prolonged crisis. In addition to Greece, Italy, Spain, Portugal, and Cyprus were all amongst the most seriously affected.

The Baltic States of Estonia, Latvia, and Lithuania all had massive economic contractions but were, however, saved a significant second dip (see Chapter 4). Their unemployment levels peaked in 2010 and then came gradually and persistently down towards their pre-crisis levels by 2017. Financial hardship increased somewhat less in these countries than might have been expected considering their initial economic contraction and increased unemployment.

Ireland and Iceland have in common an excessive bubble economy period with an unsustainable accumulation of private sector debt preceding the crisis, but unemployment and financial hardship increased at least twice as much in Ireland during the crisis. This was a result of Eurozone Ireland being more constrained by the Troika than Iceland by the International Monetary Fund (IMF), but also of different domestic policy priorities (cf. Chapters 7 and 8). Iceland could devalue its currency and recovered fast but also favoured redistribution and could rely on a dual-earner model as an insurance mechanism, while Ireland had a less protective unemployment benefit system, pursued austerity to a greater extent, and also had a lower prevalence of dual-earner households.

Spain and Portugal experienced similar levels of economic contraction, but of the two unemployment and financial hardship increased far more in Spain. The unemployment consequences of the crisis in Spain were indeed exceptional, and despite significant progress in strengthening the Spanish welfare state in the decade leading up to the crisis, the capabilities to tackle such a deep crisis were still limited, as shown in Chapter 6. A key for understanding Portugal's better outcome is that it had a significantly higher employment level before the crisis started and could maintain that better through the crisis as compared with Spain.

Moving on to more northern parts of Europe, Finland and Sweden experienced similar degrees of economic contraction (7 per cent and 6 per cent respectively), but unemployment increased modestly in both countries and heightened financial hardships were avoided. Chapters 9 and 13 show the decisive importance of a comprehensive and resourceful welfare state for protecting levels of living in deep-crisis situations. While Sweden benefited from a floating currency and strong domestic demand, Finland, with the euro, had a much tougher ride through the crisis.

Next in the rank of scale of economic contraction among our country case studies are Denmark and the UK, with around 5 per cent decline of their economies. Of the two Denmark had the larger increase of unemployment but its increase of financial hardship was less than that of the UK. Again the welfare state is a vital part of the story here, with Denmark's comparatively generous unemployment benefits with long duration playing an important role. The UK experienced a larger increase of financial hardship than expected from the scale of its economic contraction. Austerity policies served to increase the financial burdens of the unemployed and other benefit recipients (cf. Chapter 10) and low-income groups in general were particularly hard hit in the UK.

Norway had a 'smooth ride' through the Great Recession and enjoys both a very robust welfare state and sizable resources through its large oil fund. Norway also offers important lessons about the functioning of a Keynesian welfare state and a coordination system between labour market partners and government for averting deep-crisis effects when recession hits (cf. Chapter 12).

Looking at the broader context and patterning, a trend of convergence in welfare developments was to some extent evident in Europe in the decades leading up to 2008. Poverty was being reduced and the EU had set a common goal of significantly reducing poverty and social exclusion in its member states by 2020. The Great Recession disrupted that progress. Convergence in the pre-crisis period was particularly strong amongst some of the Eastern European countries. Although they were faced with a setback by the crisis, they typically returned quite robustly to their catch-up development in the latter part of the crisis period. At the same time, some of the Mediterranean countries had either not improved or decisively worsened their position by 2015. That makes for an increased divergence within the EU, with Mediterranean countries lagging further behind the Nordic and North-Western countries. These concurrent forces of convergence and divergence seem set to change the welfare landscape of Europe for some time to come.

## 15.2 How the Burdens were Shared

Our key tool, developed in this book, for assessing the welfare consequences of the Great Recession is a composite indicator of financial hardship, based on income poverty, material deprivation, and difficulties in making ends meet. This indicator has allowed us to focus in a direct way on select socio-economic groups and see how they were impacted, both across Europe as a whole and in individual country cases.

The decisive story here, looking across 30 countries as Ólafsson and Stefánsson do in Chapter 2, is that the lowest three income deciles (the 30 per cent with the lowest income) experienced by far the largest increase of financial hardship during the crisis years. These are the same groups that had the highest financial hardship levels before the crisis started. The middle-income groups were significantly less impacted by increased financial hardship while the top-income groups were barely affected at all. The recovery from the initially increased hardship was also more protracted amongst the lowest income groups while the top-income groups had more or less fully recovered from their very modest difficulties by 2015. Hence we can conclude that the lowest income groups bore the brunt of welfare consequences in Europe as a whole.

The analyses also looked at how other socio-economic groups fared, such as the unemployed, immigrants, disability pensioners, single parents, those with the lowest educational level, and various age groups. It turns out that the unemployed fared particularly badly. Disability pensioners and families with children faced increased hardship as well, while the elderly were relatively well protected against increased financial hardship. Some of these specific outcomes have much to do with differential effects and preferences of European welfare states in protecting populations against crisis consequences, to which we now turn.

## 15.3 How the Welfare State Made a Difference

The book's analyses clearly underline the potential of the contemporary welfare state for reducing or even averting increased financial hardship during such a deep crisis as the Great Recession. The emergence of modern welfare states produced a completely different institutional environment for social protection of populations, compared to what prevailed during the Great Depression of the 1930s. That is the main reason why the hard times of the Great Recession were not as consequential for levels of living as those of the 1930s.

During the crisis and its aftermath we have not seen a major shift in the political economy paradigm, even though financial regulation has been strengthened, both nationally and in the context of the EU (not least in the Eurozone). The globalized neoliberal paradigm that has been predominant for decades appears more or less intact. No major shift towards a more mixed Keynesian and welfare-oriented capitalism is evident in Western countries in general. Indeed, the initial Keynesian-inspired demand-oriented responses were in many cases replaced by austerity measures that in turn weakened the respective welfare states. Most of our country case studies of Part II report increased targeting and conditionality of welfare benefits, both amongst the more and less advanced welfare states.

What can be argued on the basis of our analyses is that the crisis shows the importance or even success of the welfare state in protecting nations' living standards and particularly those of the more vulnerable in society. But both the capability and commitment to averting increased financial hardship varied between countries (see Chapters 2 and 14).

The Nordic and Continental countries (Austria, Belgium, France, Germany, Luxembourg, the Netherlands, and Switzerland) share the features of comprehensive and resourceful social protection systems and as a consequence experienced significantly less increase of financial hardship from 2007 to peak level, as compared with other groups of welfare states. This may partly be a result of less extensive economic contractions in such countries, with their more regulated institutional environments, which provided a different context for the financial crisis triggered in the more liberal market economies (cf. lessons from the 'varieties of capitalism' (VoC) school; see Hall & Soskice, 2001, and Chapters 11 to 13).

Particularly striking is the fact that the liberal regime countries (Ireland and the UK) experienced similar levels of increased financial hardship as the more economically impacted Mediterranean countries and they also had a similarly drawn-out path of recovery up to 2015. This indicates weaker protective capabilities of the Irish and UK welfare states. One striking feature of hardship developments in these countries is how heavily the unemployed were impacted. Given a weak level of protection from unemployment benefits and activation measures in those countries (see Chapters 5, 6, 7, and 10; as well as Esser et al., 2013), this should come as no surprise. Since the unemployment benefit system is the decisive element in the automatic stabilizing feature of the welfare state this weakness may also have had its economic cost, in deepening the contraction and increasing financial hardship. The dual role of the welfare state for protecting living standards and maintaining demand levels through crises in the Keynesian sense are equally important. With weak unemployment protection the complementarity between the social protection system and the economy is partially lost.

An alternative example from the Nordic context is to be found in the Icelandic and Danish cases. While Iceland does not have as generous unemployment benefit replacement rates as the other Nordic countries, these were supplemented with additional benefits from social assistance. An important complementary effect also came from the fact that Iceland has universal access to pre-school care for children and long-term care services, which has facilitated the very high employment participation of women. Thus most households have two earners and only rarely did unemployment hit both at the same time (this applies to the other Nordic countries as well). Greatly increased activation and job creation measures also helped in the Icelandic context, as well as favourable expansion of tourism after 2010. In Denmark the hardship position of the unemployed actually reduced during the crisis years. Inadequate unemployment protection as well as a low rate of female employment participation were causal in both the Mediterranean countries and, to some extent, Ireland and the UK, rendering unemployed people more vulnerable to increased financial hardship as compared to the Nordic countries and also the North-Western Continental countries.

This variation between welfare states in comprehensiveness and resources for protecting living standards is what we would predict from the 'regime' and 'families of nations' studies of welfare states. A recent study by Birnbaum and colleagues (2017) highlights the differences in what they call 'generational welfare contracts' in the richest OECD countries. They distinguish between pro-old, pro-work, and pro-child characteristics of social protection systems.

Our results on financial hardship developments during the Great Recession show that the older population (65+) appears to have been by far the best protected age group; in most cases their financial hardship level in fact came down during the crisis period. This is partly a demographic effect in the sense that the oldest cohorts are continuously being replenished by new cohorts that have been able to earn more generous pension rights, either via public or private pensions. The conclusion is that it is far easier and more straightforward to protect the elderly during times of crisis. The pro-child and pro-work features seem to be much more important if we want to better harness the population as a whole against the effects of economic crises. Since children and the unemployed suffered increased financial hardship in most cases, particularly in the less advanced welfare states, the indication is that there is substantial room for improvement with regard to the protective function for working-age groups.

Hence we can argue that there is still considerable work to be done if we want to make European welfare states more balanced from a generational perspective. As Birnbaum and colleagues (2017) show, the more balanced generational protection systems carry the potential to create win-win situations for societal development.

In principle, a well-advanced and efficient welfare state should be able to avert any increase of financial hardship during a deep crisis, that is, if it lives fully up to its goal of being an effective insurance system—which is in fact needed, given capitalism's propensity towards instability (Keynes, 1936; Minsky, 1986). Contemporary welfare states are somewhat adrift of such a goal, as our survey of financial hardship developments during the Great Recession shows—but some much more so than others and some more now than before the cutbacks during the crisis.

## 15.4 How Politics Mattered

The Great Recession was caused by the signature market failure of letting the bubble get out of hand in the decade leading up to 2008 (Epstein & Wolfson, 2013; Reinhart & Rogoff, 2009). Regulators and governments failed too, by allowing all this to happen.

When the crisis hit, governments were typically landed with the task of muddling through the crisis, both in the macro contexts of economy and finance and in the micro context of individuals' welfare. Unless one adheres to the tenets of libertarian laissez-faire politics, that was the self-evident way forward in the crisis situation. And indeed that is how all European governments progressed. Theirs was the task of leading their nations out of the crisis. Governments, however, reacted differently and indeed had different capacities to manage their way out of the crisis (see Chapters 3 and 4).

As is shown in the book, particularly in Chapters 4 and 14 and in the country case studies of Part II, different debt levels, welfare regimes, currency regimes, and various other political economy conditions shaped the available options for governments in each case. Ideological propensities also mattered in the choices and policy reactions.

Here we only reflect on how the emphasis on austerity policies related to financial hardship developments during the crisis (cf. Chapter 14).

Countries which applied larger doses of austerity policies are also those that saw the greatest increases of financial hardship levels, both in the initial experience from 2007 to peak level and as regards the overall development pattern from 2007 to 2015. Those with milder applications of austerity had a significantly more modest increase of financial hardship and those with more balanced policies saw the least impact on hardship, if only by a margin. The exceptions to this pattern are the Baltic countries where austerity measures had immediate negative effects on financial hardship at the beginning but which then entered a strong recovery. Countries that had higher public debt levels before the crisis hit had a larger increase of financial hardship during the crisis period.

There may, of course, be mediating factors at work here, not least the depth of the crisis effect. Towards the end of Chapter 14 the relationship between financial hardship increases, welfare regimes, and austerity was analysed with control for depth of crisis. That analysis confirms both the austerity emphasis and welfare regime characteristics have significant independent effects. The book's findings also emphasize the relevance of pre-crisis debts levels, currency regimes, labour market coordination, domestic demand management, and other country-specific political economy conditional factors.

## 15.5 Crises and the Political Economy of Welfare Futures

The Great Recession has been a trying time for governments in Europe and elsewhere. Revenues came down, debts accumulated, growth was lost, financial hardship of populations increased, and political turmoil escalated. Yet, the more comprehensive and effective welfare states managed to cushion the worst consequences of the crisis and did quite well in some cases. The weaker and less resourceful welfare states, however, did not rise to the task of providing adequate social protection. Looked at over time though, we know that the welfare state is an important institution and can be an able provider of last resort for households. Our results confirm this, while underlining variations. For the point is that even the most heavily impacted countries during the Great Recession were better sheltered against population hardship than was the case during the Great Depression of the 1930s. Hence, welfare states can work and can live up to their ideals—if they are comprehensive in their coverage, adequately funded, and efficiently organized.

This notwithstanding, the welfare state remains in a precarious and to some extent contradictory situation as the crisis gradually eases (Taylor-Gooby et al., 2017). Despite the fact that governments typically took on greatly increased debt in order to save banks and stimulate and resurrect the economy, and even reduced tax revenues in the crisis situation, political support for welfare states is not stable. Arguments for curtailing or cutting expenditures of the welfare state still linger on the political agenda. This should not surprise us. The welfare state was always a political project. Its future will depend on general political currents and country-specific political conditions.

Despite the negative experiences of growing boom and bust cycles since the early 1980s (Reinhart & Rogoff, 2009), libertarians remain on the same ideological track, emphasizing tax cuts, unrestrained markets, and reduced roles for governments, which inevitably would erode welfare states (Blyth, 2013). They do not seem to link the devastating experiences of the Great Recession with the failures of unrestrained financial markets. Centre and left parties, historically more in favour of the welfare state, often appear somewhat confused and weak, perhaps exhausted by their role of defending an institutional structure which, as a programme, now appears old and jaded. It may be tiring to play a defence game for too long while competitors are continually on the attack. On top of that is increased political turmoil, with new parties on the right and left frequently issuing contradictory messages about welfare futures.

The Great Recession has been used as an example of how economic paradigms continue to be important triggers of economic crisis, but also how policy responses to the different crises have been designed. The Nordic experiences illustrate how different policy paradigms over time have informed and inspired policymakers to pursue very diverse kinds of policies. This is not only true for Keynesian support of welfare state expansion and Schumpeterian-inspired active labour market policies (ALMP), the latter being a social investment approach, but also for neoliberal deregulation reforms and more recent supply-side orientation. The Swedish policy responses to the two crises (of the early 1990s and the Great Recession) illustrate well some of the tensions between different paradigms, or within paradigms for that matter (Cronert & Palme, 2017; see also Chapter 13), but also show how different kinds of paradigms can be combined to include policy instruments aimed at supply *and* demand at the same time, as well as egalitarian human capital investment.

This urges us to consider how social sciences can inform the design of good, possibly synthesized, policy paradigms in the aftermath of the Great Recession.

Predictions are always difficult to make, especially about the future, which is why public policy should hope for the best and plan for the worst. One lesson from the comparison of the two Swedish crises is that domestic demand levels are of critical importance for mitigating (or aggravating) external shocks. Denmark, while entrenched within the Nordic institutional and policy environment, provides another example of how inadequate demand management increased financial hardship during the crisis. The countries that employed harsh austerity policies (such as the Mediterranean and liberal regime countries) generally suffered the most serious welfare consequences of the crisis, especially when they also had weak welfare states to rely on.

Another lesson is that governments with public finances in good shape provide room for action in terms of responding to external shocks and sheltering the population from severe financial hardship. Moreover, high employment rates in combination with adequate unemployment insurance provide a good recipe for protecting people in hard times—thus the automatic stabilizers would work effectively. However, social insurance does not protect newcomers to the labour market, and this implies that social safety-nets as minimum income guarantees are needed as a complement.

In the post-crisis situation there is no one generally accepted roadmap for welfare futures as there was for European nations following the Great Depression and World War II. Then the plan was to build a mixed economy welfare state to replace an unrestrained market and a warfare state. Even if no viable alternative has yet emerged as a replacement there are some interesting ideas around. The social investment agenda can be seen as an attempt to carve out some new building blocks for a new paradigm beyond Keynesianism and neoliberalism (Hemerijck, 2017; Morel, Palier, & Palme, 2012). The European Pillar of Social Rights is recognition of a missing component in European integration (European Commission, 2017d).

There are also good reasons to continuously improve and recalibrate the existing policy instruments so as better to achieve higher levels of living for the worse off and enhance security and a better functioning of capitalism in the unstable environment of global competition. Unrestrained globalized markets will only aggravate risks and inequalities if nations allow their social protection systems to be eroded.

APPENDIX

# Financial Hardship Indicator

## Concept and Method

*Kolbeinn Stefánsson*

This book uses most conventional measures of welfare, living standards, hardship, and poverty. But a special indicator of financial hardship has an important role in assessing changes of hardship through the crisis years and in relating these to various political economy background factors. Since the indicator is not a standard measure we explain it in this Appendix and compare it to a number of other similar indicators.

The financial hardship indicator is a composite measure derived through latent class analysis from various grades of low income, material deprivation, and difficulties making ends meet. The method entails dividing individuals into two classes, those suffering financial hardship and those not suffering financial hardship, on the basis of correlations between these variables.

### A.1 On Latent Class Analysis

First we must acknowledge that this indicator does not stem from us but rather from the original contribution of Pasi Moisio (2004), who proposed latent class analysis as a way to provide a discrete classification of people as either poor or non-poor on the basis of poverty measures that reflected different aspects of a multidimensional understanding of poverty (more on this in section A.2). Others have also built on Moisio's approach, most notably Nolan and Whelan (2011) in their book *Poverty and Deprivation in Europe* (see also Dewilde, 2004; and Whelan & Maître, 2005).

Latent class analysis falls within what Lazarsfeld (Lazarsfeld & Henry, 1968) termed latent structure analysis (LSA). A range of other methods such as latent factor, latent trait, and latent profile analysis are examples of LSA (McCutcheon, 1987). What LSA methods share is that they exploit the relationship among observed variables to shed light on some underlying unmeasured construct. What latent class analysis does specifically is to use the relationship among discrete categorical variables to define the underlying distribution of a sample into discrete population groups, in our case those suffering financial hardship and those that are not.

Moisio, on whose work we are building, was working with a somewhat different concept, that is, the poor and the non-poor. For Moisio, latent class analysis offered a solution to a problem posed by the inherent multidimensionality of poverty. If poverty is truly multidimensional, as most researchers would agree, then it must be operationalized through a set of measurements that tap different dimensions. How can we then aggregate these different measurements to estimate the extent of poverty?

One way to grasp this problem is to contrast these measurements to parallel measures of a unidimensional construct. In the latter case we may still be unable to measure the construct directly and all our indirect measures are likely to be imperfect, but insofar as they all measure the same thing they can be aggregated in a fairly straightforward manner. Measures of multidimensional constructs, however, will not be measuring the same thing insofar as they tap different dimensions of the underlying construct, but different things that share a relationship to that construct.

There are, of course, numerous ways to jointly use the different measures of a multidimensional construct. One is to rely on the overlap between different indicators and mark as consistently poor those who are both deprived and below a specific income threshold (Lyte et al., 2001). Another is to tally different indicators together, much like Eurostat does with its composite indicator of being 'At Risk of Poverty or Social Exclusion' (Eurostat, n.d.). This is not the place to do an extensive review of the advantages and limitations of different approaches. Suffice to say that both approaches have produced useful findings. One way to look at the latent class approach is that it is a more sophisticated method to derive a composite indicator than the aforementioned approaches as it uses the relationship among the indicators to derive the composite indicator and, more importantly, provides a way to gauge whether the observed measures do in fact have such a relationship that allows them to jointly sort sample members into subgroups.

To put it simply: a set of variables tapping into different dimensions of a multidimensional construct will be correlated among themselves. These correlations are symmetric rather than asymmetric as none have causal priority as the relationship among them rises from their shared relationship with the underlying construct rather than from causal relationships among themselves. Latent class analysis uses these correlations to sort the sample into latent groups. The sorting mechanism is that of local independence, that is, once we have sorted the sample into the latent classes there will be no correlation among the observed variables within any given class. The reasoning is fairly straightforward, once one accounts for the unobserved distribution of classes that gives rise to the relationship among the observed variables, the relationship among those variables should break down.

## A.2 Poverty, Economic Vulnerability, and Financial Hardship

Moisio formulated his approach in terms of poverty. This makes good sense, especially when basing/grounding it in the multidimensionality of the poverty concept. The concept of poverty nevertheless poses a problem in terms of the supposed symmetry of statistical relationships among the observed variables. This problem becomes apparent when we examine Peter Townsend's classical formulation of relative poverty:

> Individuals, families and groups in the population can be said to be in poverty when they lack the resources to obtain the type of diet, participate in the activities and have the living conditions and amenities which are customary, or at least widely encouraged, or approved, in the societies to which they belong. (Townsend, 1979, p. 31)

This definition seems to entail a causal relationship, that is, deprivation in terms of diet, participation, and living condition resulting from a lack of resources. It may well be that having a causal relationship built into the definition of poverty accounts for at least some of the difficulty in reaching a consensus on the measurement of poverty, seeing that causality cannot be measured directly and is in fact not a statistical concept (Goldthorpe, 2001). The issue here, however, is rather that this definition, which Moisio argues is central to poverty research, seems to grant causal priority to resources and, as Moisio points out, resources tend to be operationalized in terms of incomes. This implies that the relationship between low incomes and other measures in his model are not entirely the product of their shared relationship to the latent structure, but that the other variables in his model are in fact determined to some extent by incomes.

While this is undoubtedly the case this is not necessarily a problem if we think of our latent structures in terms other than poverty. Doing so also makes sense since even if incomes are used to estimate the latent classes there are nevertheless some with fairly high incomes who will be allocated to the 'poor' class. And given Townsend's definition of poverty we would be loath to regard anyone in, say, the top decile as being poor even if our model assigned them to the 'poor' class, though we could easily agree that they are somehow afflicted.

It is, of course, interesting in this context that Lyte and colleagues (2001) and Nolan and Whelan (2011) refrain from using the concept of poverty, conceptualizing their latent classes in terms of economic vulnerability instead. While we think that this is better than doing so in terms of poverty we have some issues with the concept of economic vulnerability as well. Our primary concern is that vulnerability implies risk of hardship rather than hardship per se. Risks are by definition latent. We can think of them as an underlying distribution of probabilities of something happening. In this case, the underlying probability of suffering financial hardship. Such underlying probabilities are difficult to measure. One issue is that vulnerabilities do not necessarily manifest. In short, one may be highly vulnerable economically for extended periods of time without ever suffering financial hardship, if only by sheer luck. In any case, given our operationalization it seems to us that our latent classes are determined by manifest conditions rather than underlying probabilities. Thus it seems more appropriate to us to think of our latent classes in terms of financial hardship.

The concept of financial hardship is not burdened by the causal priority of incomes in the same way as the concept of poverty. Low incomes are certainly a contributing factor to financial hardship but so are many other things. One's fixed expenditures may drive one into financial hardship if one's income drops, even if the resulting income is still relatively high. One may have a fairly high income yet have such extensive needs that it does not suffice (though this may be rather rare). Past choices may impose burdens as do past spells of low income, even if one's income is relatively good in the cross-section. And of course, some people are simply bad at managing their money.

Financial hardship as here conceived and measured is easily interpreted in the context of crisis, since crises reduce levels of living and increase hardship—and more so for some than others.

McCutcheon lists a number of plausible interpretations of latent classes. The reason most congruent to our approach is 'Functional interdependence of elements', which 'involves the interrelatedness of variables that are likely to be jointly present (or absent) due to their significance for the system under study' (McCutcheon, 1987, p. 12). In some ways the variables in our model tap different aspects of financial hardship, with incomes reflecting resources, material deprivation capturing to some extent the deterioration of resources over time that may not recover quickly with rising incomes, and ability to make ends meet capturing the subjective experience of hardship (see Berthoud & Bryan, 2011). Such things interact in ways that produce financial hardship for some.

## A.3 Fitting the Model

Our latent class model of financial hardship is based on three indicators from the European Union Statistics on Income and Living Conditions (EU-SILC) dataset, that is, equivalized disposable incomes, ability to make ends meet, and material deprivation, all measured at the household level. The income variable was coded into four categories and the other two variables coded into dichotomous variables (see Table A.1 for details). We used the entire dataset including all countries and all years, for a total of Z respondents in X country-year cross-sectional samples. Having a single model for all

**Table A.1.** Coding of financial hardship variables for the latent class model

| | | | |
|---|---|---|---|
| 1. | Incomes | | |
| | Equivalized disposable incomes | > = 70% | = 1 |
| | (modified OECD* equivalence scale) | > = 60%, <70% | = 2 |
| | relative to median. | > = 50%, <60% | = 3 |
| | | <50% | = 4 |
| 2. | Ability to make ends meet | | |
| | Is the household able to make ends meet? | 3–6 | = 1 |
| | 1) With great difficulty; 2) with difficulty; 3) with some difficulty; 4) fairly easily 5) easily; 6) very easily | 1–2 | = 2 |
| 3. | Material deprivation | | |
| | Eurostat's material deprivation scale | 0–2 items | = 1 |
| | Cannot afford to: | >2 items | = 2 |
| | 1) pay rent, mortgage, or utility bills | | |
| | 2) keep home adequately warm | | |
| | 3) meet unexpected expenses | | |
| | 4) eat meat or proteins regularly | | |
| | 5) go on holiday | | |
| | 6) have a television set | | |
| | 7) have a washing machine | | |
| | 8) have a car | | |
| | 9) have a telephone | | |

*Note*: Model fit is assessed using AIC and BIC: AIC = $-2\ln(L) + 2p$, where ln(L) is the log likelihood and p is the number of estimated model parameters, and BIC = $-2\ln(L) + p*\ln(N)$, where N is the total number of observations. The lower both the AIC and BIC are, the better the model fits the data.
* = Organisation for Economic Co-operation and Development.

**Table A.2.** Model fit

| | AIC | BIC | Estimated parameters | Residual DF |
|---|---|---|---|---|
| Model 1 | 8998456 | 8998596 | 11 | 4 |
| Model 2 | 12662788 | 12662980 | 15 | 8 |
| Model 3 | 14570097 | 14570340 | 19 | 28 |

observations facilitates interpretation and comparisons over time and space; however, it should be kept in mind that the latent structures of financial hardship likely differ from one country to the next and are unlikely to be invariant over time. For the analysis itself we used the poLCA package for R (Linzer & Lewis, 2011).

Table A.2 shows model 1 and we compare it to other two models we examined as potential alternatives. For model 2 we coded income as a binary variable, that is, whether respondents were above or below 60 per cent of the median equivalized disposable income, but used the full range of response options for ability to make ends meet. Model 3 uses the same categorization of incomes as model 1 but also uses the full range of response options for ability to make ends meet. Both alternative models fit the data considerably worse as evinced by their higher Akaike information criterion (AIC) and Bayesian information criterion (BIC) statistics. We considered whether we would be better off with any of the indicators left out of the model. Dropping each of them produced models with negative residual degrees of freedom, which is indicative of model misspecification. Adding more latent classes to the model had the same effect. We also considered the simplest possible model, namely coding deprivation, ability to make ends meet, and incomes as binary variables, keeping the same thresholds for deprivation and making ends meet as given in Table A.1, while setting the threshold for incomes at 60 per cent of the median income. In this model the number of estimated parameters used up all the degrees of freedom. Thus we have a two-class model, with the estimated class population share of our hardship class being 23.9 per cent whereas the predicted class membership is 19.8 per cent. As a general rule of thumb, the closer these two estimates the better.

Our model as described in Table A.1 is quite similar to that used by Nolan and Whelan (2011). It contains objective and subjective indicators as well as absolute and relative ones. From our perspective this is as it should be. A multidimensional concept of financial hardship entails all these elements. Hardship and experiences thus can be thought to result in a fairly straightforward manner from the consumption standards of one's society and the pressures and expectations they generate, but, much like as for poverty, there is an absolute component that captures the effect of generally rising living conditions even if one's position within one's 'local' distribution does not change.

In Table A.3 we look at the conditional item response probabilities, that is, the distribution of our latent classes over the variables from which it was derived. About 85.2 per cent of those not in hardship have incomes above 70 per cent of median income, 97.8 per cent do not suffer material deprivation, and 89.7 per cent have little or no difficulty making ends meet. The pattern is less clear for the hardship class. It is most clear for ability to make ends meet, as 17.5 per cent of those in hardship have little or no difficulty and 82.5 per cent do. Whereas very few people who were materially deprived

**Table A.3.** Conditional item response probabilities

| | | | | |
|---|---|---|---|---|
| **Income** | <50% | > = 50% to <60% | > = 60% to <70% | > = 70% |
| Class 1: Hardship | 25.7 | 14.6 | 14.5 | 45.1 |
| Class 2: No hardship | 4.7 | 4.2 | 6 | 85.2 |
| **Material deprivation** | Not deprived | Deprived | | |
| Class 1: Hardship | 34.2 | 65.8 | | |
| Class 2: No hardship | 97.8 | 2.2 | | |
| **Ability to make ends meet** | Little or no difficulty | Difficulty | | |
| Class 1: Hardship | 17.5 | 82.5 | | |
| Class 2: No hardship | 89.7 | 10.4 | | |

found themselves in the no hardship class, some 34.2 per cent of those in financial hardship did not suffer material deprivation, though an overwhelming majority of 65.8 per cent did.

The picture is least clear when it comes to incomes. While the vast majority of those not in hardship had incomes above 70 per cent of median income, it is also the case that the largest portion among those in hardship had incomes above that threshold, though this was not quite the majority. This is to some extent simply a matter of the different sizes of our classes and different sizes of the income groups, with the above 70 per cent group accounting for the vast majority of the population. A more detailed differentiation of those above 70 per cent of the median would reveal this, as is evident from the substantive chapters in this book where the relationship between incomes and hardship are examined in more detail. Thus, those at lower levels of income are still at a higher risk of hardship. Yet it is also worthwhile to keep in mind that incomes in the cross-section are not particularly good predictors of outcomes we would associate with poverty and by extension with financial hardship, due to income mobility and temporary setbacks or windfalls (we can think about these in terms of regression to the mean) (for a discussion of the concepts and measurements of income mobility, see Jäntti & Jenkins, 2015) as well as accumulation or deterioration of resources that are not reversed immediately with changing incomes (Berthoud & Bryan, 2011).

Overall, this suggests that having either low incomes, difficulties making ends meet, or being deprived are strongly indicative of financial hardship. Being free from any of these, however, is not a guarantee of being free of hardship due to the effects of the other two.

## A.4 Comparison of Indicators of Hardship

Lastly, we compare the financial hardship indicator to a few common indicators of hardship, to facilitate interpretation and assessment of its reliability (See Table A.4).

**Table A.4.** Six indicators of hardship compared

| | Financial hardship | Material deprivation | Making ends meet w. great difficulty | Making ends meet w. difficulty | At risk of poverty (60%) | At risk of poverty or social exclusion |
|---|---|---|---|---|---|---|
| Austria | 10 | 8.2 | 5.3 | 13.4 | 13.9 | 18.3 |
| Belgium | 15.9 | 11.6 | 8.6 | 20.5 | 14.9 | 21.1 |
| Bulgaria | 48.3 | 49.1 | 30.6 | 64 | 22 | 41.3 |
| Switzerland* | 7.8 | 4.6 | 2.8 | 11.2 | 15.6 | 18.2 |
| Cyprus | 39.7 | 34.7 | 32 | 58.8 | 16.2 | 28.9 |
| Czech Republic | 15.4 | 13.4 | 7.8 | 26.6 | 9.7 | 14 |
| Germany* | 10.8 | 10.7 | 2.6 | 7.6 | 16.7 | 20 |
| Denmark | 8.7 | 8 | 3.5 | 10.4 | 12.2 | 17.7 |
| Estonia | 13.7 | 12.8 | 4.9 | 16.2 | 21.6 | 24.2 |
| Greece | 45.9 | 40.7 | 38.2 | 77.7 | 21.4 | 35.7 |
| Spain | 23.6 | 16.5 | 14.8 | 35.2 | 22.1 | 28.6 |
| Finland | 7.3 | 7.7 | 2.5 | 7 | 12.4 | 16.8 |
| France | 14.4 | 11.1 | 4.6 | 19.9 | 13.6 | 17.7 |
| Hungary | 34.2 | 34.8 | 19.1 | 46.6 | 14.9 | 28.2 |
| Ireland | 22.1 | 19.4 | 14.9 | 32 | 16.3 | 26 |
| Iceland | 7.7 | 5 | 8.6 | 19.8 | 9.2 | 12.5 |
| Italy | 27.1 | 22.6 | 15.4 | 37.9 | 19.9 | 28.7 |
| Lithuania | 25.9 | 27.3 | 6.8 | 28.9 | 22.2 | 29.3 |
| Luxembourg | 9.6 | 4.8 | 4.2 | 12.4 | 15.3 | 18.5 |
| Latvia | 32.1 | 29.7 | 15.4 | 42.7 | 22.5 | 30.9 |
| Malta | 16.6 | 15.2 | 7.2 | 21.5 | 16.3 | 22.4 |
| Netherlands | 9.7 | 8.1 | 3.3 | 12.9 | 11.6 | 16.4 |
| Norway | 5.1 | 4.1 | 2.1 | 5.1 | 11.9 | 15 |
| Poland | 20.1 | 16.8 | 10.2 | 29.4 | 17.6 | 23.4 |
| Portugal | 26.6 | 21.6 | 20.6 | 40.4 | 19.5 | 26.6 |
| Romania | 38.2 | 39.5 | 20.2 | 45.6 | 25.4 | 37.4 |
| Sweden | 4.4 | 4 | 3.2 | 7.1 | 16.3 | 18.6 |
| Slovenia | 18.2 | 14.7 | 9.1 | 28.7 | 14.3 | 19.2 |
| Slovakia | 19.8 | 20.3 | 11.7 | 32.7 | 12.3 | 18.4 |
| UK | 14.5 | 14.1 | 6.4 | 16.4 | 16.6 | 23.5 |

*Note*: * Financial hardship for 2015.

# References

Adam, S., Browne, J., & Elming, W., 2015. The Effect of the UK Coalition Government's Tax and Benefit Changes on Household Incomes and Work Incentives. *Fiscal Studies*, 36(3), pp. 375–402.

Adema, W., Fron, P., & Ladaique, M., 2014. How Much do OECD Countries Spend on Social Protection and How Redistributive are their Tax/Benefit Systems? *International Social Security Review*, 67(1), pp. 1–25.

Agnello, L. & Sousa, R., 2014. How does Fiscal Consolidation Impact on Economic Inequality? *Review of Income and Wealth*, 60(4), pp. 702–26.

Alesina, A. & Ardagna, S., 1998. Tales of Fiscal Adjustment. *Economic Policy*, 13(27), pp. 487–545.

Alesina, A. & Ardagna, S., 2010. Large Changes in Fiscal Policy: Taxes versus Spending. *Tax Policy and the Economy*, 24(1), pp. 35–68.

Alesina, A. & Ardagna, S., 2013. The Design of Fiscal Adjustment. *Tax Policy and the Economy*, 27(1), pp. 35–68.

Alesina, A. & Giavazzi, F., 2015. The Effects of Austerity: Recent Research. NBER Reporter 2015, No. 3.

Alesina, A. & Perotti, R., 1997. Fiscal Adjustments in OECD Countries: Composition and Macroeconomic Effects. *International Monetary Fund Staff Papers*, 44(2), pp. 210–48.

Alesina, A., Barbiero, O., Favero, C., Giavazzi, F., & Paradisi, M., 2015. Austerity in 2009–13. *Economic Policy*, 25(4), pp. 383–437.

Aliber, R. & Kindleberger, C., 2011. *Manias, Panics, and Crashes: A History of Financial Crises*. 6th edition. London: Palgrave Macmillan.

Aliber, R. & Zoega, G., 2011. *Preludes to the Icelandic Financial Crisis*. London: Palgrave Macmillan.

Alsos, K. & Eldring, L., 2014. Lovfestet minstelønn i Norge? *Søkelys på arbeidslivet*, 31(3), pp. 249–66.

Andersen, J., Hede, A., & Goul Andersen, J., 2015. *Tryghedsmåling 2015. Den lange vej ud af krisen*. Copenhagen: TrygFonden.

Andersen, J., Hede, A., & Goul Andersen, J., 2017. *Tryghedsmåling 2017. Tilliden til samfundets bærebjælker*. Copenhagen: TrygFonden.

Anderson, K., 2001. The Politics of Retrenchment in a Social Democratic Welfare State Reform of Swedish Pensions and Unemployment Insurance. *Comparative Political Studies*, 34(9), pp. 1063–91.

Anttonen, A. & Karsio, O., 2016. Eldercare Service Redesign in Finland: Deinstitutionalization of Long-Term Care. *Journal of Social Service Research*, 42(2), pp. 151–66.

Arkolakis, C., Doxiadis, A., & Gelanianos, M., 2017. The Challenge of Trade Adjustment in Greece. In: Costas Meghir, Christopher A. Pissarides, Dimitri Vayanos, and Nikolaos Vettas, *Beyond Austerity: Reforming the Greek Economy*. Cambridge, MA: MIT Press, pp. 103–36.

Armingeon, K., 2012. The Politics of Fiscal Response to the Crisis of 2008–2009. *Governance*, 25(4), pp. 543–65.

Auerbach, A., Gale, W., & Harris, B., 2010. Activist Fiscal Policy. *Journal of Economic Perspectives*, 24(4), pp. 141–63.

Austin, A., 2015. *Hard Times and Capabilities: The Effects of Economic Crisis on Well-Being in the UK*. Manchester: University of Manchester Press.

Baccaro, L. & Howell, C., 2011. A Common Neoliberal Trajectory: The Transformation of Industrial Relations in Advanced Capitalism. *Politics & Society*, 39(4), pp. 521–63.

Baldwin, P., 1990. *The Politics of Social Solidarity: Class Bases of the European Welfare State 1875–1975*. New York: Cambridge University Press.

Baldwin, R. & Gros, D., 2015. *What Caused the Eurozone Crisis?* Brussels: Centre for European Policy Studies.

Baldwin, R., Beck, T., Bénassy-Quéré, A., Blanchard, O., Corsetti, G., de Grauwe, P., den Haan, W., et al., 2015. Rebooting the Eurozone: Step 1—Agreeing a Crisis Narrative. Available at: https://cepr.org/sites/default/files/policy_insights/PolicyInsight85.pdf (accessed 25 May 2018).

Ball, L., Furceri, D., Leigh, D., & Loungani, P., 2013. The Distributional Effects of Fiscal Consolidation. IMF Working Paper No. WP/13/151.

Bank of Greece, 2015. *The Governor's Report for the Year 2014*. Athens: Bank of Greece.

Barr, N., 2001. *The Welfare State as Piggy Bank: Information, Risk, Uncertainty, and the Role of the State*. Oxford: Oxford University Press.

Bartels, L. & Bermeo, N., 2014. *Mass Politics in Tough Times: Opinions, Votes and Protest in the Great Recession*. Oxford: Oxford University Press.

Baunsgaard, Thomas, and Steven A. Symansky. 2009. *Automatic Fiscal Stabilizers*. International Monetary Fund. IMF Staff Position Note 2009/23.

Beatty, C. & Fothergill, S., 2016. *The Uneven Impact of Welfare Reform: The Financial Losses to Places and People*. Sheffield: Sheffield Hallam University Centre for Regional Economic and Social Research.

Béland, D., Blomqvist, P., Goul Andersen, J., Palme, J., & Waddan, A., 2014. The Universal Decline of Universality? Social Policy Change in Canada, Denmark, Sweden, and the United Kingdom. *Social Policy and Administration*, 48(7), pp. 739–56.

Bell, T., 2016. The Referendum, Living Standards and Inequality. Available at: http://www.resolutionfoundation.org/media/blog/the-referendum-living-standards-and-inequality (accessed 30 June 2016).

Bengtsson, N., Edin, P.-A., & Holmlund, B., 2014. Löner, sysselsättning och inkomster—ökar klyftorna i Sverige? Report to the Fiscal Council No. 2014/1. Available at: http://www.finanspolitiskaradet.se/download/18.7841e2a2145d5672688a2737/1410181438711/Underlagsrapport+2014-1+Bengtsson%2C+Edin+%26+Holmlund.pdf (accessed 26 July 2018).

Bennett, F., 2013. Researching within Household Distribution: Overview, Developments, Debates and Methodological Challenges. *Journal of Marriage and Family*, 75(3), pp. 582–97.

Bennett, F., 2015. The Impact of Austerity on Women. In: L. Foster, A. Brunton, C. Deeming, & T. Haux, eds. *In Defence of Welfare II*. Bristol: Policy Press/Social Policy Association, pp. 59–61.

Berg, J. & Bech, M., 2009. *Finansernes fald. Hvordan den perfekte storm væltede de finansielle markeder*. Copenhagen: Gyldendal.

Bergmann, E., 2014. *Iceland and the International Financial Crisis: Boom, Bust and Recovery*. London: Palgrave Macmillan.

Bermeo, N. & Pontusson, J., 2012. *Coping with Crisis: Government Reactions to the Great Recession*. New York: Russell Sage Foundation.

Bernburg, J., 2016. *Economic Crisis and Mass Protest: The Pots and Pans Revolution in Iceland*. London: Routledge.

Berthoud, R. & Bryan, M., 2011. Income, Deprivation and Poverty: A Longitudinal Analysis. *Journal of Social Policy*, 40(1), pp. 135–56.

Bieler, A., 2012. Small Nordic Countries and Globalization: Analysing Norwegian Exceptionalism. *Competition & Change*, 16(3), pp. 224–42.

Birch Sørensen, P., 2010. Nedturen i dansk økonomi: Hvor meget var selvforskyldt? *Samfundsøkonomen*, 28(1), pp. 29–34.

Birnbaum, S., Ferrarini, T., Nelson, K., & Palme, J., 2017. *The Generational Welfare Contract: Justice, Institutions and Outcomes*. Cheltenham: Edward Elgar.

Björklund, A. & Jäntti, M., 2011. *Inkomstfördelningen i Sverige. SNS Välfärdsrapport 2011*. Stockholm: SNS förlag.

Blanchard, O., Dell'Ariccia, G., & Mauro, P., 2010. Rethinking Macroeconomic Policy. *Journal of Money, Credit and Banking*, 42(1), pp. 199–215.

Blanchard, O., Jaumotte, F., & Loungani, P., 2014. Labour Market Policies and IMF Advice in Advanced Economies during the Great Recession. *IZA Journal of Labour Policy*, 3(2), pp. 1–23.

Blomgren, J., Hiilamo, H., Kangas, O., & Niemelä, M., 2014. Finland: Growing Inequality with Contested Consequences. In: B. Nolan, W. Salverda, D. Checchi, I. Marx, A. McKnight, I. G. Tóth, & H. G. van de Werfhorst eds., *Changing Inequalities and Societal Impacts in Rich Countries*. Oxford: Oxford University Press, pp. 223–47.

Blomqvist, P. & Palme, J., 2016. *Universalism in Swedish Welfare Policy 1990–2014*. Uppsala: Department of Government, Uppsala University.

Blyth, M., 2002. *The Great Transformation: Economic Ideas and Institutional Change in the Twentieth Century*. New York: Cambridge University Press.

Blyth, M., 2013. *Austerity: The History of a Dangerous Idea*. Oxford: Oxford University Press.

Bochel, H. & Powell, M., 2016. *The Coalition Government and Social Policy: Restructuring the Welfare State*. Bristol: Policy Press.

Bonoli, G., 2001. Political Institutions, Veto Points, and the Process of Welfare State Adaptation. In: P. Pierson, ed., *The New Politics of the Welfare State*. Oxford: Oxford University Press, pp. 238–64.

Bozio, A., Emmerson, C., Peichl, A., & Tetlow, G., 2015. European Public Finances and the Great Recession: France, Germany, Ireland, Italy, Spain and the UK Compared. *Fiscal Studies*, 36(4), pp. 405–30.

Bradshaw, J., Ditch, J., Homles, H., & Whiteford, P., 1993. *Support for Children: A Comparison of Arrangements in Fifteen Countries*. London: HMSO.

Brady, D., 2009. *Rich Democracies, Poor People: How Politics Explain Poverty*. Oxford: Oxford University Press.

Bratsberg, B., Dølvik, J., Nergaard, K., & Raaum, O., 2015. Arbeidsinnvandring, rekruttering og fleksibilitet. In: H. Dale-Olsen, ed., *Norsk arbeidsliv i turbulente tider*. Oslo: Gyldendal Akademisk, pp. 56–82.

Brommels, M., Aronkytö, T., Kananoja, A., Lillrank, P., & Reijula, K., 2016. Valinnanvapaus ja monikanavarahoituksen yksinkertaistaminen [Freedom of Choice and the Simplification of Multi-Channel Funding]. Available at: http://urn.fi/URN:ISBN:978-952-00-3821-2 (accessed 25 October 2017).

Brønnum-Hansen, H. & Baadsgaard, M., 2008. Increase in Social Inequality in Health Expectancy in Denmark. *Scandinavian Journal of Public Health*, 36(1), pp. 44–51.

Brønnum-Hansen, H. & Baadsgaard, M., 2012. Widening Social Inequality in Life Expectancy in Denmark. *BMC Public Health*, 2012(12), p. 994.

Browne, J., 2011. *The Impact of Tax and Benefit Reforms by Sex: Some Simple Analysis*. London: Institute for Fiscal Studies.

Browne, J. & Elming, W., 2015. *The Effect of the Coalition's Tax and Benefit Changes on Household Incomes and Work Incentives*. London: Institute for Fiscal Studies.

Browne, J. & Hood, C., 2016. *Living Standards, Poverty and Inequality in the UK: 2015–16 to 2020–21*. London: Institute for Fiscal Studies.

Callan, T., Regan, M., Savage, M., & Walsh, J., 2017. *Income Distribution in Ireland through Recession, Towards Recovery*. Dublin: Economic and Social Research Institute.

Callan, T., Colgan, B., Logue, C., Savage, M., & Walsh, J. R., 2015. Distributional Impact of Tax, Welfare and Public Service Pay Policies: Budget 2016 and Budgets 2009–2016. *Quarterly Economic Commentary*. Available at: https://www.esri.ie/pubs/QEC2015WIN_SA_Callan.pdf (accessed 26 July 2018).

Cambridge Centre for Housing and Planning Research and Ipsos MORI, 2015. Evaluation of Removal of the Spare Room Subsidy: Final Report. Available at: https://www.cchpr.landecon.cam.ac.uk/Projects/Start-Year/2013/Spare-Room-Subsidy-Household-Benefit-Cap/Final-Report/Final-Report (accessed 26 July 2018).

Cameron, D., 2012. European Fiscal Responsibility to the Great Recession. In: N. Bermeo & J. Pontusson, eds., *Coping with Crisis: Government Reactions to the Great Recession*. New York: Russell Sage Foundation, pp. 91–129.

Caminada, K. & Goudswaard, K., 2010. How Well is Social Expenditure Targeted to the Poor? In: P. Saunders & R. Sainsbury, eds., *Social Security, Poverty and Social Exclusion in Rich and Poorer Countries*. Cambridge: Intersentia, pp. 97–112.

Campbell, J. & Pedersen, O., 2007. The Varieties of Capitalism and Hybrid Success: Denmark in the Global Economy. *Comparative Political Studies*, 40(3), pp. 307–32.

Cancela Outeda, C. & González Cacheda, G., 2017. The Spanish Productive Model Facing the Challenge of its Europeanization. In: J. Ramos and E. del Camp, eds., *Austerity and the Implementation of the EU-2020 Strategy in Spain*. Brussels: Peter Lang, pp. 89–212.

Cantillon, B., Chzhen, Y., Handa, S., & Nolan, B., 2017. *Children of Austerity. Impact of the Great Recession on Child Poverty in Rich Countries*. Oxford: Oxford University Press.

Capoccia, G. & Kelemen, D., 2007. The Study of Critical Junctures: Theory, Narrative, and Counterfactuals in Historical Institutionalism. *World Politics*, 59(3), pp. 341–69.

Castles, F., ed., 1989. *The Comparative History of Public Policy*. Oxford: Oxford University Press.

Castles, F., ed., 1993. *Families of Nations: Patterns of Public Policy in Western Democracies*. Dartmouth: Dartmouth Publication Co.

Castles, F., 2010. Black Swans and Elephants on the Move: The Impact of Emergencies on the Welfare State. *Journal of European Social Policy*, 20(2), pp. 91–101.

Castles, F. & Obinger, H., 2008. Worlds, Families, Regimes: Country Clusters in Europe and OECD Area Public Policy. *West European Politics*, 31(1–2), pp. 321–44.

Castles, F., Leibfried, S., Lewis, J., Obinger, H., & Pierson, C., 2010. *The Oxford Handbook of the Welfare State*. Oxford: Oxford University Press.

Central Bank of Ireland, 2016. *Residential Mortgage Arrears and Repossession Statistics*. Dublin: Central Bank of Ireland.

Central Statistics Office, 2015. *Quarterly National Household Survey, Q2 2015*. Cork: Central Statistics Office.

Central Statistics Office, 2017. *Survey on Income and Living Conditions 2016 Results*. Cork: Central Statistics Office.

Christensen, J., 2010. *How Low Can You Go? Exploring the Evolution of Personal Income Tax Policy and the Welfare State in Ireland*. Odense: NordWel and Reassess Summer School.

Christiansen, N., Petersen, K., Edling, N., & Haave, P. eds., 2006. *The Nordic Model of Welfare: A Historical Reappraisal*. Copenhagen: Museum Tusculanum Press.

Christodoulakis, N., 2015. *Greek Endgame: From Austerity to Growth or Grexit*. London: Rowman & Littlefield.

Chung, H. & Thewissen, S., 2011. Falling Back on Old Habits? A Comparison of Social and Unemployment Crisis Reactive Policy Strategies in Germany, the UK and Sweden. *Social Policy and Administration*, 45(4), pp. 354–70.

Clayton, R. & Pontusson, J., 1998. Welfare-State Retrenchment Revisited: Entitlement Cuts, Public Sector Restructuring, and Inegalitarian Trends in Advanced Capitalist Societies. *World Politics*, 51(1), pp. 67–98.

Conley, H., 2012. Economic Crisis, Austerity and Gender Equality: The UK Case. *European Gender Equality Law Review*, 2012(2), pp. 14–19.

Copelovitch, M., Frieden, J., & Walter, S., 2016. The Political Economy of the Euro Crisis. *Comparative Political Studies*, 49(7), pp. 811–40.

Crawford, R. & Johnson, P., 2015. The UK Coalition Government's Record, and Challenges for the Future. *Fiscal Studies*, 36(3), pp. 275–82.

Cronert, A. & Palme, J., 2017. Approaches to Social Investment and their Implications for Poverty in Sweden and the European Union. CROP/UiB Global Working Paper No. 4.

Crouch, C., 2009. Privatized Keynesianism: An Unacknowledged Policy Regime. *BJPIR*, 11, pp. 382–99.

Curtice, J., Phillips, M., & Clery, L. eds., 2016. *British Social Attitudes 33*. London: NatCen.

Cutler, D. & Johnson, R., 2004. The Birth and Growth of the Social Insurance State: Explaining Old Age and Medical Insurance across Countries. *Public Choice*, 120(1–2), pp. 87–121.

Daly, M., 2005. Recasting the Story of Ireland's Miracle: Policy, Politics or Profit. In: U. Becker & H. Schwartz, eds., *Employment Miracles: A Critical Comparison of the Dutch, Scandinavian, Swiss, Australian and Irish Cases versus Germany and the US*. Amsterdam: Amsterdam University Press, pp. 133–55.

Dam, N., Hvolbøl, T. S., Pedersen, E. H., Sørensen, P. B., Thamsborg, S. H., & Afdeling, O., 2011. Boligboblen der bristede: Kan boligpriserne forklares? Og kan deres udsving dæmpes. Danmarks Nationalbank Kvartalsoversigt. Available at: http://web.econ.ku.dk/pbs/Dokumentfiler/Publications%20(Danish)/Boligboblen%20der%20bristede%20Del%201%202011.pdf (accessed 26 July 2018).

Dao, M. & Loungani, P., 2010. The Human Cost of Recessions: Assessing It, Reducing It. IMF Staff Position Note No. SPN/10/17.

De Agostini, P., Hills, J., & Sutherland, H., 2014. Were We Really All in it Together? The Distributional Effects of the UK Coalition Government's Tax-Benefit Changes. Social & Policy Administration Working Paper No. 10.

De Guindos, L., 2016. *España amenazada*. Madrid: Península.

De Henau, J. & Reed, H., 2016a. 10 Years of Austerity: The Impact on Low-Income Households and Women. *Journal of Child Poverty Action Group*, 154, pp. 6–9.

De Henau, J. & Reed, H., 2016b. *A Cumulative Gender Impact Assessment of Ten Years of Austerity Policies*. London: Women's Budget Group.

De la Porte, C. & Heins, E., 2015. A New Era of European Integration? Governance of Labour Market and Social Policy since the Sovereign Debt Crisis. *Comparative European Politics*, 13(1), pp. 8–28.

De Økonomiske Råd, 2009. *Økonomi. Efteråret 2009*. Copenhagen: De Økonomiske Råd.

Del Pino, E., 2013. The Spanish Welfare State from Zapatero to Rajoy: Recalibration to Retrenchment. In: B. Field & A. Botti, eds., *Politics and Society in Contemporary Spain*. New York: Palgrave Macmillan, pp. 197–216.

Dellepiane-Avellaneda, S. & Hardiman, N., 2015. *The Politics of Fiscal Efforts in Ireland and Spain: Market Credibility vs. Political Legitimacy*. In: G. Karyotis & R. Gerodimos, eds., *The Politics of Extreme Austerity: Greece in the Eurozone Crisis*. Basingstoke: Palgrave Macmillan, pp. 198–221.

Department for Work and Pensions, 2016. Households below Average Income 1994/95 to 2014/15. Available at: https://www.gov.uk/government/statistics/households-below-average-income-199495-to-201415 (accessed 28 June 2016).

Department of Social Protection, 2011. *Pathways to Work*. Dublin: Department of Social Protection.

Department of Social Protection, 2017. *Social Inclusion Monitor 2015*. Dublin: Department of Social Protection.

Devries, P., Guajardo, J., Leigh, D., & Pescatori, A., 2011. A New Action-Based Dataset of Fiscal Consolidation. IMF Working Paper No. 11/128.

Dewilde, C., 2004. The Multidimensional Measurement of Poverty in Belgium and Britain: A Categorical Approach. *Social Indicators Research*, 68(3), pp. 331–69.

Dimakakos, A. & Skiadas, C., 2016. *Analysis of Employment and Earnings Data of Active Contributors to IKA-ETEAM in 2009–2014*. Athens: n.p.

Dölvik, J. & Martin, A. eds., 2015. *European Social Models from Crisis to Crisis: Employment and Inequality in the Era of Monetary Integration*. Oxford: Oxford University Press.

Dølvik, J., Andersen, J., & Vartiainen, J., 2017. Nordic Models in Turbulent Times: Consolidation and Flexible Adaptation. In: J. Dølvik & A. Martin, eds., *European Social Models from Crisis to Crisis: Employment and Inequality in the Era of Monetary Integration*. Oxford: Oxford University Press, pp. 246–87.

Dølvik, J., Eldring, L., & Visser, J., 2014. Setting Wage Floors in Open Markets: The Role of the Social Partners in Europe's Multilevel Governance. In: S. Evju, ed., *Regulating Transnational Labour in Europe: The Quandaries of Multilevel Governance*. Oslo: Department of Private Law, University of Oslo, pp. 131–87.

Dølvik, J., Bråten, M., Longva, F., & Steen, A., 1997. Norwegian Labour Market Institutions and Regulations. In: J. Dølvik & A. Steen, eds., *Making Solidarity Work?* Oslo: Scandinavian University Press, pp. 51–111.

Donovan, D. & Murphy, A., 2013. *The Fall of the Celtic Tiger*. Oxford: Oxford University Press.

Dukelow, F. & Considine, M., 2014. Between Retrenchment and Recalibration: The Impact of Austerity on the Irish Social Protection System. *Journal of Sociology and Social Welfare*, 40(2), pp. 55–72.

Eichengreen, B., 2008. *The European Economy since 1945: Coordinated Capitalism and Beyond*. Princeton, NJ: Princeton University Press.

Eichengreen, B., 2015. *Hall of Mirrors: The Great Depression, the Great Recession, and the Uses-and Misuses-of History*. Oxford: Oxford University Press.

Eika, T., 2008. Det svinger i norsk økonomi. *Samfunnsspeilet*, 22(5–6), pp. 98–111.

Eläkekysymysten asiantuntijatyöryhmän raportti, 2013. *Suomen eläkejärjestelmän sopeutuminen eliniän pitenemiseen* [Adaptation of the Finnish Pension System to the Increasing Life Expectation]. Helsinki: Centre for Pensions.

Elliott, L., 2015a. At Least Recession's Pain was Shared this Time. *The Guardian*, 19 October.

Elliott, L., 2015b. Fixing the Roof in the Sun, or Just Papering over the Cracks until the House Falls Down? *The Guardian*, 7 December.

Emmerson, C. & Tetlow, G., 2015. UK Public Finances: From Crisis to Recovery. *Fiscal Studies*, 36(4), pp. 555–77.

Epstein, G. & Wolfson, M. eds., 2013. *The Handbook of the Political Economy of Financial Crises*. Oxford: Oxford University Press.

Esping-Andersen, G., 1985. *Politics against Markets: The Social Democratic Road to Power*. Princeton, NJ: Princeton University Press.

Esping-Andersen, G., 1990. *The Three Worlds of Welfare Capitalism*. Princeton, NJ: Princeton University Press.

Esser, I., Ferrarini, T., Nelson, K., Palme, J., & Sjöberg, O., 2013. Unemployment Benefits in EU Member States. European Commission. Available at: http://www.ec.europa.eu/social/BlobServlet?docId=10852&langId=en (accessed 26 July 2018).

EUROMOD, 2016. Effects of Tax-Benefit Policy Changes across the Income Distributions of the EU-28 Countries: 2013–14 and 2014–15. EUROMOD Working Paper No. EM10/17.

European Commission, 2016a. The Corrective Arm. Available at: http://ec.europa.eu/economy_finance/economic_governance/sgp/corrective_arm/index_en.htm (accessed 12 October 2016).

European Commission, 2016b. The Irish GDP Revision. Available at: http://ec.europa.eu/eurostat/documents/24987/6390465/Irish_GDP_communication.pdf (accessed 18 October 2016).

European Commission, 2017a. Council Recommendation on the 2017 National Reform Programme of Ireland and Delivering a Council Opinion on the 2017 Stability Programme of Ireland. Available at: https://ec.europa.eu/info/sites/info/files/2017-european-semester-country-specific-recommendations-commission-recommendations_-_ireland_0.pdf (accessed 26 July 2018).

European Commission, 2017b. *Country Report Spain 2017*. Brussels: European Commission.

European Commission, 2017c. The ESM Stability Support Programme. Greece: First and Second Reviews. July 2017: Background Report. Institutional Paper No. 064.

European Commission, 2017d. European Pillar of Social Rights: Building a More Inclusive and Fairer European Union. Available at: https://ec.europa.eu/commission/priorities/deeper-and-fairer-economic-and-monetary-union/european-pillar-social-rights_en (accessed 13 August 2018).

Fagerberg, J., C. Å., Mjøset, L., & Skarstein, R., 1990. The Decline of Social-Democratic State Capitalism in Norway. *New Left Review*, 181, pp. 60–94.

Farnsworth, K. & Irving, Z., 2015. *Social Policy in Times of Austerity*. Bristol: Policy Press.

Featherstone, K., 2005. 'Soft' Co-ordination meets 'Hard' politics: The European Union and Pension reform in Greece. *Journal of European Public Policy*, 49(2), pp. 193–217.

Featherstone, K., 2011. The Greek Sovereign Debt Crisis and EMU: A Failing State in a Skewed Regime. *Journal of Common Market Studies*, 49(2), pp. 193–217.

Fernández-Otheo, C. M., Barroso, D. M., & Myro Sánchez, R., 2004. Desinversión y deslocalización de capital extranjero en España. *EKONOMIAZ. Revista vasca de Economía*, 55(1), pp. 106–29.

Fernández Rodríguez, C., 2014. La creación de las bases del sistema de regulación del desempleo. In: C. Fernández Rodríguez & A. Serrano Pascual, eds., *El paradigma de la flexiguridad en las políticas de empleo españolas*. Madrid: CIS, pp. 179–219.

Ferreiro, J. & Serrano, F., 2012. The Economic Crisis in Spain: Contagion Effects and Distinctive Factors. In: P. Arestis & M. Sawyer, eds., *The Euro Crisis*. Basingstoke: Palgrave Macmillan, pp. 235–68.

Ferrera, M., 1996. The 'Southern Model' of Welfare in Social Europe. *European Social Policy*, 6(1), pp. 17–37.

Ferrera, M. & Hemerijck, A., 2003. Recalibrating Europe's Welfare Regimes. In: J. Zeitlin & D. M. Trubek, eds., *Governing Work and Welfare in a New Economy: European and American Experiments*. Oxford: Oxford University Press, pp. 88–128.

Figari, F., Salvatori, A., & Sutherland, H., 2010. Stress Testing the UK Welfare System for Unemployment. *Journal of Poverty and Social Justice*, 18(3), pp. 229–42.

Flora, P. & Heidenheimer, J., 1998. *The Development of Welfare States in Europe and America*. London: Transaction Press.

Fløtten, T., Hippe, J., & Christensen, J., 2007. Den reformerte velferdsstaten. In: J. Dølvik, T. Fløtten, G. Hernes, & J. Hippe, eds., *Hamskifte: den norske modellen i endring*. Oslo: Gyldendal, pp. 69–99.

Förster, M., Llena-Nozal, A., & Nafilyan, V., 2014. *Trends in Top Incomes and their Taxation in OECD Countries*. Paris: OECD.

Friberg, J., 2016. Labour Migration: New Patterns of Labour Migration from Central and Eastern Europe and its Impact on Labour Markets and Institutions in Norway. In: J. Dølvik & L. Eldring, eds., *Comparative Social Research*, vol. 32: *Labour Mobility in the Enlarged Single European Market*. Bingley: Emerald, pp. 19–45.

Frieden, J., 2015. The Political Economy of Adjustment and Rebalancing. *Journal of International Money and Finance*, 52, pp. 4–14.

Friis, K., 2012a. Det er så yndigt at følges ad: Tilbagetrækningen fra arbejdsmarkedet set i et husstandsperspektiv. In: J. Goul Andersen & P. Jensen, eds., *Tilbagetrækning fra arbejdsmarkedet: årsager og effekter*. Copenhagen: Frydenlund Academic, pp. 137–57.

Friis, K., 2012b. Kønsforskelle i tidlig tilbagetrækning fra arbejdsmarkedet. In: J. Goul Andersen & P. Jensen, eds., *Tilbagetrækning fra arbejdsmarkedet: årsager og effekter*. Copenhagen: Frydenlund Academic, pp. 159–73.

Fritzell, J., Hols-Salén, L., Nelson, K., Palme, J. and Schön, P. 2016. *ESPN: Country Profile Sweden*. Brussels: European Commission, Directorate for Employment Social Affairs and Inclusion.

Funke, M., Schularick, M., & Trebesch, C., 2016. Going to Extremes: Politics after Financial Crises, 1870–2014. *European Economic Review*, 88(C), pp. 227–60.

Furåker, B., 1986. *Stat och arbetsmarknad. Studier i svensk rörlighetspolitik*. Lund: Arkiv förlag.

Galenianos, M., 2014. The Greek Crisis: Origins and Implications. Available at: http://dx.doi.org/10.2139/ssrn.2505455 (accessed 27 July 2018).

Gallego Calderón, R. & Subirats, J., 2011. Regional Welfare Regimes and Multi-Level Governance. In: M. León & A. Guillén, eds., *The Spanish Welfare State in European Context*. Aldershot: Ashgate, pp. 97–118.

Garrett, G., 1998. *Partisan Politics in the Global Economy*. New York: Cambridge University Press.

Gjedrem, S., 2002. Økonomiske perspektiver. *Penger og Kreditt*, 2002(1), pp. 3–10.

Gjedrem, S., 2010. En nyttig sentralbank. Speech at Norges Bank's Symposium 'What is a Useful Central Bank?', Oslo.

Goldrick-Kelly, P., 2015a. *Trends in Education Spending*, Dublin: Nevin Economics Research Institute.

Goldrick-Kelly, P., 2015b. *Trends in Health Spending*, Dublin: Nevin Economics Research Institute.

Goldthorpe, J. H., 2001. Causation, Statistics, and Sociology. *European Sociological Review*, 17(1), pp. 1–20.

González Begega, S. & Del Pino, E., 2017. Social Policy in Spain under Austerity: Assessing EU Leverage for Structural Adjustment and Welfare Reform. In: J. Ramos & E. Del Campo, eds., *Austerity and the Implementation of the EU-2020 Strategy in Spain*. Brussels: Peter Lang, pp. 279–302.

González Begega, S. & Luque Balbona, D., 2014. Goodbye to Competitive Corporatism in Spain? Social Pacting and Conflict in the Economic Crisis. *REIS*, 148, pp. 79–102.

Goul Andersen, J., 2003. The General Election in Denmark, November 2001. *Electoral Studies*, 22(2), pp. 186–93.

Goul Andersen, J., 2007. Restricting Access to Social Protection for Immigrants in the Danish Welfare State. *Benefits*, 15(3), pp. 157–69.

Goul Andersen, J., 2011. From the Edge of the Abyss to Bonanza—and Beyond: Danish Economy and Economic Policies 1980–2011. *Comparative Social Research*, 28, pp. 89–165.

Goul Andersen, J., 2012. Økonomisk bæredygtighed—politisk usikkerhed. Den danske velfærdsstat 1990–2012. *Politica*, 44(3), pp. 339–61.

Goul Andersen, J., 2013. *Krisens Navn. Bekæmper regeringen den forkerte økonomiske krise?* Copenhagen: Frydenlund Academic.

Goul Andersen, J., 2016. Stigende politisk mistillid. In: J. Goul Andersen & D. Shamshiri-Petersen, eds., *Fra Krisevalg til jordskredsvalg. Vælgere på vandring 2011–2015*. Copenhagen: Frydenlund Academic, pp. 279–323.

Goul Andersen, J., 2017. Medborgerskab under pres. In: J. Guldager & M. Skytte, eds., *Socialt arbejde*. 2nd edition. Copenhagen: Akademisk Forlag., pp. 88–137.

Goul Andersen, J., 2018. Globalisering og stigende økonomisk ulighed: økonomi eller politik. *Økonomi & Politik*, 91(1), pp. 46–64.

Goul Andersen, J., Albrekt Larsen, C., & Jensen, J., 2003. *Marginalisering og velfærdspolitik*. Copenhagen: Frydenlund.

Gourevitch, P., 1986. *Politics in Hard Times: Comparative Responses to International Economic Crises*. Ithaca, NY: Cornell University Press.

Government of Ireland, 2017. *National Reform Programme Ireland*. Dublin: Government of Ireland.

Guajardo, J., Leigh, D., & Pescatori, A., 2014. Expansionary Austerity? International Evidence. *Journal of the European Economic Association*, 12(4), pp. 949–68.

Guillén, A., 2007. Spain: Starting Periphery, becoming Centre. In: J. Kvist & J. Saari, eds., *The Europeanization of Social Protection*. Bristol: Policy Press, pp. 117–35.

Guillén, A. & González Begega, S., 2016. Spain: Welfare State. In: M. Dubnick & D. Bearfield, eds., *Encyclopedia of Public Administration and Public Policy*. New York: Taylor & Francis, pp. 3095–4000.

Guillén, A. & Pavolini, E., 2017. Spain and Italy: Regaining the Confidence and Legitimacy to Advance Social Policy. In: P. Taylor-Gooby, B. Leruth, & H. Chung, eds., *After Austerity: Welfare State Transformation in Europe after the Great Recession*. Oxford: Oxford University Press, pp. 136–54.

Hacker, J., 2004. Privatizing Risk without Privatizing the Welfare State: The Hidden Politics of Social Policy Retrenchment in the United States. *American Political Science Review*, 98(2), pp. 243–60.

Hacker, J. & Pierson, P., 2010. Winner-Take-All Politics: Public Policy, Political Organization, and the Precipitous Rise of Top Incomes in the United States. *Politics & Society*, 38(2), pp. 152–204.

Halifax, 2015. *Five Years of Generation Rent*. London: Lloyds Banking Group.

Hall, P., 1989. *The Political Power of Economic Ideas: Keynesianism across Nations*. Princeton, NJ: Princeton University Press.

Hall, P., 1993. Policy Paradigms, Social Learning, and the State: The Case of Economic Policymaking in Britain. *Comparative Politics*, 25(3), pp. 275–96.

Hall, P., 1999. The Political Economy of Europe in an Era of Interdependence. In: H. Kitschelt, P. Lange, G. Marks, & J. Stephens, eds., *Continuity and Change in Contemporary Capitalism*. New York: Cambridge University Press, pp. 135–63.

Hall, P., 2013. The Political Origins of our Economic Discontent. In: M. Kahler & D. Lake, eds., *Politics in the New Hard Times: The Great Recession in Comparative Perspective*. Ithaca, NY: Cornell University Press, pp. 129–49.

Hall, P. & Soskice, D., 2001. *Varieties of Capitalism: The Institutional Foundations of Comparative Advantage*. Oxford: Oxford University Press.

Hardiman, N., 2013. *Rethinking the Political Economy of Fiscal Consolidation in Two Recessions in Ireland*. Dublin: University College Dublin.

Hardiman, N. & MacCarthaigh, M., 2016. State Retrenchment and Administrative Reform in Ireland: Probing Comparative Policy Paradigms. *Journal of Comparative Policy Analysis*, 19(2), pp. 100–18.

Hassler, J. 2010. Sweden in Past, Current and Future Economic Crises. Report to the OECD Economics Department.

Hay, C. & Smith, N., 2013. The Story of a North Sea Bubble: The Strange Demise of the Anglo-Liberal Growth Model in the United Kingdom and Ireland. *European Political Science Review*, 5(3), pp. 401–30.

Hay, C. & Wincott, D., 2012 *The Political Economy of European Welfare Capitalism*. Basingstoke: Palgrave Macmillan.

Hemerijck, A., 2017. *The Uses of Social Investment*. Oxford: Oxford University Press.

Hermann, C., 2015. Crisis and Social Policy in Europe. *Global Social Policy*, 15(1), pp. 82–5.

Herndon, T., Ash, M., & Pollin, R., 2014. Does High Public Debt Consistently Stifle Economic Growth? A Critique of Reinhart and Rogoff. *Cambridge Journal of Economics*, 38(2), pp. 257–79.

Hick, R., 2014. From Celtic Tiger to Crisis: Progress, Problems and Prospects for Social Security in Ireland. *Social Policy and Administration*, 48(4), pp. 394–412.

Hiilamo, H., 2017. Näin SOTESta tuli sekunda [In This Way SOTE became Inferior]. Available at: https://www.hs.fi/sunnuntai/art-2000005483366.html (accessed 11 December 2017).

Himmelweit, S., 2016. Childcare as an Investment in Infrastructure. In: J. Campbell & M. Gillespie, eds., *Feminist Economics and Public Policy*. London: Routledge, pp. 83–93.

HM Government, 2018. https://www.gov.uk/universal-credit.

Honkanen, P., 2017. *Calculations on the Levels of Basic Security Benefits*. Helsinki: Kela.

Hood, A., Joyce, R., & Cribb, A., 2016. Observations. Available at: http://www.ifs.org.uk/publications/8338 (accessed 28 June 2016).

Hort, S., 2014. *Social Policy, Welfare State and Civil Society in Sweden*. Volume 1. Lund: Arkiv förlag.

Horwitz, L. & Myant, M., 2015. *Spain's Labour Market Reforms: The Road to Employment—or to Unemployment*. Brussels: European Trade Union Institute.

House of Commons Work and Pensions Committee, 2016. In-Work Progression in Universal Credit, Tenth Report of Session 2015–16, HC 549. Available at: http://www.publications.parliament.uk/pa/cm201516/cmselect/cmworpen/549/549.pdf (accessed 28 June 2016).

Huber, E. & Stephens, J., 2014. Partisan Impacts on Social Policy and Distributive Outcomes in the Eras of Welfare State Expansion and Retrenchment. APSA 2014 Annual Meeting Paper.

IMF (International Monetary Fund), 2012. Staff Report for the 2012 Article IV Consultation and First Post-Program Monitoring Discussion, International Monetary Fund.

IMF (International Monetary Fund), 2015. Fiscal Monitor, April 2015: Now is the Time: Fiscal Policies for Sustainable Growth, International Monetary Fund.

INE (Labor Institute of the private sector union GSEE in Greece), 2017. *The Greek Economy and Employment: Annual Report 2017*. Athens: Labour Institute.

Ingimundarson, V., Urfalino, P., & Erlingsdóttir, I., 2016. *Iceland's Financial Crisis: The Politics of Blame, Protest, and Reconstruction*. London: Routledge.

Innes, D. & Tetlow, G., 2015. Delivering Fiscal Squeeze by Cutting Local Government Spending. *Fiscal Studies*, 36(3), pp. 303–25.

Innocenti: UNICEF Office of Research, 2014. *Children of the Recession: The Impact of the Economic Crisis on Child Well-Being in Rich Countries*. Florence: Innocenti: UNICEF Office of Research.

Institute of Social and Economic Research, 2016. Written Evidence from ISER, University of Essex (IGF0053) to House of Commons Work and Pensions Select Committee. Available at: https://www.iser.essex.ac.uk/2016/03/15/children-were-hardest-hit-by-policy-changes-along-with-those-in-their-30s-and-early-40s-iser-evidence-to-select-committee (accessed 17 July 2016).

Ioannides, Y. & Pissarides, C., 2015. Is the Greek Debt Crisis One of Supply or Demand? *Brookings Papers on Economic Activity*, Fall, pp. 349–73.

Jansen, M., 2016. *The Challenge of Integrated Support to Long Term Unemployment*. Madrid: Fedea/JP Morgan Chase & Co. New.

Jäntti, M. & Jenkins, S., 2015. Income Mobility. In: A. B. Atkinson & F. Bourguignon, eds., *Handbook of Income Distribution*. Volume 2. Amsterdam: North Holland, pp. 807–935.

Jenkins, S., Brandonlini, A., Micklewright, J., & Nolan, B., 2013. *The Great Recession and the Distribution of Household Income*. Oxford: Oxford University Press.

Johnson, P., 2016. *The Times*, 25 June.

Jónsson, Á. & Sigurgeirsson, H., 2016. *The Icelandic Financial Crisis: A Study into the World's Smallest Currency Area and its Recovery from Total Banking Collapse*. London: Palgrave Macmillan.

Jordfald, B. & Nymoen, R., 2016. *Hva skjer nederst i lønnsfordelingen i privat sektor? Rapport nr 8–2016*. Oslo: Senter for lønnsdannelse.

Kahler, M. & Lake, D. A., 2013. *Politics in the New Hard Times: The Great Recession in Comparative Perspective*. Ithaca, NY: Cornell University Press.

Kangas, O., 2006. Politiikka ja sosiaaliturva Suomessa [Politics and Social Security in Finland]. In T. Paavonen & O. Kangas, eds., *Eduskunta hyvinvointivaltion rakentajana* [Parliament as the Builder of the Welfare State]. Helsinki: Edita, pp. 189–396.

Kangas, O., 2007. Finland: Labour Markets against Politics. In: E. Immergut, K. Anderson, & I. Schulze, eds., *The Handbook of West European Pension Politics*. Oxford: Oxford University Press, pp. 248–96.

Kangas, O. & Kalliomaa-Puha, L., 2016. *ESPN Thematic Report on Social Investment, Finland 2014–2015*. Brussels: European Commission.

Kangas, O. & Niemelä, M., 2017. Riskit, vakuutus ja sosiaalivakuutus [Risks, Insurance and Social Insurance]. In: P. Havakka, M. Niemelä, & H. Uusitalo, eds., *Sosiaalivakuutus* [Social Insurance]. Helsinki: FINVA, pp. 10–56.

Kangas, O. & Palme, J., 2005. *Social Policy and Economic Development in the Nordic Countries*. Basingstoke: Palgrave.

Kangas, O. & Palme, J., 2007. Social Rights, Structural Needs and Social Expenditures. In: J. Clasen & N. Siegel, eds., *Investigating Welfare State Change*. Cheltenham: Edward Elgar, pp. 106–29.

Kangas, O. & Pulkka, V.-V., 2016. *Ideasta kokeiluun? Esiselvitys perustulokokeilun toteuttamisvaihtoehdoista* [From an Idea to an Experiment: A Preliminary Report on Alternatives to Carry Out a Basic Income Experiment]. Helsinki: VNK.

Kangas, O., Niemelä, M., & Varjonen, S., 2014. When and Why Do Ideas Matter? *European Political Science Review*, 6(1), pp. 73–92.

Kangas, O., Palme, J., & Kainu, M., 2017. The Multifaceted Roles of the Social Investment State in Compensating, Accumulating and Multiplying Endowments over the Life Cycle. In: J. Erola & E. Kilpi-Jakonen, eds., *Social Inequality across the Generations*. Cheltenham: Edward Elgar, pp. 181–207.

Karsio, O. & Anttonen, A., 2013. Marketisation of Eldercare in Finland. In: G. Meagher & M. Szhebely, eds., *Marketisation in Nordic Eldercare: A Research Report on Legislation, Oversight, Extent and Consequences*. Stockholm: Department of Social Work, University of Stockholm, pp. 85–124.

Katsimi, M. & Moutos, T., 2010. EMU and the Greek Crisis: The Political-Economy Perspective. *European Journal of Political Economy*, 26(44), pp. 568–76.

Katzenstein, P., 1985. *Small States in World Markets: Industrial Policy in Europe*. New York: Cornell University Press.

Keeler, J., 1993. Opening the Window for Reform Mandates, Crises, and Extraordinary Policy-Making. *Comparative Political Studies*, 25(4), pp. 433–86.

Kenworthy, L., 2011. *Progress for the Poor*. Oxford: Oxford University Press.

Keynes, J. M., 1936. *The General Theory of Employment, Interest and Money*. London: Macmillan.

Kiander, J., 2001. *Laman opetukset: Suomen 1990 luvun kriisin syyt ja seuraukset* [Teachings of the Depression: Causes and Consequences of the Finnish Economic Crisis]. Saarijärvi: Gummerus.

Kingdon, J., 1984. *Agendas, Alternatives, and Public Policies*. Boston, MA: Little, Brown & Co.

Kjellberg, A., 2018. Kollektivavtalens täckningsgrad samt organisationsgraden hos arbetsgivarförbund och fackförbund. *Studies in Social Policy, Industrial Relations, Working Life and Mobility*, 2018(1), pp. 1–135.

Kleppe, P., 2003. *Kleppepakke. Meninger og minner fra et langt politisk liv*. Oslo: Aschehoug.

Korhonen, T., 2011. *Talouskriisistä rahaliittoon* [From a Recession into Monetary Union]. Helsinki: Suomen Pankki.

Korpi, W., 2003. Welfare-State Regress in Western Europe: Politics, Institutions, Globalization, and Europeanization. *Annual Review of Sociology*, 29(1), pp. 589–609.

Korpi, W. & Palme, J., 2003. New Politics and Class Politics in the Context of Austerity and Globalization: Welfare State Regress in 18 Countries, 1975–95. *American Political Science Review*, 97(3), pp. 425–46.

Krugman, P., 2012. *End this Depression Now!* New York: W. W. Norton.

Kuivalainen, S. & Nelson, K., 2011. Eroding Minimum Income in the Nordic Countries and Abroad? Reassessing the Typical Character of Nordic Social Assistance. In: J. Kvist, J. Fritzell, B. Hvinden, & O. Kangas, eds., *Changing Social Equality: The Nordic Welfare Model in the 21st Century*. Bristol: Policy Press, pp. 69–88.

Laeven, L. & Valencia, F., 2010. Resolution of Banking Crises: The Good, the Bad and the Ugly. IMF Working Paper No. WP/10/146.

Laeven, L. & Valencia, F., 2013. Systematic Banking Crises Database. *IMF Economic Review*, 61(2), pp. 225–70.

Lago Peñas, M., 2016. *Cartografia de los recortes. El gasto público en España entre 2009–2014*. Madrid: CCOO.

Lane, P., 2012. The European Sovereign Debt Crisis. *Journal of Economic Perspectives*, 26(3), pp. 49–67.

Larragy, J., O'Cinnéide, S., & O'Riain, S., 2006. *Social Foundations for an Uncertain Future, Report to Forfas*. Maynooth: Department of Sociology and Applied Social Studies.

Lazarsfeld, P. F. & Henry, N. W., 1968. *Latent Structure Analysis*. Boston, MA: Houghton Mifflin.

Leventi, C. & Matsaganis, M., 2018. Disentangling Annuities and Transfers: The Case of Greek Retirement Benefits. Available at: http://www.ecineq.org/ecineq_lux15/FILESx2015/CR2/p96.pdf (accessed 27 July 2018).

Levy, J., 2010. Welfare Retrenchment. In: F. Castles, S. Leibfried, J. Lewis, H. Obinger, & C. Pierson, eds., *The Oxford Handbook of the Welfare State*. Oxford: Oxford University Press, pp. 552–67.

Lie, E. & Vennesland, C., 2010. *Over evne. Finansdepartementet 1965–1992*. Oslo: Pax.

Lindblom, C., 1959. The Science of Muddling Through. *Public Administration Review*, 19(2), pp. 79–88.

Linzer, D. A. & Lewis, J. B., 2011. poLCA: An R Package for Polytomous Variable Latent Class Analysis. *Journal of Statistical Software*, 42(10), pp. 1–29.

Lister, R., 2006. *Women's and Children's Poverty: Making the Links*. London: Women's Budget Group.

Lucas, R., 1976. Econometric Policy Evaluation: A Critique. *Carnegie-Rochester Conference Series on Public Policy*, 1, pp. 19–46.

Lundgren, B., 2009. Testimony of Bo Lundgren Director General, Swedish National Debt Office, at the Congressional Oversight Panel, 19 March.

Lupton, R., Burchardt, T., Hills, J., Stewart, K., & Vizard, P., 2016. *Social Policy in a Cold Climate: Policies and their Consequences since the Crisis*. Bristol: Policy Press.

Lupton, R., with Burchardt, T., Fitzgerald, A., Hills, J., McKnight, A., Obolenskaya, P., Stewart, K., et al., 2015. The Coalition's Social Policy Record: Policy, Spending and Outcomes 2010–2015. Centre for Analysis of Social Exclusion, London School of

Economics, Research Report No. 4. Available at: http://sticerd.lse.ac.uk/dps/case/spcc/RR04.pdf (accessed 26 July 2018).

Lyte, R., Maître, B., Nolan, B., & Whelan, C., 2001. Persistent and Consistent Poverty in the 1994 and 1995 Waves of the European Community Household Panel Survey. *Review of Income and Wealth*, 47(4), pp. 427–49.

McCutcheon, A. L., 1987. *Latent Class Analysis*. London: Sage Publications.

MacInnes, T., 2016. More Insecure? The Changing Face of Temporary Work. Available at: https://wearecitizensadvice.org.uk/more-insecure-the-changing-face-of-temporary-work-81d5955a2502 (accessed 29 January 2018).

McKay, A., Campbell, J., Thomson, E., & Ross, S., 2013. Economic Recession and Recovery in the UK: What's Gender Got to Do with it? *Feminist Economics*, 19(3), pp. 108–23.

McNamara, K., 1998. *The Currency of Ideas: Monetary Politics in the European Union*. New York: Cambridge University Press.

Magone, J., 2016. The Politics of Troika Avoidance: The Case of Spain. In: J. Magone, B. Laffan, & C. Schweiger, eds., *Core–Periphery Relations in the European Union*. Abingdon: Routledge, pp. 205–15.

Mandelkern, R., 2016. Explaining the Striking Similarity in Macroeconomic Policy Responses to the Great Recession: The Institutional Power of Macroeconomic Governance. *Comparative Political Studies*, 49(2), pp. 219–52.

Marchal, S., Marx, I., & van Mechelen, N., 2016. Minimum Income Protection in the Austerity Tide. *IZA Journal of European Labour Studies*, 5(1), pp. 1–20.

Maskína, 2014. Fyrrum atvinnuleitendur, November-December 2013 (Report for Directorate of Labour). Available at www.vinnumalastofnun.is/files/Konnun-VMST_764137556.pdf (accessed 14 February 2014).

Matsaganis, M., 2011. The Welfare State and the Crisis: The Case of Greece. *Journal of European Social Policy*, 21(5), pp. 501–12.

Matsaganis, M., 2013. Prerequisites to the Revival of Public Health Care in Greece. In: S. Kalyvas, G. Pagoulatos, & H. Tsoukas, eds., *From Stagnation to Forced Adjustment: Reforms in Greece 1974–2010*. Oxford: Oxford University Press, pp. 133–50.

Matsaganis, M., 2017. The Contorted Politics of Guaranteed Minimum Income in Greece. Paper presented at ESPAnet Annual Conference, Lisbon, 14–16 September.

Matsaganis, M., 2018a. Income Support Policies and Labour Market Reform under Austerity in Greece. In: S. Theodoropoulou (ed.), *Labour Market Policies in the Era of Pervasive Austerity: A European Perspective*. Bristol: Policy Press, pp. 43–68.

Matsaganis, M., 2018b. Making Sense of the Greek Crisis. In: M. Castells, ed., *Europe's Crisis*. Cambridge: Polity, pp. 49–69.

Matsaganis, M. & Leventi, C., 2011. Pathways to a Universal Basic Pension in Greece. *Basic Income Studies*, 6(1), pp. 1–20.

Matsaganis, M. & Leventi, C., 2014. The Distributional Impact of Austerity and the Recession in Southern Europe, *South European Society and Politics*, 19(3), pp. 393–412.

Matsaganis, M., Leventi, C., Kanavitsa, E., & Flevotomou, M., 2017. *Towards a More Efficient Anti-Poverty Policy: Revised Report*. Athens: diaNEOsis Foundation.

Meagher, G. & Szhebely, M. eds., 2013. *Marketisation in Nordic Eldercare: A Research Report on Legislation, Oversight, Extent and Consequences*. Stockholm: Department of Social Work, University of Stockholm.

Mettler, S., 2015. Twenty Years On: Paul Pierson's Dismantling the Welfare State? *Political Science & Politics*, 48(2), pp. 270–3.

Ministry of Finance and Economy, 2016. *Skýrsla fjármála—og efnahagsráðherra um niðurfærslu verðtryggðra fasteignalána* [Report to Parliament about the Effects of the Debt Relief Programme of 2013–2014]. Reykjavik: Ministry of Finance and Economy.

Minsky, H., 1986. *Stabilizing an Unstable Economy*. New York: McGraw-Hill.

Miron, J. & Weil, D., 1998. The Genesis and Evolution of Social Security. In: M. Bordo, C. Goldin, & E. White, eds., *The Defining Moment: The Great Depression and the American Economy in the Twentieth Century*. Chicago: University of Chicago Press, pp. 297–322.

Mitsopoulos, M. & Pelagidis, T., 2011. *Understanding the Crisis in Greece: From Boom to Bust*. Basingstoke: Palgrave Macmillan.

Mjøset, L. & Cappelen, Å., 2011. The Integration of the Norwegian Oil Economy into the World Economy. *Comparative Social Research*, 28, pp. 167–263.

Moene, K. & Wallerstein, M., 1993. What is Wrong with Social Democracy. In: P. Bardhan & J. Roemer, eds., *Market Socialism: The Present Debate*. Cambridge: Cambridge University Press, pp. 219–235.

Moisio, P., 2004. A Latent Class Application to the Multidimensional Measurement of Poverty. *Quality and Quantity*, 38(6), pp. 703–17.

Morel, N., Palier, B., & Palme, J. eds., 2012. *Towards a Social Investment Welfare State? Ideas, Policies and Challenges*. Bristol: Policy Press.

Moreno, L., 2013. Spain's Catch Up with the EU Core: The Implausible Quest of a 'Flying Pig'? *South European Society and Politics*, 18(2), pp. 217–36.

Mosley, L., 2003. *Global Capital and National Government*. New York: Cambridge University Press.

Müller, W. & Gangl, M., 2003. *Transitions from Education to Work in Europe*. Oxford: Oxford University Press.

Muñoz del Bustillo, R. & Antón, J., 2015. Turning Back before Arriving? The Weakening of the Spanish Welfare State. In: D. Vaughan-Whitehead, ed., *The European Social Model in Crisis: Is Europe Losing its Soul?* Cheltenham: Edward Elgar, pp. 451–506.

Murphy, M., 2012. Interests, Institutions and Ideas: Explaining Irish Social Security Policy. *Policy and Politics*, 40(3), pp. 347–65.

Murphy, M., 2016. Low Road or High Road? The Post-Crisis Trajectory of Irish Activation. *Critical Social Policy*, 36(3), pp. 432–52.

Myrdal, A. & Myrdal, G., 1934. *Crisis in the Population Question* [Kris i befolkningsfrågan]. Stockholm: Bonniers.

Myro, R. & Gandoy, R., 2009. Sector industrial. In: J. García-Delgado & R. Myro, eds., *Lecciones de Economía Española*. Madrid: Thompson-Reuters, pp. 217–43.

Natili, M., 2016. Changing Welfare in Southern Europe? Political Competition and the Evolution of Regional Minimum Income Schemes in Italy and Spain. *Social Policies*, 3(2), pp. 331–48.

NESC (National Economic and Social Council), 2009. *Ireland's Five-Part Crisis: An Integrated National Response*. Dublin: National Economic and Social Council.

NESC (National Economic and Social Council), 2013. *Ireland's Five-Part Crisis, Five Years on: Deepening Reform and Institutional Innovation*. Dublin: National Economic and Social Council.

Nolan, B. & Whelan, C., 2011. *Poverty and Deprivation in Europe*. Oxford: Oxford University Press.

NOU (Norges offentlige utredninger - Norway's government publications), 1992:26. En nasjonal strategi for økt sysselsetting i 1990-årene. List of Norwegian government publications available at: https://www.regjeringen.no/no/dokument/nou-ar/id1767/

NOU, 2011:1. Bedre rustet mot finanskriser.

NOU, 2013:13. Lønnsdannelsen og utfordringer for norsk økonomi.

NOU, 2016:15. Lønnsdannelsen i lys av nye økonomiske utviklingstrekk.

NOU, 2017:2. Integrasjon og tillit. Langsiktige konsekvenser av høy innvandring.

OECD (Organisation for Economic Co-operation and Development), n.d. National Accounts Data Files. Available at: http://www.oecd.org/std/na (accessed 27 July 2018).

OECD, 1981. *The Welfare State in Crisis*. Paris: OECD.

OECD, 1994. *The OECD Jobs Study: Facts, Analysis, Strategies*. Paris: OECD.

OECD, 2009. *OECD Economic Surveys: United Kingdom 2009*. Paris: OECD.

OECD, 2011a. *Divided We Stand: Why Inequality Keeps Rising*. Paris: OECD.

OECD, 2011b. *Economic Surveys: Greece*. Paris: OECD.

OECD, 2013. *Crisis Squeezes Income and Puts Pressure on Inequality and Poverty*. Paris: OECD.

OECD, 2014a. *Employment and Skills Strategies in Ireland*. Paris: OECD.

OECD, 2014b. *Society at a Glance: The Crisis and its Aftermath*. Paris: OECD.

OECD, 2016a. *Employment Outlook*. Paris: OECD.

OECD, 2016b. Social Expenditure Update. Available at: http://www.oecd.org/els/soc/OECD2016-Social-Expenditure-Update.pdf (accessed 27 July 2018).

OECD, 2016c. *Society at a Glance*. Paris: OECD.

OECD, 2016d. OECD Tax Benefit Model. Available at: http://www.oecd.org/els/benefits-and-wages.htm (accessed 27 July 2018).

OECD, 2017a. *Employment Outlook*. Paris: OECD.

OECD, 2017b. *Taxing Wages*. Paris: OECD.

Offe, C., 1984. *Contradictions of the Welfare State*. Cambridge, MA: MIT Press.

Office for National Statistics, 2016. Measuring National Well-Being: Life in the UK. Available at: https://www.ons.gov.uk/peoplepopulationandcommunity/wellbeing/articles/measuringnationalwellbeing/2016 (accessed 27 July 2018).

Ohisalo, M., 2017. *Murusia hyvinvointivaltion pohjalla: leipäjonot, koettu hyvinvointi ja huono-osaisuus* [Crumbs at the Bottom of a Welfare State: Charity Food Aid and Subjective Well-Being of the Disadvantaged]. Kuopio: Publications of the University of Eastern Finland.

Ólafsson, Þ. & Vignisdóttir, K., 2012. *Household's Position in the Financial Crisis in Iceland*. Reykjavik: Central Bank of Iceland.

Ólafsson, S., 1990. *Lífskjör á Norðurlöndum* [Level of Living in the Nordic Countries]. Reykjavík: Iðunn.

Ólafsson, S., 2008. Íslenska efnahagsundrið: Frá hagsæld til frjálshyggju og fjármálahruns [The Icelandic Economic Miracle]. *Icelandic Review of Politics and Public Administration*, 4(2), pp. 231–56.

Ólafsson, S., 2011. Icelandic Capitalism: From Statism to Neoliberalism and Financial Collapse. In: *Nordic Varieties of Capitalism: Comparative Social Research*, ed. L. Mjöset, 28 (special issue), pp. 1–52.

Ólafsson, S., 2014. Hrunið og árangur endurreisnarinnar. *Íslenska þjóðfélagið* [Icelandic Society], 5(2), pp. 95–116.

Ólafsson, S., 2016a. The Political Economy of Iceland's Boom and Bust. In: V. Ingimundarson, P. Urfalino, & I. Erlingsdóttir, eds., *Iceland's Financial Crisis: The Politics of Blame, Protest and Reconstruction*. London: Routledge, pp. 57–78.

Ólafsson, S., 2016b. The Strategy of Redistribution: Iceland's Way Out of the Crisis. In: V. Ingimundarson, P. Urfalino, & I. Erlingsdóttir, eds., *Iceland's Financial Crisis: The Politics of Blame, Protest and Reconstruction*. London: Routledge, pp. 156–83.

Ólafsson, S. & Kristjánsson, A., 2012. *Umfang kreppunnar og afkoma ólíkra tekjuhópa: Report to the Ministry of Welfare*. Reykjavik: Ministry of Welfare.

Ólafsson, S. & Kristjánsson, A., 2013. Income Inequality in Boom and Bust: A Tale from Iceland's Bubble Economy. In J. C. Gornick and M. Jäntti eds., *Income Inequality: Economic Disparities and the Middle Class in Affluent Countries*. Stanford, CA: Stanford University Press, pp. 416–38.

Ólafsson, S. & Kristjánsson, A., 2017. *Ójöfnuður á Íslandi: Skipting tekna og eigna í fjölþjóðlegu samhengi* [Inequality in Iceland: The Distribution of Incomes and Wealth in a Comparative Perspective]. Reykjavik: University of Iceland Press.

Ólafsson, S., Kristjánsson, A., & Stefánsson, K., 2012. *Mótvægisaðgerðir gegn skuldavanda, fátækt og atvinnuleysi: Report to the Ministry of Welfare*. Reykjavik: Ministry of Welfare.

O'Riain, S., 2014. *The Rise and Fall of Ireland's Celtic Tiger, Liberalism, Boom and Bust*. Cambridge: Cambridge University Press.

Ortega, E. & Peñalosa, J., 2012. *The Spanish Economic Crisis: Key Factors and Growth Challenges in the Euro Area*. Madrid: Banco de España.

Palme, J., 2003. Pension Reform in Sweden and the Changing Boundaries between Public and Private. In: G. Clark & N. Whiteside, eds., *Pension Security in the 21st Century*. Oxford: Oxford University Press, pp. 144–67.

Palme, J., 2017a. The Swedish Welfare State System: With Special Reference to Inequality and the Paradox of Redistribution. In: C. Aspalter, ed., *The Routledge Research Companion on Welfare State Systems*. London: Routledge, pp. 203–215.

Palme, J., 2017b. Welfare States Institutions in Hard Times: The Global Financial Crisis as a Stress Test in the European Laboratory. Paper presented at the MPSA Annual Conference, Chicago.

Palme, J., Bergmark, Å., Bäckman, O., Estrada, F., Fritzell, J., Lundberg, O., Sjöberg, O. and Szebehely, M. 2002. Welfare Trends in Sweden: Balancing the Books for the 1990s. *European Journal of Social Policy*, 12(4), pp. 329–46.

Parliament's Information Service, 2017. *Increases of Income Due to the Policy Changes the Sipilä Government Has Adopted*. Helsinki: Parliament's Information Service.

Pavolini, E., León, M., Guillén, A., & Ascoli, U., 2015. From Austerity to Permanent Strain? The EU and Welfare State Reform in Italy and Spain. *Comparative European Politics*, 13(1), pp. 56–76.

Pekkarinen, J. & Vartiainen, J., 1993. *Suomen talouspolitiikan pitkä linja* [The Long-Lasting Line of Finnish Economic Policy-Making]. Helsinki: WSOY.

Perbo, U., 1999. Varför fick Sverige en depression i början på 90-talet? *Ekonomisk Debatt*, 27, pp. 325–33.

Perez, S. & Matsaganis, M., 2017. The Political Economy of Austerity in Southern Europe. *New Political Economy*, 23(2), pp. 192–207, https://doi.org/10.1080/13563467.2017.1370445, accessed 24 July 2017.

Perez, S. & Matsaganis, M., 2018. Can the Welfare State as We Know it Survive? A View from the Crisis-Ridden Southern European Periphery. *Southern European Society and Politics*, 23(2), pp. 192–207.

Perrons, D., Lacey, N., Phillips, A., Wearing, S., Ashtiany, S., Biressi, A., Carter, C., et al., 2015. Confronting Gender Inequality: Findings from the LSE Commission on Gender, Inequality and Power. London School of Economics. Available at: http://eprints.lse.ac.uk/66802/ (accessed 26 July 2018).

Petmesidou, M. & Guillén, A., 2014. Can the Welfare State as We Know it Survive? A View from the Crisis-Ridden South European Periphery. *South European Society and Politics*, 19(3), pp. 295–307.

Pierson, P., 1994. *Dismantling the Welfare State? Reagan, Thatcher and the Politics of Retrenchment*. Cambridge: Cambridge University Press.

Pierson, P., 1996. The New Politics of the Welfare State. *World Politics*, 48(2), pp. 143–79.

Pierson, P., 2001. Post-Industrial Pressure on the Mature Welfare States. In: P. Pierson, ed., *The New Politics of the Welfare State*. Oxford: Oxford University Press, pp. 80–104.

Pierson, P., 2015. Reflections of the Evolution of a Research Program. *PS: Political Science & Politics*, 48(2), pp. 292–4.

Plough, N., ed. 2017. *Økonomisk ulighed i Danmark* [Inequality in Denmark]. Copenhagen: Djöf Publishers.

Pohjola, M., 2014. *Suomi uuteen nousuun* [New Growth for Finland]. Helsinki: Teknologiateollisuus.

Polanyi, K., 1944. *The Great Transformation: The Economic and Political Origins of Our Time*. Boston, MA: Beacon Press.

Pontusson, J., 2011. Once Again a Model: Nordic Social Democracy in a Globalized World. In: J. Cronin, G. Ross, & J. Schoch, eds., *What's Left of the Left: Democrats and Social Democrats in Challenging Times*. Durham, NC: Duke University Press, pp. 89–116.

Pontusson, J. & Raess, D., 2012. How (and Why) is this Time Different? The Politics of Economic Crisis in Western Europe and the United States. *Annual Review of Political Science*, 15(1), pp. 13–33.

Price, R., Dang, T.-T., & Botev, J., 2015. *Adjusting Fiscal Balance for the Business Cycle: New Tax and Expenditure Elasticity Estimates for OECD Countries*. Paris: OECD.

Prime Minister's Office, 2013. Höfuðstólslækkun húsnæðislána (The Debt Relief Program). Reykjavík: Forsætisráðuneytið.. Available at: https://www.stjornarradid.is/media/forsaetisraduneyti-media/media/Skyrslur/hofudstolslaekkun-husnaedislana.pdf

Raess, D. & Pontusson, J., 2015. The Politics of Fiscal Policy during Economic Downturns, 1981–2010. *European Journal of Political Research*, 54(1), pp. 1–22.

Reed, H. & Portes, J., 2014. *Cumulative Impact Assessment: A Research Report by Landman Economics and the National Institute of Economic and Social Research (NIESR) for the EHRC*. London: Equality and Human Rights Commission.

Rehm, P., 2016. *Risk Inequality and the Welfare State: Social Policy Preferences, Development, and Dynamics*. New York: Cambridge University Press.

Reinhart, C. & Rogoff, K., 2009. *This Time is Different: Eight Centuries of Financial Folly*. Princeton, NJ: Princeton University Press.

Reinhart, C. & Rogoff, K., 2010. Growth in a Time of Debt. *American Economic Review*, 100(2), pp. 573–8.

Rhodes, C., 2016. *The Welfare Cap*. London: House of Commons Library.

Rodríguez Cabrero, G., 2011. The Consolidation of the Spanish Welfare State (1975–2010). In: A. Guillén & M. León, eds., *The Spanish Welfare State in European Context*. Aldershot: Ashgate, pp. 17–38.

Rodríguez Zapatero, J., 2013. *El dilema. 600 días de vértigo*. Barcelona: Planeta.

Romer, C. D. & Romer, D. H., 2010. The Macroeconomic Effects of Tax Changes: Estimates Based on a New Measure of Fiscal Shocks. *American Economic Review*, 100(3), pp. 763–801.

Romer, C. D. & Romer, D. H., 2014. New Evidence on the Impact of Financial Crises in Advanced Countries. NBER Working Paper No. 21021.Available at: http://www.nber.org/papers/w21021 (accessed 27 July 2018).

Ronchi, S., 2018. Which Roads (if any) to Social Investment? The Recalibration of EU Welfare States at the Crisis Crossroads (2000–2014). *Journal of Social Policy*, 47(3), pp. 1–20.

Royo, S., 2009. Reforms Betrayed? Zapatero and Continuities in Economic Policy. *South European Society and Politics*, 14(4), pp. 435–51.

Ruggie, J. G., 1982. International Regimes, Transactions, and Change: Embedded Liberalism in the Postwar Economic Order. *International Organization*, 36(2), pp. 379–415.

Sánchez, R., 2011. Crisis económica y modelo productivo. *Información Comercial Española*, 863, pp. 79–96.

Sapir, A., 2005. *Globalization and the Reform of European Social Models*. Brussels: Bruegel.

Savage, Micheal & Callan, Tim & Nolan, Brian & Colgan, Brian, 2015. "The Great Recession, Austerity and Inequality: Evidence from Ireland," Papers WP499, Economic and Social Research Institute (ESRI).

SCB (Statistiska centralbyrån – Sweden Statistics), 2018. Rekordår og kriser – så har BNP ökat och minskat. Available at: http://www.scb.se/hitta-statistik/sverige-i-siffror/samhallets-ekonomi/bnp—bruttonationalprodukten/. Accessed at August 13 2018.

Scharpf, F., 2000. The Viability of Advanced Welfare States in the International Economy: Vulnerabilities and Options. *Journal of European Public Policy*, 7(2), pp. 190–228.

Schumpeter, J. A., 1942. *Capitalism, Socialism, and Democracy*. New York: Harper & Row.

Seely, A., 2016. *Capital Gains Tax: Recent Developments*. London: House of Common Library.

Seidman, L., 2012. Keynesian Stimulus versus Classical Austerity. *Review of Keynesian Economics*, 1(1), pp. 77–92.

Simpson, M., 2017. The Social Union after the Coalition: Devolution, Divergence and Convergence. *Journal of Social Policy*, 46(2), pp. 251–68.

Skidelsky, R., 2010. The Relevance of Keynes. *Cambridge Journal of Economics*, 35(1), pp. 1–13.

Smeeding, T., 2006. Poor People in Rich Nations: The United States in Comparative Perspective. *Journal of Economic Perspectives*, 20(1), p. 69–90.

Social Justice Ireland, 2016a. *Budget Choices: Policy Briefing*. Dublin: Social Justice Ireland.

Social Justice Ireland, 2016b. *Employment Monitor Issue 1*. Dublin: Social Justice Ireland.

Social Justice Ireland, 2016c. *Work, Unemployment and Job Creation*. Dublin: Social Justice Ireland.

Sørensen, C., 2010. Historisk uansvarlig finanspolitik og rådgivning. *Samfundsøkonomen*, 28(2), pp. 9–14.

SOS (Official Statistics of Sweden), 2006. *Social Rapport 2006*. Stockholm: Socialstyrelsen.

Spilimbergo, A., Symansky, S., Cotterelli, C., & Blanchard, O., 2008. Fiscal Policy for the Crisis. IMF Staff Position Note No. SPN/08/01.

St.melding 29 (Norway government publication), 2016–17. Perspektivmeldingen 2017. Public Report, Norway. Available at https://www.regjeringen.no/no/dokumenter/meld.-st.-29-20162017/id2546674/.

St.melding 35 (Norway government publication), 1994–5. Velferdsmeldingen. Public Report, Norway. Available at: https://www.stortinget.no/no/Saker-og-publikasjoner/Stortingsforhandlinger/Lesevisning/?p=1994-95&paid=3&wid=c&psid=DIVL443.

Standard & Poor's, 2016. *QE and Economic Inequality: The UK Experience*. London: Standard & Poor's.

Starke, P., Kaasch, A., & van Hooren, F., 2013. *The Welfare State as Crisis Manager: Explaining the Diversity of Policy Responses to Economic Crisis*. London: Palgrave Macmillan.

Statistics Finland, 2005. *Statistical Yearbook of Finland 2005*. Helsinki: Statistics Finland.

Statistics Finland, 2013. *Historiasarjat: Kansantalouden tilinpito* [Historical Series: National Accounts]. Helsinki: Statistics Finland.

Statistics Finland, 2017. *Statistical Yearbook of Finland 2017*. Helsinki: Statistics Finland.

Stefánsson, K., 2012. Umfang vinnunnar í lífi Íslendinga, 1991–2008. In: G. B. Eydal and S. Ólafsson eds., *Þróun velferðarinnar 1998–2008* [Welfare Developments 1998–2008]. Reykjavik: Social Science Research Institute, University of Iceland, pp. 89–106.

Stefánsson, K., Arnardóttir, L., & Karlsson, A., 2018. Children's Deprivation and Economic Vulnerability in Iceland 2009 and 2014. *Child-Indicators Research*, 11(3), pp. 783–803.

Steigum, E. & Thøgersen, Ø., 2015. A Crises Not Wasted: Institutional and Structural Reforms behind Norway's Strong Macroeconomic Performance. In: T. Andersen, M. Bergman, & S. Jensen, eds., *Reform Capacity and Macroeconomic Performance in the Nordic Countries*. Oxford: Oxford University Press, pp. 246–73.

Stewart, H., 2015. Be Honest about how much People are Losing, Mr Osborne. *The Observer*, 2 August.

Stiglitz, J., 2016. *The Euro: How a Common Currency Threatens the Future of Europe*. New York: W. W. Norton and Company.

Stokke, T., 1998. *Lønnsforhandlinger og konfliktløsning. Norge i et skandinavisk perspektiv*. Oslo: Fafo.

Streeck, W., 2017. *Buying Time: The Delayed Crisis of Democratic Capitalism*. London: Verso.

Streeck, W. & Schäfer, A., 2013. *Politics in the Age of Austerity*. Cambridge: Polity Press.

Sureda-Gomila, A., 2011. Real Estate Boom and Crisis in Spain. In: R. Bardhan, R. Edelstein, & C. Kroll, eds., *Global Housing Markets: Crises, Policies and Institutions*. Hoboken, NJ: John Wiley, pp. 157–72.

Svallfors, S. & Taylor-Gooby, P., 1999. *The End of the Welfare State? Response to State Retrenchment*. New York: Routledge.

Swank, D., 2001. Political Institutions and Welfare State Restructuring: The Impact of Institutions on Social Policy Change in Developed Democracies. In: P. Pierson, ed., *The New Politics of the Welfare State*. Oxford: Oxford University Press, pp. 197–237.

Swank, D., 2002. *Global Capital, Political Institutions, and Policy Change in Developed Welfare States*. New York: Cambridge University Press.

Swedish Fiscal Policy Council, 2011. *Report of the Swedish Fiscal Policy Council*. Stockholm: Swedish Fiscal Policy Council.

Taylor, J., 2000. Reassessing Discretionary Fiscal Policy. *Journal of Economic Perspectives*, 14(3), pp. 21–36.

Taylor-Gooby, P., 2004. *New Risks, New Welfare: The Transformation of the European Welfare State*. Oxford: Oxford University Press.

Taylor-Gooby, P., 2012. Root and Branch Restructuring to Achieve Major Cuts: The Social Policy Programme of the 2010 UK Coalition Government. *Social Policy and Administration*, 46(1), pp. 61–82.

Taylor-Gooby, P., 2015. Making the Case for the Welfare State. *Policy and Politics*, 43(4), pp. 597–614.

Taylor-Gooby, P., Leruth, B., & Chung, H., 2017. *After Austerity: Welfare State Transformation in Europe after the Great Recession*. Oxford: Oxford University Press.

Thelen, K., 2013. *Varieties of Liberalization and the New Politics of Social Solidarity*. Cambridge: Cambridge University Press.

Tinios, P., 2005. Pension Reform in Greece: Reform by Instalments—a Blocked Process. *West European Politics*, 28(2), pp. 402–19.

Tønder, A. & Nyen, T., 2014. *Yrkesfagene under Press*. Oslo: Universitetsforlaget.

Townsend, P., 1979. *Poverty in the United Kingdom*. Middlesex: Penguin Books.

Tranøy, B., 2000. *Losing Credit: The Politics of Liberalisation and Macro-Economic Regime Change in Norway 1980–92*. Oslo: Oslo University.

Tuomala, M., 2017. Sosiaalivakuutus ja uudelleenjako [Social Insurance and Redistribution]. In: P. Havakka, M. Niemelä, & H. Uusital, eds., *Sosiaalivakuutus* [Social Insurance]. Helsinki: FINVA, pp. 247–62.

Uusitalo, H., 1996. Economic Crisis and Social Policy in Finland in the 1990s. SPRC Discussion Paper No. 70.

Van Kersbergen, K. & Vis, B., 2014. *Comparative Welfare State Politics*. Cambridge: Cambridge University Press.

Van Kersbergen, K., Vis, B., & Hemerijck, A., 2014. The Great Recession and Welfare State Reform: Is Retrenchment really the Only Game Left in Town? *Social Policy and Administration*, 48(7), pp. 883–904.

Vartiainen, J., 2011. The Finnish Model of Economic and Social Policy: From Cold War Primitive Accumulation to Generational Conflicts? *Comparative Social Research*, 28 (special issue), pp. 53–87.

Vidal, G., 2018. Challenging Business as Usual? The Rise of New Parties in Spain in Times of Crisis. *West European Politics*, 41(2), pp. 261–86.

Weaver, K., 1986. The Politics of Blame Avoidance. *Journal of Public Policy*, 6(4), pp. 371–98.

Weir, M., Orloff, A. S., & Skocpol, T., 1988. *The Politics of Social Policy in the United States*. Princeton, NJ: Princeton University Press.

Whelan, C., Nolan, B., & Maître, B., 2016. The Great Recession and the Changing Intergenerational Distribution of Economic Stress across Income Classes in Ireland: A Comparative Perspective. *Irish Journal of Sociology*, 25(2), pp. 105–27.

Whelan, C.T. & Maître, B. 2005. 'Vulnerability and Multiple Deprivation Perspectives on Economic Exclusion in Europe: A Latent Class Analysis', *European Societies* 7(3): 423–50.

Whelan, K., 2014. Ireland's Economic Crisis: The Good, the Bad and the Ugly. *Journal of Macroeconomics*, 39(Part B), pp. 424–40.

Wilcox, S., Perry, J., & Williams, P., 2015. *UK Housing Review*. Coventry: Chartered Institute of Housing.

Women's Budget Group, 2014. Response to the Autumn Financial Statement 2014. Available at: http://wbg.org.uk/wp-content/uploads/2015/01/WBG-AFS-final.pdf (accessed 27 June 2016).

Women's Budget Group, 2016. *The Impact on Women of the 2016 Budget: Women Paying for the Chancellor's Tax Cuts*. London: Women's Budget Group.

Wren-Lewis, S., 2015. The Knowledge Transmission Mechanism and Austerity. Hans Böckler Stiftung and IMK Macroeconomic Policy Institute Working Paper No. 160-2015.

Wright, S., Dwyer, P., McNeill, J., & Stewart, A., 2016. *First Wave Findings: Universal Credit*. York: University of York for Welfare Conditionality Project.

# Index

*Note*: Table and figures are indicated by an italic *t* and *f* following the page number.

The manufacturer's authorised representative in the EU for product safety is Oxford University Press España S.A. of El Parque Empresarial San Fernando de Henares, Avenida de Castilla, 2 - 28830 Madrid (www.oup.es/en or product.safety@oup.com). OUP España S.A. also acts as importer into Spain of products made by the manufacturer.
Printed and bound by CPI Group (UK) Ltd, Croydon, CR0 4YY
14/09/2026
02216308-0013